Palgrave Macmillan Studies in Banking and Financial Institutions

Series Editor
Philip Molyneux, Bangor University, Bangor, UK

The Palgrave Macmillan Studies in Banking and Financial Institutions series is international in orientation and includes studies of banking systems in particular countries or regions as well as contemporary themes such as Islamic Banking, Financial Exclusion, Mergers and Acquisitions, Risk Management, and IT in Banking. The books focus on research and practice and include up to date and innovative studies that cover issues which impact banking systems globally.

More information about this series at
https://link.springer.com/bookseries/14678

Giuliana Birindelli · Antonia Patrizia Iannuzzi

# Women in Financial Services

## Exploring Progress towards Gender Equality

Foreword by Alessandra Perrazzelli

palgrave
macmillan

Giuliana Birindelli
Department of Management
and Business Administration
"G. d'Annunzio" University
of Chieti-Pescara
Pescara, Italy

Antonia Patrizia Iannuzzi
Department of Economics,
Management and Business Law
"Aldo Moro" University of Bari
Bari, Italy

ISSN 2523-336X ISSN 2523-3378 (electronic)
Palgrave Macmillan Studies in Banking and Financial Institutions
ISBN 978-3-030-93470-5 ISBN 978-3-030-93471-2 (eBook)
https://doi.org/10.1007/978-3-030-93471-2



This Palgrave Macmillan imprint is published by the registered company Springer Nature Switzerland AG
The registered company address is: Gewerbestrasse 11, 6330 Cham, Switzerland

*To the Other Half of the Sky*

# Foreword

Women's empowerment has the capacity to become today a relevant factor in the recovery process. A greater female participation in the labour market is, and should be recognised to be, a key driver for growth, one that would help to achieve the full potential of our economies. Moreover, as widely underlined by the economic literature, women bring unique skills and perspectives to the workplace, with different attitudes to risk and collaboration.

Gender equality should be pursued focusing on policies aimed at enhancing women's talents and skills, defining and defending women's rights, supporting their access to better quality jobs, and increasing women's representation in leadership positions. These actions should interest all sectors, with special attention to activities such as financial services, where they can also lead to significant improvements in risk management.

The growth of services, the financial sector included, is a long-term trend, which accelerated over the last decade. This trend, together with the improvements in women's educational levels, the changes in the structure of family arrangements, and the gradual reshaping of gender roles, has positively affected women's job opportunities. In the last 25 years or so, the female employment rate increased in the euro area from less than 50 to about 65%, a result in line with other advanced economies but at a level that is still much below that of men. Furthermore, women's remuneration is often below that of men in the same position and their labour market participation is generally dampened—quantitatively and qualitatively—by several structural and long-term factors, which are difficult to eradicate in the short term. Especially in financial service activities, women's participation is lagging behind: much is needed to raise it and improve on the quality of jobs.

To break the glass ceiling, or better to say the double glass ceiling clearly defined in Chapter 4 of this book, policy must act on both the supply and demand of women's labour, supporting their efforts to reach higher quality jobs. This may also trigger an increase in labour supply and in productivity. Indeed, the most recent experience is teaching us that policies that operate on labour demand are relatively inexpensive and are effective in achieving higher equality of opportunities and in promoting diversity, even if these measures alone do not suffice to foster diversity and inclusion.

Focusing on financial services, corporate management bodies can benefit from an appropriately diverse composition—not only in terms of gender, but also in terms of geographical origin, age, educational background, and professional expertise. It helps to include varied views in financial institutions, to support effective challenges, and to reduce the risk of groupthink. The diversity has relevant beneficial effects on the sound and prudent management of intermediaries, improving decision-making processes and ensuring an effective corporate governance.

Financial authorities, at the national and at the international level, should continue to devote greater attention to diversity, with respect to both their own organisation and that of supervised entities. In this book, the results of several analyses are reviewed and the adoption of different policy measures is assessed in terms of both their actual impact and the opportunities they help to open.

In line with other financial authorities, the Bank of Italy has long been supporting diversity inside and outside, applying a gradual approach and moving towards more stringent measures only when softer measures turned out to be inadequate in overcoming an enduring market failure.

Internally, targets of female representation in top positions have been combined with other initiatives, such as training and mentoring, in the attempt to achieve better work-life balances. In the Eurosystem, several approaches are being adopted; it is worth mentioning the most recent announcement by the European Central Bank of a new strategy for the 2020–2026 period, which aims at further raising the share of women at various salary levels. In the Bank of Italy, much research has been conducted on gender issues to identify best practices, mechanisms, recommendations, and policies to support wider and better female employment. Several initiatives have also been taken in the field of financial education, focusing on how to improve the financial inclusion of women.

Relating to supervised entities, in 2015, a Bank of Italy recommendation has been issued with the objective of raising the presence of women in banks' boards. As it became clear that the improvements have been less than adequate, a more stringent measure was adopted last July. A binding, though feasible, gender target has been set for top managerial positions and bodies in all banks, listed and not listed, in order for them to benefit from diversity composition in their corporate governance. Some compulsory measures, leveraging on top-down approach, can also prompt bottom-up process. The data evidence suggests that affirmative policies may induce an increase in the diversity of boards along dimensions other than the share of women in top executive positions. These are the cases of geographical origin, age, and skills.

The debate on the necessity to ensure adequate gender diversity in top positions has strengthened over recent years, but there is still a long way to go to close the gap. In the financial sector, in the private entities as well as in the supervisory authorities and central banks, women at top management levels are rather few, as shown by data reported in the chapters of this book. The pandemic crisis highlighted the scale of existing disparities and inequalities, further underscoring the need for progress in gender equality. This year, women's empowerment is a key priority for the G20 as Diversity and Inclusion is for Central banks within the G7 Finance Track. A strategy for gender equality has also been adopted by the European Commission.

In the ongoing pandemic, the increase in the burden of family care might force women out of the labour market, and a she-cession might emerge. This crisis can and should be turned into an opportunity. We experienced that new forms of work are possible: flexible and digital working arrangements may favour female labour market participation through a better balancing of work and family care responsibilities. In the meantime, the possibility of spending part of the week working from home, even if it may allow women to better balance their time and duties, cannot substitute for proper childcare arrangements. They remain fundamental to ensure productivity and not limiting career opportunities in the longer run. Flexible work arrangements must not give rise to a gender segregation trap, but should represent a way to increase female participation.

Women's empowerment is not just a matter of growth. The active participation in the labour market, the advancement of one's own potential, the acquisition of skills, and the access to economic independence are all essential requirements for the enhancement of diversity and inclusion.

The discussion among institutions is fundamental, as the law is not enough to trigger a radical change of cultural pace. Therefore, the achievement of gender equality requires public and private interventions capable of addressing the multiple dimensions that still hinder qualitatively and quantitatively higher female participation in the labour market, especially in specific sectors as the financial one. The thorough knowledge, the extensive analysis, and the development of tools are core for a full awareness of the gender gap, not limited to the establishment of quotas. This book offers a relevant step forward in this direction considering in depth the case of the financial sector.

Alessandra Perrazzelli
Deputy Governor
of the Bank of Italy
Rome, Italy

# Acknowledgements

We would like to take this opportunity to sincerely thank Alessandra Perrazzelli, Deputy Governor of the Bank of Italy, for her kindness in writing the foreword to our book. We are delighted and honoured that the book begins with her valuable comments.

Special thanks also to Philip Molyneux, series editor of the Palgrave Macmillan Studies in Banking and Financial Institutions, for the opportunity of publishing this book.

Giuliana Birindelli would like to sincerely thank the "Consorzio Universitario di Economia Industriale e Manageriale" (CUEIM) for allowing her to dedicate this last year to deepen her research activities, which are particularly significant at this stage of her academic career. Finally, Antonia Patrizia Iannuzzi would like to thank the University of Bari for contributing to the expenses of the proofreading service.

# Contents

# About the Authors

**Giuliana Birindelli** is Full Professor of Financial Markets and Institutions in the Department of Management and Business Administration, "G. d'Annunzio" University of Chieti-Pescara, Italy, where she teaches "Financial Markets and Institutions" and "Banking and Finance". She obtained her Ph.D. and her post-doctorate degree at the University of Pisa, Italy. She is a Fellow of many academic associations and scientific research centres, also as a delegate for her university. She also acts as member of editorial boards and as reviewer for many scientific journals. Additionally, she is currently serving as a member of the Bank of Italy's Board of Auditors. Her main research interests are corporate governance in banks, social and environmental performance in the banking sector, Basel framework, internal rating systems, operational risk, and compliance risk. She is the author of many publications on these topics and she has co-authored another book in the Palgrave Macmillan Studies in Banking and Financial Institutions (*Operational Risk Management in Banks. Regulatory, Organizational and Strategic Issues*).

**Antonia Patrizia Iannuzzi** is Associate Professor of Financial Markets and Institutions in the Department of Economics, Management and Business Law, "Aldo Moro" University of Bari, Italy, where she teaches the courses of "Financial Markets and Institutions" and "Management of Banking and Insurance Institutions". She holds a Ph.D. in "Banking and Finance" from the University of Roma "Sapienza" (Italy), and since 2005, she has carried out her research and teaching activities in banking and financial issues also at the Universities of Foggia and Catanzaro (Italy). She is member of several academic research projects and of three editorial boards and acts as reviewer for many scientific journals. So far, she has authored (or co-authored) numerous scientific publications on the following topics: corporate reputation and reputational risk in the banking sector, corporate governance, banking compensation, corporate social responsibility, ethical funds, single resolution mechanism, and mutual guarantee institutions.

# List of Figures

# List of Tables

CHAPTER 1

# Introduction

Gender diversity in the financial system has increased the attention of supervisors, policymakers, and academics worldwide, especially over the last decade. The issue is complex and is characterised by numerous intertwined political, social, and economic dimensions. The focus on the enhancement of women's professional value is in line with the expectations of many distinguished economists and politicians, such as Christine Lagarde, Barack Obama, and Viviane Reding, as we will see in the following chapter.

The time when the financial world was reluctant to accept any change in favour of female talent seems long gone. Initiatives to enhance women's skills and capabilities are growing in the financial sector. However, despite significant progress in the field, there is still a lot of work to be done and change is evolving slowly. In the face of such important changes, we cannot fail to ask ourselves whether such attention is the result of cultural and ethical factors alone, or whether it also implies other triggering factors closely linked to events and peculiarities of the financial system.

The answer to this question can be found by recalling the group-think phenomenon. The term "group-think" refers to the presence of a dominant decision-making group unable to explore and evaluate alternatives to the prevailing view, resulting in the failure of governance mechanisms. Group-think, which gives rise to the so-called herd behaviour, is caused



G. Birindelli and A. P. Iannuzzi, *Women in Financial Services*, Palgrave Macmillan Studies in Banking and Financial Institutions, https://doi.org/10.1007/978-3-030-93471-2_1

by a lack of diversity. In our setting of financial institutions, a lack of diversity is particularly evident in terms of female representation, especially in the boards of directors of financial firms. Indeed, the inadequate representation of women contributes to the group-think phenomenon as it reduces the exchange of views and debate among board members, negatively affecting the decision-making process. A group dominated by one gender is less efficient and successful than a group in which both genders are adequately represented. This is why group-think has been considered as one of the main causes of the 2007–2008 financial crisis, characterised by the clear dominance of men at the top of the financial sector.

Awareness of the perverse effects of male-dominated decision-making processes has accelerated attention to the benefits of diversity. The effectiveness of board monitoring and decision-making can be greatly enhanced by enriching leadership styles, talents, and viewpoints. In our specific scenario, the presence of women broadens the competencies, knowledge, and skills of the members of a decision-making group.

The positive impact of a more gender-balanced board composition has also been extensively investigated in the literature through a wealth of studies on non-financial companies and an expanding body of literature on financial companies, especially banks. So far, studies have primarily explored the relationship between the proportion of women on boards of directors and bank economic-financial performance and/or riskiness. However, we are now seeing a consolidation of research lines such as those on the relationship between the proportion of women on bank boards and corporate social responsibility (CSR) or environmental performance, which so far have been scarcely explored.

The issue of gender equality is not limited to the composition of boards and the proportion of women in governing bodies and extends to other relevant topics, such as the gender pay gap. In Europe, the formal recognition of this issue dates back to Article 119 of the Treaty of Rome (1957) establishing the European Economic Community (EEC) and requiring each Member State to ensure that men and women should receive equal pay for equal work.

The centrality of the gender gap—including the pay gap—in financial firms has given rise to many initiatives of a different nature. First of all, regulatory proposals, legal measures, recommendations, and guidelines at international, European, and national levels. A few examples are the Directive 2013/36/EU (known as CRD IV) which emphasised the need for sufficient diversification (also by gender) in the composition of the management bodies of credit institutions; another is the new set of principles by the Basel Committee on Banking Supervision, which in 2015 revised the corporate governance principles for banks, establishing a general requirement of diversification/balance in the composition of the board of directors. Also noteworthy is the Directive (EU) 2019/878 (CRD V) which revised several important remuneration principles. One of these principles concerns the need for gender-neutral remuneration policies, according to the principle "*of equal pay for male and female workers for equal work or work of equal value*".

At a national level, a few countries have decided to set a compulsory minimum percentage of women on company boards (hard quotas), whereas other countries have preferred a path with no binding conditions, characterised by the issuing of recommendations to increase the weight of women (soft quotas). Hard quotas can be established for a limited timeframe such as in Italy, where the measure was in fact extended beyond its original period of application. Additionally, other self-regulatory actions have been taken through the issuing of "charters" setting out principles to promote a more gender-balanced financial industry (emblematic examples are the UK, Italian, and Belgian charters, which we will illustrate in the book).

It is also worth mentioning the 2030 Agenda for Sustainable Development, which—as well-acknowledged—includes 17 Sustainable Development Goals (SDGs) adopted by all the United Nations Member States in 2015; within this cluster of SDGs, Goal 5 is dedicated to gender equality and empowerment of all women and girls.

In response to all these initiatives, an increasing number of indexes have been developed to track the gender diversity performance of companies such as the Bloomberg Gender-Equality Index and the Morgan Stanley Capital International Women's Leadership Index. Alongside these, methodologies have been developed to certify a company's commitment to gender equality in the workplace (for instance, the Economic Dividends for Gender Equality certification and the Winning Women Institute certification). The indexes and certifications, as we will illustrate in detail, also concern financial intermediaries, both bank and non-bank financial institutions.

To date, studies on banks (like those by the European Banking Authority) show a prevailing increase in the weight of women on boards over time, in both the role of executive and non-executive directors. Looking at the data in detail, we can note the presence of a prevailing trend of a greater intake of women on boards as non-executive directors—that is, in supervisory rather than management roles. Other emerging trends are the low proportion of women in revenue-generating roles (linked to the so-called profit and loss responsibilities) and the still low number of female Chief Executive Officers (CEOs) and board chairs. Concerning CEOs, the path to this position involves filling leadership positions that are mostly held by men, thus justifying the low number of female CEOs. Another distinctive feature of the financial industry is the so-called double glass ceiling, marked by fewer and fewer women as they move up the career ladder. More specifically, while gender balance can be observed at entry level, a double imbalance can be noticed along the career path: one in middle management positions and an even greater one in executive committee positions.

The insurance sector shows similar characteristics to the banking sector: a large gap between women employees and women in managerial positions, as well as a significant underrepresentation of women on boards of directors and in executive positions.

However, the samples considered in studies on board composition and top positions are heterogeneous just as the observation periods. Accordingly, the results should only be interpreted as dominant trends, which may not be confirmed in certain geographical areas and/or countries. Indeed, studies sometimes show very marked differences across countries, as well as divergent trends among companies within the same country.

Similar considerations can be made regarding the gender pay gap, for which there are only partial data currently available. Nevertheless, some key trends can be observed. First, the gender pay gap in the EU financial sector is still high and shows wide variability, as wage discrimination is larger in some countries compared to others. Moreover, there does not seem to be a relationship between the adoption of gender policies and the reduction of the gender pay gap. In the Nordic and Anglo-Saxon countries, which are known to be at the forefront of gender equality rankings, the pay gap between men and women remains on average high where the average value for 2010–2019 was 36.59% for Iceland; 30.17% for Norway; and 38.29% for the UK. Finally, the gender pay gap of banks and insurance companies is the highest of all other economic sectors in all EU Member States. In the light of this situation, a growing number of European countries have decided to adopt specific laws on the gender pay gap aimed, above all, at obliging larger companies to offer more information on this issue on the assumption that increasing disclosure is an effective means of mitigating this gap. Furthermore, the recent introduction of the principle of gender-neutral remuneration policy (mentioned above) will bring significant changes on this front.

Compared to other financial sectors, the representation of women in the asset management sector is even lower. There are far fewer women than men pursuing careers as portfolio and fund managers, and women-led funds remain a rarity in the investment industry. Overall, female representation in the global fund industry has essentially remained unchanged over the last twenty years. To date, it is estimated that just 1.1% of the global wealth of the asset management industry is managed by women. In this context, the recent initiative by some asset managers to promote "gender diversity" funds is very welcome. These are mutual funds that invest most of their total assets in equities and equity-related securities of companies worldwide that stand out for their gender diversity performance (such as the Nordea 1-Global Gender Diversity Fund and the Fidelity Women's Leadership Fund).

In National Central Banks, the obstacles to women's careers seem even more pronounced than in supervised financial intermediaries. The issue is more complex and sensitive for many reasons, including the gender gap (to the disadvantage of women) in economics education, which seems essential to reach top positions in these financial institutions. Another factor, marginally explored in the literature, is related to how women are perceived concerning the objectives pursued by Central Banks; whether they are considered more or less risk-averse and inflation-averse, qualifying in these cases respectively as "hawks" or "doves". Female governors seem to be a particular rarity; our reconstruction counted 67 female governors in 51 Central Banks worldwide. However, there are timid signs of change. Firstly, the European Central Bank has strengthened its gender equality policy over time, characterised by the setting of targets for the recruitment and promotion of women belonging to different seniority levels. Similarly, initiatives from National Central Banks indicate a strong focus on gender equality: examples include an increase in the number of diversity officers who formally take on the role of implementing and monitoring diversity and inclusion practices; in training to support women's career progression; in objective recruitment policies, resulting for instance in a name-blind process; and in a greater focus on the gender pay gap than in the past, resulting in a few cases in the publication of ad hoc reports.

The present book is divided into 11 chapters. The following Chapter 2, entitled "An Overview of Legal Measures, Voluntary Rules, Indexes, and

Certifications Concerning Gender Diversity in the Banking Industry", opens by exploring the growing attention to gender diversity in the financial system and its main drivers with an emphasis on banks. It first analyses the reasons behind the strong focus on gender diversity in this system, linked to the so-called group-think and the related "Lehman Sisters Hypothesis", according to which the typical risk-inclined male behaviour and its reckless outcomes could be balanced by the more cautious/less risk-inclined behaviour of women. The chapter then outlines initiatives and legal acts aimed at disseminating the culture and practice of gender equality. Detailed reference is given to capital requirements directives (CRDs) known as CRD IV and CRD V: CRD IV deals with the criterion of diversity in its broader acceptation (in terms of gender, age, geographical origin, professional background, and so on) in relation to recruitment and composition of governing bodies; CRD V deals with gender-neutral pay policies. Section 3 provides a detailed overview of the so-called hard gender quotas, which are compulsory by law, and the "soft" quotas, which are not compulsory by law but stem from self-regulatory initiatives. Section 4 describes requirements for disclosing information on gender diversity, with specific reference to the Global Reporting Initiative standards. The chapter closes with Section 5, which describes indexes that track the performance of companies that are committed to supporting gender equality and provides details on gender parity certifications and the Women's Empowerment Principles, with mention of some of the financial companies involved.

Chapter 3, entitled "Women and Bank Performance: Theoretical Background and Literature Review", intends to offer a comprehensive literature review of the existing research on the relationship between board gender diversity (BGD) and financial institutions' performance. To this end, after briefly reviewing the main theories on the role of women in the decision-making process, several sections are elaborated, each devoted to analysing a specific relationship. First, empirical studies investigating the relationship between BGD and bank economic-financial performance are examined. Given the high number of these studies, they are grouped into three categories: (1) studies revealing a positive linear relationship, (2) studies supporting a non-significant, negative, or non-linear relationship between BGD and bank performance, and (3) studies focused on Microfinance Institutions (MFIs). Then, the analysis shifts to the studies that examine the associations between BGD and bank efficiency, bank CSR/environmental performance, and bank risk-taking. Finally, the chapter is closed by a section dedicated to other areas of research on bank gender diversity that have not yet been explored in depth.

Chapter 4 ("Data on Female Representation in Banks") aims to provide data on the presence of women in financial firms, especially banks, and the evolution of this over time, drawing on several studies conducted mainly by international and European organisations. A special focus is devoted to female board members with executive and non-executive functions, chairwomen, and female CEOs. The general trend shows both an increase in the presence of women, especially as non-executive board members, most likely due to pressures resulting from the introduction of hard gender quotas in many countries, and yet a low number of female CEOs and chairs. Moreover, the data show the persistence of the low weight of women in revenue-generating roles. Despite the large differences in the data across countries, the Scandinavian countries seem to be the most oriented towards gender equality. Finally, attention is given to the "double glass ceiling" phenomenon. In this respect, studies show that despite there being a gender balance at entry levels, the relationship becomes imbalanced in middle management and even more in executive committee positions. The chapter analyses both the motivations behind this phenomenon and some supporting data.

Chapter 5, entitled "The Gender Pay Gap in the Financial Sector: Where Do We Stand?", addresses the issue of the gender pay gap within the financial system. To this end, it first reviews the main treaties and legal acts that formalise the principle of equal pay for men and women, from the Treaty of Rome to the main European directives. It then analyses the theoretical and empirical studies on the issue, which for the financial sector are still at an embryonic stage. The second part of the chapter focuses exclusively on the financial system, analysing the evolution of the gender pay gap over time and the differences across geographical areas and economic sectors. The assessment is performed using data collected by Eurostat and the European Banking Authority, and also provides a focus on the gender pay gap in the UK banking sector. Finally, the chapter explores the most recent laws on the gender pay gap passed in several European countries and the recent "gender neutrality principle" of banking remuneration practices. The chapter closes by proposing some actions that need to be taken by banks to close the existing gap.

Chapter 6 ("Gender Diversity in the Insurance Industry: Progress Made and Next Steps") can be divided into three sections. The first shows the main evidence from the few studies conducted so far on insurance companies, underlining above all a scant presence of female directors and the lack of a significant relationship between board gender diversity and corporate performance. In the second section, some data on the current presence of women in the workforce of these financial institutions, including managerial and top positions, are reported. Finally, the third section focuses on three leading insurance companies in the European market (Axa, Zurich Insurance, and Assicurazioni Generali), which are particularly attentive to gender diversity in order to highlight the progress that this sector is making towards achieving greater gender equality.

Chapter 7 ("Women in the Asset Management Sector") focuses on the role of the asset management (AM) industry in adopting and disseminating gender diversity principles. To this end, the chapter opens with a brief analysis of the rationale behind the importance of gender diversity in this industry and focuses on the still high barriers that women encounter and face. The second section analyses the main regulatory initiatives put in place by both European and US regulators to promote gender diversity in the asset management sector. The third section deals with the current adoption by mutual funds of investment strategies focused on the promotion of gender equality. This is followed by an overview of the main gender diversity funds that some important asset managers (Nordea, Fidelity, RobecoSAM, UBS Asset Management, and State Street Global Advisors) have chosen to place recently on the market. Finally, the chapter ends with an in-depth look at the main initiatives adopted by some AM trade associations (Investment Association, Finance Finland, and Assogestioni) aimed at encouraging AM firms to increase the uptake of gender diversity policies and standards.

Chapter 8 ("How Central Are Women in Central Banks?") deals with gender issues in Central Banks (CBs). In such a setting, discrimination against women and obstacles to their careers seem even more pronounced than in supervised financial intermediaries. The chapter first discusses the causes of this accentuated difficulty for women and then reviews the scarce literature on the pattern of appointments and promotions of women on CB boards, on the relations between gender and monetary policy decisions, and finally, on the influence exerted by women on the stability of the financial system and the quality of supervision. The focus then shifts to the strengthening of the gender parity policy by the European Central Bank, marked by the setting of targets for the recruitment and promotion of women, and to women governors. In the latter regard, we have tried to build a detailed picture of the women who have held such positions in CBs around the world, highlighting both how rare they still are and how patterns change across countries. Finally, the chapter offers a picture of the gender policies followed by the EU28 CBs, based on responses Central Banks provided to our survey and/or on information retrieved from the Central Banks' documents, especially their annual reports.

Chapter 9 ("Gender Diversity in Banks and Insurance Companies: The State of Art") is exclusively empirical. Indeed, it aims to provide an overview of the gender diversity policies adopted by banks and insurance companies across the world over the last 11 years (2010–2020) by using data collected from the database Refinitiv Eikon, namely: (a) the percentage of women employees; (b) the percentage of new women employees; (c) the percentage of women managers; (d) the percentage of female directors on the board; (e) the percentage of female executive members; (f) the gender pay gap; (g) flexible working hour mechanisms promoting a work-life balance; (h) the board gender diversity policy; and (i) the support to the UN-Sustainable Development Goal (SDG) 5 Gender Equality. The full sample consists of 2064 listed financial intermediaries (1427 banks and 637 insurance companies, the latter belonging to the following sub-sectors: life & health insurance, multiline insurance and brokers, property and casualty insurance, and reinsurance). Overall, the analysis shows that women are still underrepresented in managerial positions and, even more so, in executive roles in the banking and insurance sectors. However, it is important to underline that over the last 11 years there has been a rearrangement of the roles held by women in our sample. Indeed, on the one hand, the number of women employees has decreased, and on the other hand, the number of women directors, managers, and executives has increased, although with very different growth rates. In any case, the rebalancing process is still ongoing and will be so for a long time.

Chapter 10 ("A Case of Temporary (extended) "Hard Quotas": Gender Diversity in Italian Banks") analyses gender diversity in Italian banks starting from the regulatory framework—first and foremost, the Golfo-Mosca Law, which was reiterated with amendments by the 2020 Budget Law. Alongside these regulations, the chapter illustrates numerous additional initiatives, such as the establishment of an Observatory that studies and promotes gender equality by the Bank of Italy, together with the Department for Equal Opportunities of the Italian Presidency of the Council of Ministers and Italian Companies and Exchange Commission (Commissione Nazionale per le Società e la Borsa, CONSOB). Another initiative is the charter by the Italian Banking Association inviting signatories to strengthen their governance following the principles of inclusiveness and equal opportunities. Not least, the proposal by the Bank of Italy, following its 2015 diversity benchmark, to introduce a gender quota in the administrative and control bodies of banks, which recently became an integral part of the provisions on corporate governance in Italian banks. The chapter ends with an analysis and commentary on the female presence and gender pay gap in Italian banks (with a focus on listed banks) based on data extrapolated from corporate governance and remuneration policies reports.

Chapter 11 ("Proposing a Framework for Calculating an Index on Gender Equality in Financial Firms") opens by underlining the importance of a model that allows the assessment of the gender diversity of financial firms under several analysis profiles, widely discussed in the previous chapters. We propose a model of analysis that is suitable for the construction of an index of gender diversity based on a set of items predetermined according to standards, legal acts, and best practices relevant to the topic. More specifically, the framework consists of 24 items that can be divided into four categories: (1) gender balance in governance bodies and employees; (2) policies promoting gender equality; (3) transparency of the company's actions towards the community; and (4) equal compensation. In the case of comparison among intermediaries of the same country, the proposed framework can be integrated by considering further elements peculiar to each country. It is a first attempt to fill a gap in the gender diversity literature, where, to the best of our knowledge, there is no framework to calculate a gender equality index that goes beyond the composition of governance bodies and the gender of the board chair and/or CEO.

CHAPTER 2

# An Overview of Legal Measures, Voluntary Rules, Indexes, and Certifications Concerning Gender Diversity in the Banking Industry

**Abstract** The chapter opens by exploring the growing attention to gender diversity and its main drivers in the financial system, primarily in the banking sector. It first analyses the reasons behind the strong focus on gender diversity in this system, linked to the so-called group-think (considered one of the main causes of the 2007–2008 financial crisis) and the related "Lehman Sisters Hypothesis". The chapter then outlines initiatives and legal measures aimed at disseminating the culture and practice of gender equality. Detailed reference is given to CRD IV and CRD V: CRD IV deals with the criterion of diversity in its broader acceptation (in terms of gender, age, geographical origin, professional background, and so on) in relation to the recruitment and composition of governing bodies; CRD V deals with gender-neutral pay policies. Section 3 provides a detailed overview of the so-called hard gender quotas, which are compulsory by law, and the "soft" quotas, which are not compulsory by law but rather

This chapter is the result of the joint efforts of the two authors. However, Giuliana Birindelli mainly contributed to Sects. 2.1, 2.3, 2.5 and Antonia Patrizia Iannuzzi to Sects. 2.2, 2.4.



G. Birindelli and A. P. Iannuzzi, *Women in Financial Services*, Palgrave Macmillan Studies in Banking and Financial Institutions, https://doi.org/10.1007/978-3-030-93471-2_2

stem from self-regulatory initiatives. Section 4 describes requirements for disclosing information on gender diversity, with specific reference to the Global Reporting Initiative standards. The chapter closes with Sect. 5, which describes indexes that track the performance of companies committed to supporting gender equality and provides details on gender parity certifications and the Women's Empowerment Principles, with mention of some of the financial companies involved.

## 2.1 Gender Diversity in the Banking Industry: Why Is It Generating so Much Attention?

In recent years, gender diversity in the workplace has become a central topic for legislators, policymakers, and academics worldwide. Much has been done to highlight the value of diversity, raise awareness of gender disparity, establish principles of equality, and safeguard individuals' rights to diversity. Many initiatives span across employment sectors, from manufacturing to business, education, science, and politics, leading to tangible progress and setting new milestones along the way. Yet, despite the growing momentum, some sectors appear to lag behind, as if reluctant to welcome any sort of change. In this scenario, the banking and non-banking financial sector has made a lot of progress, but much still needs to be done. It must be said that many distinguished personalities from the economic and political world have publicly acknowledged the issue, underlining the value of women and the importance of a culture of inclusion within the financial industry, and are increasingly encouraging effective and sustainable actions towards this goal. We wish to recall some eloquent quotes from such illustrious personalities.

> Mark Carney, former Governor of the Bank of Canada and then former Governor of the Bank of England:
> *... having a diverse workforce [e.g., in terms of gender, ethnicity, sexual orientation] is essential to delivering our mission to promote the good of the people of the United Kingdom by maintaining monetary and financial stability.* (Carney, 2018, p. 1)

> Neelie Kroes, former Vice President of the European Commission:
> *... if change is slower than we would like, let us remember that change starts with us. It is our responsibility to use our talents – we owe it to ourselves, and to all women.* (Kroes, 2011, p. 4)

> Christine Lagarde, former Managing Director of the International Monetary Fund and present head of the European Central Bank:
> *... women's empowerment ... represents a missed opportunity in the pursuit of macroeconomic stability and inclusive growth.* (Lagarde, 2019, p. 5)
>
> Barack Obama, former US President:
> *I'm absolutely confident that, for two years, if every nation on earth was run by women, you would see a significant improvement across the board on just about everything — living standards and outcomes.* (Obama, 2019)
>
> Viviane Reding, former European Commissioner and currently sitting Member of intergroups of the European Parliament:
> *Gender equality is not an academic debate but a question of society.* (Reding, 2016)
>
> Ignazio Visco, Governor of the Bank of Italy:
> *Italy's expected potential growth for the upcoming years heavily depends on one of its key drivers, i.e., the hypotheses of female participation [in the workforce].* (Visco, 2019, p. 1, our translation from Italian)

But where has this strong focus on gender balance and women's empowerment originated? Is it just an ethical and cultural issue alone?

An interesting insight into this question comes from a famous statement by Lagarde: "*... if Lehman Brothers had been "Lehman Sisters", today's economic crisis clearly would look quite different*" (Lagarde, 2010) and from the connected "Lehman Sisters claim", which openly links the typical risk-inclined male behaviour to its reckless outcomes—especially in the presence of inadequate regulation and incentive mechanisms (van Staveren, 2014). On closer inspection, the statement hints at two important aspects. On the one hand, there is the perverse link which is especially accentuated in the largely male-dominated high finance sector. On the other hand, an adequate female component in the field could balance this attitude with more cautious/less risk-inclined behaviour and a diverse set of perspectives and skills to be used in the decision-making process. In other words, having more women in top banking positions might reduce the chances of the bank's collapse (see Chapter 3).

The theory known as the "Lehman Sisters Hypothesis" extends the issue to the broader aspect of decisional processes within a group setting and the inevitable flaws that follow under certain circumstances. Similarly to the way decision-making at individual level may be affected by an overconfidence bias, decision-making at group level may be affected by a cognitive bias. In the specific setting of a board, for example, it can lead members to fail to explore alternatives to the dominant view in the decision-making process (Janis, 1972), consolidating what is known as the group-think phenomenon.

Thus, group-think can undermine the effectiveness of governance mechanisms and result in misconduct. Misconduct, therefore, also stems from a lack of diversity and inclusion (FSB, 2018). Group-think is considered one of the major causes of the financial crisis, precisely a failure of the mechanisms of corporate governance (The High-Level Group on Financial Supervision in the European Union, 2009). Another expression used to describe the phenomenon in which individuals act collectively as part of a group, without considering individual thoughts, values, and beliefs is "herd behaviour".

Diversity, including gender diversity, seems beneficial to the banking governance review process in particular to overcome the effect of male traits, such as overconfidence, risk-taking, group-think, or herd behaviour. Diversity in all forms broadens the competencies, knowledge, views, and skills of members of a group, thus enriching the exchange of views and debate within the group, ultimately improving the decision-making process. A group dominated by a single gender is less efficient and less successful compared to a more inclusive group where both genders are adequately represented (Kamalnath, 2018). The issue of adequate representation is extremely relevant in counterbalancing the group-think phenomenon. The flaws of the processes and mechanisms underlying the functioning of a group cannot be corrected through tokenistic diversity alone, but rather by reaching a critical mass of minorities—in this case, a minimum number or threshold of women (Kanter, 1977a, 1977b; see Chapter 3).

Along the same line, the usefulness of diversity (gender diversity included) has also been stressed by the European Commission in its Green Paper on the European Union (EU) corporate governance framework, claiming diversity as an effective antidote to counteracting group-think. It mentions how the enrichment of leadership styles, talents, and viewpoints can significantly enhance effective monitoring and decision-making carried out by the boards of directors: "*Gender diversity can contribute to tackling group-think. There is also evidence that women have different leadership styles, attend more board meetings and have a positive impact on the collective intelligence of a group*" (European Commission, 2011, p. 7). Such a position on the benefits of diversity-promoting policies across industry sectors was reaffirmed one year later by the European Commission stating: "*... insufficient diversity could lead to a so-called group-think process, translating into less debate, fewer ideas and challenges in the boardroom and potentially less effective oversight of the management board or executive directors*" (European Commission, 2012, p. 6).

Since then, the promotion of equality between women and men has continued to be part of the European Commission work programmes. The focus on this issue is, among other things, the result of the principle of inclusiveness ("no one is left behind") promoted by the 2030 Agenda for Sustainable Development (European Parliament, 2019). As well known, the Agenda includes 17 Sustainable Development Goals (SDGs) which were officially adopted by all the United Nations Member States in 2015 (United Nations, 2015). Some of these SDGs (in particular, SDGs 1 to 7) can be considered an extension of the Millennium Development Goals, previously developed in 2000, especially for the least developed countries (Avrampou et al., 2019; Kumar et al., 2016). Within this cluster of SDGs, Goal 5 has the following official wording: "Achieve gender equality and empower all women and girls". For this goal, the United Nations has defined 9 targets (i.e., sub-goals) and 14 indicators (i.e., metrics to assess the level of achievement of the sub-goals).

Within the implementation of SDGs, the banking and non-banking financial sector has naturally come to play a central role.

First, the financing of goals requires the mobilisation of sufficient financial resources and strategies that increase the funding sources (United Nations, 2019). The financing gap is high; the annual gap in developing countries is estimated at $2.5 trillion (UNCTAD, 2015). Financial support is needed on several fronts. Public support must be complemented by private investments, and the financial system can make a significant contribution both by addressing investors' needs and by offering financial products and services addressing the SDGs (Weber, 2018). Microfinance and lending to women and female-owned businesses could facilitate the achievement of Goal 5 (Weber, 2018; Weber & Adnan, 2014).

In addition, financial institutions could relevantly contribute to the achievement of Goal 5 through their staff recruitment policies (at all levels), their commitment to ensuring an effective work-life balance, and policies that drive diversity and equal opportunities.

In particular, they could fulfil target 5.5 "Ensure women's full and effective participation and equal opportunities for leadership at all levels of decision-making" by focusing on indicator 5.5.2 (the proportion of women in managerial positions), target 5.a "Undertake reforms to give women equal rights to economic resources, as well as access to ownership and control over land and other forms of property, financial services, inheritance and natural resources, in accordance with national laws", and target 5.c "Adopt and strengthen sound policies and enforceable legislation for the promotion of gender equality and the empowerment of all women and girls at all levels". Further details about this issue will be given in the following chapters.

## 2.2 Guidelines and Legal Measures: A Focus on Europe

The "Lehman Sisters Hypothesis" can be considered the thread of a series of regulatory proposals, legal measures, and recommendations at international, European, and national level.

Regarding measures within the banking system, in 2015 the Basel Committee on Banking Supervision (BCBS) reviewed corporate governance principles for banks by introducing a great challenge to internal organisation and governance structure. Compared to the previous version (BCBS, 2010), where there was no reference to diversity, the new principles establish a general requirement of diversification and balance in the composition of the board of directors (BCBS, 2015, principle 2: board qualifications and composition): diversity is to be meant as diversity in skills, backgrounds, and views and should be ensured by recruitment policies that are attentive to this balance. Thus, the BCBS does not specifically refer to gender, but rather to a broader and more inclusive concept of diversity.

At a European level, the principle of diversity had already been outlined a few years earlier. In particular, Directive 2013/36/EU (known as CRD

IV[1]), on access to the activity of credit institutions and the prudential supervision of credit institutions and investment firms, affirms this requirement by emphasising the need for sufficient diversification in the composition of management bodies of credit institutions by age, sex, geographical provenance, education, and career path to guarantee a variety of experience and skills. In CRD IV, therefore, the criterion of diversity is expressed regarding specific features, including gender. The directive reasserts the application of the criterion of diversity in the context of recruitment policy (recital 60) and outlines, in Article 88(2)(a), the importance of the balance between men and women which, if not fulfilled, should stimulate appropriate measures developed by the nomination committee to achieve adequate representation of the underrepresented gender. This committee, which should be nominated in significant institutions in terms of their size, internal organisation, scope, and complexity of the activities carried out, should set a target for the participation of the underrepresented gender in the management body and should decide on the implementation policies to meet that target. The involvement of the nomination committee is envisaged in all cases, except where the management body does not have any influence on the appointment of candidates.

Article 91(12) of Directive 2013/36/EU assigns the European Banking Authority (EBA) the task of defining the concept of diversity to be followed in the selection of the components of the management body. In this respect, the EBA has stated that by improving the gender balance in positions directly below the management body, institutions will be more capable of taking gender diversity into account when recruiting members of this body (EBA, 2021).

In addition, Article 9(1) of Directive 2014/65/EU (on markets in financial instruments) assigns the issue of guidelines on the topic to the European Securities and Markets Authority (ESMA) and the EBA. In March 2018, ESMA and EBA issued said guidelines. Diversity is defined as "*the situation whereby the characteristics of the members of the management body, including their age, gender, geographical provenance and educational and professional background, are different to an extent that allows a variety of views within the management body*" (ESMA & EBA, 2018, p. 7).

[1] CRD stands for Capital Requirements Directive.

The approaches on diversity policy differ depending on the type of institution: significant versus non-significant institutions. Significant institutions are global systemically important institutions (G-SIIs) and other systemically important institutions (O-SIIs) (CRD IV, Article 131). All other institutions are non-significant. The guidelines issued by the ESMA and the EBA specify that the diversity policy for significant institutions "*should include a quantitative target for the representation of the underrepresented gender in the management body*" (ESMA & EBA, 2018, p. 30), as well as the timeframe in which to reach the target and indications on how to achieve it. Differently, the other institutions should set qualitative targets, especially where the management body is made up of less than five members. Also in this case, there is a guideline concerning those who do not hold top positions. In fact, "*institutions should implement a diversity policy for staff, including career planning aspects and measures to ensure equal treatment and opportunities for staff of different genders*" (ESMA & EBA, 2018, pp. 30 and 31). There is, therefore, a strengthening of governance rules aimed at promoting diversity, not only for gender balance but in broader terms including gender equality at all levels of the banking organisation.

Directive (EU) 2019/878 (CRD V), which amended Directive 2013/36/EU, has reviewed several important remuneration principles. One principle concerns the need for gender-neutral remuneration policies, according to the principle "*of equal pay for male and female workers for equal work or work of equal value*". The new CRD V provisions assign the EBA the task of issuing guidelines on what constitutes gender-neutral policies. Moreover, national regulators are assigned the task of collecting information on the gender pay gap from the affected firms to enable the EBA to report on the application of gender-neutral policies. Therefore, the rules of governance will also be strengthened by provisions on gender-neutral compensation: the same work, or work of equal value, must be paid regardless of the gender of the person performing the work. Given that gender pay gaps also exist in the banking sector, these forecasts should have a strong impact on gender realignment (for more information see Chapter 5). It is worth pointing out that this issue recalls one of the SDGs, in particular Goal 8, about "Decent work and economic growth", and target 8.5 ("By 2030, achieve full and productive employment and decent work for all women and men, including for young people and persons with disabilities, and equal pay for work of equal value").

In recent years, the focus on gender equality has led to many other initiatives. One is the directive on work-life balance for parents and carers (Directive (EU) 2019/1158). The directive, which regulates paternity leave and flexible working arrangements, is foreseen to have a strong impact on women's employment opportunities in terms of employment rate, salary, and career progression. The directive, together with the others mentioned above, shows a strong attention to the wider and more motivated participation of women in the professional world, particularly as a result of group-think and its harmful consequences. Alongside all these initiatives at the European/international level, several other initiatives have been promoted at a national level. As we shall see in the following section, the solutions adopted differ among countries: some have established hard quotas setting a mandatory minimum percentage of women on the company boards, while others have opted for soft quotas issuing recommendations for increasing the presence of women.

## 2.3 Gender Quotas for Boards of Directors and Self-Regulatory Initiatives in Europe

In November 2012, the European Commission submitted a proposal for a directive on gender balance (Brussels, 14.11.2012, COM[2012] 614 final 2012/0299 [COD]) concerning non-executive directors of companies listed on the stock markets. The proposal establishes that all enterprises (except for small and medium-sized ones) achieve a minimum target of 40% of the underrepresented gender on boards, setting a 2018 deadline for public sector companies and 2020 for those of the private sector. For those states that extend the application of a minimum threshold to executive directors alongside non-executive directors, the minimum target is lowered to 33%.

Indeed, many countries have introduced measures to strengthen the presence of women in positions of responsibility.

There have been several approaches adopted for implementing these initiatives: some countries have introduced binding quotas with a strict (hard quota) or no sanction system according to the "comply or explain" principle (the non-compliant company must justify why it has not complied with the legislation); other countries have adopted non-binding measures (soft quotas), recommending the respect of certain percentages of presence on the boards, thus following a voluntary approach based on recommendations within codes of good governance principles.

The scope of application is also diverse: in some cases, the provisions apply to companies listed on regulated markets, while in others they apply to all large companies (listed and unlisted) or to state-owned companies. Finally, differences are also found concerning the type of member of the governing bodies to which the provisions are addressed, given that in some cases gender balance is only required for non-executive directors and in other cases for all members regardless of their role (De Masi, 2019).

The first country to have enacted a law on gender quotas is Norway, followed by other countries which adhered to the initiative by enacting rules establishing a minimum percentage of the underrepresented gender in governing bodies. Although gender quotas are considered an effective means of dissolving barriers, discrimination, and stereotypes against women, their effectiveness and desirability may be questioned. Indeed, if we assume that women's underrepresentation is not due to discriminatory processes and men's positions of power, but rather to the choice of women, who may prefer motherhood and childcare to work and a professional career, the establishment of quotas might lead to the selection of low-skilled women, which lowers the average quality of the work team and ultimately firm performance (on these opposing views see Profeta, 2020, pp. 55–57). We will return to this point in other parts of the book, especially in Chapter 3.

Table 2.1 lists the European countries that have adopted such a law, alongside the consequences in case of non-compliance which include either sanctions of variable severity or application of the "comply or explain" principle.

Other initiatives have often been taken to encourage greater representation of women in corporate governance bodies, such as the widespread recommendations contained in corporate governance codes (as in Finland, the UK, and Sweden). Recommendations call for voluntary actions towards achieving gender balance and are often accompanied by hard quotas, meaning that in some countries both types of quotas coexist (as in Belgium, Germany, Italy, the Netherlands, and Portugal).

Other important self-regulatory initiatives have emerged with specific reference to the financial sector. First, the HM Treasury Women in Finance Charter launched by the UK government in March 2016 and addressed to financial services firms. Given the low number of women in executive positions (see Chapter 4), the charter aims to promote a more balanced financial industry, oriented towards setting internal targets

**Table 2.1** European countries with national quotas

| *Country* | *Quota target* | *Year of enactment of the law (compliance year)* | *Scope and coverage* | *Sanctions* |
|---|---|---|---|---|
| Austria | 30% | 2017 (2022) | All listed companies and those with more than 1000 employees. Exempted companies with less than 20% of total employees of the underrepresented gender | Board elections annulled |
| | 35% | 2011 (2018) | Companies in which the state has a majority stake | No sanctions for non-compliance |
| Belgium | 33% | 2011 (2017 to comply for large companies; 2019 for smaller companies; 2012 for state-owned enterprises) | Listed companies; State-owned enterprises | Suspension of remuneration of directors and appointments of women until the target is reached |
| France | 40% | 2011 (2014: quota target 20%; 2017: quota target 40%) | Listed companies; Companies with revenues or total assets over €50 million with 500 or more employees for three consecutive years; Governmental organisations | Appointments of new directors are null and void, and directors' fees may be withheld |

(continued)

**Table 2.1** (continued)

| *Country* | *Quota target* | *Year of enactment of the law (compliance year)* | *Scope and coverage* | *Sanctions* |
|---|---|---|---|---|
| Germany | 30% of non-executive board seats; 50% for state-owned enterprises | 2015 (2020; for state-owned enterprises from 2018 onward) | Listed companies subject to employee participation on boards ("co-determination"); State-owned enterprises | Annulment of new appointments |
| Iceland | 40% | 2010 (2013) | Companies with over 50 employees | Comply or explain |
| Italy (This law was extended with amendments in 2019, raising the target quota to 40% and the mandates from 3 to 6) | 33% | 2011 (application only to the first three consecutive board terms after the law's enactment, after which it expires) | Listed companies; State-owned enterprises | Notice with the obligation to comply with the legislation and financial penalties |
| The Netherlands (This law was extended in 2016 until 1 January 2020; a legal proposal introducing the obligation for listed companies to have at least one-third female members on supervisory boards was tabled in November 2020 and will be discussed in Parliament) | 30% | 2013 (2016, 2020) | Large legal entities | Comply or explain |

| *Country* | *Quota target* | *Year of enactment of the law (compliance year)* | *Scope and coverage* | *Sanctions* |
|---|---|---|---|---|
| Norway | 40% | 2003 (2008) | Public limited companies | Dissolution of the company and other public severe sanctions, like de-listing from the Oslo Stock Exchange |
| Portugal | 33.3% | 2017 (2020 for state-owned enterprises; for publicly traded companies 20% by their first general meeting in 2018; 33.3% for the first general meeting held in 2020) | State-owned enterprises; Publicly traded companies | For state-owned companies, annulment of the supervisory bodies, and the election of new ones. Publicly traded companies that do not comply will be listed on the websites of the Commission for Citizenship and Gender Equality, the Commission for Equality in Labour and Employment, and the Securities Market Commission. Moreover, fines are foreseen if non-compliance exceeds 360 days |
| Spain | 40% | 2007 (2015) | Public and private firms | Comply or explain |

*Source* Authors' elaboration on Deloitte (2019) and Hastings (2018) for the gender diversity strategy adopted and supporting women's career progression and transparency to the public on these issues. In order to promote gender diversity, it identifies four key points: (1) having a supervisor for diversity policy in the senior executive team; (2) setting internal goals for gender diversity in senior management; (3) publishing annual reports providing information on progress towards these targets; and (4) linking the remuneration of the senior executive team to the achievement of these targets as an intention of the company. The commitments of the charter have been signed by an increasing number of enterprises over time. To date, there are more than 400 signatories (Chinwala et al., 2021). They differ by size, legal form, and activity; the signatories are global banks, credit unions, insurance companies, and fintech start-ups based in the UK, America, Europe, and Asia.

In the wake of the UK Charter, another charter was launched a few years after (precisely on 19 June 2019) by the Italian Banking Association (Associazione Bancaria Italiana-ABI). The charter entitled "Women in Banks: enhancing gender diversity" (translated from the Italian "Donne in banca: valorizzare la diversità di genere") invites banking and non-banking financial institutions (associated or not) to adopt the principles contained within and to promote their implementation internally and externally to the institutions. These principles concern equal opportunities in recruitment and career development throughout the company organisation, including its highest hierarchical positions. The commitment required goes beyond the working environment: gender equality must also be promoted outside the workplace throughout society and in communities (for further details see Chapter 10). The list of member institutions (updated on 9 March 2021; see ABI, 2021) contains 37 institutions, equal to 90% in terms of total assets and 88% in terms of employees (the percentages refer to the Italian banking system).

Again, in June 2019, a Women in Finance Charter was proposed by the Belgian financial institutions, in consideration of the predominant male presence at executive and board-level positions. The Belgian "Gender Diversity in Finance" Charter reflects the aspiration of the signatories—37 as of June 2020—to achieve gender equality at all levels of the organisation. By signing the charter, each signatory company undertakes to: (1) promote the progression of women in senior roles through the identification of best practices and the setting of internal targets, the progressive achievement of which should be monitored, measured, and made public; (2) adopt and publish a strategy aiming at diversity at all levels of the organisation with the awareness that such a strategy may change from company to company also in consideration of the different starting points; (3) hold the top management of one's organisation accountable; and (4) consider appointing a diversity manager and/or one or more gender balance experts, if the company has yet to appoint such roles.

Despite the numerous compulsory and voluntary initiatives taken in the various countries, few banks so far have achieved targets that point to an effective diversity policy, according to EBA reports (see Chapter 4). In particular, institutions that promote gender diversity by ad hoc policies are 40.65% of the sample considered by EBA (2020) and those that meet their gender targets are only half at 20.14% (EBA, 2020; for more details see Chapter 4). Therefore, the importance of gender balance in businesses, including banks and other financial institutions, is at the heart of the European debate, and not only that.

## 2.4 Gender Diversity Disclosure: The Non-financial Information

The information on gender diversity to be provided to stakeholders is regulated by Directive 2014/95/EU regarding the disclosure of non-financial information addressed to large companies ("public-interest entities"), with more than 500 employees, and to other companies on a national basis.

In particular, non-financial statements should contain information on the initiatives taken to ensure gender equality (Directive 2014/95/EU, recital 7). Moreover, the information concerning diversity policies (in a broader acceptation of age, gender, and so on) of the administrative, management, and supervisory bodies of companies should be reported within the corporate governance statement (Directive 2014/95/EU, recital 19).

It is worth mentioning that, as well-acknowledged, the framework of non-financial information is set to change significantly. On 21 April 2021, the European Commission presented a proposal for a directive on the publication of corporate sustainability information (European Commission, 2021). In other words, the European Commission has adopted a proposal for a Corporate Sustainability Reporting Directive (CSRD) which would amend the reporting requirements set out in the Non-Financial Reporting Directive (NFRD). First, the proposal considerably extends the scope of the NFRD by lowering the size criteria: the proposed directive extends its scope to all large companies (whether listed or not) and all companies listed on regulated markets (including small and medium-sized enterprises but excluding listed micro-enterprises). Large companies are defined as companies that exceed at least two of the following three size criteria at the balance sheet date: balance sheet total of EUR 20,000,000; net revenue of EUR 40,000,000; average number of employees during the financial year of 250. Second, as to the content of the information (previously known as "non-financial information" and changed to "sustainability information"), the proposal introduces more detailed reporting requirements. Among the information to be provided, the directive specifies that the sustainability reporting standards shall detail the information that enterprises are to disclose about social factors, including information about "equal opportunities for all, including gender equality and equal pay for equal work, training and skills development, and employment and inclusion of people with disabilities" (Article 19b[2][b][i]). The document also emphasises the importance of communicating progress towards a more balanced gender participation in economic decision-making. Finally, a direct reference to gender is contained in the description of the diversity policy applied in relation to the company's administrative, management, and supervisory bodies (European Commission, 2021).

Because Global Reporting Initiative (GRI) standards are widely used in non-financial statements (Hoffmann et al., 2018; Raucci & Tarquinio, 2020), it may be useful to report the standards used as reference for describing the gender diversity issue, which is also linked to target 5 of SDG 5, which is to "Ensure women's full and effective participation and equal opportunities for leadership at all levels of decision-making in political, economic and public life". Table 2.2 indicates the unit and source for each relevant piece of information. The description should specify the policy followed in selecting the highest governance body and its committees, their composition, the weight of the two genders in the governance bodies, and the various categories of employees. Finally, reference should be also made to the GRI standard on equal pay, which concerns 3 of the SDG targets: target 5.1 "End all forms of discrimination against all women and girls everywhere", target 8.5 "By 2030, achieve full and productive employment and decent work for all women and men, including for young people and persons with disabilities, and equal pay for work of equal value", and target 10.3 "Ensure equal opportunity and reduce inequalities of outcome, including by eliminating discriminatory

**Table 2.2** GRI standards and gender diversity

| *Available Business Disclosures* | *Unit* | *Sources* |
|---|---|---|
| Composition of the highest governance body and its committees by:<br>i. Executive or non-executive;<br>ii. Independence;<br>iii. Tenure on the governance body;<br>iv. Number of each individual's other significant positions and commitments, and the nature of the commitments;<br>v. Gender;<br>vi. Membership of underrepresented social groups;<br>vii. Competencies relating to economic, environmental, and social topics;<br>viii. Stakeholder representation | Number | GRI Standard 102-22 |
| Nomination and selection processes for the highest governance body and its committees | N/A | GRI Standard 102-24 |
| Criteria used for nominating and selecting the highest governance body members, including whether and how:<br>i. Stakeholders (including shareholders) are involved;<br>ii. Diversity is considered;<br>iii. Independence is considered;<br>iv. Expertise and experience relating to economic, environmental, and social topics are considered | N/A | GRI Standard 102-24 |
| Percentage of individuals within the organisation's governance bodies in each of the following diversity categories:<br>i. Gender;<br>ii. Age group: younger than 30 years, 30–50 years, older than 50 years;<br>iii. Other indicators of diversity where relevant (such as minority or vulnerable groups) | % | GRI Standard 405-1 |
| Percentage of employees per employee category in each of the following diversity categories:<br>i. Gender;<br>ii. Age group: younger than 30 years, 30–50 years, older than 50 years;<br>iii. Other indicators of diversity where relevant (such as minority or vulnerable groups) | % | GRI Standard 405-1 |
| Ratio of the basic salary and remuneration of women to men for each employee category, by significant locations of operation | Ratio | GRI Standard 405-2 |

*Source* GRI (2020)

laws, policies and practices and promoting appropriate legislation, policies and action in this regard" (GRI, 2020).

Recently, some countries have shown great sensitivity to the gender pay gap and the principle "equal work, equal pay between women and men". Unfair wage inequality is illegal in several European countries. For this reason, many countries have introduced pay gap surveys and analyses to be performed by companies to discover, prevent, and erase possible gaps between women's and men's earnings and, in any case, among different segments of the staff employed, linked, for example, to religion or ethnicity (for more details on this topic see Chapter 5).

## 2.5 Indexes, Certifications, and the Women's Empowerment Principles

With the increasing attention towards gender parity in business management, several indexes have been developed to track the performance of companies in terms of gender equality, along with procedures to certify the company's commitment to pursuing gender equality in the workplace. The indexes and certifications also concern banking and non-banking financial intermediaries. The section ends by outlining a set of principles that offer guidance to enterprises in this field, known as the Women's Empowerment Principles.

### *2.5.1 Gender Equality Indexes*

Here, we describe some of the most common indexes in use today, illustrating the information they provide, where they overlap, and where they provide additional insight.

The Bloomberg Gender-Equality Index: the index is based on a standardised reporting model to capture information and data from the firms. The framework includes a set of questions grouped into five pillars. Pillar 1 "Female leadership & talent pipeline" collects information related to the number of women who are in the workforce, middle management, senior management, and the board of directors, and the number of women hired and promoted during the fiscal year. It also considers whether the positions of chair of the board and CEO are covered by a woman and whether a chief diversity officer has been appointed. Pillar 2 "Equal pay & gender pay parity" enquires on company audits on global equal pay, the resolution of any disparities emerging from the audit, the publication of any actions intended to close the gender pay gap, the number of women in the top pay quartile, the upper-middle pay quartile, the lower-middle pay quartile, and the lower pay quartile. Pillar 3 "Inclusive culture" addresses parental leave (e.g., the framework asks the minimum number of weeks of fully paid primary and secondary parental leave), insurance and benefits (e.g., insurance coverage that may be provided by the company for fertility services and gender reassignment services), family care (such as childcare services that may be provided by the company), flexibility (e.g., flexibility from the company to change both working hours and the place where employees work), and career development (e.g., whether a gender-diverse slate of candidates for all management roles is required and whether tools have been developed to reduce discriminatory behaviours). Pillar 4 "Sexual harassment policies" assesses company policies to combat sexual harassment and to manage employee complaints (e.g., does the company use an impartial external third party or an independent internal function?). Pillar 5 "Pro-women brand" concerns company suppliers (e.g., does the company have female suppliers?), products and services offered (e.g., do they allow any form of exploitation of women? Do they benefit women's health, safety, and well-being in the workplace? In the case of financial firms, is funding provided specifically to women-owned businesses? And do intermediaries keep track of repayment rates by gender?), education (referring to financial, health, or insurance education programmes directed at women in the community and not at female employees or clients), and public support for women (e.g., does the firm support non-profit organisations whose primary goal is protecting women in the workplace? Has the firm obtained gender equality certification?) (Bloomberg, 2019).

The index, which refers to companies with a high market capitalisation, is calculated by means of a methodology that multiplies the capitalisation by a score ranging from 0 to 100% (with 100% as the perfect score) which is assigned by taking into account two parameters: the disclosure of gender data (the so-called disclosure score) and the performance of the company reached in the five pillars compared to the industry peer group (the "data excellence score"). The two scores contribute to the final score with different weights; weights are also given to the pillar scores to determine the data excellence score (Bloomberg, 2021).

The latest release at the time of writing this book is for 2021 and lists a total of 380 well-known companies from 44 countries and belonging to

50 industries. The list includes many financial firms, especially banks and insurance companies (Table 2.3).

The European Women on Boards (EWoB) Gender Diversity Index: this index was developed within a "network of European networks" founded in 2013 to address gender issues. The index is measured considering four parameters: (1) the percentage of women in all leadership positions, calculated avoiding duplications if a person holds more than one position; (2) the percentage of women in the highest decision-making body, i.e., board of directors (in the unitary governance system) or supervisory board (in the two-tier governance system); (3) the percentage of women in executive functions (the decision-making level following the level indicated in point (2)); and (4) the percentage of women on board committees. Parameter 1 holds the greatest weight at 50%, followed by parameters 2 and 3 each weighing 20%, and parameter 4 weighing 10%. The index in its original version ranges from 0 to 1, where 0.5 represents the ideal value reflecting perfect gender balance. The index range, however, has been recently modified to make the result more intuitive, changing the range from 0 to 2 so that the ideal value is set at 1 (EWoB, 2020).

Unlike the Bloomberg Gender-Equality Index, the European Women on Boards Gender Diversity Index covers companies from 18 European countries (Austria, Belgium, Czechia, Denmark, Finland, France, Germany, Ireland, Italy, Luxembourg, the Netherlands, Norway, Poland, Portugal, Spain, Sweden, Switzerland, and the United Kingdom) with most companies being listed in the STOXX Europe 600 index. The percentages of companies from each country vary greatly and are the highest for the United Kingdom and France. One interesting and distinguishing feature of the EWoB Gender Diversity Index is that it produces rankings at a company, country, and industry level, providing different perspectives of factors contributing to performance in gender equality policies. Indeed, the 2020 EWoB study highlights that the greatest differences in rankings are found in inter-country comparisons rather than inter-sector comparisons, thus confirming the stronger association of gender issues to culture, beliefs, and traditions of a country rather than sector-specific characteristics.

With particular reference to the "Financial & Insurance Services" sector and its three sub-sectors (insurance, financial services, and banks), banking and non-banking financial firms are present with a total of 125 companies. The top three companies in this sector are a Swedish company

**Table 2.3** A selection of representative financial companies included in the 2021 Bloomberg Gender-Equality Index (in brackets are the company's core activity and headquarters location)

| |
|---|
| Alpha Bank (bank—Athens, Greece) |
| Ameriprise Financial Inc (financial services company—Minneapolis, Minnesota, United States) |
| Banco Commercial Português SA (private banking company—Porto, Portugal) |
| Banco Santander SA (financial services company—Madrid and Santander, Spain) |
| Bank Hapoalim BM (bank—Tel Aviv-Yafo, Israel) |
| Bank of America Corporation (multinational investment bank and financial services holding company—Charlotte, North Carolina, United States) |
| Bank Pekao SA (bank—Warsaw, Poland) |
| Barclays (multinational investment bank and financial services company—London, United Kingdom) |
| BBVA (multinational financial services company—Madrid and Bilbao, Spain) |
| BNP Paribas (bank—Boulevard des Italiens, Paris, France) |
| CaixaBank (leading financial group in retail banking —Valencia, Spain) |
| Capital One Financial Corporation (bank holding company specializing in credit cards, auto loans, banking, and savings accounts—McLean, Virginia, United States) |
| Cembra Money Bank AG (consumer finance bank—Switzerland) |
| China Life Insurance Co Ltd (life insurance company—Taiwan) |
| Citigroup Inc (multinational investment bank and financial services corporation—New York City, New York, United States) |
| Commercial International Bank (private sector bank—Cairo, Egypt) |
| Commonwealth Bank of Australia (multinational bank—Sidney, Australia) |
| Credit Suisse (global wealth manager and investment bank—Zürich, Switzerland) |
| Erste Group Bank AG (financial services provider—Vienna, Austria) |
| FinecoBank SpA (bank—Milan, Italy) |
| Grupo Financiero Banorte (financial group—Monterrey, Mexico) |
| Intesa Sanpaolo (bank—Turin, Italy) |
| Itau Unibanco Holding SA (bank—São Paulo, Brazil) |
| Jyske Bank A/S (bank—Silkeborg, Denmark) |
| KB Financial Group (life insurance provider—Seoul, South Korea) |
| Lloyds Banking Group PLC (financial services group—London, United Kingdom) |
| Malayan Banking Berhad (universal bank—Kuala Lumpur, Malaysia) |
| Mediobanca Banca di Credito Finanziario SpA (global merchant bank—Milan, Italy) |
| Mitsubishi UFJ Financial Group, Inc (Japanese bank holding and financial services company—Chiyoda, Tokyo) |
| Mizuho Financial Group (banking holding company—Ōtemachi district of Chiyoda, Tokyo, Japan) |
| Moneta Money Bank AS (bank—Prague, Czech Republic) |

(continued)

**Table 2.3** (continued)

| |
|---|
| National Australia Bank (bank—Melbourne, Australia) |
| National Bank of Canada (commercial bank—Montreal, Canada) |
| National Bank of Greece SA (banking and financial services company—Athens, Greece) |
| Provident Financial PLC (consumer finance company specialized in credit cards, vehicle finance and personal loans—Bradford, United Kingdom) |
| Prudential PLC (insurance company—London, United Kingdom) |
| QBE Insurance Group Ltd (insurance and reinsurance provider—Sydney, Australia) |
| Royal Bank of Canada (bank—Toronto, Canada) |
| Scotiabank (bank—Toronto, Canada) |
| Silicon Valley Bank (commercial bank—Santa Clara, California, United States) |
| Société Générale (investment bank and financial services company—Paris, France) |
| Standard Chartered PLC (banking and financial services company—London, United Kingdom) |
| Sumitomo Mitsui Financial Group (commercial banking company—Chiyoda City, Tokyo, Japan) |
| Sun Life Financial (life insurance company—Toronto, Canada) |
| Swedbank (bank—Stockholm County, Sweden) |
| Swiss Re AG (reinsurance and insurance company—Zürich, Switzerland) |
| Toronto-Dominion Bank (banking and financial services corporation—Toronto, Ontario) |
| UBS (investment bank and financial services company—Zürich and Basel, Switzerland) |
| UniCredit Group (bank—Milan, Italy) |
| Wells Fargo & Co (provider of banking, mortgage, investing, credit card, and personal, small business, and commercial financial services—San Francisco, California, United States) |
| Zurich Insurance Group AG (insurance provider—Zürich, Switzerland) |

*Source* http://bloomberg.com/GEI (last accessed: May 2021)

(Kinnvevik B), a Dutch company (ASR Nederland NV), and a company from the Czech Republic (RMS Mezzanine).

The FTSE Women on Boards Leadership Index Series: launched in February 2018, the series allows investors to target their investments towards companies that stand out for their gender equality and social impact. This series is based on a factor-based approach that tilts stocks to over/underweight according to gender diversity on the company's board and its social impact score. The series comprises two indexes: the FTSE All-Share® Women on Boards Leadership Index and the Russell 1000® Women on Boards Leadership Index. These two indexes are in turn based on two market capitalisation weighted indexes: the FTSE All-Share® ex Investment Trust Index and the Russell 1000® Index. The process of developing the two indexes of the series involves adjusting the constituent weightings according to two scores. One is an adjustment score for each company, which accounts for the percentage of women on the board over the Industry Classification Benchmark (ICB, a well-known industry classification taxonomy) average; the other is an adjustment score that considers social impact. The latter is based on the so-called Social Pillar score, which refers to five topics: Customer Responsibility, Health and Safety, Human Rights and Community, Labour Standards, and across all those areas, the Social Supply Chain (FTSE Russell, 2018, 2020). In essence, the construction process implies that companies with high values of these two scores will have a higher weight, and companies with lower scores will have less weight.

Regarding the presence of banks among the top 10 constituents of the two indexes, as of 31 March 2021, we recall HSBC Holdings (ICB sector is "Banks") ranked in the FTSE All-Share® Women on Boards Leadership Index (FTSE Russell, 2021a) and Bank of America (also in this case, ICB sector is "Banks") ranked in the Russell 1000® Women on Boards Leadership Index (FTSE Russell, 2021b).

The State Street Global Advisors (SSGA) Gender Diversity Index: this index was launched two years earlier, in February 2016. It tracks the performance of the highest market capitalisation US companies that stand out for their achievements in terms of gender parity on the board of directors and in senior leadership positions. Companies in the eleven sectors considered (Energy, Information Technology, Health Care, Industrials, Financials, Consumer Staples, Communication Services, Consumer Discretionary, Materials, Utilities, Real Estate) are ranked based on three ratios from an independent third party using information from the company's reports and website. In general, for the inclusion of companies in the index, the scores of companies in each sector are calculated according to criteria based on three ratios: (1) ratio of women executives to all executives; (2) ratio of women executives except those who are on the board of directors to all executives except those who are on the board of directors; and (3) ratio of women both executives and board members to all executives and board members. Executives are defined as those holding at least the position of vice president and for financial companies are defined as those holding at least the position of managing director (SSGA, 2021).

The Morgan Stanley Capital International (MSCI) Women's Leadership Index: the index is available in different configurations according to the countries and markets considered. It includes companies that stand out at national level for their commitment to pursuing gender parity on the board of directors and in leadership positions. In detail, each company must meet three requirements, namely Number of Women in Leadership Position, Percentage of Women on Board, and Discrimination and Workforce Diversity Controversy (MSCI, 2017). In particular, the requirements are the following: (1) a minimum of three female directors or, alternatively, at least one female director and one in a leadership role (i.e., chairperson, co-chairperson, executive chairperson, lead director, CEO, co-CEO, chief financial officer); (2) the share of women on the board above the average share calculated for all companies in the same MSCI country; and (3) the company not having been involved in any significant controversies related to diversity and discrimination in the workplace (MSCI, 2020).

The index is sector-neutral and the weight of each Global Industry Classification Standard (GICS) sector is equal to that assumed in the "Parent Index" (the underlying MSCI index). In addition, within each sector, the weights of the constituents are equal.

The MSCI indexes available are numerous, each characterised by the underlying index they are based on. For example, the MSCI World Women's Leadership Index, launched on 12 July 2016, is based on the MSCI World Index, which includes large and mid-cap stocks in 23 Developed Market (DM) countries worldwide (namely, Australia, Austria, Belgium, Canada, Denmark, Finland, France, Germany, Hong Kong, Ireland, Israel, Italy, Japan, the Netherlands, New Zealand, Norway, Portugal, Singapore, Spain, Sweden, Switzerland, the UK, and the US). Another example is the MSCI Europe Index (the parent index of another MSCI index on female leadership, the MSCI Europe Women's Leadership Index, likewise launched on 12 July 2016) which ranks the large and mid-cap stocks in the 15 European countries listed above. On the same day, the MSCI USA IMI Women's Leadership Index, based on the MSCI USA IMI Index, was launched. This index, unlike those described above, includes large, mid-cap, and small-cap stocks. The market considered is obviously the US market. Large, mid-cap, and small-cap stocks, in this case traded in the Canadian market, are also included in the MSCI Canada IMI Index, the parent index of the MSCI Canada IMI Women's Leadership Select Index, launched on 22 February 2018. At the end of March 2021, among the top 10 constituents, there were four financial companies (Royal Bank of Canada, Toronto-Dominion Bank, Bank Nova Scotia, and Bank Montreal; MSCI, 2021). Finally, we would like to mention two indexes based on the MSCI Japan IMI Top 700 Index, which includes large, mid-cap, and small-cap securities in the Japanese markets. They are the MSCI Japan Empowering Women Index (WIN), launched on 3 July 2017, and the MSCI Japan Empowering Women (WIN) Select Index, launched on 7 March 2018. Both select companies that stand out for their commitment to gender diversity and for their high financial quality.

### *2.5.2 Gender Equality Certifications*

Alongside indexes, gender equality certifications are becoming more widespread. In order to highlight the underlying process, we will look at two organisations that issue such certifications.

The Economic Dividends for Gender Equality (EDGE) certification: this certification—also issued to the European Central Bank (see Chapter 8)—measures the positioning of a company/organisation seeking certification against gender equality standards, set by the Swiss-based EDGE Certified Foundation. The measurement covers gender balance in terms of representation in the organisation, gender pay equity, the effectiveness of policies to promote careers inspired by equal opportunities, and inclusive culture in the workplace.

In the process, companies are required to benchmark themselves against EDGE standards and competitors, and certification is granted by a third-party certification body that guarantees impartiality (namely, there are three external accredited bodies: FLOCERT, SGS, and Intertek) after it has carried out an independent audit.

The certification is valid for two years since the pursuit of gender equality is an ongoing process and it signals the current status of this process. The certification has three levels. At the first level (Assess: Recognising Commitment), the company has undergone an independent audit on gender balance, gender pay equity, the effectiveness of equal opportunity career policies, and inclusive culture and is committed to an impactful action plan. This plan demonstrates the company's commitment to progress on gender parity under all parameters covered by the standards and to close any gaps identified in the company's assessment. The Assess level can be held for a maximum of six years, after which the company must move up to a higher level of certification if it wishes to maintain EDGE certification. In the second level (Move: Showcasing Progress), in addition to meeting all the above conditions, the company is required to achieve the EDGE global standard in some core areas (representation, pay gap, policies, and culture) and commits to further accelerate its progress. At the third level (Lead: Celebrating Success), the company reaches the EDGE global standard in all the areas and achieves gender balance successfully.[2] So far, among the financial organisations that have been certified are banks (e.g., Philippine National Bank, KBZ Bank), insurance/reinsurance companies (e.g., Insular Life Assurance Co., Allianz Suisse Versicherungs Gesellschaft AG, Swiss Reinsurance Company Ltd, and Zurich Insurance plc), asset management companies (e.g., CPP Investment Board Canada, Pictet Asset Management Ltd, and XA Investment Managers US), and supranational/government/federal institutions (e.g., the European Investment Bank, Infonavit, and Overseas Private Investment Corporation).[3]

Certification by the Winning Women Institute (WWI)[4]: this certification comes from an Italian organisation and has an underlying process that starts with a pre-audit to gather information about the company's position on gender equality in terms of gender-relevant processes and projects. The pre-audit is essentially a preliminary assessment of the company interested in obtaining certification. It consists of two analyses: the first verifies the positioning of the key performance indicators (KPIs) envisaged by the WWI certification model within the company; the second detects the perception that employees of both genders, chosen by the company from middle management positions, have regarding equal treatment of men and women in the workplace. The KPIs are part of the Dynamic Model Gender Rating developed by the WWI. The model has four areas of investigation, each of which includes qualitative and/or quantitative indicators relevant to capturing gender parity observed under multiple profiles. The areas and their respective indicators are as follows: (1) growth opportunities in the company: share of female employees; share of women managers; share of women in the management committee; share of women participants in non-compulsory training courses; (2) gender pay equity and HR processes: gender pay gap for the same job level/grade/category; difference between average women's

[2] Source: the website https://edge-cert.org/, last accessed: May 2021.

[3] The full list of the certified organisations is available at https://edge-cert.org/certified-organizations/.

[4] We would like to take this opportunity to thank Enrico Gambardella, President of the Winning Women Institute, for his kind availability to provide us with useful material on the WWI.

salaries and average men's salaries; valuing women in terms of annual promotions; share of women hired in the last 24 months; availability of services for work-life balance; (3) gender diversity policies: information actions on gender diversity in the workplace; actions in support of equal opportunities; actions aimed at surveying employees' perception of gender diversity in the workplace; actions aimed at spreading the culture of equal opportunities outside the workplace; and (4) maternity protection policies: offer of services upon return from maternity leave; presence of company policies aimed at protecting maternity in addition to what is provided for by the national collective labour agreement; offer of policies that allow benefits to be retained during maternity leave (WWI, 2018a, 2018b). The perception of employees is surveyed during dedicated workshops aimed at identifying both the company's strengths and the improvement actions. The second step of the certification process is the audit carried out by a third-party certification company (Ria Grant Thornton) according to the Dynamic Model Gender Rating, illustrated above. In this phase, the primary aim is to verify the truthfulness of the information and data collected during the pre-audit phase. The third step is the issuing of certification by the WWI if the audit results demonstrate compliance with the required standards. The certification, which the WWI communicates to the community and the market, is valid for three years. Among the companies certified by the WWI, there are financial companies, in particular the insurance companies Allianz Partners and Cardif (part of the BNP Paribas Group).

### 2.5.3 *Principles on Gender Equality*

In addition to these certification bodies, another global initiative deserving mention is the set of Women's Empowerment Principles (WEPs) launched in 2010 by UN Women and UN Global Compact. The principles provide a holistic framework for companies to embed a culture of gender equality in the workplace. The seven principles are listed in the following:

1. "Establish high-level corporate leadership for gender equality", which emphasises the importance of (a) establishing high-level gender equality and human rights policies; (b) creating a high-level task force and involving stakeholders, both internal and external to the company, in defining plans and policies to promote gender

equality; (c) setting gender equality targets and measuring progress by making managers at all levels accountable for the company's performance against the targets set; (d) ensuring that there are no factors that discriminate against women, also in terms of participation in governance bodies.

2. "Treat all women and men fairly at work – respect and support human rights and non-discrimination", which urges companies to: (a) remove all discrimination, including the gender pay gap, against women regardless of their background; (b) implement non-discriminatory recruitment and career advancement policies; (c) offer services that help with work-life balance (such as flexible working and childcare support); (d) encourage men to take parental leave.
3. "Ensure the health, safety and well-being of all women and men workers", which focuses on company policies and procedures, which should include ad hoc training courses, aimed at (a) preventing all forms of violence and sexual harassment, including domestic violence (especially for employees who work remotely); (b) ensuring equal access of workers to health insurance and tailored support for those with special needs/disabilities; (c) meeting the need to ensure safe and healthy working conditions.
4. "Promote education, training and professional development for women", which encourages women to progress in their careers and companies to develop training and awareness-raising programmes on equal rights for men and women.
5. "Implement enterprise development, supply chain and marketing practices that empower women", which includes (a) asking business partners, contractors, and suppliers to adopt the WEPs and to disclose their gender parity policies; (b) removing any harmful gender stereotypes from company materials and advertising; (c) and (most importantly, for financial intermediaries) investing in women-led businesses and seeking solutions to remove the barriers they face in accessing capital and financial products/services.
6. "Promote equality through community initiatives and advocacy", which involves carrying out and supporting gender equality programmes for the benefit of the whole community, including working with business partners, suppliers, and community leaders, interacting with stakeholders, and supporting community initiatives through philanthropy and grant programmes.

7. "Measure and publicly report on progress to achieve gender equality", which is implemented by: (a) measuring the results accomplished and the progress made in achieving gender parity; (b) surveying stakeholders regularly to monitor their expectations and needs; (c) disclosing the achievements and progress in implementing the WEPs (United Nations Entity for Gender Equality and the Empowerment of Women, 2021).

As of 1 March 2021, the WEPs have been subscribed by nearly 5000 companies from 141 countries, representing over 10 million employees. Among these companies, 180 are banks, mainly based in Asia and the Pacific (49), the Americas and the Caribbean (48), and Europe and Central Asia (44); 107 are insurance companies, based mostly in the above geographical areas with 24 in Asia and the Pacific, 29 in the Americas and the Caribbean, and 40 in Europe and Central Asia. There are only 10 asset management companies, four of which are in Asia and the Pacific, while there are 332 consumer finance companies, of which 123 are in the Americas and the Caribbean.[5]

## References

ABI—Associazione Bancaria Italiana. (2021). *Carta "Donne in banca: valorizzare la diversità di genere". Elenco degli aderenti in ordine alfabetico.* Aggiornamento al 9 marzo.

Avrampou, A., Skouloudis, A., Iliopoulos, G., & Khan, N. (2019). Advancing the sustainable development goals: Evidence from leading European banks. *Sustainable Development, 27*(4), 743–757. https://doi.org/10.1002/sd.1938

BCBS—Basel Committee on Banking Supervision. (2010, October). *Principles for enhancing corporate governance.*

BCBS—Basel Committee on Banking Supervision. (2015, July). *Guidelines: Corporate governance principles for banks.*

Bloomberg. (2019, May). *Bloomberg's gender reporting framework.*

Bloomberg. (2021). *Gender-equality index methodology.*

Carney, M. (2018, July 4). *Letter to The Rt Hon. Nicky Morgan MP, Chair of the Treasury Committee, House of Commons, Committee Office.*

[5] The complete list of the companies is available at the following link: https://www.weps.org/companies.

Chinwala, Y., Barrow, J., & Deb, S. (2021, March). *HM treasury women in finance charter: Annual Review 2020: Monitoring the progress of signatories and holding them to account.*

De Masi, S. (2019). *La diversità di genere negli organi di governo delle imprese.* Giappichelli.

Deloitte. (2019). *Women in the boardroom: A global perspective* (6th ed.).

EBA—European Banking Authority. (2020). *Report on the benchmarking of diversity practices at European Union level, under Article 91(11) of Directive 2013/36/EU (2018 Data).* EBA/REP/2020/05.

EBA—European Banking Authority. (2021, July 2). *Final report on guidelines on internal governance* (EBA/GL/2021/05).

ESMA and EBA-European Securities and Markets Authority and European Banking Authority. (2018, March 21). *Guidelines on the assessment of the suitability of members of the management body and key function holders.* ESMA71-99-598 EBA/GL/2017/12.

European Commission. (2011). *Green paper.* The EU Corporate Governance Framework. 5.4.2011 Com(2011) 164 final.

European Commission. (2012). *Action plan: European company law and corporate governance—A modern legal framework for more engaged shareholders and sustainable companies.* 12.12.2012 COM(2012) 740 final.

European Commission. (2021). *Proposal for a Directive of the European Parliament and of the Council amending Directive 2013/34/EU, Directive 2004/109/EC, Directive 2006/43/EC and Regulation (EU) No 537/2014, as regards corporate sustainability reporting.* COM (2021) 189 final.

European Parliament. (2019). *Annual strategic report on the implementation and delivery of the Sustainable Development Goals (2018/2279(INI)), resolution of 14 March.*

EWoB—European Women on Boards. (2020). *European women on boards gender diversity index.*

FSB—Financial Stability Board. (2018, April 20). *Strengthening governance frameworks to mitigate misconduct risk: A toolkit for Firms and supervisors.*

FTSE Russell. (2018). *FTSE women on boards leadership index series.* Integrate leadership in gender diversity into a broad market benchmark.

FTSE Russell. (2020, December). *FTSE women on boards leadership index.*

FTSE Russell. (2021a, March 31). *Factsheet: FTSE all-share women on boards leadership index.*

FTSE Russell. (2021b, March 31). *Factsheet: Russell 1000 women on boards leadership index.*

GRI—Global Reporting Initiative. (2020, March). *Linking the SDGs and the GRI standards.*

Hastings, P. (2018, Fall). *Breaking the glass ceiling: Women in the boardroom.*

Hoffmann, E., Dietsche, C., & Hobelsberger, C. (2018). Between mandatory and voluntary: non-financial reporting by German companies. *NachhaltigkeitsManagementForum, 26*, 47–63. https://doi.org/10.1007/s00550-018-0479-6

Janis, I. L. (1972). *Victims of groupthink: A psychological study of foreign-policy decisions and fiascoes*. Houghton Mifflin.

Kamalnath, A. (2018). Gender diversity as the antidote to 'groupthink' on corporate boards. *Deakin Law Review, 22*, 85–106. https://doi.org/10.21153/dlr2017vol22no1art723

Kanter, R. M. (1977a). *Men and women of the corporation*. Basic Books.

Kanter, R. M. (1977b). Some effects of proportions on group life: Skewed sex ratios and responses to token women. *American Journal of Sociology, 82*(5), 965–990.

Kroes, N. (2011, March 7). Don't take no for an answer. In *Conference "Women in Science, Innovation and Technology", speech*. Budapest.

Kumar, S., Kumar, N., & Vivekadhish, S. (2016). Millennium development goals (MDGs) to sustainable development goals (SDGs): Addressing unfinished agenda and strengthening sustainable development and partnership. *Indian Journal of Community Medicine, 41*(1), 1–4. https://doi.org/10.4103/0970-0218.170955

Lagarde, C. (2010, May 11). What if it had been Lehman sisters? *The New York Times* (Online). https://dealbook.nytimes.com/2010/05/11/lagarde-what-if-it-had-been-lehman-sisters/

Lagarde, C. (2019). A global imperative: Empowering women is critical for the world's economy and people. *Finance and Development, 56*(1), 5.

MSCI—Morgan Stanley Capital International. (2017, June). *MSCI women's leadership index methodology.*

MSCI—Morgan Stanley Capital International. (2020). *MSCI ESG controversies.*

MSCI—Morgan Stanley Capital International. (2021, March 31). *MSCI Canada IMI women's leadership select index (CAD).*

Obama, B. (2019) quote from Asher S (December 16, 2019). Barack Obama: Women are better leaders than men. *BBC News*. https://www.bbc.com/news/world-asia-50805822

Profeta, P. (2020). *Gender equality and public policy: Measuring progress in Europe*. Cambridge University Press.

Raucci, D., & Tarquinio, L. (2020). Sustainability performance indicators and non-financial information reporting. *Evidence from the Italian Case, Administrative Sciences, 10*(1), 1–17. https://doi.org/10.3390/admsci10010013

Reding, V. (2016). *Seminar organised by the EIB-European Investment Bank Institute*. https://institute.eib.org/2016/01/viviane-redinggender-equality-is-a-question-of-society/

SSGA—State Street Global Advisors. (2021). *SSGA gender diversity index (SSGAGDI): Index methodology.*

The High-Level Group on Financial Supervision in the European Union. (2009, February). *Report*. Brussels.

United Nations. (2015). *Transforming our world: The 2030 agenda for sustainable development*. https://www.un.org/ga/search/view_doc.asp?symbol=A/RES/70/1&Lang=E

United Nations. (2019). *The sustainable development goals report*.

United Nations Conference on Trade and Development (UNCTAD). (2015). *Investing in sustainable development goals: Part 1—Action plan for private investments in SDGs*. UNCTAD.

United Nations Entity for Gender Equality and the Empowerment of Women. (2021). *Equality means business*.

United Nations—Inter-agency Task Force on Financing for Development. (2019). *Financing for sustainable development report 2019*. https://developmentfinance.un.org/fsdr2019

van Staveren, I. (2014). The Lehman sisters hypothesis. *Cambridge Journal of Economics, 38*(5), 995–1014. https://doi.org/10.1093/cje/beu010

Visco, I. (2019, dicembre 10). *Intervento al Convegno della rivista Economia Italiana "Gender gaps in the Italian economy and the role of public policy"*. Banca d'Italia, Palazzo Koch.

Weber, O. (2018, November). *The financial sector and the SDGs: Interconnections and future directions* (Centre for International Governance Innovation Papers No. 201).

Weber, O., & Adnan, A. (2014). Empowerment through microfinance: The relation between loan cycle and level of empowerment. *World Development, 62*, 75–87. https://doi.org/10.1016/j.worlddev.2014.05.012

WWI—Winning Women Institute. (2018a). *Il Pre-Audit WWI®*.

WWI—Winning Women Institute. (2018b). *Report di valutazione pre-audit. La certificazione sulla Gender Equality come vantaggio competitivo per il business.*

CHAPTER 3

# Women and Bank Performance: Theoretical Background and Literature Review

**Abstract** This chapter offers a comprehensive literature review of the existing research on board gender diversity (BGD) and performance in banks and other financial institutions. After briefly reviewing the main theories on the role of women in the decision-making process, we analyse different relationships. First, empirical studies investigating the relationship between BGD and bank economic-financial performance are examined. Given the large number of studies, they are grouped into three categories: (1) studies revealing a positive linear relationship, (2) studies supporting non-significant, negative, or non-linear relationships between BGD and bank performance, and (3) studies focused on the Microfinance Institutions (MFIs). Then, the analysis shifts to the studies that examine the associations between BGD and bank efficiency, bank corporate social responsibility (CSR) performance and bank risk-taking. The final section of the chapter is dedicated to other areas of research on bank gender diversity that would benefit from an in-depth exploration.

This chapter is the result of the joint efforts of the two authors. However, Giuliana Birindelli mainly contributed to Sects. 3.3, 3.4 and Antonia Patrizia Iannuzzi to Sects. 3.1, 3.2,3.5, 3.6, 3.7. The authors equally contributed to Table 3.1.



G. Birindelli and A. P. Iannuzzi, *Women in Financial Services*, Palgrave Macmillan Studies in Banking and Financial Institutions, https://doi.org/10.1007/978-3-030-93471-2_3

## 3.1 Main Theories on the Role of Women in the Decision-Making Process

Before analysing the empirical literature aimed at demonstrating the positive implications of a greater presence of women in top and managerial positions, it is appropriate to explore the main economic theories underpinning these empirical studies. Indeed, the benefits of women on the boards can be explained in the light of the theories driving the debate around the influence of board gender diversity (BGD) on company performance. These theories, mentioned by all studies on BGD, not only those focusing on financial firms, are continually increasing in number. Initially, studies on BGD were based on only the three theories of agency theory, resource-dependence theory, and human capital theory (Nguyen et al., 2020). In the last five years, however, a significant number of other theories have been used. In particular, "*thirty-one different theoretical perspectives [have been] explicitly employed on this topic with twenty theories that have been utilized one time*" (Khatib et al., 2021, p. 5).

The first and most employed theory in the literature on BGD in financial firms is the agency theory which postulates that boards can better perform their monitoring role—by aligning owners' (shareholders) and agents' (managers) interests—when they are highly independent and diversified, that is when directors are of different ages and genders, and come from different countries. In this context, increasing the diversity of these governing bodies by enhancing the representation of women would improve their supervisory role and, in turn, improve the efficiency of corporate governance. In sum, by increasing their BGD, companies can minimise agency problems by decreasing the likelihood that managers pursue their own self-interests (Shettima & Dzolkarnaini, 2018; Talavera et al., 2018). These benefits will be reflected in the company's performance, which would tend towards improvement and growth.

In line with these considerations, the resource-dependence theory considers BGD a critical resource for companies because more women on the board add value and increase company performance by providing different perspectives, new skills, and competencies to the decision-making process (Adams & Ferreira, 2009). Compared to male directors, female directors have different opinions and experiences, a distinct approach to problem-solving, and more long-term and stakeholder-oriented views. This improves the firm's understanding of the market and may also enhance its image and corporate reputation (Khatib et al., 2021; Reddy & Jadhav, 2019).

Another theoretical framework often cited by the studies on BGD is the human capital theory. This perspective states that each individual has distinctive characteristics—in terms of skills, talent, and background—that distinguish him/her from others. In other words, each individual has a "diverse and unique" human capital and this aspect, in the context of corporate governance, is viewed as a key resource for the firm. Based on this assumption, this theory posits the unique capital of female directors compared to that of male board members can improve the firm's performance.

Other more recent theories applied in this field are the critical mass theory, the upper echelons theory, and the homophily perspective. The first theory arises from the original work of Kanter (1977) addressing gender diversity in group dynamics and processes. In particular, the critical mass theory postulates that a minority of board members with specific and similar characteristics (age, ethnicity, gender, nationality, tenure, etc.) will exercise their power by influencing decisions made by the board, only after reaching a certain threshold. Therefore, this theory considers BGD to be a positive trait, provided a threshold or critical mass of female representation is achieved. New views, skills, and competencies can influence group culture and firm performance in a positive way only when women reach a certain threshold level on the board. An increasing number of studies have found evidence of critical mass theory (De Masi et al., 2021), noting that bank boards need to be composed of at least 30% women in order to influence business processes and thus improve bank financial (Farag & Mallin, 2017; Kramaric & Miletic, 2017; Owen & Temesvary, 2018) and corporate social responsibility (CSR) performance (Birindelli et al., 2018), technical efficiency (Ramly et al., 2017), environmental commitment (Birindelli et al., 2019), and earnings management (Fan et al., 2019).

The upper echelons theory also posits a strong relationship between the firm's outcomes and the demographic characteristics of the top management team (Hambrick, 2007; Hambrick & Mason, 1984). Specifically, the core concept of this perspective is that top executives use their personalised lens and perspectives to make assessments and decisions (Hambrick, 2007). Said differently, the strategic situations are interpreted differently by the executives because of their different experiences, values, personalities, and other specific human factors. Thus, drawing on this theory, many studies document a strong translation of the values of women executives into the company's strategy. Since women are seen as more conservative, prudent, and more oriented towards long-term strategies, scholars suggest increasing BGD to enhance the social and economic performance of firms (Adusei et al., 2017).

Finally, more recent studies on BGD in banks have also employed the homophily perspective to formulate and corroborate their hypotheses. This theoretical perspective is based on the commonalities between individuals with respect to educational background, gender, age, and social status. The homophily perspective states that people who share common features or values are more likely to associate with each other and to establish stronger social relations (Berger et al., 2013). Some scholars find that bank performance is positive when there is a significant representation of women on the board, and a female CEO or chairperson. The affinity between women directors and women in top positions leads to better interaction, resulting in a superior corporate governance system (Glass & Cook, 2017). Similar results are found when the analysis focuses on environmental performance: firms led by female CEOs and managed by women interlinked board members are less likely than other firms to suffer environmental issues (Glass et al., 2016). Regarding the homophily perspective applied to the banking sector, while Berger et al. (2013) document that the likelihood of appointing additional female outside directors increases when there are already female executives on the bank's board, resulting in improved corporate governance, Birindelli et al. (2019) provide a novel application of this theory by arguing that the CEO's gender plays a crucial role in shaping the impact of a board's gender diversity on the bank's environmental performance. The authors reveal that a critical mass of women on the board positively impacts environmental performance only when banks are led by female CEOs. In other words, female CEOs empower the critical mass of women directors to pursue better environmental strategies (Birindelli et al., 2019).

## 3.2 Board Gender Diversity and Bank Economic-Financial Performance: A Positive Linear Relationship

Following the first studies to examine the effect of female directors on corporate performance, especially the research by Adams and Ferreira

(2009), the empirical literature has increasingly focused on this issue. Studies have mainly focused on non-financial companies, though in recent years there have also been interesting research developments specifically on the banking system. In both cases (non-financial and financial companies), there is mixed evidence and no real agreement on the impact of BGD on performance. Some papers find that a higher number of women on boards has a positive effect on financial performance, while others document a negative impact or no effects at all. Other researchers suggest that there is a non-linear association between economic performance and BGD.

Among the studies finding an overall positive linear relationship between BGD and bank performance, we can differentiate between single-country and multi-country studies. The first group includes the studies of Pathan and Faff (2013), Del Prete and Stefani (2015), Mori and Towo (2017), Agyemang-Mintah and Schadewitz (2019), Adesanmi et al. (2019), Mazzotta and Ferraro (2020), and Khan and Wang (2021). Two of these studies focus on Anglo-Saxon countries, two on Italy, one on China, and the last two on African countries.

The Anglo-Saxon studies are carried out by Pathan and Faff (2013) and Agyemang-Mintah and Schadewitz (2019). Pathan and Faff (2013) examine a sample of 212 US bank holding companies over the period 1997–2011. They only partially confirm the positive relationship between BGD and bank performance (return on average assets, ROAA; return on average equity, ROAE; and average stock return) because this relationship is only found in the pre-Sarbanes–Oxley Act (SOX) period (1997–2002). In the post-SOX (2003–2006) and the crisis period (2007–2011), the positive effect of BGD tends to weaken. As stated by these authors, "*This result is particularly important because it indicates that the inclusion of more female directors does not necessarily improve bank performance. One plausible interpretation could be that more female board members beyond a "desirable" limit reduce the possibility of the inclusion of more capable male directors*" (Pathan & Faff, 2013, p. 1574). Similarly, Agyemang-Mintah and Schadewitz (2019), considering a large sample of UK financial institutions (investment banking, insurance, mortgages, investment trust, banking services) find that having women on corporate boards contributes positively to the financial value of these institutions (as proxied by Tobin's Q) only for the pre-crisis period (2000–2006). Conversely, the presence of females on the board after the financial crisis no longer has a significant effect on the value of financial firms due to the economic downturn experienced by the entire UK economy during those years.

Del Prete and Stefani (2015) and Mazzotta and Ferraro (2020) examine the Italian banking system. The first study analyses the impact of BGD on Italian bank performance from 1995 to 2010. Due to the low presence (often close to zero) of women on the boards of these banks during the period under investigation, the two authors choose to use a dummy variable instead of the share of women.[1] This study shows that gender diversity on boards tends to have a positive effect on the quality of credit and, though less robust, on bank profitability as measured by the return on assets (ROA). Mazzotta and Ferraro (2020), instead, analyse 22 Italian listed banks in a more recent time frame (2008–2014). The first of their findings is that BGD positively affects bank performance measures (ROAE and ROAA), especially after the gender quota law (Law 120/2011, known as "Legge Golfo-Mosca", see Chapter 10) and in the aftermath of the 2007/2008 financial crisis (2011–2014). Second, a higher presence of female directors tends to damage the market performance of banks (measured by Tobin's Q), likely due to the male-centred vision by investors believing that female directors might hinder the value of the bank. Finally, the positioning of female directors on the board (executive, non-executive, or independent) has a non-neutral impact on bank performance. Indeed, it is mostly the presence of executive and independent female directors that positively affects bank performance. Taken together, the study by Mazzotta and Ferraro (2020) documents the importance of BGD in times of financial crisis by corroborating the positive effect of a gender quota law on the economic performance of banks.

The other single-country studies concentrate on China and Africa. Khan and Wang (2021) focus on a sample of 17 Chinese commercial banks from 2008 to 2019 and find that the existence of female directors alone does not positively and significantly improve the financial performance of banks. Female directors do positively influence bank performance when they are selected as independent directors. Regarding the African continent, Mori and Towo (2017) suggest that in order to maximise profitability, banks need to increase both the overall number

[1] This dummy variable is equal to 1 if there is at least one woman on the bank board two years before the time referring to the dependent variable, which is a bank performance indicator, and 0 otherwise.

of directors and the number of female directors. Focusing on 35 banks in Tanzania over the period 2009–2013, their empirical analysis shows a positive link between female board representation and bank ROA and profit margin. Based on this evidence, they conclude that "*with current changes in policy and education in emerging countries, there is a need to increase female representation in order for banks to benefit not only from their expertise but also their way of dealing with issues*" (Mori & Towo, 2017, p. 169). Likewise, Adesanmi et al. (2019) find that BGD positively affects the bank's financial performance in terms of profit margin. However, the analysis only includes 10 listed deposit money banks in Nigeria from 2008 to 2017.

Other studies confirm a positive relationship between BGD and bank performance, through a multi-country analysis. This provides an understanding of the extent to which the positive implication of board gender diversity in banks can be generalised in a framework where institutional differences are taken into account. These studies can be grouped into three categories: (a) international multi-country studies; (b) European multi-country studies, and (c) Islamic multi-country studies.

The first group includes the study of García-Meca et al. (2015). These authors conduct an empirical investigation on a sample of 159 banks in nine countries (Canada, France, Germany, Italy, the Netherlands, Spain, Sweden, the United Kingdom, and the United States) during the period 2004–2010 to analyse how female and foreign directors contribute to board behaviour and bank performance (Tobin's Q and ROA). The main findings reveal that while foreign directors harm bank performance, female directors generate a positive effect. This occurs because the presence of women on bank boards improves governance, which makes the bank more profitable. The authors state that this finding shows "*women directors are not substitutes for traditional corporate directors with identical abilities but rather that qualified women directors have unique characteristics that create additional value in banks*" (García-Meca et al., 2015, p. 210). Finally, this study also documents that the positive contribution of BGD to bank performance is stronger in countries with high investor protection levels and legal enforcement. This confirms that banking authorities consider board oversight an important complement to supervision rather than a substitute. In the same vein, using a sample of 461 large banks from countries of the Organisation for Economic Co-operation and Development (OECD), Gulamhussen and Santa (2015) assess the role of women in bank boardrooms (board of directors, supervisory board, and audit committee) by employing several bank performance measures (ROA, ROAE, net interest income, other operating income, non-interest expenses, and Tobin's Q). After controlling for bank and country-specific effects and applying a two-stage least-squares (2SLS) regression, they find that the participation of women on the board positively influences not only accounting performance measures but also loan quality and coverage of impaired loans (which improve via bank capital), and finally earnings variability (which decreases). Similar findings are also observed for the presence of women on the supervisory board and with some exceptions on the audit committee. Moreover, for a sub-sample of listed banks, the positive influence of female directors also regards the market performance of banks (Tobin's Q ratio).

The second group of multi-country analyses includes three main studies on the European continent. The first study, conducted by Mateos de Cabo et al. (2012) on a large sample of 612 banks from 20 European countries in December 2006, documents a higher presence of female directors in growth-oriented banks. The second by Andrieş et al. (2020) uses a unique, hand-collected dataset of 156 banks from Central and Eastern European (CEE) countries during 2005–2012. Their results show that banks with a chairwoman and a higher proportion of female board members record a higher level of profitability and tend to have a lower level of credit losses and a higher level of stability during the 2008 financial crisis. Again, similar conclusions are reached by Cardillo et al. (2020), who are the first to jointly analyse the impact of BGD on the probability and size of public bailouts and on bank performance. The analysis focuses on 105 banks in EU-15 countries over the period 2005–2017. The main findings suggest that BGD is positively related to bank accounting and market performance (as measured by ROA, Tobin's Q, and dividend payout ratios) and negatively related to the probability of receiving a public bailout. In other words, banks with more female directors on their boards benefit not only from better performance but as a result also from a lower probability of incurring a government bailout.

Finally, in the third group of multi-country studies, we have the recent study by Jabari and Muhamad (2021) focused on Islamic states. This work analyses 19 Islamic banks (9 Indonesian and 10 Malaysian) over 9 years (2010–2018) and finds that BGD has a positive influence on the economic performance (ROAE) of Islamic banks. However, while this is always true for the proportion of women on the board of directors (BOD), the positive impact on bank performance is only true for smaller banks when considering the proportion of female Shariah supervisory board (SSB) members. Given the differences between Islamic banks and conventional banks, this evidence could contribute to generalising the positive contribution of BGD to bank performance.

In summary, there is a wealth of studies confirming an overall positive relationship between women on boards and economic-financial performance of banks. In this context, the authors address many policy implications to the supervisory authorities around the world so they may ensure sound governance systems that focus on increased gender diversity in boardrooms to improve performance and risk-taking in banks. Yet, this should in no way be considered as a substitute for sound regulation and supervision.

### 3.2.1 *The Case of Microfinance Institutions*

Other interesting research analyses the BGD-financial performance nexus in Microfinance Institutions (MFIs), where corporate governance systems still appear under-investigated compared to other financial institutions. According to Strøm et al. (2014), "*the microfinance industry is particularly suited for studying the impact of female leadership on governance and performance because of its mission orientation, its entrepreneurial nature, diverse institutional conditions, and high percentage of female leaders*" (Strøm et al., 2014, p. 60).

Adopting a chronological approach, the paper by Mersland and Strøm (2009), studying 278 microfinance institutions from 60 countries over the period 1998–2007, documents a positive relationship between the financial performance of these institutions and the presence of a female CEO. Specifically, when MFIs are led by a female CEO, their economic performance (measured by ROA and operational self-sufficiency—OSS[2]) increases. This likely is due to the high number of female clients generally served by these institutions and to the greater ability of female CEOs to understand the needs and the most suitable products for such clients, resulting in a more profitable credit relationship. In other words, given the very high percentage of women as clients, the presence of a female CEO in MFIs tends to reduce the information asymmetry towards their clients more than a male CEO would. This positive relationship is also

[2] The OSS is defined as operating income divided by the total of financial expense, loan-loss expense, and operating expense. In this study, OSS is used to measure the financial performance of a MFI.

confirmed by the interesting matching between the percentages of female CEOs and female clients documented by this study. Indeed, the presence of a female CEO equals 23.5%, while 73% of MFI clients are women. Likewise, Strøm et al. (2014) reach similar results. Focusing on a global panel of 329 MFIs in 73 countries over eleven years (1998–2008), these authors show that a female CEO and a female chairperson on the board are positively related to the MFI performance in terms of both ROA and return on equity (ROE). Hasan et al. (2019), on the other hand, only focus on a single country. Their sample consists of 68 MFIs from Bangladesh over the period 2008–2009. Despite the smaller sample size and shorter time horizon compared to previous studies, Hasan et al. (2019) confirm the positive impact of female leadership on MFI financial performance. In particular, they show that gender diversity on the board has a positive impact on MFI performance only when the CEO is female. Taken separately, females on the board and female CEOs show a negative correlation with the financial performance of MFIs (as measured by the operational self-sufficiency), while the interaction variable (female CEO with female directors on the board) for capturing the joint effect of board gender diversity and female CEO is positive and significant.

The last paper supporting a positive correlation between BGD and MFI performance does not focus on women in apical positions, but on female managers. This research by Boubacar (2020), using data from 266 microfinance institutions located in the West African Economic and Monetary Union (WAEMU) for the period 2013–2017,[3] demonstrates that having more female managers in MFIs favours the granting of loans, especially to the female clients of these institutions. This result "*may indicate that a female manager has a better knowledge of the products women want and also sets terms that appeal to women*" (Boubacar, 2020, p. 217). Thus, according to other studies (Mori & Olomi, 2012), women participating in the decision-making process have a positive influence on the social goals of MFIs to meet the needs of the poorest and most vulnerable clients.

Lastly, Adusei et al. (2017) and Shettima and Dzolkarnaini (2018) report results that differ from the above studies (negative and non-significant respectively). Drawing on data from 494 MFIs across 76

[3] These MFIs are distributed as follows: 37 MFIs operating in Benin, 28 MFIs in Burkina Faso, 33 MFIs in the Ivory Coast, 4 MFIs in Guinea-Bissau, 23 MFIs in Mali, 22 MFIs in Niger, 83 MFIs in Senegal, and 36 MFIs in Togo.

countries over five years (2010–2014), Adusei et al. (2017) find that BGD is negatively and significantly related to the economic-financial performance of these institutions (measured by ROA and OSS). This negative impact seems more likely to occur when a MFI combines 50% or higher female representation on its board with 50% or higher female representation on its management team. Thus, the authors conclude that: "*although microfinance is a business for and by women yet excessive female representation on boards and management teams could be detrimental to the financial performance of MFIs. We, thus, recommend that there should be equitable representation of both men and women on boards and management teams of MFIs in order to promote appreciable financial performance*" (Adusei et al., 2017, p. 12). Shettima and Dzolkarnaini (2018), using a sample of 30 Nigerian Microfinance Institutions for the period 2010–2013, document a positive and significant relationship between board size and MFI performance (ROE and ROA), whereas the relationship concerning female directors on the board is negative and non-significant. Thus, their results do not support the role of BGD in influencing MFI performance.

## 3.3 Studies Supporting a Non-significant, Negative, or Non-linear Relationship Between BGD and Bank Economic-Financial Performance

Other studies find evidence of different relationships between BGD and bank economic-financial performance: non-significant, negative, or non-linear. These studies appear very heterogeneous, especially for the geographic area analysed and the time window. Accordingly, we shall separate them into the following categories:

(a) studies on the United States and Europe;
(b) studies on China and India;
(c) studies on the Middle East and North Africa (MENA) and Muslim countries.

The first group includes the research by Rodríguez-Ruiz et al. (2016), Farag and Mallin (2017), Kramaric and Miletic (2017), Dinu and Bunea (2018), Owen and Temesvary (2018), and Arnaboldi et al. (2020). The study by Farag and Mallin (2017), focusing on 99 European banks over the period 2004–2012, finds the relationship between BGD and bank performance is significant and positive for the board of directors (BOD), supervisory board (SB), and management board (MB). The diversity-performance nexus is found to be non-linear for all bodies; however, the relation for the board of directors and supervisory board takes an inverted U-shape, while it is a non-inverted U-shape for the management board. This implies that while women sitting on the BOD and SB positively influence bank performance until a certain threshold (or critical mass) is reached (beyond which appointing an additional female director tends instead to lower financial performance), the relationship is reversed for the MB where the impact on bank performance becomes positive only after reaching a critical mass (equal to 27%) of female directors. This seemingly contradictory double nexus reveals two aspects. On the one hand, the net effect of gender diversity on bank performance can be either positive or negative depending on the role played by female directors (if they are executive or not); on the other hand, a gender-balanced board is always better than an unbalanced-board (on both the female and male sides). Similar results are found by Owen and Temesvary (2018) regarding the US banking sector. Applying instrumental variables methods to data on approximately 90 US bank holding companies from 1999 to 2015, they document the presence of significant non-linearities in the relationship between bank performance (as proxied by the ROA, the revenue to expense ratio, the sharp ratio, and the stock price growth) and BGD, suggesting that the economic impact of female board representation largely depends on its existing level. Said differently, to enhance economic performance, banks need to reach a critical percentage of women sitting on their boards; the impact on economic performance only becomes positive beyond this point. Additionally, this positive effect is only observed in better-capitalised banks, or well-managed banks, suggesting that the impact of gender diversity also depends on the quality of bank management. In contrast, the studies by Arnaboldi et al. (2020) and Dinu and Bunea (2018) show the relationship between bank performance and female board representation is non-significant. Both studies focus on the European banking sector and include bank performance indicators.[4] Arnaboldi et al. (2020) use a larger sample (77 EU listed

[4] The performance indicators utilised by Arnaboldi et al. (2020) are the following: (a) SR-stock market annualised daily return; (b) SDSR-standard deviation of the SR; (c) ROA; (d) NIM-net interest margin;(e) *Z*-score as a measure of bank solvency. Dinu and

banks) and a very wide time window (2007–2015) also encompassing the years of the subprime crisis.[5] Dinu and Bunea (2018) restrict their scope to 27 Romanian banks and include only one year's data (2016). Again, in the European setting, Kramaric and Miletic (2017) consider all Croatian commercial banks over the period 2002–2014 and prove the existence of a critical mass of women on the management board determines a significant influence on bank performance in terms of net interest margin (NIM) and ROA. Finally, while these studies focus on the influence of the gender board composition on corporate results, Rodríguez-Ruiz et al. (2016) extend their analysis to all the banking institution employees on the assumption that "*examining only specific groups or management teams does not capture the larger human capital pool that determines an organization's success*" (Rodríguez-Ruiz et al., 2016, p. 108). The sample consists of 59 banks operating in Spain over the period 1999–2010. There are three main findings from this study. First, there is an inverted U-shaped relationship between gender and bank performance (ROA): recruiting more women employees enhances efficiency in the use of company assets up to a critical point equal to 43% of women in the workforce. Beyond that point, bank performance tends to decrease, probably due to cooperation problems that arise among groups that are very heterogeneous in terms of gender representation. Second, a similar relationship connects women in technical positions and bank economic performance: ROA reaches its highest value when women represent 27% of the workforce in technical jobs in the bank. Therefore, only banks with a certain degree of balance in their gender workforce composition experience better economic performance than institutions with a high concentration level of males or females. These findings are very interesting because they show that an over-recruitment of women beyond the "critical mass" point is not beneficial for bank profitability. Finally, regarding productivity (gross margin divided by the average total

Bunea (2018), instead, measure bank performance by ROA, ROE, total assets, and total loans.

[5] Arnaboldi et al. (2020) analyse several board diversity features (type, size, tenure, age of directors, BGD, employee representation, and internationalization). While some of these (size, tenure, and employee representation) have a positive impact on bank performance, no impact is found regarding the female board representation. The authors also discover a non-linear or U-shaped relationship with bank performance, but this relationship only concerns the proportion of minority representatives.

number of employees for each year), the proportion of women does not seem to increase this outcome in commercial banks.

As noted earlier, the second group comprises studies on China and India. The "Chinese" studies are carried out by Liang et al. (2013), Talavera et al. (2018), and Ting and Huang (2018). Liang et al. (2013), using a sample of the 50 largest Chinese banks from 2003 to 2010, find that the proportion of female directors on the board has no impact on either bank performance (ROA and ROE) or asset quality as measured by several proxies (NPL ratio, the stock of NPLs, the net charge-off ratio-NCO ratio, the level of NCOs). Likewise, Talavera et al. (2018), using a sample of 97 Chinese banks over a period from 2009 to 2013, do not find any relationship between the percentage of female directors and bank profitability as measured by the ROA and ROE. Differently, Ting and Huang (2018) conduct a study on the relation between the CEOs' power and any perks (any form of non-monetary compensation[6]) they receive. In other words, they investigate whether the CEO's power influences the perks that banks offer. Based on all Chinese banks from the China Banking Regulatory Commission over the period from 1999 to 2011, the authors find two interesting relationships. If, on the one hand, banks with powerful CEOs tend to have more perks, on the other hand, only BGD (among other board characteristics, including size and age of directors) effectively reduces these extra benefits providing better monitoring of the CEO's power. From this, we can deduce that fewer perks as incentives might translate into worse performance.

Studies on the Indian banking system have been carried out by Ghosh (2017), Ghosh and Ansari (2018), and Rafinda et al. (2018). In particular, Ghosh (2017), employing information on all publicly listed Indian banks (equal to 40) from 2003 to 2012, shows that female directors do not significantly affect bank performance, expressed by accounting (ROA) and market-based (Tobin's Q) measures. This could be due to over-monitoring or a lack of adequate skills in the female board members.[7] In

[6] A perk is any form of non-monetary compensation offered to employees at all levels, including—for example—travelling expenses, business entertainment expenses, overseas training expenses, board meeting expenses, company car expenses, and meeting expenses.

[7] However, when female directors are divided into executive and independent, there is some evidence that female executive directors enhance bank stability. Finally, looking across ownership, other evidence suggests that gender diversity in state-owned banks enhances stability (as measured by $Z$-score), but at the cost of lower profitability. Thus, this result

the same vein, Ghosh and Ansari (2018) examine the association between financial performance and boards of urban cooperative banks in India. Utilising cross-sectional data on 1263 banks for 2012 and employing five economic dependent variables (net interest margin, NIM; return on loans, RTL; cost of funds, CoF; cost income ratio, CIR; and non-performing loans, NPL ratio), the authors find that a greater presence of women on the boards does not have a positive impact on the economic performance of banks. On the contrary, the relationships are even negative, in that a greater gender diversity in these financial institutions exerts a dampening effect on economic performance. The only exception concerns the CIR for banks operating in low-income districts: the CIR decreases in correspondence to an increase in BGD, showing an improvement in operational efficiency. Finally, Rafinda et al. (2018), focusing on 22 banks and financial institutions in India over the period 2011–2015, find no relationship between the existence of female directors and bank performance measured by two accounting variables (ROA and ROE). However, by using the alternative measure of the ratio of operating expense to operating income (OEOI), the relationship becomes positive but is significant only at the 10% level. This weak positive relationship is likely due to greater monitoring of bank activity carried out by female directors compared to male directors.

Overall, this scarce effect of BGD on bank performance in emerging economies could be due to a combination of factors including (a) the limited presence of women on bank boards, (b) the different and less efficient governance mechanisms of banks located in these economies, and finally, (c) the fact that the inclusion of female directors is merely in compliance with regulation and does not represent the free choice of banks.

Finally, the third grouping of studies focused on the MENA and Muslim countries includes the works by Ekadah and Mboya (2012), Grassa (2016), Mohammad et al. (2018), Khan et al. (2020), and Baklouti (2020). The research by Ekadah and Mboya (2012) focuses on 32 commercial banks in Kenya for the period 1998–2009. Using two gender proxies (see Table 3.1), these authors find that board gender diversity does not affect bank performance (ROA). Specifically, the coefficients of both gender variables are negative, but not statistically significant.

indicates that ownership interacts with gender diversity in influencing bank performance. See Ghosh (2017).

These findings could be due to the male-dominated boards of Kenyan banks. Indeed, with few (or no) women sitting on the board, they may not be able to exert any influence on the bank's strategies. Indirectly, this evidence underscores the role of women as tokens in the banking industry, further validating the tokenism theory (Kanter, 1977). Similarly, Grassa (2016), focusing on 43 Islamic banks in the Gulf Cooperation Council (GCC) and Southeast Asian countries over the period 2005–2011, does not find any significant relationship between the presence of women on the Sharia board and Islamic bank credit ratings. Mohammad et al. (2018) analyse 11 Jordanian listed banks for the period 2009–2016. These authors also find no statistically significant relationship between the percentage of female top and medium-level executive managers and bank performance (ROA). Khan et al. (2020), focusing on Muslim countries, investigate whether the performance of Islamic banks (IBs) with females on the board significantly differs from that of conventional banks (CoBs). Based on a sample of 71 IBs and 120 CoBs over the period 2010–2017, they find that IBs have slightly fewer female directors on their boards compared to CoBs, and that the promotion of females in leadership positions in religiously conscious corporations (such as IBs) does not affect their economic performance. Indeed, the study shows that, compared to CoBs, the performance of IBs is not influenced by the appointment of females on the board.[8] Lastly, Baklouti (2020), using data from 42 MENA Islamic banks outside the Gulf Cooperation Council and non-Islamic countries during 2011–2018, shows that while a large-sized board of directors and the number of SSB meetings improve bank performance (ROA and ROE), the proportion of women sitting on the SSB has no impact on the financial performance of Islamic banks.

## 3.4 Board Gender Diversity and Bank Efficiency

A further and more recent strand of literature investigates the relationship between BGD and bank efficiency, stressing the idea that female board representation can be an important determinant of bank outcome. In most cases, there is a positive impact on the bank's technical efficiency,

[8] The negative relationship, hypothesised by the authors, between women directors and the performance of IBs is based, among other things, on the consideration that the presence of female directors may be interpreted as disrespectful of religious principles on behalf of IBs, adversely affecting their performance.

when the presence of women on boards increases. Only two studies find a negative relationship.

Among the works reporting a positive relationship, Andrieș et al. (2018), with a sample of 128 commercial banks from Central and Eastern European countries during the period 2005–2012, indicate that greater female representation among members of bank boards has a strong and positive impact on both cost and technical efficiency, especially for smaller banks. Hence, the absence of women in the boardroom could lead to lower technical efficiency. Similarly, Safiullah (2021), analysing a sample of 94 Islamic banks from 28 countries during the period 2003–2018, finds that gender diversity is positively associated with stability efficiency[9] estimated using the stochastic frontier approach. Adeabah et al. (2019) also document the effect of BGD on enhancing bank efficiency. Moreover, their study, focused on data from 21 banks in Ghana for the period from 2009 to 2017, documents a parabolic relationship between female directors and bank efficiency. Specifically, there is an inverted U-shaped relationship between these two variables, so that bank efficiency increases up to a maximum number of two female directors. For more than two women directors on a nine-member board, banks exhibit a decreasing return to scale. As stated by the authors: "*the optimal number of female directors on boards to achieve the highest level of efficiency for banks in the sample is two on average*" (Adeabah et al., 2019, p. 311). Finally, Ramly et al. (2017) add a further piece of evidence highlighting that the role played by women directors also matters in increasing bank efficiency. This study on 102 commercial banks from countries of the Association of Southeast Asian Nations (ASEAN) from 1999 to 2012 reveals that female board appointments alone do not assure a positive impact on bank efficiency. In other words, female directors are effective in promoting bank efficiency if they are appointed as independent directors. In addition, the authors show the importance of achieving a critical mass of independent women directors. The positive impact on cost efficiency and profit efficiency level could only be accomplished when at least one-third of the board includes independent female directors. This evidence gives a new dimension to the governance role of women directors and independent

[9] "*Stability efficiency is relatively a new measure of performance in banking and enables to capture the relative performance of how close an individual bank's financial stability is to the best performing banks among them given its production inputs and outputs condition*" (Safiullah, 2021, p. 2).

directors on bank boards, displaying the importance of both the number of women and their role in improving efficiency.

Titova (2016) and Adusei (2019), on the other hand, do not find evidence of a positive relationship between BGD and bank efficiency. However, while Titova (2016), analysing a sample of publicly traded US commercial banks and savings institutions over the period 2007–2013, finds no conclusive results, Adusei (2019), focusing on a multi-country sample of 418 MFIs over the period 2010–2014, shows that female board representation hurts the technical efficiency of these institutions. A positive relationship can be found only for larger MFIs where women on boards are more likely to promote technical efficiency rather than reducing it. This means that the size of the MFIs could play a key role in positively influencing the impact of female directors on MFIs' technical efficiency.

## 3.5 Board Gender Diversity and Bank CSR Performance and Disclosure

Compared to studies on financial performance, analyses of the relationship between BGD and non-financial performance of banks appear to be more recent and still underdeveloped. Nevertheless, a few interesting studies exist, some analysing CSR performance and others mainly focusing on the disclosure of such performance. Overall, both studies provide mixed results.

Addressing CSR performance, Al-Jaifi (2020) examines the association between BGD and a bank's environmental, social, and corporate governance performance in the ASEAN context. Focusing on a sample of 26 banks over the period 2011–2016 and using data from the Thomson Reuters-Eikon database, this study finds a positive relationship only between female directors and corporate governance performance. Conversely, the impact of BGD on environmental and social performance is not supported. This finding implies that appointing more women directors leads banks to perform better corporate governance practices. Given that female directors are considered capable of improving the board monitoring function, a higher presence of these board members makes monitoring and supervision activities better and more accurate. In the same vein, García-Sánchez et al. (2018) investigate whether BGD (and other board characteristics) impacts on CSR commitment by banks. Using a sample of 159 banks in nine countries during the period 2004–2010, their empirical evidence suggests that the greater the BGD, the better the CSR performance of banks, especially in more regulated environments and with greater investor protection. A similar positive impact on bank CSR is also generated by board independence. More recently, Gallego-Sosa et al. (2021) attempt to determine whether there are differences in commitment to the Sustainable Development Goals (SDGs) among banks with different levels of BGD. Focusing on the 30 largest banks in Europe in terms of market capitalisation, the research shows that for "Climate Action" and "Sustainable Cities and Communities" SDGs, bank commitment is stronger when there is greater female board representation. However, gender diversity does not seem to play a key role for the remaining SDGs. Shakil et al. (2021), instead, examine the moderating effect of environmental, social, and governance (ESG) controversies. In detail, this study analyses 37 US banks from 2013 to 2017 to verify whether ESG controversies moderate the BGD-ESG performance nexus. Drawing on the resource-dependence and legitimacy theories, the authors identify a significant positive relationship between BGD and bank ESG performance, although the moderating effect of ESG controversies on this relationship is not evident. Finally, Birindelli et al. (2018), focusing on a sample of 108 listed banks in Europe and the United States for the period 2011–2016, show that the relationship between BGD and a bank's ESG performance is an inverted U-shape. This means that after reaching a critical mass of women on the board, the increasing presence of female directors does not have a positive impact on a bank's sustainability performance. In sum, this study finds no support for the critical mass theory, confirming that only gender-balanced boards positively impact a bank's ESG performance.

The studies analysing the impact of BGD on bank CSR disclosure mainly focus on emerging economies and involve a smaller sample of banks. The study by Barako and Brown (2008)—one of the first to analyse this nexus—investigates the influence of board gender representation on the communication of corporate social reporting by 40 Kenyan banks. To this aim, the authors develop a CSR disclosure index based on 22 items and find that the value of this score is positively correlated with a greater presence of women on bank boards. Kiliç et al. (2015), concentrating on 25 Turkish banks over the period 2008–2012, find a significant and positive association between ownership and board composition, on the one hand, and bank CSR disclosure, on the other, under five sub-themes (environment, energy, human resources, products and customers, and community involvement). Among the board features investigated, a critical role is played by female representation: the number of female directors on the board is found to play a key role in enhancing the CSR reporting of banks. Matuszak et al. (2019) focus on 16 banks in Poland over the years 2008–2015 and analyse the impact on CSR reporting not only from female participation in management and supervisory bodies (MB and SB, respectively) of banks, but also from female leadership. The results confirm that gender diversity on the MB increases the CSR disclosure by banks, especially on human resources, and product and customer issues. Moreover, also the presence of a female chief of this board has a positive impact on CSR reporting. On the contrary, no SB variables generate a significant effect. This study sheds light on two interesting aspects. On the one hand, it uncovers the dual impact of gender diversity in a double-board system. Hence, it is interesting to understand the following question: why does MB gender diversity influence bank CSR while SB gender diversity does not? As stated by the authors, "*it can be assumed that, in the case of a model in which the MB's and SB's competencies are strictly separated, non-executive directors [including female directors] have more difficult access to information about the company and are, therefore, less effective in their tasks*" (Matuszak et al., 2019, p. 93). On the other hand, this study emphasises the importance of female leadership in the banking sector to improve bank CSR disclosure. More recently, Tapver et al. (2020) verify the association between CSR reporting of listed banks and board female representation while controlling for the impact of gender quotas. Based on a global sample of 285 commercial banks from 2005 to 2017, this study uncovers a positive association between BGD and a bank's CSR disclosure. While it would initially appear that the introduction of gender quotas does not affect this association, which remains positive also after quota corrections for banks with female representation below or above the quota, a deeper analysis shows that only above-quota female representation contributes to voluntary CSR disclosure. This suggests that introducing a gender quota system can improve CSR disclosure, especially for banks implementing this reporting voluntarily. Another interesting result is that adding more women to boards than required by quota could influence CSR reporting by banks in masculine countries but not in feminine ones. Thus, also a country's masculinity-femininity could be considered a factor influencing the association between banks CSR disclosure and female representation. Finally, Khan (2010) focusing on all the 30 private commercial banks in Bangladesh for the years 2007–2008 shows that while the percentage of non-executive members on the board and non-Bangladeshi directors are positively related to banks CSR reporting practices, no significant relationship is found for female representation on the board. In line with other studies, also in this case, the fact that women directors do not influence bank social reporting may be due to their low participation in the governing bodies of firms belonging to emerging countries (such as Bangladesh). In particular, the author affirms: "*one possible explanation of these dissimilar results would be that women empowerment in the executive level in Bangladesh is the new phenomenon and might have the restricted role to play due to the small numbers occupying the executive positions. Therefore, their role in relation to CSR issues would either be limited or unattended in most cases*" (Khan, 2010, p. 100).

### 3.5.1 Board Gender Diversity and Bank Environmental Performance

In line with the evidence presented in the previous section and with the increased attention paid by scholars in recent years, other studies have focused on bank environmental performance. The objective remains the same, to verify whether a greater presence of women on bank boards positively influences the non-financial performance.[10]

Early empirical evidence is found by Deschênes et al. (2015) who analyse the impact of certain board of director traits on CSR performance (and its components: social, governance, and environmental scores) in the largest Canadian corporations. This study does not only focus on the financial sector, though it is interesting to note that for this sector alone, the relationship between BGD and environmental performance is positive. In other words, a higher proportion of female directors favours a better environmental commitment, only for the largest Canadian banks. More recently, Gangi et al. (2019), using a sample of 142 banks from 35 countries covering the period 2011–2015, find evidence of a positive relationship between BGD and bank environmental performance. In

[10] Moreover, this interest by scholars is prompted by several theoretical studies revealing that, compared with men, women are more actively engaged in pro-environment behaviours, tend to have a better perception of environmental risks (Davidson & Freudenburg, 1996), and tend to support more often a pro-environmental legislation (Mohai & Kershner, 2002).

particular, they obtain two related results. On the one hand, the statistical analysis (difference in means) reveals that banks that are more environmentally sensitive have a higher incidence of female directors on their boards; on the other, the econometric analysis confirms this relationship indicating the incidence rate of female directors on total board members is a predictor of higher environmental engagement by banks. Thus, a board with greater openness to gender diversity contributes to increasing the bank's attention to the environment.

Birindelli et al. (2019) focus on women in leadership positions. Analysing 96 listed banks in Europe, Middle East, and Africa (EMEA) from 2011 to 2016, this study shows that when banks are led by male CEOs, the relationship between BGD and environmental performance is an inverted U-shape which may indicate the importance of gender-balanced boards (Schwartz-Ziv, 2017). On the contrary, in the few cases where banks are led by a female CEO, there is a positive impact on environmental performance when the share of women on the board exceeds a threshold of 31%. Thus, this study corroborates the critical mass theory and the homophily perspective for the banking sector, but only when banks are led by female CEOs.

Opposite findings are reported by Gallego-Sosa et al. (2020). This study, analysing 52 banks from the most polluting Western regions between 2009 and 2018, finds that the gender effect on environmental performance is very negligible. Specifically, none of the gender variables have a significant coefficient. Thus, the key conclusion is that there are no significant differences in the environmental commitment by banks based on BGD. This result could be due to the underrepresentation of women on the board, which prevents women directors from playing a significant role in bank policies and performance.

## 3.6 Women on Boards and Bank Risk-Taking

Given that women are generally considered more conservative and less inclined to take extreme risks, other scholars have recently promoted a further line of research aimed at empirically testing whether a greater presence of women on boards or in leadership positions reduces risk-taking by banks. Also in this case, there are mixed results. These empirical studies can be divided into three categories: (1) those that prove that BGD reduces bank risk; (2) those that reveal no evidence that women influence bank risk, and (3) those that document a positive association between female board representation and bank riskiness.

The first category includes the highest number of studies, which are mainly focused on US and European banks; they are mostly multi-country studies. Using a time-based criterion, the first study is carried out by Muller-Kahle and Lewellyn (2011). Focusing on 74 US financial institutions involved in subprime lending during the period 1997–2005, they find that the board structures of those firms were significantly different from those that were not involved in this credit activity. The boards of directors of subprime lenders were busier, had a shorter tenure, and were less balanced in terms of gender. Moreover, the study shows a negative linkage between BGD and the subprime lending business model. In other words, the higher the percentage of women on the board, the less likely a bank tends to focus on subprime lending. This evidence suggests that BGD can positively influence the firm's business model by leading banks to take less risky strategic decisions. Similarly, Mateos de Cabo et al. (2012), employing a large sample of 612 banks from 20 European countries, prove that a greater female board representation characterises lower-risk banks (proxied by the standard deviation of ROAA and the log of equity on total assets) confirming the risk aversion hypothesis of women directors. In the same vein, Palvia et al. (2015), using a large panel of US commercial banks over the years 2007–2010, report a strong positive relationship between women-led banks and higher levels of capital (in terms of both tier-1 capital and capital ratio). In particular, "*the magnitudes of the estimated coefficients suggest that capital ratios are approximately 0.4 percentage-units higher for banks with female CEOs and for banks in which either the CEO or board Chair is female*" (Palvia et al., 2015, p. 583). Thus, female leaders tend to behave more conservatively. Moreover, these authors reveal another interesting linkage: in smaller banks, the presence of female CEOs and chairs negatively affects the bank's propensity to fail during the financial subprime crisis. Hence, in small banks led by women, the likelihood of failure is significantly lower, suggesting that female CEOs and chairs are more cautious in taking risks, at least in these banks.[11] Overall, these findings provide support for the view that female leaders may promote more

[11] In larger banks, the propensity to fail does not appear to be associated with the gender of the bank's CEO and/or board chair.

conservative strategies and less risky financial decisions. This is particularly important for smaller banks which may be less able to absorb external shocks. Accordingly, focusing on a sample of 461 large banks from OECD countries, Gulamhussen and Santa (2015) find, after controlling for bank and country-specific effects, that both the presence and the percentage of female directors on boards have a negative relationship with bank risk-taking measures (namely, loan loss reserves, loan loss provisions, impaired loans ratio, and *Z*-score). Similar results are found for female presence on the supervisory board and, to a lesser extent, on the audit committee. Chan et al. (2016), focusing on 16 listed commercial banks in China from 2003 to 2011, also find that a higher proportion of female directors on the board reduces both the idiosyncratic[12] and total risk of banks (as measured by the standard deviation of the daily stock returns). This result is consistent with studies documenting that female directors provide different perspectives in problem-solving and a more cautious and varied perspective of risk management. More recently, Sahay et al. (2017) show similar results across about 800 banks from 72 countries during the years 2003–2013: controlling for relevant bank and country-specific factors, they find that women on the board of directors are associated with higher *Z*-scores and lower levels of non-performing loans (NPLs). Thus, a greater presence of female directors improves the stability of the bank as it reduces its risk profile. Sghaier and Hamza (2018), instead, focus on a specific investment decision, mergers and acquisitions (M&A). In particular, they study the effect of BGD and women in leadership positions (CEO, chief financial officer-CFO, and board chair) on the risk profile (RP) of acquiring banks. For a sample of 112 European acquiring banks from 2000 to 2015, they note a negative correlation between the percentage of women on the board as directors or chairs and the evolution of the RP of the acquiring bank. This result asserts that women are more risk-averse and less overconfident than their male counterparts. They also notice that the presence of at least three women on the board of directors negatively affects the risk profile of the acquiring bank, suggesting that increasing gender diversity within the board of directors could be a means to improve oversight. Likewise, Gangi et al. (2019), focusing on a sample of 142 banks from 35 countries from 2011 to 2015, find that BGD is a negative predictor of bank risk as measured by *Z*-score.

[12] As is well known, idiosyncratic risk relates to intrinsic factors that can have a negative impact on individual securities or specific asset classes.

Similarly, Cardillo et al. (2020), investigating 105 European listed banks over thirteen years (2005–2017), find that BGD reduces bank risk-taking and, ultimately, the probability that a bank needs a public bailout to avoid liquidation. This impact of BGD is very significant when considering that "*an increase by one standard deviation in gender diversity decreases the probability of a bailout by at least 2.44%, a significant reduction considering that the unconditional probability of a public bailout is approximately 18.7% from 2008 to 2013, the period when most of the bailouts (95% of the sample) take place*" (Cardillo et al., 2020, p. 3).

The study by Gallucci et al. (2020) additionally verifies the moderating effect of the country's masculinity dimension. Using data on 110 listed banks from four European countries (Germany, Italy, Spain, and Switzerland) over the period 2008–2017, this study not only confirms a negative relationship between women on the board and bank risk (as measured by the standard deviation of ROA), but it also reveals that in countries characterised by a high masculinity dimension, female bank directors become even more risk-averse than usual.[13] Birindelli et al. (2020) corroborate the negative relationship between BGD and bank riskiness, but only when other conditions are verified. Based on a sample of 215 listed banks from 40 countries over the period 2008–2016, this study documents that BGD negatively impacts bank risk only when banks are sound and until their boards reach a critical mass of women. Conversely, when banks are unsound, female directors do not have a significant and positive role in reducing risk.[14]

Other scholars relate bank risk exclusively to women in leadership positions (especially, the CEO). For example, the study by Skała and Weill (2018), based on a unique dataset of 365 Polish cooperative banks (42% of which are led by female CEOs), finds that banks headed by female CEOs are less risky. Indeed, these banks report higher capital adequacy and equity to assets ratios. This evidence supports the view that female bank CEOs are more risk-averse than men. In the same vein, Palvia et al. (2020), using a large panel of 6971 US commercial banks over the period 2007–2017, show two interrelated results. First, banks with female CEOs and board chairs are associated with better lending performance in the

[13] In other words, the country-level masculinity has a negative moderating effect on the relationship between BGD and risk-taking, leading women serving on the board to become even more risk-averse.

[14] In the study, sound banks show a level of risk below the median risk for the sample, while unsound banks are characterised by a level of risk above the median.

aftermath of severe real estate price shocks. Second, female-led banks with high real estate exposure are associated with lower default risk in the same period. As a whole, these empirical findings provide evidence that female CEOs and board chairs constrain bank risk-taking and that the behavioural differences between women and men may have important implications for bank performance.

Other authors explore the association between BGD and bank risk-taking in an emerging market context. Bunea and Dinu (2020), considering 25 Romanian banks at the end of 2018, prove that banks with more female directors have a higher total level of own funds, and thus, they are less risky. Abou-El-Sood (2019) focuses on a sample of 82 banks listed in countries belonging to the Gulf Cooperation Council from 2002 to 2014. In line with other research, this study shows that banks with more female board directors take on a lower-risk profile. Nevertheless, this linkage ceases when banks enjoy higher levels of regulatory capital ratio. In this case, indeed, female directors make decisions to invest in riskier positions contradicting the belief that female directors are generally risk-averse. So, "*risk aversion is attenuated as female directors perceive the opportunities inherent in capital adequacy and the rewards of risk-taking*" (Abou-El-Sood, 2019, p. 35). Another relevant finding is that female directors tend to undertake less risky positions in Islamic banks compared to conventional banks.

A further strand of studies analyses women's risk aversion in finance by examining the relationship between the default of borrowers and female lenders (Bellucci et al., 2011). In this context, some studies reveal that the default rates for loans originated by female loan officers tend to be lower than those associated with loans originated by male loan officers, especially when lending to women (Beck et al., 2013). Additionally, due to their greater risk aversion, female loan officers tend to restrict credit availability to new, "un-established" borrowers more than their male counterparts (Bellucci et al., 2010). This in turn could have a positive impact on the bank's risk. Therefore, in addition to increasing gender diversity on boards, another channel through which banks could reduce their riskiness profile is to allocate more women to executive/lending roles.

To the best of our knowledge, the second category of studies (revealing no impact of women on bank risk-taking) includes the following works. The first is the research by Adams and Ragunathan (2015), which, analysing 350 US financial institutions for the period 2006–2009, documents two interesting results. On the one hand, during the subprime crisis, banks with more female directors do not engage in fewer risk-taking activities nor have lower risk than other banks, suggesting that there is no causal relationship between board gender diversity and risk. On the other hand, banks with greater BGD experience better financial performance. In sum, although women directors in finance may have similar levels of risk appetite or aversion than men directors, greater BGD matters because it allows banks to perform better during a financial crisis. Talavera et al. (2018), using a sample of 97 Chinese banks from 2009 to 2013, do not find any relationship between the percentage of female directors and bank risk as measured by *Z*-score and NPL ratio. Similarly, Sheedy and Lubojanski (2018), studying approximately 36,000 survey responses from ten banks headquartered in Australia, Canada, and the UK, do not find evidence for the hypothesised positive association between female gender and desirable risk management behaviour. Said differently, they find no evidence to support the "Lehman Sisters Hypothesis", i.e., "*that recruiting more females into the financial services industry will improve risk management practices*" (Sheedy & Lubojanski, 2018, p. 914). This could be because females who succeed in financial services do not conform to traditional female stereotypes characterised by less risk-taking. Thus, hiring more females is not likely to lead to better risk management.[15] Lastly, Khan et al. (2020) focus on 71 Islamic banks (IBs) and 120 conventional banks (CoBs) operating in eleven Muslim countries between 2010 and 2017. Again, the analysis shows that the presence of females on boards is not significantly associated with a higher or lower credit risk either in CoBs or IBs.

Finally, the third category of research (positive linkage between BGD and bank riskiness) incorporates three main studies. The first is that by Berger et al. (2014) which, using difference-in-difference estimation and focusing on the entire population of German bank executive officers over the period 1994–2010, uncovers a positive effect of female gender on bank riskiness as measured by the risk-weighted assets to total assets

[15] Conversely, based on the authors' opinion, to improve risk management banks should hire/retain a larger number of senior workers and those with lower risk tolerance because seniority seems to be significantly and positively associated with desirable risk management behaviour. For the authors, the risk management conduct is "desirable" when risk managers "*respect and prioritise risk policy/limits, are willing to question the risk framework, identify/report risk issues and accept accountability for the risk management framework*" (Sheedy & Lubojanski, 2018, p. 903).

(RWA/TA) ratio and by a Herfindahl–Hirschman Index for loan portfolio concentration, albeit at a low level of statistical significance. In sum, this study provides evidence that female executives increase the portfolio risk of German banks. More recently, Farag and Mallin (2017) achieve similar results. Their study, concentrating on 99 European banks from 17 countries over the period 2004–2012, finds that female directors on the management board are not risk-averse. Indeed, they document that appointing a female director beyond a critical mass of 24% increases bank risk. However, the degree of risk-taking of female directors may vary based on their roles (non-executive or executive), and female executive directors may have the same risk-taking behaviour as their male counterparts. Lastly, Rafinda et al. (2018), focusing on 22 banks and financial institutions in India over the period 2011–2015, show BGD has a positive and significant impact on bank risk measured by $Z$-score. Thus, female board directors lead to higher risk-taking. For the authors, this result might be due to the lack of experience of women as board directors which might result in higher risk-taking.

There is further recent research that falls in the middle of these studies in that it reveals both a greater and lower propensity of women directors towards risk-taking depending on the power they hold (Abou-El-Sood, 2021). Specifically, when banks have a strong regulatory capital base that increases the investment opportunities, female directors undertake risky investments as they perceive the positive incentives resulting from their decisions. On the contrary, women directors invest in less risky assets during a financial crisis and when the CEO has more equity ownership. In these circumstances, women directors hold less power and thus they do not invest in risky positions, also to avoid penalties inherent to risky investment decisions.

## 3.7 Other Under-Investigated Research Lines on Gender Diversity

In this last section, it is worth illustrating other studies providing initial empirical evidence that should be investigated further as they address little-explored research issues on BGD (Baker et al., 2020; Nguyen et al., 2020). Indeed, "*despite the growth in research in this area, [there are still] important gaps in the literature, recent efforts to fill them, and broad directions for future research*" (Girardone et al., 2021, p. 9). The new lines of research on BGD in banks can be summarised in the following:

(a) the relationship between BGD and sanctions and misconducts by banks;
(b) the relationship between BGD and bank accounting policies;
(c) the relationship between BGD and banks' M&As;
(d) the BGD as a consequence of specific bank drivers.

The first research area includes the study by Arnaboldi et al. (2021), which investigates the impact of BGD on bank misconduct proxied by the number of fines issued by US regulators to EU listed banks during 2007–2018. Based on 83 publicly listed banks operating in 21 EU countries, the authors find that greater female representation significantly reduces the frequency of misconduct fines, equivalent to $7.48 million savings per year. Moreover, this linkage appears more robust when female directors reach a critical mass (i.e., at least three), the bank is smaller and has women in leadership roles (CEO and/or chairperson). Finally, the authors reveal that "*the mechanism through which gender diversity affects board effectiveness in preventing misconduct stems from the ethicality and risk aversion of the female directors, rather than their contribution to diversity*" (Arnaboldi et al., 2021, p. 1).

The second research line is opened by García-Sánchez et al. (2017). Considering a large sample of 159 banks from nine countries over the period 2004–2010, this study documents that BGD and financial expertise on boards have a positive effect on accounting conservatism and the earnings quality in banks. In addition, institutional factors play a significant role. In contexts of enhanced regulation and investor protection, BGD and financial expertise of directors have more influence on accounting conservatism and bank earnings quality. In the same vein, more recently, Fan et al. (2019) investigate the impact of BGD on bank earnings management based on 91 bank holding companies (BHCs) during 2000–2014. They find that women on bank boards affect earnings management through a non-linear relationship. Particularly, there is an inverted U-shaped relationship between women on boards and bank earnings management, which becomes more evident when women directors sit on audit or nomination committees. This means that the influence of women directors on earnings management changes from positive to negative reaching the threshold of three or more women directors. "*This evidence confirms the notion from tokenism/critical mass theory that the minority gender (women directors) cannot fully play their role in a group (a board) until a certain threshold or critical mass is reached*" (Fan et al., 2019, p. 18).

The third new strand of studies is carried out by Tampakoudis et al. (2020). Given that sound governance mechanisms, including managerial pay incentives and board gender composition, may contribute to the success of bank mergers by preventing managers from pursuing value-destroying acquisitions (Hagendorff et al., 2007), this study, using a unique, hand-collected dataset on 1130 M&As announced by US banks between 2003 and 2018, explores the effect of BGD on the economic impact on these transactions. The authors find a significant negative relationship between female board membership and shareholder wealth in acquiring banks, especially during the years 2012–2018 (i.e., after the subprime crisis). However, this effect becomes even more negative when the number of women on the board increases. In fact, attaining a critical mass of female directors (i.e., going from one or two women to at least three women) is associated with lower bidder returns than those obtained by completely male boards. These effects suggest that the presence of female directors on bank boards is not a determinant of value creation in a bank's M&As. Thus, in the authors' opinion, businesses and regulators should be cautious when they advocate BGD in the banking sector.

Lastly, a few other studies provide insight into BGD as the result of bank characteristics. In this case, BGD is no longer the main independent explanatory variable, but rather the dependent variable. In this field, we can mention the study by Mateos de Cabo et al. (2012) aimed at identifying organisational features that could predict female presence on bank boards. Based on 612 European banks from 20 countries, these authors show that the proportion of women on the board is higher for banks having low risk and leverage, large boards, and growth orientation.

It is worth mentioning that in other recent studies, BGD is interacted with other independent variables to ascertain the moderating role of women on boards and the interaction effects of this variable in the banking sector. These studies are essentially those by Proença et al. (2020) and Stefanovic and Barjaktarovic (2021). The first analyses the effect of

BGD on the relationship between political connections and bank performance, proxied by two accounting measures (ROAA and ROAE) and one risk measure reflecting the quality of the bank's assets (loan loss provisions to total loans, LLPTL). Interestingly, this study reveals that female directors, although a minority, have a higher rate of political connections than men in European Central Bank-supervised banks. Moreover, by examining the non-linear (quadratic) effects of the interaction terms between BGD and political connections, BGD tends to attenuate the negative impact of political connections on bank performance. In other words, when gender diversity is high (at least greater than 14%), there is a U-shaped relationship between political connections and bank performance; that is, the former variable reduces the latter only to a certain point. This means that "*the differentiating characteristics of women such as greater ethical sensitivity and greater risk aversion, mitigate the negative effects of political connections on banking performance, making the institution's interests privileged over personal ones*" (Proença et al., 2020, p. 1019). In contrast, Stefanovic and Barjaktarovic (2021) investigate the moderating role of gender on the relationship between management structure and bank performance as measured by ROA, ROE, equity to assets ratio, and net income. The main objective of these authors is to accurately capture the potential influence of BGD and board structure on bank economic-financial outcomes by studying multiple-interaction relationships between several gender variables (female gender of the president of the executive board; number and ratio (%) of female members on the executive board; female gender of the chair of the board of directors; number and ratio (%) of female members on boards of directors). In summary, this study yields two main findings: (a) the relationship between gender diversity and financial performance is indirect and, most importantly, (b) BGD does not improve bank economic performance per se but interacting with another gender, socio-demographic, and board structure variable.

Table 3.1 reviews all the studies illustrated in the chapter, divided by the topic investigated, providing an overview of the state of advancement of research on BGD in banks.

**Table 3.1** Studies on BGD in banks

| *Authors* | *Objectives* | *Sample and years* | *Main data sources* | *Methodology* | *Gender proxy*[16] | *Results (Limited to gender issues)* |
|---|---|---|---|---|---|---|
| **BGD and bank economic-financial performance** | | | | | | |
| Mersland and Strøm (2009) | To examine the relationship between firm performance and corporate governance in microfinance institutions (MFIs) | 278 MFIs in 60 counties over the 1998–2007 period | Rating reports from 5 rating agencies (MicroRate, Microfinanza, Planet Rating, Crisil, and M-Cril) | 3SLS (three-stage least squares) (random effects) | • Female CEO: dummy variable equal to 1 if the CEO is female, 0 otherwise | a. When MFIs are led by a female CEO, their financial performance increases |
| Ekadah and Mboya (2012) | To analyse the effect of BGD on bank performance | 32 commercial banks in Kenya over the 1998–2009 period | Central Bank Kenya (CBK), and the Banking Survey Reports | Stepwise regression | • The proportion of female directors<br>• Dummy variable: 1 if the bank has at least one female director and 0 otherwise | a. BGD does not affect bank performance (ROA)<br>b. The boards of commercial banks in Kenya are strongly male-dominated |

16 The gender variables have been described by indicating the symbols/terms used in the studies, where present.

| *Authors* | *Objectives* | *Sample and years* | *Main data sources* | *Methodology* | *Gender proxy* | *Results (Limited to gender issues)* |
|---|---|---|---|---|---|---|
| Pathan and Faff (2013) | To examine whether the board structure (size and composition, including BGD) in banks is related to performance | 212 large US bank holding companies over the 1997–2011 period (2194 bank-year observations) | BankFocus, Refinitiv, and banks' annual reports | GMM (generalised method of moments) | • Female directors: the % of directors who are female | a. While BGD improves bank performance in the pre-SOX period (1997–2002), this impact is weakened in both the post-SOX (2003–2006) and crisis periods (2007–2011) |
| Liang et al. (2013) | To explore the influence of a comprehensive set of board characteristics (size, composition, and functioning of the board) on bank performance and asset quality | The 52 largest Chinese banks over the 2003–2010 period | Banks' annual reports, the Almanac of China's Finance and Banking, China Statistical Yearbook, and China City Statistical Yearbook | OLS (ordinary least squares) + GMM | • Female directors: the proportion of female directors on the board | a. The proportion of female directors on the board has no impact on either bank performance (ROA and ROE) or asset quality |

(continued)

**Table 3.1** (continued)

| *Authors* | *Objectives* | *Sample and years* | *Main data sources* | *Methodology* | *Gender proxy* | *Results (Limited to gender issues)* |
|---|---|---|---|---|---|---|
| Strøm et al. (2014) | To investigate the relationships between female leadership, firm performance, and corporate governance of MFIs | 329 Microfinance Institutions (MFIs) in 73 countries over the 1998–2008 period | Rating reports from 5 rating agencies (MicroRate, Microfinanza, Planet Rating, Crisil, M-Cril)[17] | Probit + OLS + Heckman model | • Female CEO: dummy variable equal to 1 if the CEO is female, 0 otherwise<br>• Female chair: dummy variable equal to 1 if the board chair is female, 0 otherwise<br>• Female directors: dummy variable equal to 1 if one or more of the board directors are female, 0 otherwise<br>• # Female directors: number of female directors<br>• Female directors' fraction: female directors as a fraction of all directors<br>• Dumfemdir ≥3: dummy variable equal to 1 if the female directors total three or more | a. Female CEOs or female chairpersons are positively related to the MFIs' performance in terms of both ROA and ROE |

[17] This is an updated version of the dataset used by Mersland and Strøm (2009).

| *Authors* | *Objectives* | *Sample and years* | *Main data sources* | *Methodology* | *Gender proxy* | *Results (Limited to gender issues)* |
|---|---|---|---|---|---|---|
| Del Prete and Stefani (2015) | To investigate the effects of BGD on bank riskiness and economic performance | Approximately 1000 Italian banks for the 1995–2010 period (15,000 bank-year observations) | Bank of Italy's databases, and banks' balance sheet | Panel data regression (fixed effects) | • Dummy female: 1 if there is at least one woman on the bank boards<br>• Share of women: % of women on each kind of bank board (administrative and supervisory boards) | a. BGD tends to have a positive effect on credit quality and, although less robust, the same on bank profitability<br>b. Beneficial effects due to the level of female participation in the top Italian bank boards |
| Gulamhussen and Santa (2015) | To analyse whether women in the boardrooms (board of directors, supervisory board, and audit committee) have a positive influence on accounting and market performance and risk-taking in banks | 461 large banks from OECD countries[18] in 2006 | BankFocus, bank websites, and Refinitiv | 2SLS (two-stage least squares) | • The proportion of women on the board of directors (FBOARD), on the supervisory board (FSUP), and on the audit committee (FAUDIT)<br>• A dummy equal to 1 if the bank has at least one female director on the board (DBOARD), on the supervisory board (DSUP), and on the audit committee (DAUDIT) | a. The presence and % of female directors in the boardrooms both have a positive influence on bank performance<br>b. The presence and % of female directors in the boardrooms both have a negative influence on risk-taking |

(continued)

18 The countries are Australia, Austria, Belgium, Canada, Denmark, France, Germany, Greece, Ireland, Island, Italy, Japan, Luxembourg, Mexico, the Netherlands, Norway, Poland, Portugal, Spain, Sweden, Switzerland, Turkey, the UK, and the US.

**Table 3.1** (continued)

| *Authors* | *Objectives* | *Sample and years* | *Main data sources* | *Methodology* | *Gender proxy* | *Results (Limited to gender issues)* |
|---|---|---|---|---|---|---|
| García-Meca et al. (2015) | To analyse the effect of board diversity (gender and nationality) on bank performance and the role played by institutional factors (regulatory and investor protection levels) on this linkage | 159 banks in 9 countries[19] over the 2004–2010 period (877 bank-year observations) | Compustat, EIRIS, and the Spencer & Stuart Board Index | GMM | • %Women: % of female directors on the boards | a. BGD increases bank performance<br>b. In contexts of weaker regulation and lower investors protection, board diversity has less influence on bank performance |
| Rodríguez-Ruiz et al. (2016) | To examine the dynamics of the gender diversity-performance relationship in the banking sector;<br>To verify whether banks with an equal gender distribution and a higher % of qualified women have better corporate outputs | 59 Spanish commercial banks over the 1999–2010 period | Statistical Yearbook of Spanish Banks | Panel data regression (random effects) | • The % of women in the workforce<br>• The proportion of qualified women (% of females with technical skills over the total number of women)<br>• The Blau index[20] | a. There is an inverted U-shaped relationship between both the number of female employees and women in technical positions and the bank's financial performance (ROA)<br>b. The proportion of women in the workforce does not affect productivity |

[19] The countries are Canada, France, Germany, Italy, the Netherlands, Spain, Sweden, the UK, and the US.

[20] The authors also use the "Blau index" as an alternative measure of board diversity. This index is calculated as the percentage of board members in each category (male/female) and it ranges from 0 to 0.5. The last value occurs when the board is equally balanced.

| *Authors* | *Objectives* | *Sample and years* | *Main data sources* | *Methodology* | *Gender proxy* | *Results (Limited to gender issues)* |
|---|---|---|---|---|---|---|
| Kramaric and Miletic (2017) | To investigate the influence of gender diversity in the boardroom on bank performance | 33.61 Croatian banks per year, over the 2002–2014 period (437 bank-year observations) | Banks' annual reports, bank websites, and Banks Bulletin of Croatian National Bank | Panel data regression (fixed effects) + static pooled model | • Five dummy variables equal to 1 (0 otherwise): (1) if there are no women on the management/supervisory board (uniform group); (2) if there are up to 20% of women on the management/supervisory board (skewed group); (3) if women make up between 20 and 40% of the management/supervisory board (tilted group); (4) if at least 40% of the management/supervisory board is women (balanced group); (5) if the chairperson of the management/supervisory board is female | a. When the critical mass of 20–40% of women on the management board is reached, the bank performance improves |

(continued)

**Table 3.1** (continued)

| *Authors* | *Objectives* | *Sample and years* | *Main data sources* | *Methodology* | *Gender proxy* | *Results (Limited to gender issues)* |
|---|---|---|---|---|---|---|
| Adusei et al. (2017) | To investigate whether: (a) increasing representation of female board members translates into increasing representation of women in management teams; (b) gender diversity on the board and management team impacts on the financial performance of MFIs; (c) management gender diversity moderates the relationship between BGD and the financial performance of MFIs | 494 MFIs across 76 countries over the 2010–2014 period | www.mixmarket.org, World Bank, and the United Nations Development Program | Panel data regression (fixed effects) | • Board gender diversity: % of female directors out of the total number of directors<br>• Management gender diversity: % of women managers out of the total number of managers<br>• Critical mass for board gender diversity: % of female directors divided by all directors ≥50%<br>• Critical mass for management gender diversity: % of women managers divided by all managers ≥50%<br>• Interaction term at threshold level: % of female directors divided by all directors ≥50% multiplied by the % of women managers divided by all managers ≥50% | a. The increase in the number of female directors triggers an increase in female managers<br>a. BGD is negatively and significantly related to the MFI's financial performance<br>b. The financial performance collapse is more likely when a MFI combines a 50% or higher female representation on its board with a 50% or higher female representation on its management team |

| *Authors* | *Objectives* | *Sample and years* | *Main data sources* | *Methodology* | *Gender proxy* | *Results (Limited to gender issues)* |
|---|---|---|---|---|---|---|
| Ghosh (2017) | To explore whether BGD impacts bank behaviour | All publicly listed Indian banks (40) over the 2003–2012 period | Indian Central Bank Prowess database | Mean difference (*t*-test) + dynamic panel data | • D_Women: dummy equal to 1 if a bank has a woman on its board, 0 otherwise<br>• Sh_Women: the number of women directors divided by all board directors | a. BGD does not significantly affect bank performance (ROA and Tobin's Q)<br>b. Only female executive directors enhance the bank's stability (*Z*-score)<br>c. In state-owned banks, BGD enhances stability but at the cost of lower profitability |
| Mori and Towo (2017) | To examine the effect of board composition on profitability for banks in Tanzania | 35 banks in Tanzania over the 2009–2013 period (175 bank-year observations) | Banks' annual reports and bank websites | SUR (seemingly unrelated regression) | • Any-woman: dummy variable equal to 1 if there is one woman on the board and 0 otherwise<br>• Women: number of women directors | a. There is a positive linkage between women representation on boards and banks' ROA and profit margin |
| Farag and Mallin (2017) | To investigate the influence of BGD on both bank financial fragility and performance | 99 European banks over the 2004–2012 period | Banks' annual reports, BankFocus, Thomson One Banker, and Refinitiv | GMM | • Female: % of female directors sitting on the board of directors<br>• FemaleSB: % of female directors sitting on the supervisory board<br>• FemaleMgtB: % of female directors sitting on the management board<br>• The Blau index | a. The relationship between BGD and bank performance (ROA) is significant and positive for the board of directors (BOD), the supervisory board (SB), and the management board (MB)<br>b. However, while for the BOD and SB the diversity-performance nexus is non-linear and has an inverted U-shape, for the MB, the linkage is non-linear but the U-shape is not inverted |

(continued)

**Table 3.1** (continued)

| *Authors* | *Objectives* | *Sample and years* | *Main data sources* | *Methodology* | *Gender proxy* | *Results (Limited to gender issues)* |
|---|---|---|---|---|---|---|
| Ghosh and Ansari (2018) | To examine whether board size and gender-diverse boards affect bank financial performance;<br>To verify whether these linkages vary across high-income/low-income districts of India | 1263 urban cooperative banks in India in 2012 (cross-sectional data) | N.A | OLS | • Sh_WOMEN: the number of women directors divided by board size<br>• D_WoC: dummy variable equal to 1 if a bank is woman-owned, 0 otherwise | a. Gender diversity exerts a dampening impact on bank performance<br>b. There is a differential impact of board size and board diversity across high- and low-income districts |
| Talavera et al. (2018) | To examine the effects of board diversity (in terms of age and gender) on bank profitability and risk | 97 Chinese banks over the 2009–2013 period | Banks' annual reports | Fixed effect instrumental variable approach<br>+<br>GMM | • Female directors: % of female directors | a. No relationship between the % of female directors and bank performance (ROA and ROE) |
| Rafinda et al. (2018) | To examine the impact of BGD on the sustainability of bank performance and risk | 22 banks and financial institutions in India over the 2011–2015 period (110 bank-year observations) | BankFocus, banks' annual reports, and Spencer Stuart | Pooled panel data regression | • The total number of female directors divided by the total number of board directors | a. Foreign directors lead the company into worse performance<br>b. Female directors have no impact on the company's performance (ROA and ROE), except for the ratio of operating expense to operating income |
| Ting and Huang (2018) | To examine the relationship between the power and perks (any form of non-monetary compensation) of CEOs | Chinese banks over the 1999–2011 period (all financial institutions from the China Banking Regulatory Commission) | Banks' annual reports | GMM | • Percentage of female directors | a. Banks with powerful CEOs provide more perks<br>b. Only gender-diverse boards effectively reduce the CEOs' power and perks |

| *Authors* | *Objectives* | *Sample and years* | *Main data sources* | *Methodology* | *Gender proxy* | *Results (Limited to gender issues)* |
|---|---|---|---|---|---|---|
| Owen and Temesvary (2018) | To study the impact of the boards' gender composition on bank performance; To verify whether the impact of greater BGD depends on the bank and board's characteristics | 90 US bank holding companies over the 1999–2015 period (1600 bank-year observations) | BankFocus, Compustat, CRSP (Center for Research in Security Prices), and BoardEx | Instrumental variables methods | • Female share on the board<br>• The Blau index | a. There is a non-linear, U-shaped relationship between BGD and various measures of bank performance (ROA, revenue to expense ratio, Sharpe ratio, and annual stock price growth). Female board representation has a positive effect once the threshold level of gender diversity is achieved<br>b. Only better-capitalised banks benefit from this positive effect |
| Shettima and Dzolkarnaini (2018) | To examine the effect of board characteristics on MFIs performance | 30 MFIs in Nigeria over the 2010–2013 period (120 firm-year observations) | Microfinance Information eXchange (MIX) database, and annual reports of MFIs | GLS (generalised least squares) | • Board diversity: the absolute number of female directors<br>• % Board Diversity: % of female directors | a. There is a positive and significant relationship between board size and the MFIs performance (ROE and ROA)<br>b. There is a negative and non-significant linkage between female directors and the MFIs' performance |
| Mohammad et al. (2018) | To analyse the potential effect of gender diversity on the financial performance of Jordanian banks listed on the Amman Stock Exchange | 11 Jordanian banks over the 2009–2016 period | Companies Guide from the Amman Stock Exchange (ASE), and direct phone and e-mail contact with the banks | OLS | • WOMENBOD: % of women on the boards of directors<br>• WOMENEXEC: % of women that are part of the top and medium-level executive management | a. There is no statistically significant relationship between the percentage of women on boards and bank financial performance (ROA)<br>b. This result also applies to the percentage of women in top and medium-level executive management positions |

(continued)

**Table 3.1** (continued)

| *Authors* | *Objectives* | *Sample and years* | *Main data sources* | *Methodology* | *Gender proxy* | *Results (Limited to gender issues)* |
|---|---|---|---|---|---|---|
| Dinu and Bunea (2018) | To study the influence of female directors on bank financial performance | 27 Romanian banks | Banks' annual reports, bank websites, and the National Bank of Romania website | ANOVA test + regression analysis | • %_Women_board_of_ directors: the number of women divided by total members of the board of directors<br>• %_Women_directorate/ steering committee: the number of women divided by total members of the directorate/steering committee | a. The influence of women directors on bank performance (ROA and ROE) is not significant<br>b. This result is justified by the poor representation of women at the level of the Romanian banks' boards of directors |
| Adesanmi et al. (2019) | To examine the effect of BGD on the financial performance of Nigerian banks | 10 listed deposit money banks in Nigeria over the 2008–2017 period | Banks' annual reports | Pooled OLS | • Board gender diversity: female directors divided by the total number of directors | a. Both gender diversity and independence of boards positively affect the financial performance (profit margin) of deposit money banks in Nigeria |
| Agyemang-Mintah and Schade-witz (2019) | To examine whether having women on the boards can impact financial firm value during the pre-/post-global financial crisis periods | 63 UK financial institutions[21] for the 2000–2011 period (756 firm-year observations) | Refinitiv | Panel data regression (random and fixed effects) | • Gender: the number of women on bank board | a. The presence of women on the boards of UK financial institutions has a positive and statistically significant impact on firm value (Tobin's Q) but only during the pre-crisis period (2000–2006)<br>b. After the financial crisis, BGD no longer has a significant effect on firm value likely due to the economic downturn experienced by the entire UK economy during those years |

[21] These institutions belong to the investment banking, insurance, mortgage, investment trust, and banking services sectors.

| *Authors* | *Objectives* | *Sample and years* | *Main data sources* | *Methodology* | *Gender proxy* | *Results (Limited to gender issues)* |
|---|---|---|---|---|---|---|
| Hasan et al. (2019) | To investigate the possible impact of various governance attributes on the MFIs' financial performance | 68 MFIs from Bangladesh over the 2008–2009 period | Annual reports of MFIs, Bangladesh Microfinance Statistics 2009, desk-reports of partner Organisations maintained by PKSF (Palli Karma-Sahayak Foundation) | OLS | • FDB: % of female members on the board<br>• FCEO: dummy variable equal to 1 if the CEO is female<br>• FCFB: interaction variable between FCEO and FDB | a. Women on the board and female CEOs have a negative linkage with MFI's financial performance (operating income divided by total financial expenses, loan loss expenses, and operating expenses)<br>b. The interaction variable (FCFB-female CEO with female directors) for capturing the joint effect of BGD and female CEOs has a positive and significant impact on the MFI's performance |
| Mazzotta and Ferraro (2020) | To investigate the effects of BGD on bank economic performance, considering the implementation of gender quota laws; To test the potential impact of female directors and their roles on bank boards | 22 Italian listed banks over the 2008–2014 period (131 bank-year observations) | Corporate governance reports of banks, BankFocus, and Refinitiv | Panel data regression (fixed effects) + GMM | • FEMALE: the number of female directors divided by the number of directors on the board<br>• FEDIR: the number of female executive directors divided by the number of directors on the board<br>• FNEDIR: number of women on the board who do not have an executive role divided by the number of directors on the board<br>• FIND: number of women on the board who have an independent role divided by the number of directors on the board | a. There is a positive relationship between BGD and performance accounting measures (ROAE and ROAA)<br>b. There is a non-neutral impact of the presence of female directors on boards<br>c. There is a significant and negative effect of BGD on market measures (Tobin's Q) |

(continued)

**Table 3.1** (continued)

| *Authors* | *Objectives* | *Sample and years* | *Main data sources* | *Methodology* | *Gender proxy* | *Results (Limited to gender issues)* |
|---|---|---|---|---|---|---|
| Andrieş et al. (2020) | To investigate whether banks with more female directors or chairwomen display lower risk and higher performance | 156 banks from 17 CEE countries[22] over the 2005–2012 period | Banks' annual reports, other corporate documents, bank websites, BankFocus, and World Bank | Panel data regression (fixed effects) + GMM | • Women on board: % of females among members of the banks' boards<br>• Chairwoman: dummy variable equal to 1 if the chairperson of the board is female<br>• The Blau and the Shannon indexes[23] | a. Banks with a chairwoman and a higher proportion of female directors record a higher level of profitability (ROE and ROA) and stability (*Z*-score, but only during the financial crisis) and a lower level of credit losses (impaired loans to gross loans ratio, NPL and loan loss provisions to total loans ratio)<br>b. The regulatory framework affects the relationship between BGD and bank performance and risk<br>c. Banks with a chairwoman or a higher proportion of female directors show a higher profitability and stability if they are established in a country with a tolerant regulatory environment |

[22] The countries are Albania, Bosnia and Herzegovina, Bulgaria, Croatia, the Czech Republic, Estonia, Hungary, Latvia, Lithuania, Macedonia, Montenegro, Poland, Romania, Serbia, Slovakia, Slovenia, and the Ukraine.

[23] The Shannon index is calculated as follows: $-\sum_{i=1}^{n} P_i * log\ P_i$, where P is the share of board members in each category (male/female) and n is the total number of directors sitting on the board. The values range from 0 to 0.69, where the latter figure corresponds to the greatest possible degree of diversity. The Shannon index is more sensitive to small changes in the board gender diversity because it is a logarithmic measure.

| *Authors* | *Objectives* | *Sample and years* | *Main data sources* | *Methodology* | *Gender proxy* | *Results (Limited to gender issues)* |
|---|---|---|---|---|---|---|
| Khan et al. (2020) | To examine whether the presence of female directors is smaller for Islamic banks (IBs) than for conventional banks (CoBs);<br>To examine how the performance of IBs with women on the board differs from that of conventional banks | 71 IBs + 120 CoBs operating in 11 Muslim countries over the 2010–2017 period (1528 bank-year observations) | BankFocus, banks' annual reports, World Bank, and Bank Regulation and Supervision Database | DID (difference in differences) + panel data regression (random effects) | • Female ratio: female directors divided by the total number of directors | a. IBs have only slightly fewer female directors on their boards compared to their conventional counterparts<br>b. The presence of female directors on the board does not affect differently the performance (risk-adjusted return, i.e., ROAA divided by standard deviation of ROAA over the last three years) of IBs and CoBs |
| Cardillo et al. (2020) | To examine the impact of BGD on the probability and size of the public bailouts of banks;<br>To examine the linkage between BGD and bank performance | 105 banks in EU-15 countries over the 2005–2017 period | Public Support Measures in Europe and the United States, European Commission, Global Trade Alert from CEPR, BankFocus, and World Bank | OLS + PSM (propensity score matching) + IV-estimation methods | • Gender diversity: % of female directors on the board | a. Banks with more BGD are less likely to receive a public bailout. When this happens, they receive a lower amount of bailout funds than their counterparts with less BGD<br>b. BGD is positively linked to bank performance as proxied by ROA, Tobin's Q, and dividend payout ratios |
| Arnaboldi et al. (2020) | To examine whether board features and diversity (including gender diversity) play a role in explaining bank performance | 77 listed banks from 20 EU countries over the 2007–2015 period | BoardEx, BankFocus, and Refinitiv | Mean difference (t-test) + panel data regression (fixed effects) + GMM | • DBOARDWOM: dummy equal to 1 if both genders are represented on the board, and 0 if the board consists exclusively of men<br>• BOARDWOM: number of women on the board<br>• BOARDWOM2: fraction of women on the board | a. The boards of the top performing banks have, on average, more female directors<br>b. There is no impact of board gender diversity on bank performance (stock return, ROA, net interest margin, *Z*-score) and riskiness (standard deviation of stock return) |

(continued)

**Table 3.1** (continued)

| *Authors* | *Objectives* | *Sample and years* | *Main data sources* | *Methodology* | *Gender proxy* | *Results (Limited to gender issues)* |
|---|---|---|---|---|---|---|
| Boubacar (2020) | To explore the existence of a relationship between the presence of women in the top management and the performance of MFIs in West African Economic and Monetary Union (WAEMU) countries | 266 MFIs in WAEMU countries over the 2013–2017 period (1183 MFI-year observations) | Microfinance Information eXchange (MIX) | Panel data regression (random effects) | • Women_board: % of women on the board<br>• Women_managers: % of women managers | a. The proportion of women on the board has a negative and significant impact on the effectiveness of MFIs in terms of reducing operational costs<br>b. The presence of female managers does not affect MFIs' financial performance<br>c. Women in the top management positions have a positive impact on the MFIs' social performance in terms of more credit being granted to the female clients of MFIs |
| Jabari and Muhamad (2021) | To examine the influence of gender diversity on the board of directors (BOD) and the Shariah supervisory board (SSB) on the financial performance of Islamic banks | 9 Islamic banks (Indonesia and Malaysia) over the 2010–2018 period | Fitch Connect, World Bank, and banks' annual reports | OLS + panel data regression (random effects) | • DW BOD: dummy variable equal to 1 when at least one woman sits on the BOD, and 0 otherwise<br>• DW SSB: dummy variable equal to 1 when at least one woman sits on the SSB, and 0 otherwise<br>• PW BOD: % of women directors sitting on the BOD<br>• PW SSB: % of women directors sitting on the SSB | a. There is a positive relationship between the proportion of women on the BOD and bank performance (ROAE)<br>b. Concerning the proportion of women among the SSB members, the positive impact on bank performance is verified only for smaller banks |

| *Authors* | *Objectives* | *Sample and years* | *Main data sources* | *Methodology* | *Gender proxy* | *Results (Limited to gender issues)* |
|---|---|---|---|---|---|---|
| Baklouti (2020) | To examine the effect of the characteristics of the Shariah supervisory board (SSB) on the financial performance of Islamic banks | 42 Islamic banks spread over 12 countries[24] in the Middle East and North Africa (MENA) region, excluding the Gulf countries and some non-Islamic countries over the 2011–2018 period | Banks' annual reports, BankFocus, and the FRED website | Panel data regression (random effects) + GLS | • SSB women: the proportion of women on the SSB | a. While a large-sized board of directors and a number of SSB meetings improve bank performance (ROA and ROE), the proportion of women sitting on the SSB has no impact on the financial performance of Islamic banks |
| Khan and Wang (2021) | To explore corporate governance and its impacts on bank financial performance | 17 commercial banks in China over the 2008–2019 period (170 bank-year observations) | CSMAR (China Stock Market & Accounting Research) database | GMM | • Female board representation: % of female directors on the board<br>• Interaction variable of independent directors and female board members | a. The presence of female directors does not improve bank financial performance (ROA)<br>b. Female directors improve bank performance when they are selected as independent directors |

(continued)

24 The banks in the sample are from Tunisia, Algeria, Egypt, Jordan, Palestine, the Syrian Arab Republic, the Sudan, Lebanon, Yemen, Iraq, the UK, and Sri Lanka.

**Table 3.1** (continued)

| *Authors* | *Objectives* | *Sample and years* | *Main data sources* | *Methodology* | *Gender proxy* | *Results (Limited to gender issues)* |
|---|---|---|---|---|---|---|
| Grassa (2016) | To investigate whether Islamic banks with strong corporate governance benefit from higher credit ratings compared to Islamic banks with weaker governance;<br>To verify whether Shariah governance can affect the credit ratings of Islamic banks | 43 Islamic banks in GCC and Southeast Asian countries over the 2005–2011 period (bank-year observations range between 94 and 120) | Banks' annual reports, Zawya database, and BankFocus | Ordered logit model + simultaneous equation approach | • Women directors: % of women sitting on the board of directors<br>• SB women: % of women sitting on the Shariah board | a. Banks' credit ratings are positively associated with the % of women directors, but not with the % of women sitting on the Shariah board |
| **BGD and bank risk-taking** | | | | | | |
| Muller-Kahle and Lewellyn (2011) | To examine whether board configuration plays a role in determining the decision to specialise in subprime lending by financial institutions | 74 US financial institutions over the 1997–2005 period (275 firm-year observations) | US Department of Housing and Urban Development (HUD), Thomson One Financial, SEC DEF 14A proxy statements filed with the Securities and Exchange Commission | Logistic panel regression (random effects) | • Board gender diversity: the proportion of women divided by the total number of directors | a. BGD is negatively associated with the decision to specialise in subprime lending<br>b. "Outside director busyness" (average number of director positions held by outside directors of the firm) is positively associated with subprime lending |

| *Authors* | *Objectives* | *Sample and years* | *Main data sources* | *Methodology* | *Gender proxy* | *Results (Limited to gender issues)* |
|---|---|---|---|---|---|---|
| Mateos De Cabo et al. (2012) | To identify the organisational characteristics that could be predictive of the presence of women on the bank boards | 612 banks from 20 European countries[25] | BankFocus | Poisson regression | • The proportion of female directors on the board | a. The proportion of women on the board is higher for lower-risk banks (risk is measured by the standard deviation of ROAA and the equity on total assets), for banks with larger boards, and for those with a growth orientation (measured by the growth rate of total assets) |
| Berger et al. (2014) | To investigate how executive board characteristics (size, age, gender, education, and tenure composition) affect the portfolio risk of financial institutions | The entire population of German bank executive officers over the 1994–2010 period | Deutsche Bundesbank | DID (difference in differences) | • The proportion of female board members | a. Younger executives and BGD increase bank portfolio risk (although the latter effect is weaker in terms of both statistical and economic significance) |

(continued)

[25] The countries are Austria, Belgium, Cyprus, Czech Republic, Denmark, Finland, France, Germany, Sweden, Greece, Hungary, Ireland, Italy, Luxemburg, the Netherlands, Poland, Portugal, Slovenia, Spain, and the UK.

**Table 3.1** (continued)

| *Authors* | *Objectives* | *Sample and years* | *Main data sources* | *Methodology* | *Gender proxy* | *Results (Limited to gender issues)* |
|---|---|---|---|---|---|---|
| Adams and Ragunathan (2015) | To examine the relationship between BGD on the one hand and various types of risk-taking activities in banks (such as the use of mortgage-backed securities) and the overall bank risk on the other | 350 US financial institutions over the 2006–2009 period | Compustat Federal Reserve Bank National Information Center, the bank's proxy filing (from EDGAR Company Filings), BoardEx, and CRSP (Center for Research in Security Prices) | OLS + 2SLS | • Fr(Women): the number of female directors divided by board size | a. There is no causal relationship between BGD and bank risk<br>b. Female directors may have similar levels of risk appetite or risk aversion to male directors<br>c. Banks with more BGD have better performance during the subprime crisis |
| Palvia et al. (2015) | To examine whether bank capital ratios and default risk are associated with the gender of the Chief Executive Officers (CEOs) and board chairs | 6729 US commercial banks over the 2007–2010 period (22,978 bank-year observations) | SNL Financial, reports on the bank's condition and income (bank call reports) available from the Federal Financial Institutions Examination Council (FFIEC) | Mean difference (t-test) + 2SLS + logistic panel regression | • Female CEO: dummy variable that equals 1 for banks that have a female CEO<br>• Female Chair: dummy variable that equals 1 for banks that have a female board chair<br>• Female CEO or chair: dummy variable that equals 1 for banks that have either a female CEO or a female board chair | a. Female-led banks (banks with female CEOs or board chairs) exhibit higher levels of equity capital<br>b. Female CEOs and chairwomen reduce the bank's default risk during the financial crisis, only for smaller banks |

| *Authors* | *Objectives* | *Sample and years* | *Main data sources* | *Methodology* | *Gender proxy* | *Results (Limited to gender issues)* |
|---|---|---|---|---|---|---|
| Gulamhussen and Santa (2015) | To analyse whether the presence of women in boardrooms (board of directors, supervisory board, and audit committee) has a positive influence on bank accounting and market performance and risk-taking | 461 large banks from OECD countries in 2006 | BankFocus, bank websites, and Thomson Reuters | 2SLS | • The proportion of women on the board (FBOARD), on the supervisory board (FSUP), and on the audit committee (FAUDIT)<br>• A dummy equal to 1 if the bank has one female director on the board (DBOARD), on the supervisory board (DSUP), and the audit committee (DAUDIT) | a. There is a negative relationship between the presence of women on the board and bank risk-taking (loan loss reserve, loan loss provision, impaired loans, and the *Z*-score)<br>b. Similar findings are found for female presence on the supervisory board and audit committee |
| Chan et al. (2016) | To examine the impact of directors' socioeconomic background (including BGD) on banks' risk-taking behaviour | 16 listed commercial banks in China over the 2003–2011 period | Bloomberg, BankFocus, banks' annual reports, and Refinitiv | GLS + GMM | • Gender diversity is proxied by the % of female directors sitting on the board | a. A higher proportion of female directors on the board decreases both the idiosyncratic (standard deviation of the residual obtained from the two-factor market model) and the total risk of banks (standard deviation of the daily stock returns) |

(continued)

**Table 3.1** (continued)

| *Authors* | *Objectives* | *Sample and years* | *Main data sources* | *Methodology* | *Gender proxy* | *Results (Limited to gender issues)* |
|---|---|---|---|---|---|---|
| Farag and Mallin (2017) | To investigate the influence of BGD on both bank financial fragility and performance | 99 European banks over the 2004–2012 period | Banks' annual reports, BankFocus, Thomson One Banker, and Datastream | GMM | • Female: % of female directors sitting on the board of directors<br>• FemaleSB: % of female directors sitting on the supervisory board<br>• FemaleMgtB: % of female directors sitting on the management board<br>• The Blau index | a. Appointing a female director beyond the critical mass of 24% increases the level of bank risk (impaired loans divided by gross loans, %)<br>b. Role (non-executive or executive) influences the degree of risk-taking of female directors<br>c. Female and male executive directors may have the same risk-taking behaviour |
| Sahay et al. (IMF) (2017) | To examine the female representation in leadership positions in banks and bank supervision agencies worldwide; To examine the linkage between BGD and bank stability and riskiness | About 800 banks in 72 countries[26] over the 2003–2013 period | BoardEx, BankFocus, Refinitiv, and IMF World Economic Outlook (WEO) database | Pooled OLS + panel data regression (fixed effects) | • The share of women directors on bank boards | a. Women on the board of directors are associated with higher *Z*-scores and lower levels of non-performing loans (NPLs) |

[26] More than half of the banks in the sample are from the US, more than 20% are from Europe, and the rest are from Asia, the Americas, and Africa.

| *Authors* | *Objectives* | *Sample and years* | *Main data sources* | *Methodology* | *Gender proxy* | *Results (Limited to gender issues)* |
|---|---|---|---|---|---|---|
| Talavera et al. (2018) | To examine the effects of board diversity (in terms of age and gender) on bank profitability and risk | 97 Chinese banks over the 2009–2013 period | Banks' annual reports | Fixed effects instrumental variable + GMM | • Female directors: % of female directors on bank boards | a. There is no relationship between the percentage of female directors and bank risk as measured by the *Z*-score and NPL ratio |
| Sheedy and Lubo-janski (2018) | To investigate the risk management behaviour among the financial service staff and the linkage with the female gender | 36,000 survey responses from 10 banks headquartered in Australia, Canada, and the UK over 26 months (July 2014–August 2016) | Survey | Survey + two-step regression model + mean difference (t-test) | • Gender distribution by business line (BL) and seniority | a. There is little evidence of a positive association between the female gender and desirable risk management behaviour<br>b. Women who succeed in financial services do not conform to traditional female stereotypes characterised by less risk-taking |
| Sghaier and Hamza (2018) | To investigate the influence of gender diversity in the boardroom and in the top management positions on the risk profile (RP) of acquiring banks | 112 European acquiring banks over the 2000–2015 period | Thomson One Banker database and banks' annual reports | 2SLS | • Women: % of women directors on the board<br>• Women top: dummy variable equal to 1 if either the CEO, CFO, or chair is a woman, and 0 otherwise<br>• 3 women: dummy variable equal to 1 if there are more than 3 women on the board, and 0 otherwise | a. There is a negative correlation between the % of women directors on the board or a female chair and the evolution of the RP of the acquiring banks<br>b. The presence of at least three women on the board of directors negatively affects the RP of the acquiring banks |

(continued)

**Table 3.1** (continued)

| *Authors* | *Objectives* | *Sample and years* | *Main data sources* | *Methodology* | *Gender proxy* | *Results (Limited to gender issues)* |
|---|---|---|---|---|---|---|
| Rafinda et al. (2018) | To examine the impact of BGD on the sustainability of bank performance and risk | 22 banks and financial institutions in India over the 2011–2015 period (110 bank-year observations) | BankFocus, banks' annual reports, and Spencer Stuart | Pooled panel data regression | • Total number of female directors divided by the total number of board directors | a. BGD has a positive and significant impact on bank risk measured by the *Z*-score of Asset Risk (ZSA) |
| Skała and Weill (2018) | To investigate the relationship between CEO gender and bank risk | 365 Polish cooperative banks over the 2008–2012 period (2037 bank-year observations) | Banks' annual reports, and the Polish Statistical Office's (GUS) data on the different regions (Local Data Bank) | Regression analysis | • Female CEO: dummy variable equal to 1 if the CEO is a woman, 0 otherwise | a. Banks headed by female CEOs report higher capital adequacy and equity to assets ratios<br>b. Banks headed by female CEOs are less risky |
| Gangi et al. (2019) | To analyse the impact of effective corporate governance mechanisms on environmental engagement and risk-taking of banks | 142 banks from 35 countries[27] over the 2011–2015 period (655 bank-year observations) | Thomson Reuters' ASSET4 and World Bank | Mean difference (t-test) + Heckman's two-stage model | • B_GD: the % of female directors divided by total board directors | a. BGD is a negative predictor of bank risk as measured by the *Z*-score |

[27] The countries are Australia, Austria, Belgium, Brazil, Canada, Chile, China, Colombia, Denmark, France, Germany, Greece, Hong Kong, Hungary, India, Ireland, Israel, Italy, Kuwait, Malaysia, Norway, Oman, the Philippines, Puerto Rico, Russia, Singapore, South Africa, Spain, Sweden, Switzerland, Taiwan, Thailand, Turkey, the UK, and the US.

| *Authors* | *Objectives* | *Sample and years* | *Main data sources* | *Methodology* | *Gender proxy* | *Results (Limited to gender issues)* |
|---|---|---|---|---|---|---|
| Abou-El-Sood (2019) | To investigate the association between BGD and bank risk-taking in an emerging market context | Listed banks in the GCC countries over the 2002–2014 period (50 publicly traded conventional banks + 32 Islamic banks for a total number of 780 bank-year observations) | Banks' annual reports, BankFocus, GulfBase database, and Hawkamah Institute for Corporate Governance | 2SLS | • FEM: the ratio of female directors divided by the total number of directors on the bank board<br>• FEMD: dummy variable equal to 1 if the board has a female member, and 0 otherwise | a. Banks with more female board directors assume a lower-risk profile when the regulatory capital adequacy is low<br>b. In banks with higher levels of the regulatory capital ratio, female directors make decisions to invest in more risky positions<br>c. Female directors tend to undertake less risky positions in Islamic banks compared to conventional banks |
| Palvia et al. (2020) | To examine the association between bank risk-taking and the gender of the CEO and chairperson of the board | 6971 US commercial banks over the 2007–2017 period (54,312 bank-year observations) | Banks' annual reports (from Federal Financial Institutions Examination Council-FFIEC) and SNL Financial Federal Housing Finance Agency (FHFA) | Panel data regression (fixed effects) + GMM | • Female CEO: dummy variable equal to 1 for banks that have a female CEO<br>• Female chair: dummy variable equal to 1 if the bank's board chair is a woman<br>• Female CEO or chair: dummy variable equal to 1 if either the bank CEO or the board chair is a woman | a. Banks with female CEOs and board chairs are associated with a better lending performance in the aftermath of severe real estate price shocks<br>b. Female-led banks with a high level of real estate exposure are associated with a lower default risk in the aftermath of real estate price shocks |

(continued)

**Table 3.1** (continued)

| *Authors* | *Objectives* | *Sample and years* | *Main data sources* | *Methodology* | *Gender proxy* | *Results (Limited to gender issues)* |
|---|---|---|---|---|---|---|
| Khan et al. (2020) | To examine how to differentiate the performance and the riskiness of Islamic banks (IBs) with women on the board compared to conventional banks (CoBs) | 71 IBs + 120 CoBs operating in eleven Muslim countries over the 2010–2017 period (1528 bank-year observations) | Banks' annual reports, BankFocus, World Bank, and Bank Regulation and Supervision Database | DID (difference in differences) + panel data regression (random effects) | • Female ratio: female directors divided by the total number of directors | a. The presence of women on the boards is not significantly associated with a higher or lower credit risk in both CoBs and IBs |
| Gallucci et al. (2020) | To verify whether a country's masculinity affects the relationship between a bank's board gender diversity and risk-taking | 110 banks from Germany, Italy, Spain, and Switzerland over the 2008–2017 period (13,200 bank-year observations) | Bank annual reports, bank websites, and BankFocus | Moderated multiple regression | • Gender diversity: % of female directors on the board | a. BGD is significantly and negatively linked to bank risk as measured by the standard deviation of ROA<br>b. Country-level masculinity has a negative moderating effect on the relationship between BGD and risk-taking leading women directors to become even more risk-averse |
| Cardillo et al. (2020) | To examine the impact of BGD on the probability and size of public bailouts of banks;<br>To examine the linkage between BGD and bank performance | 105 banks in EU-15 countries over the 2005–2017 period | Public Support Measures in Europe and the United States, European Commission, Global Trade Alert from CEPR, BankFocus, and World Bank | OLS + PSM + IV-estimation methods | • Gender Diversity: % of female directors on the board | a. BGD reduces bank risk-taking and ultimately, the probability that a bank needs a public bailout to avoid liquidation |

| *Authors* | *Objectives* | *Sample and years* | *Main data sources* | *Methodology* | *Gender proxy* | *Results (Limited to gender issues)* |
|---|---|---|---|---|---|---|
| Bunea and Dinu (2020) | To analyse the influence of the structure of the board of directors on capital demands and risk management undertaken in the Romanian banking system | 25 Romanian banks in 2018 | Banks' annual reports | Regression analysis + ANOVA | • Gender diversity: % of female directors on the board | a. Banks with more female directors have a higher level of total funds; thus, they are less risky |
| Birindelli et al. (2020) | To examine the relationship between female directors and bank risk, and whether such a relationship varies across both sound and unsound banks, with or without a critical mass of female directors | 215 listed banks from 40 countries[28] over the 2008–2016 period | Refinitiv Eikon, Deloitte, European Corporate Governance Institute, and World Bank | Panel data regression (fixed effects) + GMM | • Female directors: % of female directors on the board<br>• Mass (critical mass of female directors): dummy variable equal to 1 if three or more female directors serve on the board, 0 otherwise | a. Increasing the number of female directors does not reduce bank risk when banks are unsound<br>b. Conversely, when banks are sound, female directors have a significant and positive role in reducing risk but only until reaching a critical mass of women |

(continued)

[28] The countries are Australia, Austria, Bahrain, Belgium, Brazil, Canada, Denmark, Egypt, France, Germany, Hong Kong, Hungary, India, Indonesia, Ireland, Israel, Italy, Japan, Jordan, Kuwait, Malaysia, the Netherlands, Nigeria, Norway, Oman, the People's Republic of China, the Philippines, Poland, Portugal, Qatar, Russia, Singapore, South Africa, Spain, Sweden, Switzerland, Thailand, Turkey, the UK, and the US.

**Table 3.1** (continued)

| *Authors* | *Objectives* | *Sample and years* | *Main data sources* | *Methodology* | *Gender proxy* | *Results (Limited to gender issues)* |
|---|---|---|---|---|---|---|
| Abou-El-Sood (2021) | To examine whether and how female directorship is effective in reducing the excessive risk-taking of banks | 195 US commercial banks over the 2002–2018 period (2738 bank-year observations) | BankFocus, Proxy statements filed at the SEC, and Centre for Research in Security Prices (CRSP) | 2SLS + DID (difference in differences) | • The ratio of female directors to the total number of directors on the board<br>• A dummy variable equal to 1 if there are three or more female directors on the board, and 0 otherwise | a. Women directors undertake risky investments when they perceive the positive incentives of their decisions. This happens when the bank has a strong regulatory capital base that increases investment opportunities<br>b. Women directors invest in less risky assets during a financial crisis and when the CEO has more power because of his equity ownership. In these circumstances, women directors hold less power, and therefore, they do not invest in risky positions |
| **BGD and bank efficiency** | | | | | | |
| Titova (2016) | To analyse the relationship between cost efficiency and a set of board-related characteristics | Sample of US commercial banks and savings institutions over the 2007–2013 period (unbalanced panel from 1181 to 1256 bank-year observations) | Bloomberg | Stochastic frontier analysis (SFA) + data envelopment analysis (DEA) | • Female executives (number of female executives, as a % of the total executives)<br>• Women on the board (number of women on the board of directors, as a % of board size) | a. There is no relationship between board gender diversity and bank efficiency |

| *Authors* | *Objectives* | *Sample and years* | *Main data sources* | *Methodology* | *Gender proxy* | *Results (Limited to gender issues)* |
|---|---|---|---|---|---|---|
| Ramly et al. (2017) | To examine the role of independent women directors in improving bank efficiency | 102 commercial banks from ASEAN countries[29] over the 1999–2012 period (1108 bank-year observations) | Banks' annual reports and BankFocus | DEA + GMM | • The % of women directors on the board<br>• The Blau index | a. Women directors promote bank efficiency if they are appointed as independent directors<br>b. The positive impact on cost efficiency and profit efficiency level can only be achieved when one-third of the board is made up of independent women directors |
| Andrieş et al. (2018) | To study the influence of female directors on two alternative measures of bank efficiency (cost and technical efficiency) | 128 commercial banks from Central and Eastern European countries[30] over the 2005–2012 period | Annual reports, Financial Statements, and Reports on capital adequacy and risk management of banks, bank websites, RiskMetrics, BoardEx, and others (WEF, SBRS, GFDB, WDI)[31] | DEA + instrument variables | • No female on boards: dummy variable equal to 1 if a bank has no women on the boards and 0 otherwise<br>• Women on boards: % of women on bank board of directors<br>• Women on SB: % of women on bank supervisory board<br>• Women on MB: % of women on bank management boards<br>• Blau and Shannon indexes | a. A greater female representation among members of bank boards has a strong and positive impact on both cost and technical efficiency, especially in small banks |

(continued)

[29] The countries are Malaysia, Indonesia, Thailand, the Philippines, and Singapore.

[30] The countries are Albania, Bosnia and Herzegovina, Bulgaria, Croatia, Czech Republic, Estonia, Hungary, Latvia, Lithuania, Macedonia, Montenegro, Poland, Romania, Serbia, Slovakia, Slovenia, and the Ukraine.

[31] WEF: World Economic Forum; SBRS: the World Bank Survey of Bank Regulation and Supervision; GFDB: the Global Financial Development Database of World Bank; WDI: World Development Indicators.

**Table 3.1** (continued)

| *Authors* | *Objectives* | *Sample and years* | *Main data sources* | *Methodology* | *Gender proxy* | *Results (Limited to gender issues)* |
|---|---|---|---|---|---|---|
| Adeabah et al. (2019) | To analyse bank efficiency under board gender diversity;<br>To examine the determinants of bank efficiency | 21 banks in Ghana over the 2009–2017 period (148 bank-year observations) | Banks' annual reports | DEA + panel data regression | • BGD: the number of female directors excluding 0 | a. There is an inverted U-shaped linkage between female directors and bank efficiency. Bank efficiency increases up to a maximum number of two female directors<br>b. For more than 2 women directors on a 9-member board, banks exhibit a decreasing return to scale |
| Adusei (2019) | To verify whether BGD promotes the bank's technical efficiency and whether this relationship is moderated by the size of MFIs | 418 MFIs over the 2010–2014 period | Microfinance Information Exchange (MIX) market (www.mixmarket.org) and World Bank | DEA + probit + logit + GLM | • WOB: % of female directors on the board<br>• WOB dummy: dummy variable equal to 1 if the median percentage of female directors on the board of the MFI is above the sample median, and 0 otherwise | a. BGD damages the technical efficiency of MFIs<br>b. A positive relationship can only be found for larger MFIs<br>c. The size of the MFIs plays a key role in positively influencing the impact of female directors on MFIs' technical efficiency |
| Safiullah (2021) | To examine whether Shariah board governance helps Islamic banks to become more efficient in terms of stability | 94 Islamic banks from 28 countries[32] over the 2003–2018 period | Banks' annual reports, Fitchconnect, BankFocus, and World Bank | Stochastic frontier analysis (SFA) + PSM (propensity score matching) + 2SLS + GMM | • Shariah board members' gender diversity: % of female directors on the Shariah boards | a. Shariah board members' gender diversity improves stability efficiency in Islamic banks<br>b. This effect is more pronounced during the crisis period |

[32] The countries are Bangladesh, Maldives, Pakistan, Sri Lanka, Malaysia, Indonesia, Brunei Darussalam, Thailand, Bahrain, Kuwait, Oman, Qatar, Saudi Arabia, the United Arab Emirates, Egypt, Iraq, Jordan, Lebanon, Palestine, the Syrian Arab Republic, Tunisia, Yemen, Turkey, the UK, Kenya, Nigeria, South Africa, and the Sudan.

| *Authors* | *Objectives* | *Sample and years* | *Main data sources* | *Methodology* | *Gender proxy* | *Results (Limited to gender issues)* |
|---|---|---|---|---|---|---|
| **BGD and bank CSR performance** | | | | | | |
| Barako and Brown (2008) | To examine the influence of gender and board representation on the communication of corporate social reporting by Kenyan banks | 40 Kenyan banks | Banks' annual reports and the Central Bank Supervision report | Multiple regression analysis | • Women representation on board: ratio of women directors divided by the total number of directors | a. A higher level of women representation on boards improves corporate social voluntary disclosure |
| Khan (2010) | To explore the potential effects of corporate governance elements (including BGD) on bank CSR disclosure | All private commercial banks (equal to 30) in Bangladesh over the 2007–2008 period | Banks' annual reports | Content analysis + Multiple regressions analysis | • % of women directors divided by the total number of directors | a. Non-executive or non-Bangladeshi directors are positively linked to bank CSR reporting<br>b. No significant relationship is found between women representation on the board and bank disclosure |
| Kilic et al. (2015) | To analyse the trend of CSR reporting in the Turkish banking industry;<br>To investigate the impact of ownership and board structure on banks' CSR reporting | 25 Turkish banks over the period 2008–2012 | Annual reports and CSR/sustainability reports of banks | Content analysis + panel data regression (random and fixed effects) + LSDV (least-squares dummy variables) | • FEMALE_MEMB: number of female directors on the board | a. There is a significant positive effect of size, ownership diffusion, board composition, and board gender diversity on bank CSR disclosure |

(continued)

**Table 3.1** (continued)

| *Authors* | *Objectives* | *Sample and years* | *Main data sources* | *Methodology* | *Gender proxy* | *Results (Limited to gender issues)* |
|---|---|---|---|---|---|---|
| Birindelli et al. (2018) | To examine the impact of the main board characteristics, including a critical mass of female directors, on bank ESG performance | 108 listed banks in Europe and the United States over the 2011–2016 period (406 bank-year observations) | Thomson Reuters-Refinitiv and World Bank | Panel data regression (fixed effects) | • WOMEN BOD: % of women on the board of directors<br>• MASS WB (critical mass of women on the BOD): dummy variable equal to 1 if boards have at least 3 women members, 0 otherwise | a. The relationship between women on the BOD and bank's ESG performance is an inverted U-shape. Therefore, the critical mass theory for banks is not supported, confirming that only gender-balanced boards positively impact a bank's sustainability performance |
| García-Sánchez et al. (2018) | To examine whether board independence and BGD impact the CSR commitment of banks | 159 banks in 9 countries[33] over the 2004–2010 period (877 bank-year observations) | Thomson One Analytics, Ethical Investment Research Services (EIRIS), and Spencer & Stuart Board Index | Factorial analysis + panel data regression | • %Female: % of female directors on the board | a. Banks with more independent directors and more female members on their boards are inclined towards socially responsible behaviour<br>b. The positive effects are greater in environments with a stronger regulation and investor protection |

33 The countries are Canada, France, Germany, Italy, the Netherlands, Spain, Sweden, the UK, and the US.

| *Authors* | *Objectives* | *Sample and years* | *Main data sources* | *Methodology* | *Gender proxy* | *Results (Limited to gender issues)* |
|---|---|---|---|---|---|---|
| Matuszak et al. (2019) | To investigate the extent and trend of CSR reporting in commercial banks in Poland; To examine the link between corporate governance characteristics of management and supervisory bodies (MB and SB, respectively) and banks' CSR disclosure | 16 Polish commercial banks over the 2008–2015 period (144 bank-year observations) | Annual reports and CSR/sustainability reports of banks | Content analysis + panel data regression (random and fixed effects) | • ShareWomMB: the share of female members on the MB<br>• CMBWom: dummy variable equal to 1 if the chair of the MB is a woman and 0 otherwise<br>• ShareWomSB: the share of female members on the SB<br>• CSBWom: dummy variable equal to 1 if the chair of the SB is a woman and 0 otherwise | a. Gender diversity on the MB increases the banks' CSR disclosure<br>b. The presence of a female chair of the MB has a positive impact on CSR reporting<br>c. None of the SB variables generate a significant outcome on bank CSR disclosure |
| Al-Jaifi (2020) | To examine the association between board gender diversity and environmental, social, and corporate governance performance of banks in the ASEAN context | 26 banks from 5 ASEAN[34] countries over the 2011–2016 period (130 bank-year observations) | Refinitiv (ASSET4 Thomson Reuters-Datastream database) | OLS + panel data regression (random and fixed effects) + GMM | • Gender: the total number of female directors on the board divided by the total number of directors | a. BGD positively influences corporate governance performance, although it has no impact on the bank's environmental and social performance |

(continued)

[34] The countries are Malaysia, Singapore, Thailand, Indonesia, and the Philippines.

**Table 3.1** (continued)

| *Authors* | *Objectives* | *Sample and years* | *Main data sources* | *Methodology* | *Gender proxy* | *Results (Limited to gender issues)* |
|---|---|---|---|---|---|---|
| Shakil et al. (2021) | To investigate the BGD-ESG performance nexus in banks;<br>To verify the moderating role (contingency effects) of ESG controversies on this nexus | 37 US banks over the 2013–2017 period | Refinitiv | Panel data regression (random and fixed effects) + GMM | • GED: % of women on the bank board | a. There is a significant positive relationship between BGD and bank ESG performance<br>b. ESG controversies do not play a moderating role in this relationship |
| Tapver et al. (2020) | To examine the association between CSR reporting and female representation on boards while controlling for the impact of gender quotas | Global sample of 285 commercial banks over the 2005–2017 period[35] (the bank-year observations range from 861 to 1018) | Refinitiv | Logistic panel regression (fixed effects) | • %wom: % of women on the board<br>• %wex1: % of women on the board exceeding the mandatory quota<br>• dwhigh: dummy variable equal to 1 if the % of women on the board is higher than the quota, 0 otherwise | a. There is a positive association between the proportion of women on the board and the banks' CSR disclosure<br>b. This positive association remains after the quota corrections for the banks with either below- or above-quota in terms of female representation |

35 The banks are headquartered in many countries (both developed and developing). The countries are the following: Australia, Austria, Belgium, Bermuda, Canada, China, the Czech Republic, Cyprus, Denmark, France, Germany, Greece, Hong Kong, Hungary, India, Indonesia, Ireland, Italy, Japan, Malaysia, the Netherlands, Norway, the Philippines, Poland, Portugal, Russia, Singapore, South Korea, Spain, Sweden, Thailand, Turkey, the UK, and the US.

| *Authors* | *Objectives* | *Sample and years* | *Main data sources* | *Methodology* | *Gender proxy* | *Results (Limited to gender issues)* |
|---|---|---|---|---|---|---|
| | | | | | • dwlow: dummy variable equal to 1 if the % of women on the board is lower than the quota, 0 otherwise<br>• dweq: dummy variable equal to 1 if the % of women on the board is equal to the quota, 0 otherwise<br>• %wex2: % of women on the board exceeding the female workforce participation in the country | c. Including more women on boards than required by the quota could positively affect bank CSR reporting in "masculine" countries and not in "feminine" countries |
| Gallego-Sosa et al. (2021) | To explore whether gender diversity on the board of directors can characterise companies with different degrees of engagement with the Sustainable Development Goals (SDGs) | The 30 largest banks in Europe from 13 countries[36] in 2017 | Annual reports, corporate governance reports, and sustainability reports of banks | Descriptive and inferential statistical analyses + mean difference (t-test) | • Dum1: dummy variable equal to 0 if there are no women on the board of directors, and 1 otherwise<br>• Dum3: dummy variable equal to 0 if there are fewer than 3 women on the board of directors, and 1 otherwise<br>• Nwom: number of women on the board of directors<br>• Pwom: proportion of female directors, calculated as the ratio of the number of women on the board compared to the Blau index | a. Banks with a larger female representation on the board show a greater commitment to the SDGs designed to improve environmental performance and the equitable development of cities<br>b. Concerning the remaining SDGs, BGD does not offer a way of differentiating between the banks |

(continued)

[36] The countries are Spain, France, Italy, Sweden, Germany, Denmark, Ireland, Hungary, the Netherlands, Poland, Austria, Czech Republic, and Portugal.

**Table 3.1** (continued)

| *Authors* | *Objectives* | *Sample and years* | *Main data sources* | *Methodology* | *Gender proxy* | *Results (Limited to gender issues)* |
|---|---|---|---|---|---|---|
| **BGD and bank environmental performance** | | | | | | |
| Deschênes et al. (2015) | To examine if board characteristics have an impact on the CSR score of companies, including banks | The 60 largest public Canadian firms over the 2004–2008 period | Thomson Reuters, banks' annual reports, and Michael Jantzi Research Associates | OLS | • The % of female directors serving on the board | a. The CSR score is positively linked to the % of women and independent directors<br>b. Only for the financial sector, the relationship between BGD and environmental performance is positive |
| Gangi et al. (2019) | To analyse the impact of corporate governance mechanisms on the banks' environmental engagement and risk-taking | 142 banks from 35 countries[37] over the 2011–2015 period (655 bank-year observations) | Refinitiv and World Bank | Mean difference (t-test) + Heckman's two-stage model | • The incidence of female directors on the total board directors | a. Banks that are more environmentally sensitive have larger boards with a higher incidence of independent and female directors among the total board members |

[37] The countries are Australia, Austria, Belgium, Brazil, Canada, Chile, China, Colombia, Denmark, France, Germany, Greece, Hong Kong, Hungary, India, Ireland, Israel, Italy, Kuwait, Malaysia, Norway, Oman, the Philippines, Puerto Rico, Russia, Singapore, South Africa, Spain, Sweden, Switzerland, Taiwan, Thailand, Turkey, the UK, and the US.

| *Authors* | *Objectives* | *Sample and years* | *Main data sources* | *Methodology* | *Gender proxy* | *Results (Limited to gender issues)* |
|---|---|---|---|---|---|---|
| Birindelli et al. (2019) | To analyse the connections between women leaders (in terms of both female directors and female CEOs) and bank environmental performance | 96 listed banks in the EMEA (Europe, Middle East, and Africa) region over the 2011–2016 period | Refinitiv, World Bank, the Global Gender Gap Index, the World Economic Forum, Deloitte, and the European Corporate Governance Institute | Panel data regression (random effects) + 2SLS | • Women on the board of directors: the total number of women on the board of directors (minus the CEO, if applicable) divided by the total number of board members<br>• A critical mass of women: dummy variable that is equal to 1 if the boards have at least 3 women on them, 0 otherwise<br>• CEO woman: dummy variable that is equal to 1 if the CEO is a woman, 0 otherwise | a. When the banks are led by male CEOs, there is an inverted U-shaped relationship between BGD and environmental performance<br>b. In the few cases where banks are led by a woman CEO, there is a U-shaped linkage between BGD and environmental performance<br>c. The positive impact on environmental performance emerges when the share of women on the board exceeds a threshold of 31% |
| Gallego-Sosa et al. (2020) | To verify whether BGD is a differentiating factor among banks with distinct environmental performance scores | 52 banks (28 in Europe and 24 in North America) over the 2010–2018 period | Refinitiv | Panel data regression (random and fixed effects) | • Dum1: dummy variable equal to 0 if there are no women on the board, 1 otherwise<br>• Dum3: dummy variable equal to 0 if there are fewer than 3 women on the board, 1 otherwise<br>• The number of women on the board<br>• Pwom: number of women on the board divided by the total number of board members | a. A greater presence of women on bank boards has no significant effect on banks' environmental performance<br>b. This finding can be due to the underrepresentation of women on bank boards |

(continued)

**Table 3.1** (continued)

| *Authors* | *Objectives* | *Sample and years* | *Main data sources* | *Methodology* | *Gender proxy* | *Results (Limited to gender issues)* |
|---|---|---|---|---|---|---|
| | | | | | • Dum30: dummy variable equal to 0 if fewer than 30% of the board members are women, 1 otherwise<br>• Dum40: Dummy variable equal to 0 if less than 40% of the board members are women, 1 otherwise<br>• An index reflecting the diversity of the board of directors. Its value ranges between 0 and 0.5 (0.5 indicates a perfect balance) | |
| **Other "minor" (or under-investigated) research lines** | | | | | | |
| Arnaboldi et al. (2021) | To examine the relationship between BGD and bank misconduct | 83 publicly listed banks operating in 21 EU countries over the 2007–2018 period | Banks' annual reports, BoardEx, Bloomberg, BankFocus, Refinitiv Eikon, Violation Tracker, the websites and press releases of the US regulatory agencies, and the World Economic Forum Global Gender Gap Report (2018) | Negative binomial model + probit model + event study | • Female Director: dummy variable equal to 1 if the gender of at least one board director is female, 0 otherwise<br>• Female Director %: the proportion of female directors on the board<br>• Δ Female Director %: the change in the proportion of female directors on the board each year<br>• Critical Mass (≥3): dummy variable equal to 1 if the number of female directors on the board is at least 3, 0 otherwise | a. A higher proportion of women on the board reduces the frequency of misconduct fines<br>b. This negative linkage appears to be more robust when the number of female directors reaches a critical mass (i.e., there are at least 3), when the bank is smaller, or when it is led by women in leadership roles (CEO and/or chair) |

| *Authors* | *Objectives* | *Sample and years* | *Main data sources* | *Methodology* | *Gender proxy* | *Results (Limited to gender issues)* |
|---|---|---|---|---|---|---|
| | | | | | • Critical Mass ($\geq 2$): dummy variable equal to 1 if the number of female directors on the board is at least 2, 0 otherwise<br>• Critical Mass (=1): dummy variable equal to 1 if the number of female directors on the board is 1, 0 otherwise<br>• Female CEO: dummy variable equal to 1 if the gender of the chief executive officer (CEO) is female, 0 otherwise<br>• Female Chair: dummy variable equal to 1 if the gender of the board chair is female, 0 otherwise<br>• Female Leader: dummy variable equal to 1 if the gender of the CEO and/or the chair/president (board leadership) is female, 0 otherwise | |

(continued)

Table 3.1 (continued)

| *Authors* | *Objectives* | *Sample and years* | *Main data sources* | *Methodology* | *Gender proxy* | *Results (Limited to gender issues)* |
|---|---|---|---|---|---|---|
| Fan et al. (2019) | To examine the impact of BGD on bank earnings management | 91 bank holding companies (BHCs) over the 2000–2014 period (4823 bank-year observations) | BoardEx, banks' call reports, and the CRSP (the Center for Research in Security Prices) | Panel data regression + GMM | • %_Women: the proportion of women directors or women independent directors<br>• N_Women: the number of women directors or women independent directors<br>• The Blau index | a. There is an inverted U-shaped relationship between BGD and bank earnings management: the influence of women directors on earnings management changes from positive to negative when there are 3 or more women directors<br>b. This inverted U-shaped effect is more evident if women sit on audit or nomination committees. It is moderated if women directors have higher education levels and more board experience. This is unchanged during the 2007–2009 financial crisis |
| García-Sánchez et al. (2017) | To analyse whether BGD affects accounting conservatism and earnings quality in the banking sector | 159 banks from 9[38] countries over the 2004–2010 period (877 bank-year observations) | Compustat, Stuart Board Index, and EIRIS | GMM | • Women: % of female directors on the board<br>• Several gender interaction variables | a. There is a positive monitoring role held by female directors concerning accounting conservatism and earnings quality in banks<br>b. In environments with stronger regulation and investor protection, BGD has more influence on the conservatism and earnings quality of banks |

[38] The countries are Canada, France, Germany, Italy, the Netherlands, Spain, Sweden, the UK, and the US.

| *Authors* | *Objectives* | *Sample and years* | *Main data sources* | *Methodology* | *Gender proxy* | *Results (Limited to gender issues)* |
|---|---|---|---|---|---|---|
| Tampakoudis et al. (2020) | To explore the effect of BGD on the economic impact of bank mergers and acquisitions (M&As) | 1130 M&A deals announced by US banks over the 2003–2018 period | Banks' annual reports on Form 10-K (SEC website) and Bloomberg | Event study + OLS + 2SLS | • Percentage of women on the board<br>• The number of women on the board<br>• Boards with at least 1 woman: dummy variable equal to 1 if the board consists of at least one woman and 0 otherwise<br>• The Blau index | a. There is a significant negative relationship between female board membership (including a critical mass of women directors) and shareholder wealth in acquiring banks, especially during the years 2012–2018 (i.e., after the subprime crisis)<br>b. BGD is not a determinant of value creation in the M&As of banks |
| Stefanovic and Barjak-tarovic (2021) | To explore the factors moderating the indirect relationships between BGD and its effect on bank performance | All banks (27) operating in Serbia in 2017 | National Bank of Serbia Database | Moderation analysis with a bootstrapping method + OLS | • Chair of the executive board: dummy variable equal to 1 if the chairperson is female, and 0 otherwise<br>• Chair of the board of directors: dummy variable equal to 1 if the chairperson is female, and 0 otherwise<br>• Presence of female members on the board and on the executive board: a dummy variable for each board equal to 1 if at least one woman is present | a. The relationship between top management gender structure and bank financial performance is indirect<br>b. Bank economic performance is not improved by BGD per se, but by interaction with other gender, socio-demographic, and board structure variables |

(continued)

**Table 3.1** (continued)

| *Authors* | *Objectives* | *Sample and years* | *Main data sources* | *Methodology* | *Gender proxy* | *Results (Limited to gender issues)* |
|---|---|---|---|---|---|---|
| | | | | | • The % of female members on the board and the executive board<br>• The number of female members of the board and on the executive board | |
| Proença et al. (2020) | To investigate the role of BGD in explaining the effects of the board members' political connections on the banking performance in the Eurozone | 83 banks supervised by the European Central Bank (ECB) over the 2013–2017 period | Banks' annual reports, bank websites, LinkedIn, BankFocus, and World Bank | GMM | • Women on board: % of women on the board<br>• Shannon index | a. Women directors, albeit in the minority, have a higher rate of political connections than men<br>b. BGD mitigates the negative impact of political connections on bank performance |

## References


Abou-El-Sood, H. (2019). Corporate governance and risk taking: The role of board gender diversity. *Pacific Accounting Review, 31*(1), 19–42. https://doi.org/10.1108/PAR-03-2017-0021

Abou-El-Sood, H. (2021). Board gender diversity, power, and bank risk taking. *International Review of Financial Analysis, 75*, 101733. https://doi.org/10.1016/j.irfa.2021.101733

Adams, R. B., & Ferreira, D. (2009). Women in the boardroom and their impact on governance and performance. *Journal of Financial Economics, 94*(2), 291–309. https://doi.org/10.1016/j.jfineco.2008.10.007

Adams, R. B., & Ragunathan, V. (2015). *Lehman sisters*. FIRN Research Paper, University of New South Wales, Sydney. Retrieved from https://papers.ssrn.com/sol3/papers.cfm?abstract_id=3046451

Adeabah, D., Gyeke-Dako, A., & Andoh, C. (2019). Board gender diversity, corporate governance, and bank efficiency in Ghana: A two-stage data envelope analysis (DEA) approach. *Corporate Governance. The International Journal of Business in Society 19*(2), 299–320. https://doi.org/10.1108/CG-08-2017-0171

Adesanmi, A. D., Sanyaolu, O. A., Isiaka, M. A., & Fadipe, O. A. (2019). Empirical analysis of board diversity and the financial performance deposit money banks in Nigeria. *Accounting, 5*(4), 127–134. https://doi.org/10.5267/j.ac.2019.5.001

Adusei, M. (2019). Board gender diversity and the technical efficiency of microfinance institutions: Does size matter? *International Review of Economics & Finance, 64*(C), 393–411. https://doi.org/10.1016/j.iref.2019.07.008

Adusei, M., Akomea, S. Y., & Poku, K. (2017). Board and management gender diversity and financial performance of microfinance institutions. *Cogent Business & Management, 4*(1), 1360030. https://doi.org/10.1080/23311975.2017.1360030

Agyemang-Mintah, P., & Schadewitz, H. (2019). Gender diversity and firm value: Evidence from UK financial institutions. *International Journal of Accounting & Information Management, 27*(1), 2–26. https://doi.org/10.1108/IJAIM-06-2017-0073

Al-Jaifi, H. A. (2020). Board gender diversity and environmental, social and corporate governance performance: Evidence from ASEAN banks. *Asia-Pacific Journal of Business Administration, 12*(3/4), 269–281. https://doi.org/10.1108/APJBA-12-2018-0222

Andrieş, A. M., Căpraru, B., Mínguez-Vera, A., & Nistor, S. (2018). *Gender diversity on boards and bank efficiency across Emerging Europe*. Retrieved from SSRN https://ssrn.com/abstract=3041477 or https://doi.org/10.2139/ssrn.3041477

Andrieş, A. M., Mehdian, S., & Stoica, O. (2020). Gender diversity, banks' performance, and stability across Central and Eastern European Countries. *Journal of East European Management Studies, 25*(3), 469–502. https://doi.org/10.5771/0949-6181-2020-3-469

Arnaboldi, F., Casu, B., Gallo, A., Kalotychou, E., & Sarkisyan, A. (2021). Gender diversity and bank misconduct. *Journal of Corporate Finance*, 101834. https://doi.org/10.1016/j.jcorpfin.2020.101834

Arnaboldi, F., Casu, B., Kalotychou, E., & Sarkisyan, A. (2020). The performance effects of board heterogeneity: What works for EU banks? *The European Journal of Finance, 26*(10), 897–924. https://doi.org/10.1080/1351847X.2018.1479719

Baker, K. H., Pandey, N., Kumar, S., & Haldar, A. (2020). A bibliometric analysis of board diversity: Current status, development, and future research directions. *Journal of Business Research, 108*, 232–246. https://doi.org/10.1016/j.jbusres.2019.11.025

Baklouti, I. (2020). Is the Sharia supervisory board a friend or an enemy of Islamic banks? *Journal of Islamic Marketing*. https://doi.org/10.1108/JIMA-04-2020-0118

Barako, D. G., & Brown, A. M. (2008). Corporate social reporting and board representation: Evidence from the Kenyan banking sector. *Journal Management Governance, 12*, 309–324. https://doi.org/10.1007/s10997-008-9053-x

Beck, T., Behr, P., & Guettler, A. (2013). Gender and banking: Are women better loan officers? *Review of Finance, 17*(4), 279–1321. https://doi.org/10.1093/rof/rfs028

Bellucci, A., Borisov, A., & Zazzaro, A. (2010). Does gender matter in bank–firm relationships? Evidence from small business lending. *Journal of Banking & Finance, 34*(12), 2968–2984. https://doi.org/10.1016/j.jbankfin.2010.07.008

Bellucci, A., Borisov, A., & Zazzaro, A. (2011). Do male and female loan officers differ in small business lending? A review of the literature. In G. Calcagnini & I. Favaretto (Eds.), *The economics of small business* (pp. 195–219). Springer-Verlag.

Berger, A. N., Kick, T., Koetter, M., & Schaeck, K. (2013). Does it pay to have friends? Social ties and executive appointments in banking. *Journal of Banking & Finance, 37*(6), 2087–2105. https://doi.org/10.1016/j.jbankfin.2013.01.040

Berger, A. N., Kick, T., & Schaeck, K. (2014). Executive board composition and bank risk taking. *Journal of Corporate Finance, 28*(C), 48–65. https://doi.org/10.1016/j.jcorpfin.2013.11.006

Birindelli, G., Chiappini, H., & Savioli, M. (2020). When do women on board of directors reduce bank risk? *Corporate Governance. The International Journal of Business in Society, 20*(7), 1307–1327. https://doi.org/10.1108/CG-03-2020-0089

Birindelli, G., Dell'Atti, S., Iannuzzi, A. P., & Savioli, M. (2018). Composition and activity of the board of directors: Impact on ESG performance in the banking system. *Sustainability, 10*(12), 4699. https://doi.org/10.3390/su10124699

Birindelli, G., Iannuzzi, A. P., & Savioli, M. (2019). The impact of women leaders on environmental performance: Evidence on gender diversity in banks. *Corporate Social Responsibility and Environmental Management, 26*(6), 1485–1499. https://doi.org/10.1002/csr.1762

Boubacar, H. (2020). Women's presence in top management and the performance of microfinance institutions in West Africa. *International Journal of Social Economics, 47*(2), 207–222. https://doi.org/10.1108/IJSE-06-2019-0365

Bunea, M., & Dinu, V. (2020). The relationship between the boards characteristics and the risk management of the Romanian banking sector. *Journal of Business Economics and Management, 21*(5), 1248–1268. https://doi.org/10.3846/jbem.2020.12694

Cardillo, G., Onali, E., & Torluccio, G. (2020). Does gender diversity on banks' boards matter? Evidence from public bailouts. *Journal of Corporate Finance.* https://doi.org/10.1016/j.jcorpfin.2020.101560.

Chan, S.-G., Koh, E. H. Y., Zaini, M., & Karim, Z. A. (2016). The Chinese banks' directors and their risk-taking behavior: A corporate governance and finance perspective. *Chinese Management Studies, 10*(2), 291–311. https://doi.org/10.1108/CMS-10-2015-0226

Davidson, D. J., & Freudenburg, W. R. (1996). Gender and environmental risk concerns: A review and analysis of available literature. *Environment and Behavior, 28*(3), 302–339. https://doi.org/10.1177/0013916596283003

Del Prete, S., Stefani, M. L. (2015, June). *Women as 'gold dust': Gender diversity in top boards and the performance of Italian banks*. Bank of Italy, Working Papers N° 1014. Retrieved from https://www.bancaditalia.it/pubblicazioni/temi-discussione/2015/20151014/en_tema_1014.pdf?language_id=1

Deschênes, S., Rojas, M., Boubacar, H., Prud'homme, B., & Ouedraogo, A. (2015). The impact of board traits on the social performance of Canadian firms: *Corporate governance. The International Journal of Business in Society, 15*(3), 293–305. https://doi.org/10.1108/CG-08-2014-0097

De Masi, S., Słomka-Gołębiowska, A., & Paci, A. (2021). Women on boards and monitoring tasks: An empirical application of Kanter's theory. *Management Decision, 59*(13), 56–72. https://doi.org/10.1108/MD-10-2019-1450

Dinu, V., & Bunea, M. (2018). The impact of the gender diversity on the Romanian banking system performance. *Transformations in Business and Economics, 17*(2), 137–147.

Ekadah, J. W., & Mboya, J. (2012). Effect of board gender diversity on the performance of commercial banks in Kenya. *European Scientific Journal, 8*(7), 128–148. https://doi.org/10.19044/esj.2012.v8n7p%25p

Fan, Y., Jiang, Y., Zhang, X., & Zhou, Y. (2019). Women on boards and bank earnings management: From zero to hero. *Journal of Banking & Finance, 107*(C), 105607. https://doi.org/10.1016/j.jbankfin.2019.105607

Farag, H., & Mallin, C. (2017). Board diversity and financial fragility: Evidence from European banks. *International Review of Financial Analysis, 49*(C), 98–112. https://doi.org/10.1016/j.irfa.2016.12.002

Gallego-Sosa, C., Fernández-Torres, Y., & Gutiérrez-Fernández, M. (2020). Does gender diversity affect the environmental performance of banks? *Sustainability, 12*(23), 10172. https://doi.org/10.3390/su122310172

Gallego-Sosa, C., Gutiérrez-Fernández, M., Fernández-Torres, Y., & Nevado-Gil, M. T. (2021). Corporate social responsibility in the European banking sector: Commitment to the 2030 agenda and its relationship with gender diversity. *Sustainability, 13*(4), 1731. https://doi.org/10.3390/su13041731

Gallucci, C., Santulli, R., & Tipaldi, R. (2020). Women on bank boards and risk-taking: A cross countries analysis on the moderating role of masculinity. *Corporate Ownership & Control, 17*(3), 71–83. https://doi.org/10.22495/cocv17i3art5

Gangi, F., Meles, A., D'Angelo, E., & Daniele, L. (2019). Sustainable development and corporate governance in the financial system: Are environmentally friendly banks less risky? *Corporate Social Responsibility and Environmental Management, 26*(3), 529–547. https://doi.org/10.1002/csr.1699

García-Meca, E., García-Sanchez, I.-M., & Martinez-Ferrero, J. (2015). Board diversity and its effects on bank performance: An international analysis. *Journal of Banking & Finance, 53*, 202–214. https://doi.org/10.1016/j.jbankfin.2014.12.002

García-Sánchez, I.-M., Martínez-Ferrero, J., & García-Meca, E. (2017). Gender diversity, financial expertise and its effects on accounting quality. *Management Decision, 55*(2), 347–382. https://doi.org/10.1108/MD-02-2016-0090

García-Sánchez, I.-M., Martínez-Ferrero, J., & García-Meca, E. (2018). Board of directors and CSR in banking: The moderating role of bank regulation and investor protection strength. *Australian Accounting Review, 28*(3), 428–445. https://doi.org/10.1111/auar.12199

Ghosh, S. (2017). Why is it a man's world, after all? Women on bank boards in India. *Economic Systems, 41*(1), 109–121. https://doi.org/10.1016/j.ecosys.2016.05.007

Ghosh, S., & Ansari, I. (2018). Board characteristics and financial performance: Evidence from Indian cooperative banks. *Journal of Co-Operative Organization and Management, 6*(2), 86–93. https://doi.org/10.1016/j.jcom.2018.06.005

Girardone, C., Kokas, S., & Wood, G. (2021). Diversity and women in finance: Challenges and future perspectives. *Journal of Corporate Finance,* 101906. https://doi.org/10.1016/j.jcorpfin.2021.101906

Glass, C., & Cook, A. (2017). Do women leaders promote positive change? Analyzing the effect of gender on business practices and diversity initiatives. *Human Resource Management, 57*(4), 823–837. https://doi.org/10.1002/hrm.21838

Glass, C., Cook, A., & Ingersoll, A. R. (2016). Do women leaders promote sustainability? Analysing the effect of corporate governance composition on environmental performance. *Business Strategy and the Environment, 25*(7), 495–511. https://doi.org/10.1002/bse.1879

Grassa, R. (2016). Corporate governance and credit rating in Islamic banks: Does Shariah governance matters? *Journal of Management & Governance, 20*, 875–906. https://doi.org/10.1007/s10997-015-9322-4

Gulamhussen, M. A., & Santa, F. S. (2015). Female directors in bank boardrooms and their influence on performance and risk-taking. *Global Finance Journal,* 28(C), 10–23. https://doi.org/10.1016/j.gfj.2015.11.002

Hagendorff, J., Collins, M., & Keasey, K. (2007). Bank governance and acquisition performance. *Corporate Governance: An International Review, 15*(5), 957–968. https://doi.org/10.1111/j.1467-8683.2007.00601.x

Hambrick, D. C. (2007). Upper echelons theory: An update. *Academy of Management Review, 32*(2), 334–343. https://doi.org/10.2307/20159303

Hambrick, D. C., & Mason, P. A. (1984). Upper echelons: The organization as a reflection of its top managers. *Academy of Management Review, 9*(2), 193–206. https://doi.org/10.5465/amr.1984.4277628

Hasan, T., Quayes, S., & Khalily, B. (2019). Role of governance on performance of microfinance institutions in Bangladesh. *Eurasian Economic Review, 9*(1), 91–106. https://doi.org/10.1007/s40822-018-0102-8

Jabari, H. N., & Muhamad, R. (2021). Gender diversity and financial performance of Islamic banks. *Journal of Financial Reporting and Accounting, 19*(3), 412–433.https://doi.org/10.1108/JFRA-03-2020-0061

Kanter, R. M. (1977). Some effects of proportions on group life: Skewed sex ratios and responses to token women. *American Journal of Sociology, 82*(5), 965–990. http://www.jstor.org/stable/2777808

Khan, H. U. Z. (2010). The effect of corporate governance elements on corporate social responsibility (CSR) reporting: Empirical evidence from private commercial banks of Bangladesh. *International Journal of Law and Management, 52*(2), 82–109. https://doi.org/10.1108/17542431011029406

Khan, I., & Wang, M. (2021). Evaluating corporate performance and bank productivity in China: The moderating role of independent directors. *Sustainability, 13*(6), 3193. https://doi.org/10.3390/su13063193

Khan, M. H., Fraz, A., Hassan, A., & Abedifar, P. (2020). Female board representation, risk-taking and performance: Evidence from dual banking systems. *Finance Research Letters, 37*(C), 101541. https://doi.org/10.1016/j.frl.2020.101541

Khatib, S. F. A., Abdullah, D. F., Elamer, A. A., & Abueid, R. (2021). Nudging toward diversity in the boardroom: A systematic literature review of board diversity of financial institutions. *Business Strategy and the Environment, 30*(2), 985–1002. https://doi.org/10.1002/bse.2665

Kiliç, M., Kuzey, C., & Uyar, A. (2015). The impact of ownership and board structure on corporate social responsibility (CSR) reporting in the Turkish banking industry. *Corporate Governance. The International Journal of Business in Society, 15*(3), 357–374. https://doi.org/10.1108/CG-02-2014-0022

Kramaric, T. P., & Miletic, M. (2017). Critical mass in the boardroom of Croatian banks. *South East European Journal of Economics and Business, 12*(1), 22–37. https://doi.org/10.1515/jeb-2017-0002

Liang, Q., Xu, P., & Jiraporn, P. (2013). Board characteristics and Chinese bank performance. *Journal of Banking & Finance, 37*(8), 2953–2968. https://doi.org/10.1016/j.jbankfin.2013.04.018

Mateos de Cabo, R., Gimeno, R., & Nieto, M. J. (2012). Gender diversity on European banks' boards of directors. *Journal of Business Ethics, 109*(2), 145–162. https://doi.org/10.1007/s10551-011-1112-6

Matuszak, Ł, Różańska, E., & Macuda, M. (2019). The impact of corporate governance characteristics on banks' corporate social responsibility disclosure: Evidence from Poland. *Journal of Accounting in Emerging Economies, 9*(1), 75–102. https://doi.org/10.1108/JAEE-04-2017-0040

Mazzotta, R., & Ferraro, O. (2020). Does the gender quota law affect bank performances? Evidence from Italy. *Corporate Governance. The International Journal of Business in Society, 20*(6), 1135–1158. https://doi.org/10.1108/CG-08-2019-0252

Mersland, R., & Strøm, R. Ø. (2009). Performance and governance in microfinance institutions. *Journal of Banking & Finance, 33*(4), 662–669. https://doi.org/10.1016/j.jbankfin.2008.11.009

Mohai, P., & Kershner, D. (2002). Race and environmental voting in the US Congress. *Social Science Quarterly, 83*(1), 167–189. https://doi.org/10.1111/1540-6237.00077

Mohammad, S. J., Abdullatif, M., & Zakzouk, F. (2018). The effect of gender diversity on the financial performance of Jordanian banks. *Academy of Accounting and Financial Studies Journal, 22*(2), 1–11.

Mori, N., & Olomi, D. (2012). The efficacy of boards on the performance of microfinance institutions: Evidence from Tanzania and Kenya. *Research Report for Development, 12*(2), 157–167.

Mori, N., & Towo, G. (2017). Effects of boards on performance of local and foreign-owned banks in Tanzania. *African Journal of Economic and Management Studies, 8*(2), 160–171. https://doi.org/10.1108/AJEMS-06-2016-0090

Muller-Kahle, M. I., & Lewellyn, K. B. (2011). Did board configuration matter? The case of US subprime lenders. *Corporate Governance: An International Review, 19*(5), 405–417. https://doi.org/10.1111/j.1467-8683.2011.00871.x

Nguyen, T. H. H., Ntim, C. G., & Malagila, J. K. (2020). Women on corporate boards and corporate financial and non-financial performance: A systematic literature review and future research agenda. *International Review of Financial Analysis, 71*, 101554. https://doi.org/10.1016/j.irfa.2020.101554

Owen, A. L., & Temesvary, J. (2018). The performance effects of gender diversity on bank boards. *Journal of Banking and Finance, 90*, 50–63. https://doi.org/10.1016/j.jbankfin.2018.02.015

Palvia, A., Vähämaa, E., & Vähämaa, S. (2015). Are female CEOs and chairwomen more conservative and risk averse? Evidence from the banking industry during financial crisis. *Journal of Business Ethics, 131*(3), 577–594. https://doi.org/10.1007/s10551-014-2288-3

Palvia, A., Vähämaa, E., & Vähämaa, S. (2020). Female leadership and bank risk-taking: Evidence from the effects of real estate shocks on bank lending performance and default risk. *Journal of Business Research, 117*, 897–909. https://doi.org/10.1016/j.jbusres.2020.04.057

Pathan, S., & Faff, R. (2013). Does board structure in banks really affect their performance? *Journal of Banking & Finance, 37*, 1573–1589. https://doi.org/10.1016/j.jbankfin.2012.12.0

Proença, C., Augusto, M., & Murteira, J. (2020). Political connections and banking performance: The moderating effect of gender diversity. *Corporate Governance. The International Journal of Business in Society, 20*(6), 1001–1028. https://doi.org/10.1108/CG-01-2020-0018

Rafinda, A., Rafinda, A., Witiastuti, R. S., Suroso, A., & Trinugroho, I. (2018). Board diversity, risk and sustainability of bank performance: Evidence from India. *Journal of Security and Sustainability Issues, 7*(4), 793–806. https://doi.org/10.9770/jssi.2018.7.4(15)

Ramly, Z., Chan, S., Mustapha, M. Z., & Sapiei, N. S. (2017). Women on boards and bank efficiency in ASEAN-5: The moderating role of the independent directors. *Review of Managerial Science, 11*, 225–250. https://doi.org/10.1007/s11846-015-0186-4

Reddy, S., & Jadhav, A. M. (2019). Gender diversity in boardrooms—A literature review. *Cogent Economics & Finance, 7*(1), 1–11. https://doi.org/10.1080/23322039.2019.1644703

Rodríguez-Ruiz, Ó., Rodríguez-Duarte, A., & Gómez-Martínez, L. (2016). Does a balanced gender ratio improve performance? The case of Spanish banks (1999–2010). *Personnel Review, 45*(1), 103–120. https://doi.org/10.1108/PR-07-2014-0143

Safiullah, M. (2021). Stability efficiency in Islamic banks: Does board governance matter? *Journal of Behavioral and Experimental Finance, 29*(C), 100442. https://doi.org/10.1016/j.jbef.2020.100442

Sahay, R., Čihák, M., N'Diaye, P., Barajas, A., Kyobe, A., Mitra, S., Mooi, Y. N., & Yousefi, S. R. (2017). *Banking on women leaders: A case for more?* International Monetary Fund Working Paper, WP/17/199. Retrieved from https://www.imf.org/en/Publications/WP/Issues/2017/09/07/Banking-on-Women-Leaders-A-Case-for-More-45221

Schwartz-Ziv, M. (2017). Gender and board activeness: The role of a critical mass. *Journal of Financial and Quantitative Analysis, 52*(2), 751–780. https://doi.org/10.1017/S0022109017000059

Sghaier, A., & Hamza, T. (2018). Does boardroom gender diversity affect the risk profile of acquiring banks? *Managerial Finance, 44*(10), 1174–1199. https://doi.org/10.1108/MF-09-2017-0373

Shakil, M. H., Tasnia, M., & Mostafiz, M. I. (2021). Board gender diversity and environmental, social and governance performance of US banks: Moderating role of environmental, social, and corporate governance controversies. *International Journal of Bank Marketing, 39*(4), 661–677. https://doi.org/10.1108/IJBM-04-2020-0210

Sheedy, E., & Lubojanski, M. (2018). Risk management behaviour in banking. *Managerial Finance, 44*(7), 902–918. https://doi.org/10.1108/MF-11-2017-0465

Shettima, U., & Dzolkarnaini, N. (2018). Board characteristics and microfinance institutions' performance: Panel data evidence from Nigeria. *Journal of Accounting in Emerging Economies, 8*(3), 369–386. https://doi.org/10.1108/JAEE-01-2017-0006

Skała, D., & Weill, L. (2018). Does CEO gender matter for bank risk? *Economic Systems, 42*, 64–74. https://doi.org/10.1016/j.ecosys.2017.08.005

Stefanovic, N., & Barjaktarovic, L. (2021). Gender makes the difference: The moderating role of gender on the relationship between management structure and performance in banking. *Gender in Management: An International Journal, 36*(1), 18–38. https://doi.org/10.1108/GM-09-2019-0162

Strøm, R. Ø., D'Espallier, B., & Mersland, R. (2014). Female leadership, performance, and governance in microfinance institutions. *Journal of Banking & Finance, 42*(C), 60–75. https://doi.org/10.1016/j.jbankfin.2014.01.014

Talavera, O., Yin, S., & Zhang, M. (2018). Age diversity, directors' personal values, and bank performance. *International Review of Financial Analysis, 55*, 60–79. https://doi.org/10.1016/j.irfa.2017.10.007

Tampakoudis, I., Andrikopoulos, A., Nerantzidis, M., & Kiosses, N. (2020). Does boardroom gender diversity affect shareholder wealth? Evidence from bank mergers and acquisitions. *International Journal of Finance & Economics*. https://doi.org/10.1002/ijfe.2323

Tapver, T., Laidroo, L., & Gurvitš-Suits, N. A. (2020). Banks' CSR reporting—Do women have a say? *Corporate Governance. The International Journal of Business in Society, 20*(4), 639–651. https://doi.org/10.1108/CG-11-2019-0338

Ting, H.-I., & Huang, P.-K. (2018). CEOs' power and perks: Evidence from Chinese banks. *Journal of Economics and Business, 97*, 19–27. https://doi.org/10.1016/j.jeconbus.2018.02.003

Titova, Y. (2016). Are board characteristics relevant for banking efficiency? Evidence from the US. *Corporate Governance. The International Journal of Business in Society, 16*(4), 655–679. https://doi.org/10.1108/CG-09-2015-0124

CHAPTER 4

# Data on Female Representation in Banks

**Abstract** This chapter aims to provide data on the representation of women in financial firms, especially banks, and the evolution of this over time, drawing on several studies conducted mainly by international and European organisations. A special focus is devoted to female board members with both executive and non-executive functions, chairwomen, and female CEOs. The general trend shows, on the one hand, an increase in the presence of women, particularly as non-executive board members, most likely due to pressures resulting from the introduction of gender quotas in many countries, and on the other hand, a low number of female CEOs and chairs. Moreover, the data show the persistence of a low number of women in revenue-generating roles (the so-called roles associated with "profit and loss responsibilities"). Despite the large differences in the data across countries, the Scandinavian countries seem to be the most oriented towards gender equality. Finally, attention is given to the "double glass ceiling" phenomenon. In this respect, studies show that despite the existence of a gender balance at entry levels, the relationship

This chapter is the result of the joint efforts of the two authors. However, Giuliana Birindelli mainly contributed to Sects. 4.1, 4.2, 4.3.1, 4.4, and Antonia Patrizia Iannuzzi to Sects. 4.3.2, 4.5.



G. Birindelli and A. P. Iannuzzi, *Women in Financial Services*, Palgrave Macmillan Studies in Banking and Financial Institutions,
https://doi.org/10.1007/978-3-030-93471-2_4

becomes increasingly imbalanced in middle management and especially in executive committee positions. The chapter analyses both the motivations behind this phenomenon and some supporting data.

## 4.1 Introduction: A Brief Overview of Gender Data from the International Monetary Fund

So far, studies on women in the banking sector have typically portrayed this industry as an area dominated by men. But is it still so? Indeed, representation of women in different job positions has changed over the years. It would be interesting, however, to assess in detail the direction in which this has gone and whether the gap between men and women has narrowed or not. Let's first start from a global perspective by looking into two International Monetary Fund (IMF) studies, and then focus on the European setting through studies by the European Banking Authority (EBA).

In the first study by the International Monetary Fund (IMF, 2017) assessing the composition of the board of directors in 749 banks across 72 countries from 2001 to 2013, the presence of women in 2013 was just over 12%, with only a 2% presence of female CEOs belonging to 15 from a total of 749 banks (7 of these 15 banks are from the United States). Underrepresentation is common across geographical areas (America, Europe, Asia, and Africa) and types of banks (commercial, investment, cooperative, bank holding companies, real estate and mortgage banks, and securities firms) considered. The only exception is seen in savings banks, featuring a distinctive trend with on average more than 45% of women on their boards. Regarding the overall period examined (2001–2013), the IMF underlines a growing weight of women on the boards of directors across many geographical areas and various types of banks. For instance, the average percentage grows from 2 to 14% in East Asia and from 4 to 18% in Central Asia and Europe. Looking at the 2013 percentages calculated at the country level (Table 4.1), the highest values (above 20%) are found for the developed economies: North America, Developed Asia and Pacific, and Europe. In particular, the countries that stand out for the first two areas are, respectively, Canada with a 27.5% average and Australia with a 25.3% average. In Europe, we find that there are countries characterised by a significant presence of women, such as Lithuania (23.1%) and France (24.2%), but there are also several countries with even higher percentages: Sweden (36.8%), Finland (46.5%), and Norway

**Table 4.1** Share of women on bank boards (as a percentage of total board members): summary statistics at country level, 2013

| *Country* | *Total assets to gross domestic product (GDP) (%)* | *Number of banks* | *Share of women (Mean)* | *Country* | *Total assets to gross domestic product (GDP) (%)* | *Number of banks* | *Share of women (Mean)* |
|---|---|---|---|---|---|---|---|
| Argentina | 1.9 | 1 | 8.3 | Mexico | 8.5 | 3 | 6.6 |
| Australia | 204.9 | 10 | 25.3 | Morocco | 45.0 | 1 | 10.0 |
| Austria | 91.2 | 6 | 12.9 | Netherlands | 14.4 | 6 | 16.2 |
| Belgium | 67.9 | 5 | 11.7 | Nigeria | 33.2 | 9 | 23.0 |
| Canada | 203.7 | 14 | 27.5 | Norway | 99.4 | 6 | 47.6 |
| Chile | 29.9 | 2 | 0.0 | Oman | 36.7 | 2 | 10.1 |
| China | 30.4 | 6 | 9.1 | Pakistan | 2.4 | 1 | 0.0 |
| Colombia | 17.8 | 1 | 0.0 | Peru | NA | 1 | 0.0 |
| Cyprus | 232.1 | 2 | 8.4 | Philippines | 44.9 | 6 | 12.9 |
| Denmark | 209.4 | 5 | 19.1 | Poland | 12.8 | 2 | 6.7 |
| Egypt | 9.6 | 2 | 11.3 | Portugal | 128.7 | 5 | 7.9 |
| Finland | 5.9 | 2 | 46.5 | Qatar | 81.1 | 3 | 0.0 |
| France | 153.3 | 8 | 24.2 | Korea | 47.0 | 3 | 5.6 |
| Germany | 83.8 | 7 | 11.7 | Russia | NA | 3 | 14.8 |
| Greece | 43.9 | 7 | 17.5 | Saudi Arabia | 9.0 | 2 | 0.0 |
| Hong Kong | 37.3 | 4 | 4.6 | Singapore | 273.8 | 4 | 5.6 |
| Hungary | 36.3 | 1 | 0.0 | South Africa | 73.7 | 7 | 17.7 |
| India | 15.9 | 15 | 10.6 | Spain | 209.6 | 6 | 15.8 |
| Indonesia | 0.7 | 1 | 6.2 | Sri Lanka | 7.1 | 1 | 0.0 |
| Ireland | 83.6 | 3 | 12.1 | Sweden | 347.0 | 5 | 36.8 |
| Israel | 116.1 | 6 | 18.5 | Switzerland | 376.3 | 11 | 10.4 |
| Italy | 148.0 | 13 | 16.5 | Taiwan | 231.0 | 15 | 5.5 |
| Japan | 59.7 | 23 | 2.7 | Thailand | 58.4 | 4 | 17.8 |
| Kenya | 17.2 | 2 | 17.4 | Togo | 516.8 | 1 | 16.7 |
| Lebanon | 123.4 | 2 | 14.2 | Turkey | 57.1 | 8 | 12.1 |
| Lithuania | 4.5 | 1 | 23.1 | United Arab Emirates | 22.2 | 5 | 0.0 |
| Luxembourg | 195.6 | 1 | 0.0 | United Kingdom | 281.5 | 45 | 18.8 |
| Malaysia | 36.0 | 5 | 4.2 | United States | 94.6 | 426 | 12.0 |
| Malta | 102.7 | 1 | 0.0 | Vietnam | 4.6 | 1 | 10.0 |
| Mauritius | 31.0 | 1 | 9.1 | | | **749 (Total)** | **12.1 (Mean)** |

*Source* IMF (2017)

(47.6%). In the developing economies, only one country exceeds 20%: Nigeria, in West Africa, with a percentage of 23.0%. However, many countries in Africa exceed the average of the total sample (equal to 12.1%): Kenya (17.4%), South Africa (17.7%), and Togo (16.7%). Keeping within Asia, a few countries exceed the sample average: Israel (18.5%), Lebanon (14.2%), the Philippines (12.9%), and Thailand (17.8%). Only few countries in Asia and other countries with developing economies (Pakistan, Qatar, Saudi Arabia, Sri Lanka, and the United Arab Emirates in Asia; Chile, Colombia, and Peru in Latin America and the Caribbean) have no women on boards. On the other hand, even banks in a few European countries show boards exclusively dominated by men (Hungary, Luxembourg, and Malta: see Table 4.1). Taken together, these data show that, despite the general increase in the participation of women on bank boards in many regions, there are still wide gaps between developed and developing economies, and among regions and countries. In any case, it is worth noting that women's shares may not be representative at a country level, given the small number of banks observed in certain countries.

Regarding the type of banks, the highest increase in the observation period is found for savings banks, which already had a high share of women in 2001, thus almost doubling the proportion of female directors.

These considerations agree with those in the 2018 IMF study (IMF, 2018). The sample of banks considered is substantially the same and confirms the low shares of women in leadership positions and as female CEOs.

## 4.2 Gender Diversity Data: A Focus on the European Banking System

The gap evidenced at the international level is found again, albeit in a smaller size, a few years later in a study on the countries of the European Union (EU) and European Economic Area (EEA). The research considers a sample of 873 institutions (credit institutions and investment firms) from 29 countries, analysed on the basis of data collected by the competent authorities, and transmitted to the European Banking Authority in 2015 under Article 91(11) of Directive 2013/36/EU (EBA, 2016). The research shows that just 35.53% of the sample adopted a diversity policy, and only 24.54% specifically developed a gender diversity policy.

Moreover, female executive directors account for 13.63% of individuals in that role, and female CEOs account for 11.06% of total CEOs. In more than two-thirds of the sample (69.42%), executive directors belong to one gender alone.

There is a higher presence of female non-executive directors (18.90%), even if this increase can be justified by the higher number of non-executives compared to executives (6372 and 2869, respectively). This higher number justifies the broad percentage (60.82%) of institutions that have at least one non-executive director of both genders. Of all the boards of directors considered in the sample, the chair is female only in 8.06% of cases.

In cases of executive and non-executive directors, the maximum age of women is usually below 50 years; women are mostly between 30 and 40 years of age for executive directors, and below 30 years for non-executive directors (EBA, 2016, Figures 6 and 7).

The representation of women according to the institutions' size changes if we consider directors with management or supervisory functions. In fact, the former role is more present in smaller credit institutions (total balance sheet less than €1 billion) and the latter in larger (total balance sheet greater than or equal to €30 billion) and significant institutions.

This same study also highlights the increase in appointments of female executive and non-executive directors over time: the percentage of newly recruited directors in 2014, compared to the 2010–2013 average, rises for women, and lowers for men, though the male representation remains much higher. At a country level, the countries show very different behaviours: a few significantly increase the representation of women in 2014 compared to the previous four-year period, as seen in Belgium, Hungary, Romania, and Sweden in terms of executive directors, and Denmark, Croatia, Lithuania, and Iceland for non-executive directors. Others show a strong reduction, as seen in Finland, Luxembourg, and Malta in terms of executive women and Hungary for non-executive women (EBA, 2016, Figures 10 and 11).

A curious note is that, contrary to common thinking, the presence of executive women on bank boards is often higher in poorer rather than richer economies, according to the level of GDP per capita. In the EBA report (EBA, 2016), the EU country average for female executive directors is 13.63%, with the highest level being in Bulgaria (40.35%). Values well above the average can also be found in Croatia (32.20%), Lithuania

(29.41%), Latvia (24.69%), and Romania (25%). Another singular note is the greater weight of women in executive versus non-executive positions in all these countries (EBA, 2016, p. 14).

From analysing compliance with CRD IV and based on the findings from the EBA study, the European Commission claims that there is ample room for improvement to empower women in the workplace (European Commission, 2016). In particular, most institutions that had fixed a gender diversity objective have still not achieved it nor have indicated the timing by which they plan to pursue it. According to EBA feedback following the first CRD diversity benchmarking, the results highlight "*the need for both institutions and supervisors to make further efforts to ensure that the required diversity policies are properly put in place*" (European Commission, 2016, p. 9).

The second EBA exercise on diversity practice benchmarking was released in 2020. In 2019, competent authorities had sent the EBA information on a sample of 834 credit institutions and investment firms as of September 2018. Therefore, compared to the previous report, it presents a few changes in terms of the sample size (in consequence of mergers occurring meanwhile) and some of the countries considered.

Regarding the adoption of the diversity policy, the 2020 report features a higher number of institutions that adopted that policy. The percentage, calculated on the total sample, rises from 35.53% (EBA, 2016) to 58.39% (EBA, 2020). In both cases, the number of institutions that, in addition to having a diversity policy, promote gender diversity by setting targets related to the underrepresented gender is stable: 69.06% in the 2016 report and 69.61% in the 2020 report (percentages are calculated in relation to the total number of institutions that have a diversity policy in place). However, these percentages differ greatly when calculated with respect to the total sample considered in each report, being 24.54 and 40.65% in the first and second report, respectively.

The differences among countries are considerable; in some, diversity policies have been adopted by all institutions, though with very different approaches to promoting gender diversity, while other institutions still have no diversity policy at all. Again, there are countries with percentages of institutions that have a diversity policy equal to or very close to those of institutions that simultaneously set gender objectives; conversely, there are other countries where these two percentages differ considerably.

In the 2016 EBA report, only two countries (Denmark and Iceland) had diversity policies across all their institutions, with gender being included in policies only in the Icelandic institutions. In the 2020 EBA report, countries with 100% of institutions having a diversity policy increase to 4; they are Denmark, Iceland, Croatia, and Lithuania. Again, Iceland remains the only country with a gender diversity policy adopted across all its institutions, followed by Denmark featuring gender policies across 95.83% of its institutions, Lithuania in 66.67%, and Croatia in 18.75%. Focusing on the significant institutions (on their definition see Chapter 2, Sect. 2.2), the number rises from 4 to 15. Therefore, all significant institutions based in 15 countries have a diversity policy. Among them, all institutions based in 9 countries also have a gender diversity policy. In the remaining 6 countries, the gap between the two percentages (one referring to diversity policy and the other to gender diversity policy) varies considerably, from a minimum of 7.69% in Austria to a maximum of 66.67% in Slovenia.

In the 2016 report, Hungary and Slovakia still did not have any institutions with a diversity policy; however, data from the 2020 EBA report show that some of their institutions are moving in that direction though, to date, Hungary has still no gender policy. In Liechtenstein, which appears only in the 2020 report, both percentages (referred to institutions with diversity policy and institutions with gender diversity policy) are zero.

In the 2020 report, other countries have similar percentages. The difference between the percentage of institutions with a diversity policy and that of institutions with a gender diversity policy is less than 5% in 5 countries (Belgium, Germany, Greece, Spain, and Norway). In two of these countries (Greece and Spain), the two percentages coincide. On the contrary, in several countries, the difference between the two percentages is rather high: in 12 countries, the difference is equal to or greater than 20% (Austria, Bulgaria, Estonia, Finland, Ireland, Luxembourg, Latvia, Poland, Sweden, Slovenia, Slovakia, and the UK).

In the previous EBA report (EBA, 2016), the gaps between the two percentages are generally more frequent and wider, except for 5 countries (Estonia, France, Iceland, Ireland, and Lithuania) where the two percentages are identical.

There has been clear progress in the number of institutions that have set a 0% quantitative target for the underrepresented gender. In fact, in 2015, as many as 92 institutions had this inappropriate practice in place (EBA, 2016, p. 8), which has not been observed any longer in 2018 (EBA, 2020, p. 14).

In 2018, 339 institutions set a target percentage for the underrepresented gender (40.65% of the sample), with 168 (20.14% of the sample) claiming to have met their target (EBA, 2020, p. 15). On the other hand, if we remove institutions with a target equal to 0% in 2015, only just over 210 institutions (24.54% of the sample) had some type of target (even general and not set necessarily as a percentage) in that year; of those, 90 (10.42% of the sample) had reached the target (EBA, 2016, p. 8). Overall, this shows a significant progress in the number of both institutions with a gender target and those that reach their target. Nonetheless, a great deal of effort is still required, since in 2018 just over 40% of the total sample considered had a gender diversity policy.

Shifting from diversity policies to diversity practices, the EBA 2020 report presents the information on women sitting on the boards of directors and divides the sample according to the governance structure: countries with a one-tier structure, like Belgium, Ireland, Sweden, and the UK, and countries with a two-tier structure, like Austria, Iceland, and the Netherlands. Moreover, in addition to reporting the management body in its two functions (management function and supervisory function, corresponding respectively to executive and non-executive directors), it also reports on the staff representatives, therefore elected by the staff. This last piece of information is absent in the previous EBA report.

As in the first report, EBA (2020) provides lower figures for women executive directors compared to those for non-executive directors. This confirms the prevalence of women in supervisory rather than management functions. In particular, the percentages of executive women in credit institutions in countries with one-tier and two-tier systems are 14.65 and 15.80%, respectively, compared to 24.36 and 21.02% for non-executive women. Looking at the data in more detail, the presence of genders within the management body at a country level is more balanced in the Scandinavian and Eastern European Member States. This is probably due "*to the fact that the inclusion of women in the workforce and the availability of childcare facilities have been greater in the past in those regions*" (EBA, 2020, p. 21). Among the Scandinavian countries, Norway has percentages above 40% in the two-tier system, while Sweden has percentages between 35 and 37%. Among the Eastern European countries, the situation indicated for 2015 on the greater weight of female executives compared to non-executives in poor countries is repeated, such as in the cases of Bulgaria and Romania. Moreover, Slovenia has the highest percentage of executive women (50%) in the one-tier system together with Iceland, followed by Bulgaria (40.91%), and Norway (40.85% in the two-tier system).

Despite the discrepancies indicated (greater granularity of the data for 2018), the percentages in the two reports show a greater weight of women in both roles: the difference is +1.02 and +2.17 for executive women, and +5.46 and +2.12 for non-executive women in the two governance systems (one-tier structure and two-tier structure, respectively, see Table 4.2). However, the representation of women is still limited. This is even more true for investment firms, which compared to credit institutions still feature the lowest female representation, as in the previous report (EBA, 2016, p. 11; 2020, p. 20).

Much higher is the presence of women among staff representatives: the percentages rise to 42.42% and 35.05% in the one-tier and two-tier system, respectively. However, these selections take place beyond the diversity policies adopted by the institutions and are required only in some countries.

The percentage of female CEOs, already very low in 2015, decreases from 11.06% in 2015 to 8.53% in 2018, while the percentage of institutions featuring executive directors of only one gender slightly drops from 69.42% in 2015 to 66.95% in 2018.

The weight of female chairpersons is growing, although it remains low at 8.06% in 2015 and 9.49% in 2018. There is also growth from 60.82 to 70.78% in the number of institutions with at least one non-executive director of both genders.

The presence of young women on the boards in the two functions (management and supervision) is confirmed: the age groups in which women are most represented remain up to 50 years of age (the age groups being less than 30, between 30 and 40, and between 41 and 50 years of age). However, in 2018, there are no executive women under the age of 30, unlike in 2015 (EBA, 2020, Figures 10 and 11; see also Table 4.2).

Concerning the gender representation by institution's size, the situation has changed from 2015 to 2018.

The lower representation of executive women in 2015 is mostly observed for large and significant institutions, while in 2018 it is mainly observed for small institutions. As evidence of this change, in 2015, 54.24% of small credit institutions (total balance sheet less than €1 billion) have no women executives, and this percentage rises to 68.57% in 2018. On the contrary, larger credit institutions (total balance sheet greater than or equal to €30 billion) show a general strengthening of

**Table 4.2** EBA reports: a comparison between the main indicators

| | *EBA (2016)* | *EBA (2020)* |
|---|---|---|
| Percentage of institutions with diversity policy | 35.53 | 58.39 |
| Percentage of institutions with gender diversity policy | 24.54 | 40.65 |
| Percentage of institutions meeting their gender targets | 10.42 | 20.14 |
| Percentage of female executive directors | 13.63 | 1-tier system: 14.65<br>2-tier system: 15.80 |
| Percentage of female non-executive directors | 18.90 | 1-tier system: 24.36<br>2-tier system: 21.02 |
| Percentage of female CEOs | 11.06 | 8.53 |
| Percentage of institutions with executive directors of only one gender | 69.42 | 66.95 |
| Percentage of female chairpersons | 8.06 | 9.49 |
| Percentage of institutions with at least one non-executive director of both genders | 60.82 | 70.78 |
| Percentage of female executive directors by age group | <30: 16.67<br>30–40: 20.25<br>41–50: 16.80<br>51–60: 10.90<br>61–70: 6.25<br>>70: 3.13 | <30: 0.00<br>30–40: 19.44<br>41–50: 19.00<br>51–60: 13.60<br>61–70: 7.72<br>>70: 2.56 |

| | *EBA (2016)* | *EBA (2020)* |
|---|---|---|
| Percentage of female non-executive directors by age group | <30: 40.00 | <30: 40.00 |
| | 30–40: 27.58 | 30–40: 32.51 |
| | 41–50: 26.45 | 41–50: 32.20 |
| | 51–60: 21.11 | 51–60: 26.85 |
| | 61–70: 10.11 | 61–70: 16.03 |
| | >70: 4.50 | >70: 7.25 |
| Percentage of significant institutions without female executive directors | 60.34 | 50.63 |
| Percentage of significant institutions without female non-executive directors | 18.72 | 10.46 |
| Percentage of significant institutions with boards with over 25% executive women | 17.31 | 25.52 |
| Percentage of recently recruited female executive directors | Executive female directors recruited in 2010–2013: 15.17 | Executive female directors recruited in 2015–2016: 18.29 |
| | Executive female directors recruited in 2014: 19.39 | Executive female directors recruited in 2017–2018: 21.18 |
| Percentage of recently recruited female non-executive directors | Non-executive female directors recruited in 2010–2013: 18.52 | Non-executive female directors recruited in 2015–2016: 27.65 |
| | Non-executive female directors recruited in 2014: 22.15 | Non-executive female directors recruited in 2017–2018: 27.99 |

*Source* EBA (2016, 2020)

the female component; the percentage of institutions without executive women drops from 63.81% in 2015 to 52.25% in 2018, while executive women exceed 25% of the members of the management board in 14.28% of the institutions in 2015, a percentage that rises to 22.52% in 2018. Similarly, the decrease and increase for significant institutions are as follows: from 60.34 to 50.63% for boards without executive women and from 17.31 to 25.52% for boards with more than 25% executive women. In any case, given the high number of institutions without women and the exceedingly small number of those where males are the underrepresented gender (executive women exceed 50% only in 2.51% of significant institutions), measures still need to be taken to strengthen female participation, especially in significant institutions subject to more stringent regulatory requirements.

Like in 2015, in 2018, non-executive women are more present in the largest and significant institutions, yet measures should be implemented to enlarge their participation: for example, significant institutions without non-executive women are 10.46% in 2018 (18.72% in 2015), while the percentage is 33.63% (38.05% in 2015) in smaller institutions.

As in the previous EBA report, recruitment policies have led to a greater weight of women in both management and supervisory functions. If we compare the percentages of women recruited in 2017–2018 with those recruited in the previous two years, the percentages increase, even though there is a strong imbalance in favour of men (EBA, 2020, Figure 14). In this case, too, the countries show different trends. Some have increased the number of women executives recruited over time, such as Finland; others have reduced it, such as Bulgaria, Iceland, and Liechtenstein; others have expanded the proportion of non-executive women, such as Cyprus; others have lowered it, such as Liechtenstein and Malta (EBA, 2020, Figure 16). The reasons underlying these different trends have not been analysed: "*No further analysis of the underlying drivers that may well be found in past cultural values, the inclusion of women in the workforce, working conditions and the availability of childcare facilities has been done*" (EBA, 2020, p. 25).

Finally, if we compare the recruitment policies adopted since 2010 (EBA, 2016, Figure 10; 2020, Figure 14), there is increasing attention brought to the female component of boards in executive and non-executive roles. As already pointed out, however, the predominance of men over women remains strong.

Table 4.2 shows the main indicators of the two EBA reports, illustrated above.

As we can see, much progress has been made for the representation of women in the workforce of the samples examined. The institutions surveyed have increasingly adopted a gender diversity policy over time, met their gender targets, and consolidated the proportion of female executive and non-executive directors. However, there are still clear signs of a path to be completed and of strong obstacles for women to advance their careers and reach leadership positions. A focus on these difficulties will be made in the following pages, where we will draw on evidence from other studies.

## 4.3 Other Data

### *4.3.1 Women in Top Positions*

The evolution of the number of women in top positions has been the research topic of studies focusing on women on the board and female members of executive committees (ExCo) in the financial services industry (Oliver Wyman, 2014, 2016, 2020). The sample of companies under observation changes over time with more than 150 companies in the 2014 report, 381 in the 2016 report, and 468 in the last report. In all cases, they are international samples. The observation period has also expanded from 11 years (2003–2013) to 14 years (2003–2016), and finally to 17 years (2003–2019).

The data from the 3 reports (see Table 4.3) show that the increase of women directors has strengthened over time, from 67% (first and second report) to over 100% (third report). The trend of boards without women shows similar evidence, falling by 52%, 44%, and then almost by 60%; likewise, the trends for boards with more than 30% women have a growth rate increasing from 187% (first report) to 311% (third report).

The same trends can be seen in the female component of the executive committees: the presence of women has gradually grown at higher rates over time from the initial 30% rate to the final 82% rate; the number of committees without women has fallen over the years, initially decreasing by 29% and then twofold. Finally, committees with more than 30% female

**Table 4.3** Women directors and female executive committee members

| | *First report (2003–2013)* | *Second report (2003–2016)* | *Third report (2003–2019)* |
|---|---|---|---|
| Quota of women directors on boards | From 12 to 20% (+Δ67%) | From 12 to 20% (+Δ67%) | From 11 to 23% (+Δ109%) |
| Quota of female members of executive committees | From 10 to 13% (+Δ30%) | From 11 to 16% (+Δ45%) | From 11 to 20% (+Δ82%) |
| Boards without women | From 29 to 14% (−Δ52%) | From 34 to 19% (−Δ44%) | From 37 to 15% (−Δ59%) |
| Executive committees without women | From 49 to 35% (−Δ29%) | From 41 to 25% (−Δ39%) | From 46 to 19% (−Δ59%) |
| Boards with more than 30% female representation | From 8 to 23% (+Δ187%) | From 9 to 23% (+Δ156%) | From 9 to 37% (+Δ311%) |
| Executive committees with more than 30% female representation | From 5 to 11% (+Δ120%) | From 8 to 19% (+Δ137%) | From 9 to 26% (+Δ189%) |

*Source* Oliver Wyman (2014, 2016, 2020)

representation have shown increasing growth rates, reaching almost 190% in the last report (Table 4.3).

The increase rate for female representation on executive committees is lower than on boards, similarly to the decrease rate of executive committees without women and the increase rate of executive committees with a percentage of women above 30%. In this context, the two components (women on boards and executive committees) tend to increase their weight, especially after 2008 (Oliver Wyman, 2020, Exhibit 1), but the gap between them remains unchanged at 3% since 2013 and there seems to be no incentive to reduce it. The increase in women on the board is due to, among other things, the introduction of quotas in many countries. On the contrary, this is not true for executive committee members for which "pink" quotas rarely apply. Growing trends in women's representation on boards are undeniably important signs, but an equally important objective is to try to increase the number of women in executive positions as a variety of perspectives and skills can truly lead to improved decision-making processes in companies.

Therefore, it seems that the path followed in the representation of the female gender at the two hierarchical levels (women on the boards of directors and executive committees) does not represent an evolution towards egalitarianism, but rather towards "constrained feminisation" (Ferrary, 2017) resulting from government-imposed diversity quotas or a growing awareness towards gender issues on behalf of stakeholders.

Taking a deeper look into the data, the ExCo level positions show a mixed distribution of roles, particularly in favour of support and compliance functions. As shown in Table 4.3, in 2019, 20% of executive committee members are women, yet the highest representations of women are in the roles of head of human resources (where women predominate over men), marketing, legal, and compliance. However, there have been improvements in the presence of women leading revenue-generating roles, the so-called roles associated with "profit and loss responsibilities" (e.g., head of a business unit, division, or region), which involve working hours that are often changeable and therefore difficult to reconcile with family commitments. Among other things, these are job positions from which CEOs normally draw. In 2019, there was only a 6% presence of female CEOs; the weight of female chairs was higher, but still low at 9%.

As noted by the EBA, the Scandinavian countries are those most oriented towards gender diversity. In particular, the female components in executive committees are very high in Norway and Sweden, although in recent years the highest growth rates have been seen in Asian countries, such as Israel and India (Oliver Wyman, 2014, Exhibit 2; 2016, Exhibit 2; 2020, Exhibit 3).

There are significant differences among countries in terms of both the number of women on executive committees and its growth rate. As identified in the reports, the combination of the two variables allows the classification of the countries into four groups, namely "hitting a ceiling", "beyond the ceiling", "stuck in the mud", and "getting there" (Oliver Wyman, 2016). This representation is no longer provided in the 2020 report, but it can be reconstructed on the basis of data available in the 2016 and 2020 reports.

Based on such classification, we can identify a first group, which includes countries with high percentages of women (above 20%), but with negative or low growth rates; this is especially the case for Norway, Sweden, Thailand, and Poland. In these countries, it seems that "the ceiling has been hit" and that the process has come to a standstill, either due to insufficient women on the path to an executive career or because high targets of female representation have already been reached.

A second group can be identified with those countries showing a high female presence on executive committees and high growth rates; they are the most virtuous countries that go "beyond the ceiling", such as Israel, Australia, and Finland.

A third group is made up of countries where there are few women on the executive committees (share less than or equal to 20%) and the rates of change in 2016–2019 are low or negative. This is the case for Italy, the United Arab Emirates, Austria, Brazil, Turkey, China, Japan, and South Korea and these are "stuck in the mud" countries, the most worrying ones. The reasons for the difficulty of women's advancement are diverse, such as the insensitivity of political power to the issue, inadequate support for working mothers, and so on.

Finally, other countries have few women on bank executive committees but high growth rates between 2016 and 2019, such as in the Netherlands, Nigeria, India, Spain, Colombia, and Switzerland. These are countries that can be defined as "getting there", because even if they start from a position of low female participation, they have consistent rates of increase that, if maintained, will help to achieve a significant representation of women in a few years (Fig. 4.1).

### *4.3.2 Comparisons with the United States of America: A Few Brief Considerations*

The issue of gender diversity is global, although there are different nuances and connotations in individual countries. Focusing on the Deloitte Center for Financial Services' proprietary analysis and custom segmentation of 107 financial services institutions' data from BoardEx, Deloitte conducted interesting research on the evolution of women in US financial companies. In particular, Deloitte concentrated on those institutions that represent, in each sector, the top 25 banking, insurance, asset management, and commercial real estate companies by asset size, in addition to some payment services companies belonging to the banking sector (Rogish, Sandler, Shemluck, Danielecki, & Ramsay, 2020). The study covers a considerable time horizon (1998–2019 with projections up to

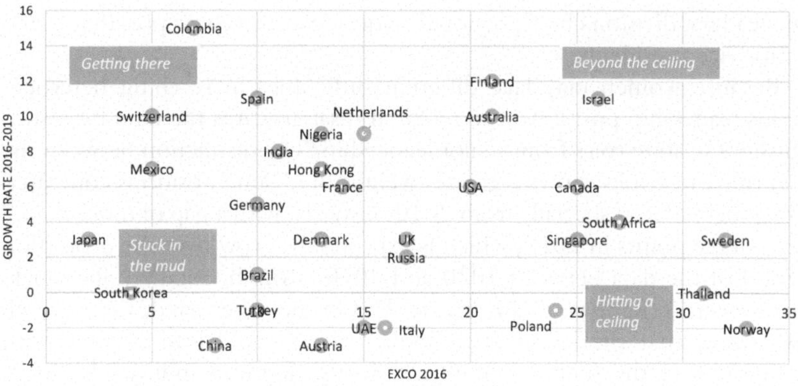


**Fig. 4.1** Countries by women on executive committees in 2016 and percentage growth rate 2016–2019 (*Source* Authors' elaboration on reports by Oliver Wyman)

2030) and focuses on leadership roles, where women seem to outperform men on many skills, such as relationship orientation, collaboration, teamwork, incisive and effective communication, innovation, and personal growth (Zenger & Folkman, 2019).

The period under observation documents the increase in the number of women in leadership roles. The growth recorded by the financial industry was slow but continuous over time and has accelerated since 2013. However, the percentage of women in leadership roles never exceeds 22%, confirming the need for ongoing efforts (Rogish, Sandler, Shemluck, Danielecki, & Ramsay, 2020, Figure 1). Neither do growth projections appear encouraging according to forecasts that estimate that parity will not be reached before 2085 and that the financial industry will still be well below the balance in 2030 (Kerpen, 2018).

The leadership roles considered in the study include both C-suite and senior leaders. The former roles refer to the high-ranking executive-level managers (with "C" standing for Chief), such as chief executive officer, chief financial officer, chief operating officer, chief marketing officer, and chief information officer. Among C-suite roles, there are many new job titles created over the last ten years where women have a significant weight (among these: chief inclusion and diversity officer, chief sustainability officer, and so on). The study refers to senior leaders such as business line leaders, division chiefs, regional leaders, executive vice presidents, and senior vice presidents.

Because women may face different difficulties in reaching heterogeneous leadership positions, the research disaggregates the data by distinguishing C-suite roles from senior leadership. The distinction between the two role categories shows a greater weight of C-suite positions compared to senior leaders, especially from 2010 onwards, with a gap of more than 7 percentage points in 2019, which is expected to grow over the projection period of the data between 2020 and 2030 (Rogish, Sandler, Shemluck, Danielecki, & Ramsay, 2020, Figure 3). On the other hand, the research also warns that the so-called multiplier effect could lead to significant expansions of the senior component in organisations induced by more women added to the C-suite. This effect could be a lever on which to act with concomitant strategies aimed at strengthening gender diversity.

An in-depth look at CEOs shows a small number of women in these positions. In line with Oliver Wyman's reports (see Sect. 4.3.1), CEOs are recruited from highly prestigious positions. In particular, the path to becoming a CEO includes leadership roles in the areas of first lines of business, finance, and operations. As the presence of women in these positions is low, the small number of female CEOs is justified (Rogish, Sandler, & Shemluck, 2020). In other words, women leaders often take on positions of responsibility that are outside the path to CEO, especially, in talent, marketing, administration, legal, and risk/compliance, as indicated in Table 4.4.

A focus on 39 companies in the financial industry based in North America belonging to three sub-sectors (banking and consumer finance, asset management and wholesale banking, and insurance; see McKinsey & Company, 2018) highlights increased difficulties for women to reach C-suite positions in these sub-sectors compared to the entire US financial industry. The higher value of C-suite women for the US industry is also reflected in the report by Rogish, Sandler, Shemluck, Danielecki, and Ramsay (2020).

Moreover, compared to their male counterparts, women lose ground at every stage of their career. Despite the number of women and men at entry being almost identical, the gender gap increases considerably in favour of men as they progress through their career, moving from manager to senior manager/director, vice president, senior vice president, and finally, C-suite. The gender gap in favour of men exceeds 60% in the case of C-suite. This trend is greatly affected by the severe penalisation

**Table 4.4** Discrepancy between responsibilities of women leaders and career path to CEO

| *Leadership responsibilities* | *Distribution of leadership roles across categories (%)* | *Share of women leaders in these areas (%)* | *Percentage of CEOs who held roles in these areas in one of the prior two roles (%)* |
|---|---|---|---|
| Line of business | 50 | 9 | 62 |
| Finance | 8 | 21 | 40 |
| Operations | 3 | 11 | 38 |
| Portfolio management | 2 | 10 | 12 |
| Regional business unit | 13 | 14 | 8 |
| Strategy | 2 | 17 | 7 |
| Marketing and business development | 3 | 48 | 5 |
| Legal | 5 | 33 | 4 |
| Technology | 5 | 22 | 2 |
| Risk/compliance | 5 | 27 | 1 |
| Talent | 3 | 66 | 1 |
| Administration | 2 | 39 | 1 |

*Source* Rogish, Sandler, and Shemluck (2020)

suffered by women of colour, who disappear at higher levels of employment (McKinsey & Company, 2018, Exhibit 1, and Table 4.5). Thus, difficulties in promotion for women appear immediately from the first promotion and increase at every stage of the career (Table 4.5).

In the three sub-sectors considered, the trends show some important differences. Upon entry, there is a situation of substantial gender equality, except for the insurance sector characterised by a significantly higher percentage of women (mostly white) compared to men. The insurance sector also shows a smaller gap between men and women in promotions, although largely in favour of men. By contrast, the widest gaps are in asset management and wholesale banking. However, the gaps are essentially the same in the last position (C-suite) at 68%, 67%, and 69%, respectively, in asset management and wholesale banking, banking and consumer finance, and insurance. At all levels, the weight of people of colour is much lower than that of white people and in general becomes lower as the levels increase (McKinsey & Company, 2018, p. 6).

**Table 4.5** Employees by level (percentage share) in North American financial services firms

| | *Entry-level* | *Manager* | *Senior manager/director* | *Vice president* | *Senior vice president* | *C-suite*[a] |
|---|---|---|---|---|---|---|
| White men | 31 | 43 | 49 | 60 | 70 | 73 |
| Men of colour | 18 | 17 | 14 | 14 | 10 | 8 |
| White women | 30 | 27 | 28 | 21 | 17 | 17 |
| Women of colour | 21 | 13 | 9 | 5 | 3 | 1 |

[a]The sum of the figures of the C-suite positions is not 100% due to rounding off
*Source* McKinsey & Company (2018)

## 4.4 Double Glass Ceiling

As seen so far, the presence of women in the financial industry is equal to that of men at the entry level but drastically decreases at increasing levels of the career path.

The reasons for the difficulties in promoting women are linked both to subjective factors such as perceptions, convictions, behaviours of women, and to factors related to business policies (McKinsey & Company, 2018).

In the former case, women approach their career with many concerns about not being able to balance work and family commitments, having to make numerous compromises, and bearing mounting pressure as they advance in their careers. This attitude may eventually undermine their determination, making them settle for less ambitious positions. On the other hand, women also lack role models to inspire them as there are few women in leadership positions to activate a self-sustaining process, increasingly delaying the rise of women in their careers. Lack of support, advice, and sponsorship also hinders promotion. Women receive less advice on career advancement and organisational policies than men, whereas the support of managers and senior leaders on these issues would be very useful to increase their motivation towards professional growth and more ambitious goals.

Among the influencing factors at a firm-level, it is appropriate to introduce accountability for supporting career progression for both genders. This requires establishing the collection of data on several dimensions for gender representation at all levels of the organisation and for all career advancements for both men and women employees. However, creating such a system also presupposes setting up a multidimensional data collection that includes the definition of targets in the form of measurable key performance indicators to be achieved in the gender balance in the organisation and the career development path of men and women. Accountability facilitates the promotion of women, especially if the targets are linked to the compensation system of those who bear the responsibility (McKinsey & Company, 2018).

Finally, it is worth mentioning that a crucial aspect of promotion at the highest level depends on the cultivation of inter-company networks, which is essential for generating business or "rainmaking". However, networks are male-dominated and the challenges faced by women in cultivating them are numerous and considerable (Blair-Loy, 2001).

The social, cultural, and psychological obstacles to women's career advancement that are invisible but difficult to overcome are collectively known as the "glass ceiling" phenomenon, which is a term coined by Morrison et al. (1992). In the banking industry, we speak more properly of a "double glass ceiling" to indicate two barriers in career progression (Ferrary, 2017).

The population of employees in the banking industry is predominantly made up of women, who in many cases exceed 50% of all staff, although there are significant differences among countries; Sweden is the most feminised country and Japan the least feminised (Ferrary, 2017). However, female representation decreases as the hierarchy rises. In particular, the first glass ceiling concerns the transition to middle management and the second to executive committees (see Fig. 4.2).

The very low probability of progression for women from middle to senior levels is further confirmed by a study on US firms. This probability, measured as the ratio of the probability of a woman being promoted to the probability of a man being promoted, is 45% in the financial services sector, which is the lowest value across all other industries (Oliver Wyman, 2014, Exhibit 4).

Despite the data supporting the existence of the glass ceiling, the awareness of such a phenomenon is more present among women and much less among men. In fact, most women share the perception of

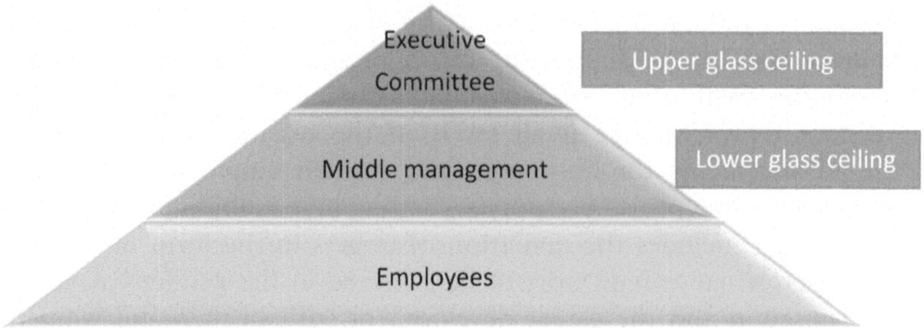


**Fig. 4.2** Double glass ceiling in the banking industry

financial services as an industry where women struggle to reach senior leadership or have the same promotion opportunities as men (Oliver Wyman, 2014, Exhibit 5).

As in the 2017 study by Ferrary, a study by the Financial Times (Noonan et al., 2017) confirms Sweden as the country with the largest female population in banks (see Table 4.6). In the world's largest banks (reported in Table 4.6), just over half of the staff are women, but the proportion falls to around 39 and 23% for middle management and senior roles, respectively. This demonstrates the need to continue to support initiatives to help women achieve a level playing field (also) in promotions.

The differences among banks are significant. In particular, consistently with the terminology used by Ferrary (Ferrary, 2017), by combining the percentages of women in middle management and executive committees, we can classify banks into four categories: (1) "feminine", i.e., banks with high percentages of women at both levels, where promotion to the first level therefore favours the rise to the second level (e.g., Citi, National Australia Bank, and Swedbank); (2) "masculine", i.e., banks with low percentages of women at both levels (e.g., MUFG and Mizuho); (3) "macho", i.e., banks with high levels of promotion to middle management, but much lower shares of women on executive committees (e.g., Société Générale and BBVA); and (4) "amazonian", i.e., banks with below-average shares of women in middle management and above-average shares of women on executive committees (the only one is Barclays).

A glass ceiling can also be found among insurance companies (Table 4.7) and asset management companies (Table 4.8), especially in the transition from middle management to senior positions. Women account for

**Table 4.6** Female employees, women in middle and senior roles in banks (year 2016)

| | *Women total (%)* | *Women mid (%)* | *Women senior (%)* |
|---|---|---|---|
| Citi | 51.4 | 42.0 | 43.2 |
| National Australia Bank | 54.0 | 53.0 | 35.0 |
| Swedbank | 73.5 | 50.4 | 34.0 |
| RBS | 50.8 | 44.0 | 34.0 |
| Bank of America | 51.9 | 49.0 | 32.0 |
| Erste | 65.4 | 49.5 | 29.7 |
| ANZ | 53.7 | 43.3 | 29.2 |
| Nordea | 54.9 | 43.0 | 28.0 |
| BNP Paribas | 53.0 | N.A | 26.0 |
| JPMorgan | 54.4 | 45.0 | 25.8 |
| HSBC | 51.9 | 46.0 | 25.0 |
| Standard Chartered | 46.0 | N.A | 25.0 |
| Barclays | 52.0 | 39.0 | 24.0 |
| UBS | 39.0 | 40.0 | 23.0 |
| Société Générale | 59.1 | 44.2 | 21.3 |
| Deutsche Bank | 41.5 | 32.8 | 21.3 |
| Goldman Sachs | 36.9 | 31.0 | 21.2 |
| BBVA | 54.1 | 49.0 | 21.0 |
| Unicredit | 57.0 | 32.0 | 19.0 |
| Credit Suisse | 35.0 | N.A | 19.0 |
| Morgan Stanley | 38.0 | 22.0 | 16.0 |
| Nomura | 38.0 | N.A | 16.0 |
| Daiwa | N.A | N.A | 8.9 |
| MUFG | 50.8 | 16.2 | 4.5 |
| Mizuho | 54.2 | 16.0 | 3.0 |
| SMBC | 51.0 | N.A | N.A |

*Source* Data from the *Financial Times* (https://ig.ft.com/managements-missing-women-data/)

just over 50% of the workforce in insurance companies, but as in banks, only 37% and 23% take up a role in middle management and senior levels. In asset management companies, which are populated by fewer women at entry, women seem to obtain more promotions in middle management and senior positions (the percentages within the sample are 44.5% and 25.6%, respectively).

For insurance companies, we can distinguish "feminine" (in particular Aviva and Axa), "masculine" (Generali), and "macho" (Lloyd's of London) companies, while there are no "amazonian" companies. Finally, among the asset management firms, it is worth mentioning the "macho"

**Table 4.7** Female employees, women in middle and senior roles in insurance companies (year 2016)

| | *Women total (%)* | *Women mid (%)* | *Women senior (%)* |
|---|---|---|---|
| Zurich | 51.1 | N.A | 29.4 |
| Aviva | 53.3 | 41.0 | 29.0 |
| Allianz | 52.4 | N.A | 28.0 |
| Axa | 52.7 | 41.8 | 27.7 |
| Metlife | 48.9 | 38.0 | 25.0 |
| Lloyd's of London | 53.0 | 50.1 | 20.0 |
| Prudential Plc | 53.7 | N.A | 20.0 |
| Swiss Re | 46.7 | 34.0 | 16.0 |
| Generali | 49.0 | 23.0 | 13.0 |
| Munich Re | 54.0 | 31.0 | N.A |
| Allstate | 56.0 | N.A | N.A |

*Source* Data from the *Financial Times* (https://ig.ft.com/managements-missing-women-data/)

**Table 4.8** Female employees, women in middle and senior roles in asset management companies (year 2016)

| | *Women total (%)* | *Women mid (%)* | *Women senior (%)* |
|---|---|---|---|
| Legg Mason | 43.2 | 42.0 | 32.0 |
| Aberdeen Asset Management | 43.7 | 43.7 | 30.0 |
| Schroders | 39.9 | 41.0 | 29.0 |
| Franklin Templeton | 42.4 | 36.0 | 27.0 |
| BlackRock | 38.9 | N.A | 26.3 |
| Fidelity International | 41.9 | 40.0 | 25.0 |
| Amundi | 44.7 | 35.0 | 23.1 |
| Union Investment | 44.3 | 76.0 | 20.0 |
| Baillie Gifford | 48.8 | 42.0 | 18.0 |
| Dodge & Cox | 48.3 | N.A | N.A |

*Source* Data from the *Financial Times* (https://ig.ft.com/managements-missing-women-data/)

Union Investment and four "amazonian" firms (Franklin Templeton, Legg Mason, Aberdeen Asset Management, and Schroders).

## 4.5 Some Final Remarks

The data contained in the numerous reports and studies analysed above show an overall positive trend of women on the board of directors in the role of both executive and non-executive directors. The data show a greater recruitment of female non-executive directors with supervisory and non-management functions. Other trends are the female prevalence on boards compared to executive committees (evidence that is linked to the previous one), the low weight of women in revenue-generating roles (the so-called roles associated with "profit and loss responsibilities"), and the constantly low number of female CEOs and chairs. Concerning the CEOs, research has outlined that the path to this role assumes leadership positions that are mostly held by men. Since boards of directors are more feminised than executive committees, banks are mostly "constrained feminists"; stakeholder pressure and the imposition of gender quotas seem to be the main drivers of women's presence on boards.

The glass ceiling in financial services is still in place. As stated by Ferrary (2017), it is actually a "double" glass ceiling, marked by fewer and fewer women as they move up the ladder. There is a gender balance at entry, but this becomes an imbalance in middle management positions and an even greater imbalance in executive committee positions.

However, because the samples and the observation periods considered in the studies change, the data should be interpreted only as dominant trends, which may not be confirmed for all countries. In fact, differences among countries and among companies within the same country may be very marked.

In the studies considered, the Nordic countries appear to be the most advanced in hiring and promoting women. It is not surprising that they occupy top positions in the World Economic Forum's ranking of countries, which takes into account national gender gaps using economic (Economic Participation and Opportunity), education (Educational Attainment), health (Health and Survival), and political (Political Empowerment) criteria. In the Global Gender Gap Index 2020 rankings, Iceland, Norway, Finland, and Sweden are in first, second, third, and fourth place, respectively (World Economic Forum, 2019). According to the EBA (2020), all Icelandic institutions have a gender diversity policy and feature the highest percentage of executive women. Given that the score varies between 0 (minimum) and 1 (maximum), the World Economic Forum's report states that "*The global top ten features four Nordic countries (Iceland,1st, Norway 2nd, Finland 3rd and Sweden 4th)*" (p. 8) and that "*Iceland is once again the most gender-equal country in the world for the 11th time in a row. It has closed almost 88% of its overall gender gap, further improving since last year. Iceland is followed by Norway*

*(2nd, 84.2%), Finland (3rd, 83.2%) and Sweden (4th, 82.0%)*" (p. 6). In the following 2021 report (World Economic Forum, 2021), Iceland is confirmed for the twelfth time as the most gender-equal country in the world and the ranking of the top 10 countries continues to be dominated by the Nordic countries, with Iceland, Norway, Finland, and Sweden in the top five.

The position of the Nordic countries towards gender equality also emerges from the Eurobarometer on gender equality (European Commission, 2017). Among all responses in the survey, particularly significant—in our opinion—is the approval/disapproval rate obtained for two specific statements: "the most important role of a man is to earn money" (QC1.3) and "the most important role of a woman is to take care of her home and family" (QC1.4). Sweden and Denmark are the countries with the highest disapproval of both statements. Finland is also among the countries expressing high disapproval. Iceland does not appear, as the survey was addressed to countries of the European Union alone.

## References

Blair-Loy, M. (2001). It's not just what you know, it's who you know: technical knowledge, rainmaking, and gender among finance executives. In S. Vallas (Ed.), *The transformation of work*. Research in the Sociology of Work 10:51–83. https://doi.org/10.1016/S0277-2833(01)80021-2

EBA—European Banking Authority. (2016). *Report on the benchmarking of diversity practices at the European Union level*. EBA-Op-2016–10 | 08 July 2016.

EBA—European Banking Authority. (2020). *Report on the benchmarking of diversity practices at European Union level, under Article 91(11) of Directive 2013/36/EU (2018 Data)*. EBA/REP/2020/05.

European Commission. (2016). *Report from the Commission to the European Parliament and the Council on benchmarking of diversity practices under Directive 2013/36/EU. 8.12.2016*. COM(2016) 774 final, 2016. Brussels

European Commission. (2017, June). *Special Eurobarometer 465*. Report. Gender Equality 2017.

Ferrary, M. (2017). *Gender diversity in the banking industry. An international comparison*. SKEMA Observatory on the Feminization of Companies

IMF—International Monetary Fund. (2017). *Banking on women leaders: A case for more?* Prepared by Sahay, R., Čihák, M., N'Diaye, P., Barajas, A., Kyobe, A., Mitra, S., Mooi, Y. N., & Yousefi, S. R. Working paper. WP/17/199.

IMF—International Monetary Fund. (2018). *Women in finance: A case for closing gaps*. Prepared by Sahay, R., Čihák, M., & other IMF Staff. September, SDN/18/05.

Kerpen, C. (2018, December 11). How will we reach gender parity in leadership? One workplace at a time. *Forbes*. Retrieved from https://www.forbes.com/sites/carriekerpen/2018/12/11/we-need-more-women-in-charge/?sh=24bdf90323f5

McKinsey & Company. (2018, September). Closing the gap. Leadership perspectives on promoting women in financial services.

Morrison, A. M., White, R. P., & Van Velsor, E. (1992). *Breaking the glass ceiling: Can women reach the top of America's largest corporations?* Addison-Wesley.

Noonan, L., Smith, A., Blood, D., & Stabe, M. (2017, April 4). Women still miss out on management in finance. *Financial Times*. Retrieved from https://ig.ft.com/managements-missing-women-data/

Oliver Wyman. (2014). *Women in financial services.*

Oliver Wyman. (2016). *Women in financial services.*

Oliver Wyman. (2020). *Women in financial services. A panoramic approach.*

Rogish, A., Sandler, S., & Shemluck, N. (2020). Diversifying the path to CEO in financial services. How prioritizing gender diversity and inclusion in leadership development and succession planning could improve outcomes. *Deloitte Insights*.

Rogish, A., Sandler, S., Shemluck, N., Danielecki, P., & Ramsay, T. (2020, July). Within reach? Achieving gender equity in financial services leadership. *Deloitte Review*. Issue 27.

World Economic Forum. (2019). Global gender gap report 2020.

World Economic Forum. (2021, March). Global gender gap report 2021.

Zenger, J., & Folkman, J. (2019, June 25). Research: Women score higher than men in most leadership skills. *Harvard Business Review*. Retrieved from https://www.iwecfoundation.org/news/research-women-score-higher-than-men-in-most-leadership-skills/

CHAPTER 5

# The Gender Pay Gap in the Financial Sector: Where Do We Stand?

**Abstract** This chapter addresses the issue of the gender pay gap within the financial system. To this end, it first reviews the main treaties and legal acts that formalise the principle of equal pay for men and women from the Treaty of Rome to the main European directives. It then analyses the theoretical and empirical studies on the issue, which for the financial sector are still in an embryonic phase. The second part of the chapter focuses exclusively on the financial system, analysing the evolution of the gender pay gap over time and the differences across geographical areas and economic sectors. The assessment primarily addresses data collected by Eurostat and the European Banking Authority (EBA). It also provides a focus on the gender pay gap in the UK banking sector. Finally, the chapter explores the most recent laws on the gender pay gap passed in several European countries and the novel "gender neutrality principle" of banking remuneration practices. The chapter ends by proposing some actions that need to be taken by banks to close the existing gender pay gap.

This chapter is the result of the joint efforts of the two authors. However, Giuliana Birindelli mainly contributed to Sects. 5.2, 5.3.3, and Antonia Patrizia Iannuzzi to Sects. 5.1, 5.3.1, 5.3.2, 5.4, 5.5.



G. Birindelli and A. P. Iannuzzi, *Women in Financial Services*, Palgrave Macmillan Studies in Banking and Financial Institutions, https://doi.org/10.1007/978-3-030-93471-2_5

## 5.1 The Principle of Equal Pay for Equal Work for Women and Men

In Europe, the formal recognition of equal pay for men and women came with the Treaty of Rome. This officially marked the birth of the European Economic Community (EEC) in March 1957. The principle was specifically addressed in Article 119, requiring each Member State to ensure that men and women receive equal pay for equal work. Moreover, this statement is in line with Article 117 of the same Treaty, affirming the need to improve the living and working conditions of the workforce to overcome inequalities and create a more effective and fairer common market.

Between 1958 and 1989, the issue of equal pay for men and women was further supported by a number of decisions made in the courts in Europe that outlined important principles that were later transcribed into European Union (EU) legislation. A relevant example is the 1976 Defrenne judgement in which the Brussels Labour Court unequivocally affirmed the principle of equal pay as one of the foundations of the European Union, recognising that this provision has the dual function of protecting companies against competitive disadvantages and of promoting social progress, as well.[1]

In more recent years, a further step towards equal pay for men and women was taken with the Treaty of Amsterdam, signed on 2 October 1997. Among its articles, Articles 2 and 3 are the most relevant as they define women's rights as fundamental and confirm the principles previously set out in the Treaty of Rome. Importantly, the Treaty of Amsterdam claims that equality between men and women is a "mission" of the European Union, delegating the task of identifying the most appropriate actions to eliminate discrimination based on sex to each Member State. In this regard, Article 119 of the Treaty of Amsterdam is of great significance (Table 5.1). It was the beginning of "gender mainstreaming" within the European Union, which is a long-term strategic approach

[1] Specifically, Ms. Defrenne was a flight attendant for the Belgian airline Sabena. She claimed to suffer from direct sex-based discrimination as she received lower pay than her male colleagues with the same qualifications. She therefore brought an action against Sabena, her employer, to obtain compensation since the discrimination she suffered was a clear breach of Article 119 of the Treaty of Rome.

**Table 5.1** Gender pay equality principle in the European Treaties and Pacts

| | |
|---|---|
| Treaty of Rome 1957 | **Article 119**:<br>Each Member State shall during the first stage ensure and subsequently maintain the application of the principle that men and women should receive equal pay for equal work. For the purpose of this Article, "pay" means the ordinary basic or minimum wage or salary and any other consideration, whether in cash or in kind, which the worker receives, directly or indirectly, in respect of his employment from his employer. Equal pay without discrimination based on sex means:<br>(a)that pay for the same work at piece rates shall be calculated on the basis of the same unit of measurement<br>(b) that pay for work at time rates shall be the same for the same job |
| Treaty of Amsterdam 1997 | **Article 119**:<br>1. Each Member State shall ensure that the principle of equal pay for male and female workers for equal work or work of equal value is applied<br>2. For the purpose of this Article, "pay" means the ordinary basic or minimum wage or salary and any other consideration, whether in cash or in kind, which the worker receives directly or indirectly, in respect of his employment, from his employer. Equal pay without discrimination based on sex means:<br>(a) that pay for the same work at piece rates shall be calculated on the basis of the same unit of measurement<br>(b) that pay for work at time rates shall be the same for the same job<br>3. The Council, acting in accordance with the procedure referred to in Article 189b, and after consulting the Economic and Social Committee, shall adopt measures to ensure the application of the principle of equal opportunities and equal treatment of men and women in matters of employment and occupation, including the principle of equal pay for equal work or work of equal value |

(continued)

**Table 5.1** (continued)

| | |
|---|---|
| Charter of Fundamental Rights of the European Union<br>2000 | **Article 23**:<br>Equality between men and women must be ensured in all areas, including employment, work, and pay. The principle of equality shall not prevent the maintenance or adoption of measures providing for specific advantages in favour of the underrepresented sex |
| Treaty on the Functioning of the European Union (TFEU)<br>2012 (TEC is the old Treaty establishing the European Community) | **Article 157** (ex Article 141 TEC):<br>1. Each Member State shall ensure that the principle of equal pay for male and female workers for equal work or work of equal value is applied<br>2. For the purpose of this Article, “pay” means the ordinary basic or minimum wage or salary and any other consideration, whether in cash or in kind, which the worker receives directly or indirectly, in respect of his employment, from his employer. Equal pay without discrimination based on sex means:<br>(a) that pay for the same work at piece rates shall be calculated on the basis of the same unit of measurement<br>(b) that pay for work at time rates shall be the same for the same job<br>3. The European Parliament and the Council, acting in accordance with the ordinary legislative procedure, and after consulting the Economic and Social Committee, shall adopt measures to ensure the application of the principle of equal opportunities and equal treatment of men and women in matters of employment and occupation, including the principle of equal pay for equal work or work of equal value<br>4. With a view to ensuring full equality in practice between men and women in working life, the principle of equal treatment shall not prevent any Member State from maintaining or adopting measures providing for specific advantages in order to make it easier for the underrepresented sex to pursue a vocational activity or to prevent or compensate for disadvantages in professional careers |

| | |
|---|---|
| European Pact for Gender Equality (2011–2020) | Annex:<br>The Council of the European Union acknowledges that equality between women and men is a fundamental value of the European Union and that gender equality policies are vital to economic growth, prosperity, and competitiveness (...). The Council therefore reaffirms its commitment to fulfil EU ambitions on gender equality as mentioned in the Treaty and in particular to:<br>1. close the gender gaps in employment and social protection, including the gender pay gap, with a view to meeting the objectives of the Europe 2020 Strategy, especially in three areas of great relevance to gender equality, namely employment, education and promoting social inclusion in particular through the reduction of poverty, thus contributing to the growth potential of the European labour force<br>2. promote better work-life balance for women and men throughout the life-course, so as to enhance gender equality, increase women's participation in the labour market and contribute to meeting the demographic challenges (...) |

*Source* European Treaties and Pacts

to promoting gender equality at all levels and in all public and private sectors.[2]

Subsequently, Article 23 of the Charter of Fundamental Rights (CFR) of the European Union proclaimed in Nice in 2000 reaffirmed that equality between men and women must be ensured in all areas including employment, work, and pay. To this end, the right of women to paid maternity leave was introduced for the first time (Article 33, CFR).

More recently, the Treaty of Lisbon of 2007 (which came into force in 2009) has further contributed to the issue of equal pay for men and women. It consolidates the Treaty on the European Union (TEU) and the Treaty on the Functioning of the European Union (TFEU) into a single document (dated 2012). It calls on the European Parliament and the Council to adopt specific measures to defend the principle of equal pay for men and women "*for equal work or work of equal value*" (Article 157, sub-section 1, TFEU). It also provides for the possibility for Member States to adopt measures "*providing for specific advantages in order to make it easier for the underrepresented sex to pursue a vocational activity or to prevent or compensate for disadvantages in professional careers*" (Article 157, sub-section 4, TFEU). Furthermore, by including the Charter of Fundamental Rights of the European Union in the annexes, the new wording of the TFEU gives this document a legally binding character within the European legal order.

Finally, as for the gender pay gap (GPG), we should also mention the "European Pact for Gender Equality" (2011–2020). This is where the EU Council affirms that policies to promote gender equality are vital for economic growth. Additionally, it reaffirms its commitment to closing the gaps in employment, social protection, and pay following the EU Treaties.

[2] The concept of "gender mainstreaming" was first proposed in 1985 at the Third World Conference on Women in Nairobi. The idea was then developed and endorsed in 1995 at the Fourth World Conference on Women in Beijing. In 1997, the Economic and Social Council (ECOSOC) defined gender mainstreaming as: "*the process of assessing the implications for women and men of any planned action, including legislation, policies or programmes, in all areas and at all levels. It is a strategy for making women's as well as men's concerns and experiences an integral dimension of the design, implementation, monitoring and evaluation of policies and programmes in all political, economic and societal spheres so that women and men benefit equally and inequality is not perpetuated. The ultimate goal is to achieve gender equality*". To further explore the gender mainstreaming concept, see Woodward (2001) and the United Nations (2002). To analyse the impact of the COVID-19 pandemic on this strategic approach, see EC (2021).

### 5.1.1 The European Directives on the Gender Pay Gap

Concerning the legislative acts that have focused on the issue of the gender pay gap at the European level, it is worth mentioning, first and foremost, Directive 75/117/EEC. This has the merit of having implemented the principle of equal pay for men and women as laid down in Article 119 of the Treaty of Rome. Subsequently, the gender pay gap was also addressed by other directives introducing, among other things, the concept of "direct discrimination" (Directive 76/207/EEC), the principles of equal treatment between men and women also in the context of self-employed activities—including those in the agricultural sector (Directive 86/613/EEC)—and, finally, the obligation to adopt measures to promote the improvement of occupational safety and the health of pregnant workers, workers who have recently given birth and workers who are breastfeeding (Directive 92/85/EEC).

More recently, two other European directives have addressed the issue of equality between men and women, including pay, in an even more incisive manner. The first is Directive 2002/73/EC (amending Directive 76/207/EEC). This broadened the concept of discrimination, distinguishing between direct and indirect discrimination. While direct discrimination occurs "*where one person is treated less favourably on grounds of sex than another is, has been or would be treated in a comparable situation*", indirect discrimination ensues "*where an apparently neutral provision, criterion or practice would put persons of one sex at a particular disadvantage compared with persons of the other sex, unless that provision, criterion or practice is objectively justified by a legitimate aim, and the means of achieving that aim are appropriate and necessary*" (Article 2, Directive 2002/73/EC). Direct discrimination, in turn, can be implicit, i.e., through reference to gender-specific situations (e.g., pregnancy), or explicit, i.e., through an explicit reference to gender. The second piece of legislation is Directive 2006/54/EC. In addition to reaffirming that the principle of equal pay for equal work (or work of equal value) is an important aspect of the principle of equal treatment between men and women and an essential and indispensable part of the "*acquis Communautaire*" (recital 8 and Article 2, Directive 2006/54/EC), it also introduces an obligation for the Member States to address the problem of unequal pay through flexible working time arrangements, allowing women and men to better reconcile work and family life. This requires appropriate provisions on parental leave benefiting both parents, as well as the creation of accessible and affordable childcare facilities and care for dependent family members. To date, Directive 2006/54/EC is still the main legal reference on equal treatment between men and women and equal pay, having introduced a more organic and uniform legislative framework resulting from the unification of pre-existing legislation and constant updating in line with developments in European case-law.

## 5.2 Main Evidence from the Literature

The literature on the GPG is still in an embryonic phase, especially when referring exclusively to the financial sector (Yanadori et al., 2018). At present, studies focus mainly on non-financial firms (Yanadori et al., 2018), and primarily on those in the United States (Chamberlain, 2016), England (Amadxarif et al., 2020), Australia (Yanadori et al., 2018), Austria, and Germany (Bergmann et al., 2019). On the other hand, works that carry out multi-country analyses are still low in number (Amado et al., 2018; Boll & Lagemann, 2019). Overall, these studies agree that the gender pay gap (i) still exists but has narrowed over the years—also in the banking sector (Usmonova, 2020)—and (ii) still presents important differences at the country level (Amado et al., 2018; Boll & Lagemann, 2019). This dynamic is attributable, above all, to improvements in the level of women's education, training, and experience (Jarrell & Stanley, 2004; Stanley & Jarrell, 1998; Weichselbaumer & Winter-Ebmer, 2005). However, there are still numerous critical issues that need to be solved. On the one hand, the gap is greater when women are recruited from outside the firm—that is, by external recruitment (rather than by internal promotion). This reveals a kind of wage discrimination that is based on power and not on market logic (Schneider et al., 2021). On the other hand, evidence suggests that the reduction of the gender pay gap only concerns aggregate measures. When it is segmented by age group, the gap appears to increase alongside the increase in the age of the workers (Chamberlain, 2016; Goldin, 2014). Moreover, while the gap tends to be zero among the lowest pay ranges as a result of the targeted minimum wage (Bargain et al., 2019), it remains high among the highest wage classes (Butcher et al., 2016).

A greater divergence is found regarding the metrics for measuring the GPG (Amado et al., 2018), as well as the factors that explain this gap. While some studies (Alkadry & Tower, 2006; Costa Dias et al., 2018) reconduct the gender pay gap mainly to differences in terms of human capital (level of education, extent of responsibilities assigned, and experience acquired over time), other research associates it mainly with a lower representation/employment rate of women (Blau & Kahn, 2017), especially in traditionally higher paid sectors (Lewis & Oh, 2009), or labour market differences (differences in years of experience and working hours, see Costa Dias et al., 2018). Finally, further studies attribute the gender pay gap to differences in the positions held. Women are particularly underrepresented in the highest-paid executive positions (Chamberlain, 2016; Yanadori et al., 2018). However, beyond these explanations, the main critical issue lies in the existence of a still rather high "unexplained" wage gap (Boll & Lagemann, 2019; Chamberlain, 2016), i.e., the part of the wage gap that scholars fail to trace back to any component of job position, labour market, and/or human capital (Amadxarif et al., 2020). This circumstance constitutes one of the main reasons for expanding knowledge on this topic, especially intending to nullify, or at least limit, the GPG on which various factors act individually or jointly (age, nature of the contract, qualifications possessed, parenting, etc.).

The financial sector is among the industries with the highest gender pay gap (Bergmann et al., 2019; Greenfield et al., 2016; Usmonova, 2020; Yildirmaz et al., 2019). Based on the US Census American Community Survey microdata for bank employees from 2001 to 2017, the GPG in US banks appears to decrease following the subprime mortgage crisis and invert trend thereafter. It can be hypothesised that this dynamic was triggered by greater demand for female skills during the crisis years. This led to an increase in the average salary of female directors, fading away once the economy and the financial market began to stabilise after the crisis. Similar evidence is also found for the UK financial sector. Based on data from the Labour Force Survey-LFS (specifically, data for the post-recession phase), Healy and Ahamed (2019) compare the pay gap in the financial sector with that of other economic sectors. They find that it is still quite resilient in the financial services sector and it is also higher at the upper end of the wage distribution, as previously noted by other authors (Bell & Reenen, 2014). As Healy and Ahamed state: "*the irony is that the more successful and better paid the woman, the greater the penalty in pay she suffered compared to her male comparator. While the pay gap was less at the lower earnings distribution, it has remained almost unchanged over the period*" (Healy & Ahamed, 2019, p. 321). In other words, women in finance manage to overcome discrimination in access to top positions by breaking the glass ceiling and they are forced to suffer further discrimination in terms of salary. Thus, this makes them dual victims.

Economic downturn seems to produce other interesting effects on the GPG in financial firms. On the one hand, during an economic downturn—when corporate performance is poor—the bonuses of CEOs of banks characterised by a higher board gender diversity decline more sharply, showing that a greater presence of women directors has a disciplining effect on the CEO's substantial compensation. On the other hand, however, the greater presence of women directors no longer has a reducing effect on the overall gender pay gap as it did during the crisis (Owen & Temesvary, 2019). The issue of bonuses and variable pay in the banking sector is also the focus of the study by Bergmann et al. (2019). The authors believe that the gender pay gap in banks and insurance companies is mainly attributable to the components of total remuneration which are mostly negotiated on an individual basis and thus subject to greater discrimination.

More recent studies shed light on the role of women in remuneration committees and the influence of female directors in formulating good remuneration practices. Although these studies focus on non-financial sectors, it is useful to cite them to identify new research lines to enrich the literature on the GPG in banks. In this regard, the study by Alkalbani et al. (2019) is interesting. It shows that a greater presence of women in remuneration committees can reduce the shareholder dissent in terms of say-on-pay, provided that the representation of women is above 30%. This finding further supports the critical mass theory, i.e., that women directors can exert a significant influence on corporate decisions when they reach a minimum threshold. The analysis by Alkalbani et al. (2019) extends to the companies belonging to the UK FTSE 350 from 2003 to 2015. It would be interesting to develop similar research exclusively on banks for which there is still a lack of thorough studies on remuneration committees (Dell'Atti et al., 2013). Additionally, a further line of inquiry into the GPG in banks could be to analyse this phenomenon jointly with the ethnic pay gap. A recent study (Amadxarif et al., 2020), using data from the UK Labour Force Survey, finds that ethnic minority women workers in the UK experience a greater pay gap than both white women and ethnic minority men.

Finally, another strand of research focuses on the pay gap between different top positions (e.g., CEO/vice presidents-VPs; CEO/other board members) and the role played by the CEO gender in these dynamics. It seems that in companies managed by female CEOs, the pay gap between CEO and VP is smaller than in companies managed by male CEOs. This is a circumstance that would be reflected in better economic performance (Vieito, 2012).

## 5.3 Data on Gender Pay Inequality in the Financial Sector

In this section, we analyse some data on the gender pay gap in the financial sector first at the EU level and then with a view specifically on UK banks. We will draw useful insights into the extent to which the gender pay gap affects women embarking on careers in the banking sector.

### 5.3.1 *Eurostat Data*

An interesting insight into the gender pay gap in the European financial sector can be gained by analysing data from the European Union statistics office, Eurostat.[3] Table 5.2, which displays data on the "unadjusted gender pay gap" in the financial sector within European countries from 2010 to 2019, allows us to make several interesting observations.

Our first consideration concerns the 2010–2019 average values for each European country. Regardless of the countries that have the value for only one year (Ireland, Montenegro, North Macedonia, Albania, and Turkey), the mean values of the unadjusted gender pay gap vary from a minimum of 16.01% (in Belgium) to a maximum of 41.19% (in the Czech Republic), reflecting different levels of wage discrimination across countries. Another consideration is that there does not seem to be a relationship, at least in the financial sector, between the adoption of gender policies and the reduction of the gender pay gap. In fact, in the Nordic and Anglo-Saxon countries, which are known to be at the forefront of gender equality rankings (e.g., WEF, 2021), the pay gap between men and women remains quite high on average (36.59% in Iceland, 30.17% in Norway, and 38.29% in the UK). Nonetheless, the data in

[3] https://ec.europa.eu/eurostat/statistics-explained/index.php?title=Gender_pay_gap_statistics#Highest_gender_pay_gap_in_financial_and_insurance_activities.

**Table 5.2** "Unadjusted gender pay gap" in the financial sector (banks and insurance companies; years 2010–2019; % values)[4]

| | *2010* | *2011* | *2012* | *2013* | *2014* | *2015* | *2016* | *2017* | *2018* | *2019* | *Mean 2010/2019* | *% Δ 2019–2010* |
|---|---|---|---|---|---|---|---|---|---|---|---|---|
| Belgium | 22.1 | 21.6 | 21.2 | 20.8 | 20.2 | 17.0 | 13.5 | 10.2 | 6.9 | 6.6 | 16.01 | −70.14 |
| Bulgaria | 24.5 | 20.8 | 25.5 | 24.9 | 23.1 | 22.7 | 22.3 | 24.2 | 25.9 | 29.5 | 24.34 | 20.41 |
| Czech Republic | 42.1 | 44.3 | 45.1 | 40.9 | 41.4 | 40.9 | 40.4 | 39.5 | 39 | 38.3 | 41.19 | −9.03 |
| Denmark | 23.0 | 22.3 | 21.3 | 21.4 | 20.6 | 20.0 | 19.5 | 18.9 | 18.2 | 17.4 | 20.26 | −24.35 |
| Germany (until 1990 former territory of the Federal Republic of Germany-FRG) | 30.0 | 30.1 | 29.6 | 29.3 | 28.7 | 27.8 | 26.2 | 25.0 | 24.2 | 24.2 | 27.51 | −19.33 |
| Estonia | 43.9 | 41.1 | 44.9 | 45.0 | 42.3 | 35.4 | 34.8 | 40.2 | 33.9 | 29.1 | 39.06 | −33.71 |
| Ireland | : | : | : | : | : | : | : | : | 28.1 | : | 28.10 | |
| Greece | 17.8 | : | : | : | 16.8 | : | : | : | 17.0 | : | 17.20 | −4.49 |
| Spain | 22.5 | 22.8 | 21.9 | 22.6 | 18.1 | 17.6 | 19.0 | 16.1 | 15.0 | 15 | 19.06 | −33.33 |
| France | 30.7 | 29.6 | 30.2 | 30.7 | 30.9 | 30.7 | 31.1 | 31.6 | 32.0 | 31.3 | 30.88 | 1.95 |

[4] The gender pay gap in its unadjusted form represents the difference between average gross hourly earnings of male paid employees and of female paid employees as a percentage of average gross hourly earnings of male paid employees. In detail, it is calculated based on the following formula: GPG = [(average gross hourly earnings of male paid employees – average gross hourly earnings of female paid employees)/average gross hourly earnings of male paid employees] expressed in %. The average earnings used for the GPG are calculated as arithmetic means. The GPG is calculated for enterprises with at least 10 employees, which include all persons who have a direct employment contract with the enterprise or local unit and receive remuneration, regardless of the type of work performed, the number of hours worked (part-timers are included), and the duration of the contract (fixed or indefinite). The unadjusted gender pay gap for the EU is calculated as the weighted mean of the gender pay gaps in the EU Member States, where the number of employees in the Member States represents the weight.

| | 2010 | 2011 | 2012 | 2013 | 2014 | 2015 | 2016 | 2017 | 2018 | 2019 | Mean 2010/2019 | % Δ 2019–2010 |
|---|---|---|---|---|---|---|---|---|---|---|---|---|
| Croatia | 7.0 | : | : | 12.1 | 21.0 | : | 4.9 | 24.9 | 24.7 | 24.8 | 17.06 | 254.29 |
| Italy | 21.7 | 22.2 | 23.4 | 24.9 | 22.4 | 22 | 18.1 | 18.3 | 23.5 | 22.7 | 21.92 | 4.61 |
| Cyprus | 27.3 | 26.1 | 25.4 | 24.6 | 24.4 | 23.6 | 22.1 | 21.2 | 19.5 | 20.2 | 23.44 | −26.01 |
| Latvia | 37.6 | 33.5 | 35.2 | 30.6 | 34.8 | 30.9 | 28.8 | 34.2 | 33.5 | 32 | 33.11 | −14.89 |
| Lithuania | 44.3 | 40.8 | 40.0 | 39.9 | 39.9 | 37.2 | 35.7 | 34.2 | 32.1 | 36.3 | 38.04 | −18.06 |
| Luxembourg | 26.0 | 25.7 | 24.0 | 23.0 | 22.5 | 23.8 | 24.5 | 24.3 | 25.3 | 24.5 | 24.36 | −5.77 |
| Hungary | 38.6 | 37.2 | 38.7 | 38.0 | 36.8 | 23.9 | 34.2 | 38 | 33.4 | 36 | 35.48 | −6.74 |
| Malta | 30.6 | 29.1 | 28.1 | 28.1 | 27.3 | 30.0 | 29.9 | 27.5 | 26.5 | 25.3 | 28.24 | −17.32 |
| Netherlands | 23.9 | 30.2 | 29.3 | 28.4 | 28.3 | 29.8 | 30.1 | 30.1 | 29.2 | 25.8 | 28.51 | 7.95 |
| Austria | 30.3 | : | : | : | 30.4 | 30.3 | 27.1 | 28.4 | 28.2 | 28 | 28.96 | −7.59 |
| Poland | 38.5 | 37.7 | 36.9 | 36.8 | 36.7 | 33.6 | 30.4 | 30.4 | 30.8 | 30.8 | 34.26 | −20.00 |
| Portugal | 25.9 | 25.8 | 22.9 | 22.1 | 21.6 | 22.8 | 21.8 | 20.7 | 19.9 | 23.6 | 22.71 | −8.88 |
| Romania | 17.8 | 21.9 | 17.7 | 21.7 | 20.9 | 24.6 | 30.1 | 29.5 | 32.6 | 32.4 | 24.92 | 82.02 |
| Slovenia | 22.8 | 22.2 | 21.7 | 22.5 | 23.7 | 23.3 | 22.5 | 23.9 | 24.3 | 24 | 23.09 | 5.26 |
| Slovakia | 37.1 | 37.6 | 35.1 | 35.3 | 35.4 | 38.0 | 36.2 | 34.9 | 33.9 | 31.4 | 35.49 | −15.36 |
| Finland | 36.4 | 35.3 | 35.3 | 35.0 | 34.2 | 32.6 | 32.0 | 30.9 | 30.4 | 28.2 | 33.03 | −22.53 |
| Sweden | 32.3 | 31.4 | 30.0 | 28.9 | 27.7 | 26.0 | 26.3 | 24.5 | 24.2 | 25.4 | 27.67 | −21.36 |
| Iceland | 32.2 | 34.2 | 34.9 | 38.1 | 38.8 | 37.3 | 39.3 | 39.1 | 35.4 | : | 36.59 | 9.94 |
| Norway | 31.4 | 31.8 | 29.9 | 29.8 | 29.9 | 31.0 | 29.7 | 29.4 | 28.6 | : | 30.17 | −8.92 |
| Switzerland | 32.0 | 31.5 | 31.1 | 31.1 | 31.0 | 30.6 | 30.5 | 30.3 | 32.7 | : | 31.20 | 2.19 |
| United Kingdom | 43.6 | 39.4 | 42.3 | 39.2 | 39.0 | 37.2 | 35.8 | 34.7 | 33.4 | : | 38.29 | −23.39 |
| Montenegro | : | : | : | : | 18.1 | : | : | : | : | : | 18.10 | : |
| North Macedonia | : | : | : | : | 15.3 | : | : | : | : | : | 15.30 | : |
| Albania | : | : | : | : | : | : | : | : | 6.2 | : | 6.20 | : |
| Serbia | : | : | : | : | 12.9 | : | : | : | 20.1 | : | 16.50 | : |
| Turkey | : | : | : | : | 9.8 | : | : | : | : | : | 9.80 | : |

*Source* Authors' elaboration on Eurostat data

the table are encouraging, showing a narrowing of the GPG in most European countries (in 21 out of 30, equal to 70%).[5] In some cases, the contraction is very significant (like in Belgium, where GPG falls by over 70%, see Table 5.2).

Table 5.3 highlights the gender pay gap for the financial sector compared to other industries based on data for 2019 (the only year for which data are available).[6] The GPG of banks and insurance companies emerges as the highest of all other economic sectors across the EU Member States with an average of 26.5%. More specifically, the gender pay gap in financial and insurance activities in 2019 ranges from 6.6% in Belgium to 38.3% in Czechia. Next in the ranking is the "Information and communication sector" with an average value of 19.7%, which is 6.8 percentage points lower than the financial sector. Finally, it is also worth noting that no country features a negative gender pay gap for the financial sector (Table 5.3, section K). Conversely, negative figures are reported in nine EU Member States for "Water supply, sewerage, waste management, and remediation activities" (Table 5.3, section E), in thirteen countries for the "Construction" sector (Table 5.3, section F) and in two countries for the "Real Estate activities" (Table 5.3, section L). This means that in these economic sectors, some women employees are paid more than men.

We must note that the data in these two tables (Tables 5.2 and 5.3) are based on an indicator that can offer only a partial picture of the gender pay gap. First, the GPG is based solely on the difference in average hourly earnings, whereas if it had also considered average annual earnings, the gap would have been wider since women usually work fewer hours. In such a case, its value would have been higher in countries with higher female unemployment rates. Because of this important limitation, GPG is defined as "unadjusted" or "unexplained". Moreover—as we shall recall—the GPG is composed of an "explicable" part (e.g., attributable to production characteristics, such as educational qualification) and an "inexplicable" part (e.g., individual characteristics of employed men and

[5] The value of 30 refers to the countries whose % change in GPG can be calculated from 2010 to 2019. See Table 5.2.

[6] However, as Eurostat points out, these are provisional data until the benchmark figures, taken from the Structure of Earnings Survey, become available in December 2024.

**Table 5.3** "Unadjusted gender pay gap" in the EU in 2019: a comparison between the financial industry and other economic sectors (% values)

| | *Business economy (B to N)* | *Manufacturing (C)* | *Electricity, gas, steam, and air conditioning supply (D)* | *Water supply, sewerage, waste management, and remediation activities (E)* | *Construction (F)* | *Information and communication (J)* | *Financial and insurance activities (K)* | *Real estate activities (L)* | *Professional, scientific, and technical activities (M)* |
|---|---|---|---|---|---|---|---|---|---|
| Belgium | 9.9 | 10.4 | 5.9 | 11.8 | 7.2 | 11.0 | 6.6 | 9.9 | 5.2 |
| Bulgaria | 14.0 | 22.7 | 8.2 | 5.6 | −11.5 | 22.4 | 29.5 | −7.5 | 16.5 |
| Czechia[a] | 14.4 | 24.1 | 17.5 | 5.3 | 7.4 | 30.5 | 38.3 | 9.0 | 24.8 |
| Denmark | 14.3 | 10.2 | 16.0 | 4.8 | 7.0 | 15.6 | 17.4 | 9.0 | 18.6 |
| Germany | 22.5 | 22.8 | 20.5 | 3.7 | 11.2 | 24.4 | 24.2 | 17.1 | 27.6 |
| Estonia | 23.2 | 25.2 | 16.6 | 7.7 | 13.0 | 25.5 | 29.1 | 14.3 | 11.6 |
| Spain | 16.9 | 17.0 | 15.1 | 10.5 | −8.3 | 12.0 | 15.0 | 14.9 | 18.7 |
| France | 14.0 | 14.0 | 9.8 | −2.9 | −9.7 | 15.3 | 31.3 | 14.1 | 23.0 |
| Croatia | 13.0 | 21.6 | 0.7 | −3.5 | −17.6 | 12.6 | 24.8 | 2.2 | 16.6 |
| Italy[b] | 14.7 | 14.6 | | | | 15.8 | 22.7 | | 24.9 |
| Cyprus[c] | 17.5 | 24.4 | 0.0 | −16.7 | −1.0 | 15.8 | 20.2 | −36.8 | 28.7 |
| Latvia | 21.5 | 22.8 | 1.4 | 16.6 | 5.1 | 31.5 | 32.0 | 18.4 | 27.6 |
| Lithuania | 15.0 | 24.6 | 9.1 | 11.6 | −2.9 | 30.2 | 36.3 | 14.3 | 17.2 |
| Luxembourg[b] | 10.9 | 10.3 | | | −8.7 | 17.6 | 24.5 | 13.9 | 20.9 |
| Hungary[d] | 15.4 | 22.9 | 20.5 | 10.5 | −2.8 | 23.7 | 36.0 | 7.2 | 17.0 |
| Malta[b, c] | 14.8 | 23.6 | | 19.9 | 4.3 | 15.0 | 25.3 | 23.1 | 24.2 |
| Netherlands | 20.4 | 17.1 | 11.3 | −1.4 | 9.2 | 16.1 | 25.8 | 16.6 | 20.6 |
| Austria | 21.6 | 20.9 | 13.6 | 8.3 | 8.2 | 20.3 | 28.0 | 28.4 | 27.5 |

(continued)

**Table 5.3** (continued)

| | *Business economy (B to N)* | *Manufacturing (C)* | *Electricity, gas, steam, and air conditioning supply (D)* | *Water supply, sewerage, waste management, and remediation activities (E)* | *Construction (F)* | *Information and communication (J)* | *Financial and insurance activities (K)* | *Real estate activities (L)* | *Professional, scientific, and technical activities (M)* |
|---|---|---|---|---|---|---|---|---|---|
| Poland | 15.4 | 18.4 | 5.1 | −0.4 | −8.7 | 28.2 | 30.8 | 7.6 | 19.2 |
| Portugal | 17.1 | 18.4 | 0.2 | −28.4 | −13.5 | 14.3 | 23.6 | 11.4 | 19.7 |
| Romania[d] | 11.6 | 22.8 | 8.5 | 3.1 | −10.3 | 26.2 | 32.4 | 0.0 | 3.3 |
| Slovenia | 9.9 | 14.0 | 1.6 | −24.2 | −27.0 | 19.5 | 24.0 | 3.3 | 12.2 |
| Slovakia | 19.0 | 25.4 | 12.0 | −1.0 | 8.0 | 27.7 | 31.4 | 17.0 | 13.1 |
| Finland | 15.9 | 8.5 | 18.0 | 2.8 | 1.5 | 13.2 | 28.2 | 17.2 | 15.0 |
| Sweden | 8.7 | 3.3 | 5.8 | −4.9 | −2.9 | 8.7 | 25.4 | 6.5 | 11.2 |
| **Mean values** | **15.7** | **18.4** | **9.9** | **1.7** | **−1.8** | **19.7** | **26.5** | **9.6** | **18.6** |

*Note* Data refer to enterprises employing 10 or more employees (NACE Rev. 2 B to S (-O)). Only for Czechia, data refer to enterprises employing 1 or more employees (NACE Rev. 2 B to S). Data are not available for Ireland, Greece, Iceland, Norway, and Switzerland

[a]The definition differs (see metadata, https://ec.europa.eu/eurostat/cache/metadata/en/sdg_05_20_esmsip2.htm)

[b]Confidential data (for Italy, sections D, E, F, L; for Luxembourg, sections D, E; for Malta, section D)

[c]Unreliable data (for Cyprus, sections D, E, F, L; for Malta, section L)

[d]Break-in series

[e]Estimated data for all sections

*Source* Authors' elaboration on Eurostat data

women, as well as sectoral and occupational gender segregations[7]). To provide a complete picture of the gender pay gap, Eurostat has developed a new synthetic indicator: the "Gender Overall Earnings Gap" based on the combination of three factors: (a) the average hourly earnings, (b) the monthly average of the number of hours paid, and (c) the employment rate based on the average earnings of all women of working age—whether employed or not—compared to men. Table 5.4 shows the dynamics of this new indicator for all EU countries from 2002 to 2018 for all private enterprises (financial and non-financial). At present, there are still no Eurostat estimates for this indicator by industrial sector.

### 5.3.2 Data from the European Banking Authority

As part of its latest benchmarking exercise on diversity policies in credit institutions and investment firms published in February 2020, the EBA included a new and final paragraph (entitled "*Gender and remuneration of the management body*") aimed at providing a first overview of the gender pay gap in the European financial sector. In particular, the data reported refer to the remuneration of the members of the management body in 2018 based on a representative sample of 834 financial institutions belonging to the EU and the European Economic Area (EEA). The main empirical findings drawn from the EBA study (EBA, 2020a) are the following:

(a) The remuneration of male members of the management body in most financial institutions is higher than that of female members.
(b) Coherently with what has been said beforehand, the institutions in which the remuneration of female directors is higher than that of male directors are very few.

[7] The term "sectoral gender segregation" refers to the concentration of one sex in certain economic activities, while "occupational gender segregation" refers to the concentration of one sex in certain occupations. Both these phenomena may explain part of the difference in earnings of men and women if one sex tends to concentrate in low-paying economic sectors or occupations and the other sex tends to concentrate in high-paying sectors or occupations. In general, there is a trend for a greater presence of women in low-paying sectors compared to men, but also in low-paying occupations due to the "glass ceiling" phenomenon. This is "*a metaphor to describe an invisible barrier that keeps women from rising beyond a certain level in an enterprise's hierarchy*" (Leythienne & Ronkowski, 2018, p. 8; on the "glass ceiling" see also Chapter 4).

**Table 5.4** "Gender overall earnings gap" in the private sector (industry, construction, and services[8]; % values)

| | *2002* | *2006* | *2010* | *2014* | *2018* |
|---|---|---|---|---|---|
| European Union—27 countries (from 2020) | : | : | 33.2 | 31.6 | : |
| European Union—28 countries (2013–2020) | : | 44.3 | 41.1 | 39.6 | : |
| Euro area—19 countries (from 2015) | : | : | 41.5 | 40.6 | : |
| Belgium | : | 38.6 | 35.9 | 31.1 | 26.4 |
| Bulgaria | 28.2 | 24.5 | 23.5 | 22.8 | 24.1 |
| Czechia | 42.3 | 43.1 | 41.0 | 40.4 | 36.0 |
| Denmark | | 29.9 | 25.7 | 26.4 | 25.1 |
| Germany (until 1990 former territory of the FRG) | | 47.7 | 45.4 | 45.2 | 41.9 |
| Estonia | | 38.9 | 32.2 | 38.4 | 32.6 |
| Ireland | 49.0 | 47.5 | 34.6 | 36.8 | 35.7 |
| Greece | | 51.6 | 45.2 | 41.4 | 40.5 |
| Spain | 55.4 | 47.6 | 38.0 | 35.7 | 33.0 |
| France | | 35.2 | 33.2 | 31.0 | 31.0 |
| Croatia | | : | 23.0 | 24.4 | 25.5 |
| Italy | | 47.5 | 44.3 | 43.7 | 43.0 |
| Cyprus | | 43.1 | 33.7 | 26.9 | 25.2 |
| Latvia | | 27.4 | 16.1 | 22.8 | 25.7 |
| Lithuania | 24.6 | 27.4 | 12.3 | 19.2 | 20.4 |
| Luxembourg | | 43.0 | 38.4 | 32.5 | 23.2 |
| Hungary | 37.0 | 33.2 | 32.7 | 32.0 | 32.8 |
| Malta | | 61.9 | 56.3 | 43.9 | 39.4 |
| Netherlands | 53.3 | 55.1 | 49.5 | 33.4 | 44.2 |
| Austria | | 50.8 | 46.7 | 44.9 | 44.2 |
| Poland | 30.1 | 33.6 | 29.6 | 31.5 | 30.7 |
| Portugal | | 26.4 | 27.8 | 26.1 | 20.6 |
| Romania | 32.5 | 24.7 | 29.9 | 26.8 | 25.3 |
| Slovenia | 24.8 | 21.4 | 12.8 | 19.6 | 21.0 |
| Slovakia | 41.3 | 44.1 | 37.5 | 37.3 | 35.5 |
| Finland | | 29.9 | 27.0 | 24.1 | 24.6 |
| Sweden | 27.1 | 32.3 | 30.2 | 26.2 | 23.5 |
| Iceland | | 40.6 | 32.8 | 34.0 | 31.2 |
| Liechtenstein | | | : | : | : |
| Norway | | 35.6 | 34.4 | 31.5 | 28.9 |
| Switzerland | | : | 45.7 | 44.5 | 43.1 |
| United Kingdom | 53.3 | 50.2 | 47.6 | 45.0 | 42.5 |
| Montenegro | | : | : | 26.0 | : |
| North Macedonia | | : | 39.5 | 39.6 | : |

(continued)

[8] Except for public administration, defence, and compulsory social security.

**Table 5.4** (continued)

| | *2002* | *2006* | *2010* | *2014* | *2018* |
|---|---|---|---|---|---|
| Albania | | : | : | : | : |
| Serbia | | : | : | 32.0 | 29.4 |
| Turkey | | 65.9 | 60.4 | 57.9 | : |

*Source* Authors' elaboration on Eurostat data

(c) This divergence can be only partly explained by the limited presence of female CEOs and chairs (equal to 8.53 and 9.49% respectively)—functions for which a higher remuneration is generally paid.

(d) There is further evidence showing that the roles performed do not fully justify the differences in remuneration. Moreover, this appears to be more evident for the category of non-executive directors compared to executive directors. The average gender pay gap for non-executive directors is higher than the respective value for board executive members (Table 5.5).[9]

(e) The distribution by percentile of the gender pay gap shows that the remuneration of female directors (both executive and non-executive) is higher than that of men only at the 10th percentile. This is in correspondence roughly with the presence of female CEOs or chairpersons. The GPG, in this case, is negative for both categories of director.

(f) At the 25th percentile, no gender pay difference exists (the GPG is 0). Meanwhile, the GPG tends to increase more for non-executive members at the highest percentiles (75th and 80th percentiles, see Table 5.5).

[9] However, as the EBA warns, these results should be interpreted with caution. Overall remuneration depends on several aspects, including differences in remuneration levels across EU and EEA Member States, the size and complexity of the financial institution, the role held (CEO, executive director, chairperson, non-executive director, employee representative, etc.), additional responsibilities (e.g., chairing committees), and the specific skills and experience needed and available on the market (e.g., IT experts with sufficient banking knowledge are particularly in demand). For this reason, the EBA states that: "*to avoid any influence on the analysis of different pay levels in Member States or based on the complexity of the institution or its performance, the pay gap was calculated in terms of percentages for each institution where there are both male and female members of a given function in the management body*" (EBA, 2020a, p. 37).

**Table 5.5** Gender pay gap for executive and non-executive directors (mean and percentile values; % values)

| *Role* | *Mean* | *p10* | *p25* | *p50* | *p75* | *p80* |
|---|---|---|---|---|---|---|
| Executive directors | 16.71 | −31.12 | 0.00 | 14.78 | 35.09 | 40.33 |
| Non-executive directors | 18.69 | −6.76 | 0.00 | 13.55 | 35.64 | 42.42 |

*Source* EBA (2020a)

(g) Overall, the pay differences between male and female executive directors can be explained as largely driven by the higher pay that is usually awarded to top managers, including CEOs. However, in some institutions with pay ratios that fall within the highest percentiles, the pay gap is likely to be caused by factors other than having a male CEO.

(h) Concerning non-executive directors, the magnitude of the differences between the 10th percentile and the 80th percentile can be partly driven by the gender of the chairperson. This may suggest that male non-executive directors do indeed receive systematically higher remuneration than female non-executive directors belonging to the same institution.[10]

### *5.3.3 A Focus on the UK Banking Sector*

The UK was one of the first European countries to introduce a legislative requirement for larger companies to disclose details of their gender pay gap (see below). The analysis of employee data from the Government Digital Service website specifically refers to the UK banking system[11] for

[10] "*However* – the EBA states – *a more detailed data collection is required to analyse whether this is the case or whether there are other factors that have led to the differences observed*" (EBA, 2020a, p. 38).

[11] More in detail, data are referred to the following Standard Industrial Classification (SIC) codes: 64110 (Central banking) e 64191 (banks—deposit taking; discount houses—monetary intermediation; money order activities; national saving bank; postal giro and postal savings bank activities).

the last four reporting years (2017–2021, see Table 5.6).[12] This evidences some interesting dynamics.

(a) In all reporting years (2017–2021), the average hourly pay for men is always higher than that paid to women. The value of the variable "*Diff Mean Hourly Percent*" (mean % difference between male and female hourly pay) is always positive, although slightly decreasing over time.
(b) This gap is accentuated when bonus pay is taken into account. In this case, the remuneration awarded to male employees is much higher than that given to women employees. Furthermore, an analysis of the trend of the variable "*Diff Mean Bonus Percent*" shows a slight increase over the years 2017–2021. The only positive fact is the trend of the variable "*Female Bonus Percent*" (% of female employees who are paid a bonus) increasing from almost 70% in reporting year 2017–2018 to over 80% in reporting year 2020–2021 (% increase of 25.56%).
(c) The gender pay gap widens in the upper-income classes. While the difference between men and women is approximately 23% in favour of the latter (more women than men) in the lower quartile (value given by the difference between 61.92 and 38.08%, see Table 5.6, column "Mean 2017–2021"), the gap becomes in favour of men and increases to 47% in the top quartile (value given by the difference between 73.28 and 26.72%, see Table 5.6, column "Mean 2017–2021"). This indicates that while women are more numerous in the lower wage categories, they are outnumbered in the upper ones. This is equivalent to saying that the percentage of men who are paid more is much higher than that of women.
(d) The middle pay classes show a more balanced presence of men and women. The differences in the lower-middle and upper-middle

[12] The first reporting year is 2017–2018, the second is 2018–2019, and so on. For each year, companies are required to communicate their remuneration and gender pay gap data by 30 March (for most public authority employers) or 4 April (for private, voluntary, and all other public authority employers) of the following year. For example, if a private company had a headcount of 250 employees on 5 April 2017, it should have reported and published its gender pay gap information by 4 April 2018. This is displayed as a submission for the 2017/2018 reporting year. The same rationale is behind the other reporting years. Therefore, gender pay gap data for the 2020/2021 reporting year run until March/April 2021.

**Table 5.6** Gender pay gap in UK banks (reporting year; % values)

| | *2017–2018* | *2018–2019* | *2019–2020* | *2020–2021* | *Mean 2017–2021* | *% Δ 2021–2017* |
|---|---|---|---|---|---|---|
| *Banks submitted after the deadline* | 8.33 | 8.57 | 0 | 0 | *4.23* | |
| *Diff Mean Hourly Percent* | 35.06 | 34.54 | 34.59 | 34.00 | *34.55* | *−3.02* |
| *Diff Median Hourly Percent* | 33.13 | 31.85 | 30.61 | 31.41 | *31.75* | *−5.19* |
| *Diff Mean Bonus Percent* | 52.83 | 50.69 | 55.06 | 53.82 | *53.10* | *1.87* |
| *Diff Median Bonus Percent* | 48.66 | 39.73 | 51.74 | 49.04 | *47.29* | *0.78* |
| *Male Bonus Percent* | 67.19 | 70.16 | 71.85 | 83.60 | *73.20* | *24.43* |
| *Female Bonus Percent* | 66.80 | 69.35 | 71.72 | 83.88 | *72.94* | *25.56* |
| *Male Lower Quartile* | 38.08 | 37.53 | 38.28 | 38.43 | *38.08* | *0.93* |
| *Female Lower Quartile* | 61.92 | 62.47 | 61.72 | 61.57 | *61.92* | *−0.57* |
| *Male Lower Middle Quartile* | 48.16 | 47.44 | 46.63 | 47.93 | *47.54* | *−0.47* |
| *Female Lower Middle Quartile* | 51.84 | 52.56 | 53.37 | 52.07 | *52.46* | *0.44* |
| *Male Upper Middle Quartile* | 60.05 | 57.55 | 57.90 | 58.84 | *58.59* | *−2.03* |
| *Female Upper Middle Quartile* | 39.95 | 42.45 | 42.10 | 41.16 | *41.41* | *3.05* |

| | 2017–2018 | 2018–2019 | 2019–2020 | 2020–2021 | Mean 2017–2021 | % Δ 2021–2017 |
|---|---|---|---|---|---|---|
| *Male Top Quartile* | 73.97 | 73.31 | 72.89 | 72.95 | *73.28* | *−1.38* |
| *Female Top Quartile* | 26.03 | 26.69 | 27.11 | 27.05 | *26.72* | *3.93* |

*Notes* *Diff Mean Hourly Percent*: Mean % difference between male and female hourly pay (negative = women's mean hourly pay is higher). *Diff Median Hourly Percent*: Median % difference between male and female hourly pay (negative = women's median hourly pay is higher). *Diff Mean Bonus Percent*: Mean % difference between male and female bonus pay (negative = women's mean bonus pay is higher). *Diff Median Bonus Percent*: Median % difference between male and female bonus pay (negative = women's median bonus pay is higher). *Male Bonus Percent*: % of male employees who are paid a bonus. *Female Bonus Percent*: % of female employees who are paid a bonus. *Male Lower Quartile*: % of males in the lower hourly pay quarter. *Female Lower Quartile*: % of females in the lower hourly pay quarter. *Male Lower Middle Quartile*: % of males in the lower-middle hourly pay quarter. *Female Lower Middle Quartile*: % of females in the lower-middle hourly pay quarter. *Male Upper Middle Quartile*: % of males in the upper-middle hourly pay quarter. *Female Upper Middle Quartile*: % of females in the upper-middle hourly pay quarter. *Male Top Quartile*: % of males in the top hourly pay quarter. *Female Top Quartile*: % of females in the top hourly pay quarter

*Source* Authors' elaboration on data from https://gender-pay-gap.service.gov.uk/viewing/download

quartiles are lower. In other words, within these specific quartiles payments to men and women are more similar.

(e) UK banks have shown a positive attitude to disclosing their gender pay gap. In the first reporting year, which corresponds to the first year of application of the disclosure requirement (2017–2018), 92% of all UK banks sent what was requested by the deadline (Table 5.6).

The comparison between the GPG in the UK banking system and that of all other economic sectors evidences additional interesting considerations[13]:

(a) Both the overall gender pay gap and the bonus gap are considerably higher in the UK banking sector compared to all other economic sectors. While at the end of 2018 the average gender pay gap across all UK companies is approximately 14%, it rises to 35% in the banking sector. The difference between the two sectors (financial and non-financial) is slightly wider when only bonus pay is considered. In this case, the gender pay gap is 36% for UK non-financial firms compared to 59% for the banking sector. In summary, UK banks appear to be further behind non-financial firms in closing the gender pay gap, especially if this concerns the bonus payments.

(b) The size of the company (in terms of number of employees) does not have a significant impact on the extent of the GPG. Specifically, the gender pay gap in UK banks appears to be only slightly larger in small banking institutions compared to larger ones.

(c) Overall, even in UK banks, the large gender pay gap is mainly determined by the low number of women in top or senior positions. All UK banks have a quartile index[14] above zero, showing that there is a higher proportion of men paid above the median compared to the overall workforce. Moreover, the gender pay gap tends to increase as employees move from the lower to the upper quartiles of the statistical distribution of this gap.

[13] Data are referred to the Central Bank and to all banking institutions. Any company with a pay gap above 100% is excluded. See https://www.pwc.co.uk/services/human-resource-services/gender-pay/spotlight-on-banking.html.

[14] "*The quartile index shows the relative distribution of men and women in the quartile ranges. A positive value indicates that there is a higher proportion of men in the upper and upper middle quartiles compared to the overall workforce*". See PwC (2019).

## 5.4 Actions to Close the Pay Gap

The contrast to the gender pay gap has been claimed by all supervisory authorities and policymakers, not just banking ones (Healy & Ahamed, 2019). This phenomenon, however, is not based on ethical and social justice reasons alone (see SDG target 8.5 of the 2030 Agenda for Sustainable Development). There is empirical evidence showing that reducing this gap also has important positive impacts in terms of economic value creation both for the firm and at the macro-economic level. Some estimates by the European Commission suggest that "*a decrease of the GPG of 2% points will result in an increase in total GDP of some EUR 34 billion, equivalent to EUR 67.71 per capita across the EU*" (Del Monte, 2013, p. 24). The main route followed by the authorities has been to oblige firms to increase their disclosure on this gap on the assumption that market discipline can act here (Bennedsen et al., 2019; Healy & Ahamed, 2019). By being obliged to inform the market about their gender pay gap, firms are pressured to reduce the gap to avoid disclosing compromising information that could lead to reputational sanctions. A recent study by Austin et al. (2021) confirms this assumption. By using an experimental methodology, they show that investors are more likely to invest in companies that disclose a smaller gender pay gap (or at least some pay equity) than in companies that do not disclose any information or that have a rather high gender pay gap. This indicates that disclosing pay equity makes companies more attractive to investors as it enables them to better assess the firm's remuneration policies.

In this section, we first analyse the main legislative measures adopted in some countries to reduce the gender pay gap and then we focus on the new principle of gender-neutral remuneration that has recently been introduced in the banking sector.

### 5.4.1 *The Most Recent Legislative Measures*

Among the latest measures taken at the national level, one of the most interesting is the law approved in Iceland in 2017.[15] It obliges public and private institutions, companies, banks, and any employer with 25 employees or more to ensure equal pay and qualifications between men

[15] Specifically, it is an amendment to the "Act on Equal Status and Equal Rights of Women and Men" adopted in 2008.

and women and to obtain an ISO-based "Pay Equality Certification", under penalty of paying a fine of up to 50 thousand Icelandic Krona (approximately €450). This law, which came into force in January 2018, will operate in full force at the end of 2025. The deadline is set for 2020 for large companies and 2025 for smaller companies.[16]

Following this law, in recent years, France, Belgium, Austria, Portugal, and Spain have taken steps to enshrine the principle of equal pay. They have implemented new reporting standards at the legislative level. As an incentive to close the pay gap, they have passed laws ranging from strengthening controls to requiring adequate disclosure of the company pay structure (Amadxarif et al., 2020). As an example, in Germany on 30 March 2017, the Bundestag passed legislation requiring companies with more than 200 employees to provide—upon request by the employees—information on the gender pay levels for the same work or for work of equal value. For companies with more than 500 employees, the obligation to produce gender equality data is triggered regardless of an explicit request as the companies must regularly produce reports on their pay to demonstrate the effective "alignment" of the salaries paid to men and women with the same job as well as to demonstrate all actions taken to eliminate any pay differentials.

A similar route was chosen in England where the Equality Act 2017 introduced a requirement for all private and third sector companies with more than 250 employees to produce a gender pay gap report.[17] An interesting aspect of this reporting concerns the extent of its transparency. Companies are required to publish relevant data both on their website

[16] Iceland also holds another record: it is the most gender-equal country in the world according to the World Economic Forum's reports (see Chapter 4). Iceland's record goes back a long way. As early as 1980, the country elected the world's first woman as President of the Republic (Vigdís Finnbogadóttir). Furthermore, "*Iceland is one of the few countries where women have been in the highest institutional positions in the country for almost as long as men in the past 50 years. A woman has been in a head-of-state position in 23.5 of the past 50 years, second only to Bangladesh, where women have been in this role for over 27 years*" (WEF, 2021, p. 32). It currently has a female prime minister (Katrín Jakobsdóttir, since 30 November 2017) as well as a very high percentage of women parliamentarians and ministers (39.7 and 40%, respectively). See WEF (2021).

[17] The doctrine tends to consider that it is necessary to extend this disclosure obligation to smaller companies with fewer than 250 employees. For more details, see Amadxarif et al. (2020).

and on a special government portal[18] created by the British government so that anyone can freely consult the data of any company.[19] In addition, English companies subject to this obligation must also produce a "written statement" (except for public authority employers) confirming the truthfulness of their data on the gender pay gap and explaining the reasons behind the gap.[20] Companies may additionally publish an "action plan" to inform the community of the measures that they intend to take to close the gap. Finally, there is also a monitoring system required by the Equality and Human Rights Commission (EHRC)[21] and a series of sanctions in case of non-compliance. This includes the publication of the names of non-compliant companies on the website of the commission as part of a name and shame policy.[22]

In France, there is an obligation to publish gender pay data. Companies with 50 or more employees are obliged to publish the data on their websites. Spain has moved in the same direction where companies with 50 or more employees must keep a pay register available to their workers' representatives, as well as account for significant differences (more than 25%) in gender pay. In Sweden, according to the 2008 Discrimination Act, employers with more than 10 employees must conduct pay audits (containing detailed information on gender pay gaps). Companies with more than 25 employees are also required to provide a gender equality plan. Non-compliant employers are obliged to remedy their non-fulfilment, while an e-learning platform is made available to employees to increase their knowledge and awareness on the topic.

In contrast, the US has chosen the path of voluntary reporting. In 2016, the last major piece of US legislation on gender pay equity (*The*

[18] See https://gender-pay-gap.service.gov.uk/.

[19] See https://gender-pay-gap.service.gov.uk/viewing/search-results?t=1&search=&orderBy=relevance.

[20] The "written statement" is not required from public authority employers unless they are not listed on Schedule 19 to the Equality Act 2010. Moreover, English law requires this statement to be signed by an "appropriate person" who will depend on the type of employer involved. For more details, see https://www.gov.uk/guidance/the-gender-pay-gap-information-employers-must-report#snapshot-date.

[21] It is a public but independent body responsible for ensuring compliance with reporting requirements and for ensuring that the published information is correct.

[22] See www.equalityhumanrights.com/en/pay-gaps/gender-pay-gap-our-enforcement-action#:~:text=Coronavirus%3A%20suspension%20on%20gender%20pay,for%20the%202019%2F20%20year.

*White House Equal Pay Gap*) was passed, urging companies to provide detailed data on their remuneration policies and the compensation paid to all workers.[23] Despite the voluntary nature of this disclosure, several US companies (including some large banks) have started to provide their data, especially in the light of the significant pressure from institutional investors. One example is the company "Pax World Management", which has assets under management totalling approximately $4.1 billion.

Finally, other countries such as Italy are in an "experimental phase". This is because they are in the process of adopting a similar piece of legislation. Italy, which is among the countries with the highest gender pay gap, is currently in the approval phase (bill No. 615 of 11 May 2018).[24] This reiterates the obligation for companies with more than 100 employees to produce a biennial report on the aspects related to equal opportunities in the workplace, including remuneration (an obligation already provided for in Article 46 of Legislative Decree No. 198 of 2006). For companies below the size threshold, the regime is voluntary. In addition, Italian law provides not only for the publication of both compliant and non-compliant companies on the website of the Ministry of Labour and Social Policies (in Italian Ministero del Lavoro e delle Politiche Sociali) but also for the possibility of obtaining an equal employment opportunity certification (a sort of "pink label" for virtuous companies). This is to be awarded to companies that comply with certain minimum parameters in terms of equal pay and work-life balance.[25]

[23] Previously, in 2009, the Obama administration promoted the Lilly Ledbetter Fair Pay Act. In 1963, John F. Kennedy signed The Equal Pay Act.

[24] This proposal introduces amendments to Article 46 of the Code of Equal Opportunities for Men and Women (Legislative Decree No. 198 of 11 April 2006) concerning the staff situation report. Further amendments to this article were also made by Legislative Decree No. 5 of 25 January 2010 implementing Directive 2006/54/EC on the principle of equal opportunities and equal treatment of men and women in matters of employment.

[25] Italian law tightens the penalties providing for the suspension of tax benefits for one year for companies that do not send their biennial report within a 12-month period. An ongoing comprehensive overview of the gender pay equality laws in force worldwide, including sanctions for non-compliant companies, is being carried out by PricewaterhouseCoopers (https://www.pwc.ch/en/insights/hr/global-gender-pay-compass.html).

### 5.4.2 *The "Gender Neutrality Principle" in Bank Remuneration Practices*

In the financial sector, the main legal act specifically addressing the issue of gender pay equality is Directive No. 878 of 2019, otherwise known as Capital Requirement Directive (CRD) V. Recital 9 recalls that "*the principle of equal pay for male and female workers for equal work or work of equal value is laid down in Article 157 of the Treaty on the Functioning of the European Union (TFEU). That principle needs to be applied in a consistent manner by institutions*". It follows that credit institutions and investment firms will be called upon (after the directive has been transposed into national law) to apply this principle consistently. This will be done by formulating and implementing a "gender-neutral remuneration policy". The concept of a "gender-neutral remuneration policy" (a novelty introduced, for the first time, by CRD V) requires the policy to be mandatorily based on equal pay for male and female workers for equal work or for work of equal value. Accordingly, banks and investment firms shall comply with this additional principle of gender neutrality in the light of the new legal provisions, thereby contributing to the pursuit of full equality among all staff. Because the EU regulation does not specify the corporate roles to which this principle should be applied, it is assumed that it extends beyond the top management to all levels of employee. At the application level, the implementation of this principle requires banks to describe the duties of their staff and to identify equal positions or positions of equal value concerning the responsibilities, activities, and time required to perform them. This analysis is also necessary to assess the level of effectiveness of the application of the principle of equal pay, particularly in the context of the periodic review of remuneration policies required for corporate bodies. The regulator requires the board of directors—and the remuneration committee, where established—to analyse gender neutrality of remuneration policies and to verify the gender pay gap and its evolution over time as part of this periodic review. In the case where inequality is evidenced, banks are required to document the reasons for the gender pay gap and to take appropriate corrective actions unless they can demonstrate that the gender pay gap is due to circumstances other than failure to apply the principle of gender pay equity. Finally, the directive also specifies that the principles and measures to be adopted by the bank to ensure the neutrality of its remuneration policies should be duly justified and formalised in the remuneration policy submitted to the shareholders' meeting.

A more comprehensive overview of how the principle of gender neutrality should be applied in the bank remuneration policy is provided by the EBA's latest guidelines on sound remuneration policies, drafted in compliance with the provisions of CRD V (EBA, 2021a).[26] First, the guidelines reiterate the meaning of this principle (as already stated in Article 157, TFEU): men and women—but also any other identified gender[27]—performing the same work, or work of equal value, are entitled to the same remuneration. This equality is not limited to the basic salary but it must extend to any other compensation, in cash or in kind, that the worker receives directly or indirectly in connection with his/her employment from his/her employer.[28] The EBA states that "*a gender neutral remuneration policy should ensure that all aspects of the remuneration policy are gender neutral, including the award and pay out conditions for remuneration*" (EBA, 2021a, p. 27). Concerning the fixed part of the remuneration, in compliance with the principle of pay neutrality, it should reflect the professional experience, organisational responsibility, level of education, seniority, skills, and expertise possessed by the individual employee, as well as any external constraints (economic and/or cultural) including the salary level of the geographical area in which he/she resides.

As for the scope of application of this principle, the guidelines expressly state that it applies to all staff members, and therefore not only to members of the bank's management and control bodies. In addition, the

[26] The latest EBA document—while recalling the Charter of Fundamental Rights of the European Union, the European Convention for the Protection of Human Rights and Fundamental Freedoms, and the Universal Declaration of Human Rights—reiterates the need to avoid any discrimination in working conditions by ensuring equal opportunities for all genders at all levels including succession plans, training policies, and career prospects. See EBA (2021a).

[27] This refers, for example, to transgender people. As stated by the EBA, "*the principle of gender neutrality should apply to all genders*" (EBA, 2021a, p. 90).

[28] However, the principle of equal treatment does not prevent Member States from maintaining or adopting measures providing for specific advantages in order to make it easier for the underrepresented sex to pursue a vocational activity or to prevent or compensate for disadvantages in professional careers.

gender-neutral remuneration principle should promote sound and effective risk management. This means that it should contribute to ensuring that the bank's remuneration policy is consistent both with the overall business strategy and, above all, with all the main financial and non-financial risks (credit, market, operational, liquidity, reputational risks, etc.) that are assumed by the bank. At the same time, financial institutions are required to ensure that their remuneration policies are gender-neutral, especially where contracts are formalised on an individual basis.[29] In particular:

(a) Financial institutions have the responsibility of demonstrating that their remuneration policy is gender-neutral. This implies that where there are substantial differences between the average remunerations of male and female staff or members of the management body, institutions are required to document the main reasons demonstrating that the difference does not result from a non-gender-neutral remuneration policy (EBA, 2020b).
(b) Financial institutions are required to document and describe individual job positions, to define salary categories, or to set up a job classification system that considers the type of activities and tasks assigned to each staff member. This must be in agreement with the principle of gender equality. It is noteworthy to mention that such a system allows both the bank itself and the supervisory authorities to monitor the application of the principle of equal pay concerning gender more effectively.
(c) The gender pay gap should be constantly monitored as part of the review of the remuneration policy, which falls under the responsibility of the supervisory function and the remuneration committee (if there is one). In addition, this review should take place separately for members of the management body, identified staff,[30] and other staff.

[29] In contrast, if remuneration is subject to collective bargaining where pay contracts are applicable regardless of the sex of the staff, it is easier to check whether remuneration policies are applied in a gender-neutral manner. However, the EBA specifies that it is up to the financial institution to ensure that its remuneration policies are gender-neutral as this is not the responsibility of the social partners (EBA, 2021a).

[30] By identified staff the EBA means those members of staff whose professional activities have a material impact on the bank's risk profile. For more details, see EBA (2021b).

(d) For such monitoring, banks may use the annual gross remuneration of the staff as the measuring unit. This should be based not only on the remuneration awarded but also on the working time arrangements, on the holiday time awarded, and on any other financial and non-financial benefits. This calculation should be made separately for each country in which the bank operates.
(e) Financial institutions should have policies in place that facilitate the reintegration of staff after maternity, paternity, or parental leave.

Other provisions appear to be less binding as they are left to the bank's decision. More specifically, when determining staff remuneration, the EBA states that such institutions may (but are not obliged to) consider, in a gender-neutral manner, other aspects including:

(a) the employees' level of education, skills, commitment and responsibility, the work performed, and the nature of the tasks involved;
(b) the work location and the local cost of living;
(c) the hierarchical level of the staff and whether the staff have managerial responsibilities;
(d) the scarcity of staff available in the labour market for specialised positions;
(e) the nature of the employment contract (whether it is open-ended or fixed-term);
(f) the professional experience of the staff and whether they hold any professional certifications;
(g) specific benefits, including the payment of any family and additional child allowances to staff members with spouses and dependants.

These derogations are foreseen because, in essence, the EBA accepts that some pay differentiation is possible, although it should not lead to discrimination.

Finally, other provisions are directly addressed to the competent authorities supervising credit institutions. These authorities are responsible for ensuring compliance with the principle of gender pay equality by the financial institutions that they supervise. More specifically, supervisors should ensure that the remuneration policies, practices, and processes of financial institutions are adequate and periodically reviewed, so that:

(a) governance arrangements and processes for the design and monitoring of the remuneration policy are in place;
(b) there is an adequate exchange of information among all internal bodies and functions, as well as within the team involved in the design, implementation, and monitoring of the remuneration policy;
(c) an annual review of remuneration policies and practices and its main outcomes, including whether the remuneration policy is gender-neutral, is implemented;
(d) a remuneration committee with sufficient powers and resources to perform its functions is established (especially where required by a regulator);
(e) remuneration policies are developed taking into account internal capital and liquidity adequacy assessment processes.

## 5.5 What Can Banks Do to Reduce Their Gender Pay Gap?

As the reduction of GPG is universally required by supervisory authorities, policymakers, investors, and stakeholders, banks are facing the unavoidable challenge of revising their remuneration policies. Although there are several actions and strategies to be taken in this regard, perhaps the most relevant is to address underlying prejudice and discrimination by introducing cultural change. Only once gender equality has become part of a solid cultural basis, strategies to reduce the gender pay gap can truly bear fruit. Examples of such actions are as follows (Greenfield et al., 2016):

1. Conducting a regular process of self-assessment of the gender pay gap. It would be suitable for banks to conduct, at least annually, an in-depth analysis of their gender pay gap. In conducting this analysis, it is important to distinguish between fixed and variable pay, the latter being the most affected in the total remuneration. In addition, it would be advisable not to use simplistic approaches based on averages of salaries paid or on the difference between means. Instead, a robust statistical approach, such as multiple regression, would ensure that legitimate differences in pay, job-related skills, performance, experience, education, and so on are adequately taken into account.

2. Redefining—and periodically reviewing—the roles and functions attributed to all employees. This makes it easier to set up homogeneous groups of employees of different sexes with the same functions and implement more accurate monitoring of the gender pay gap.
3. Implementing a monitoring and remediation system focused on the gender pay gap. Equally important is the management of the pay gap. To this end, banks should identify a team dedicated exclusively to assessing and monitoring this gap. The team (or the remuneration committee) should conduct (or oversee) the pay equity assessment, identify groups with unexplained pay gaps, conduct targeted research on specific employees potentially requiring a pay adjustment, document explanations for making (or not making) adjustments, and ensure that adjustments are being made.
4. Increasing disclosure and reporting on the gender pay gap both within the firm and externally. Disclosure is a powerful tool for alignment since it makes the participants in an organisation aware of the existence of the gap and induces management to address it. Otherwise, it may become difficult to recruit high-level and competent staff.

## References

Alkadry, M. G., & Tower, L. E. (2006). Unequal pay: The role of gender. *Public Administration Review, 66*(6), 888–898. https://www.jstor.org/stable/4096605

Alkalbani, N., Cuomo, F., & Mallin, C. (2019). Gender diversity and say-on-pay: Evidence from UK remuneration committees. *Corporate Governance: An International Review, 27*(5), 378–400. https://doi.org/10.1111/corg.12292

Amado, C. A. F., Santos, S. P., & São José, J. M. S. (2018). Measuring and decomposing the gender pay gap: A new frontier approach. *European Journal of Operational Research, 271*(1), 357–373. https://doi.org/10.1016/j.ejor.2018.05.023

Amadxarif, Z., Angeli, M., Haldane, A. G., & Zemaityte, G. (2020, July). *Understanding pay gaps* (Staff Working Paper No. 877). Bank of England.

Austin, C. R., Bobek, D. D., & Harris, L. L. (2021). Does information about gender pay matter to investors? An experimental investigation. *Accounting,*

*Organizations and Society, 90*, 101193. https://doi.org/10.1016/j.aos.2020.101193

Bargain, O., Doorley, K., & Van Kerm, P. (2019). Minimum wages and the gender gap in pay: New evidence from the UK and Ireland. *Review of Income and Wealth, 65*(3), 514–539. https://doi.org/10.1111/roiw.12384

Bell, B., & Reenen, J. V. (2014). Bankers and their bonuses. *Economic Journal, 124*(574), F1–F21. https://doi.org/10.1111/ecoj.12101

Bennedsen, M., Simintzi, E., Tsoutsoura, M., & Wolfenzon, D. (2019). *Do firms respond to gender pay gap transparency?* (NBER working papers 25435). https://doi.org/10.3386/w25435

Bergmann, N., Scheele, A., & Sorger, C. (2019). Variations of the same? A sectoral analysis of the gender pay gap in Germany and Austria. *Gender Work & Organization, 26*(5), 668–687. https://doi.org/10.1111/gwao.12299

Blau, F. D., & Kahn, L. M. (2017). The gender wage gap: Extent, trends, and explanations. *Journal of Economic Literature, 55*(3), 789–865. https://doi.org/10.1257/jel.20160995

Boll, C., & Lagemann, A. (2019). The gender pay gap in EU countries—New evidence based on EU-SES 2014 data. *Intereconomics, 54*(2), 101–105. https://doi.org/10.1007/s10272-019-0802-7

Butcher, T., Mumford, K., & Smith, P. N. (2016, September). *Workplaces, low pay and the gender earnings gap in Britain* (Report for the Low Pay Commission). https://pure.york.ac.uk/portal/files/49861737/LPC_low_pay_and_gender_gaps.pdf

Chamberlain, A. (2016). *Demystifying the gender pay gap: Evidence from Glassdoor salary data*. Glassdoor. https://www.glassdoor.com/research/app/uploads/sites/2/2016/03/Glassdoor-Gender-Pay-Gap-Study-3.pdf

Costa Dias, M., Joyce, R., & Parodi, F. (2018, February). *The gender pay gap in the UK: Children and experience in work* (Institute for Fiscal Studies Working Paper 18/02). https://ifs.org.uk/uploads/publications/wps/MCD_RJ_FP_GenderPayGap.pdf

Del Monte, M. (2013). *European added value assessment: Application of the principle of equal pay for men and women for equal work of equal value*. European Parliament. https://op.europa.eu/en/publication-detail/-/publication/98a2b7d9-eb87-490b-81cb-987deea0d078

Dell'Atti, A., Intonti, M., & Iannuzzi, A. P. (2013). The effectiveness of remuneration committees in European banks: Regulation and best practices. *Journal of Financial Regulation and Compliance, 21*(4), 373–396. https://doi.org/10.1108/JFRC-11-2012-0046

EBA—European Banking Authority. (2020a). *Report on the Benchmarking of Diversity Practices at European Union level Under Article 91(11) of Directive 2013/36/EU (2018 data)*. EBA/REP/2020/05.

EBA—European Banking Authority. (2020b, October 29). *Consultation Paper on Draft Guidelines on sound remuneration policies under Directive 2013/36/EU*. EBA/CP/2020/24.

EBA—European Banking Authority. (2021a, July 2). *Draft guidelines on internal governance under Directive 2013/36/EU*. EBA/GL/2021/05.

EBA—European Banking Authority. (2021b, January 21). *Draft Regulatory Technical Standards on criteria to identify categories of staff whose professional activities have a material impact on an investment firm's risk profile or assets it manages under Directive (EU) 2019/2034 (IFD) of the European Parliament and of the Council on the prudential supervision of investment firms*. EBA/RTS/2021/02.

EC—European Commission. (2021). *2021 report on gender equality in the EU*.

Goldin, C. (2014). A grand gender convergence: Its last chapter. *American Economic Review, 104*(4), 1091–1119. https://doi.org/10.1257/aer.104.4.1091

Greenfield, G., Levine, B., & Gaertner, S. (2016). *Pay equity in financial services*. Mercer Institute. https://www.oliverwyman.com/content/dam/oliver-wyman/global/en/2016/june/WiFS/WiFS_2016_PAYEQUITY_Pages.pdf

Healy, G., & Ahamed, M. M. (2019). Gender pay gap, voluntary interventions and recession: The case of the British financial services sector. *British Journal of Industrial Relations, 57*(2), 302–327. https://doi.org/10.1111/bjir.12448

Jarrell, S. B., & Stanley, T. D. (2004). Declining bias and gender wage discrimination? A meta-regression analysis. *Journal of Human Resources, 39*(3), 828–838. https://doi.org/10.2307/3558999

Lewis, G. B., & Oh, S. S. (2009). A major difference? Fields of study and male-female pay differences in federal employment. *The American Review of Public Administration, 39*(2), 107–124. https://doi.org/10.1177/0275074008317158

Leythienne, D., & Ronkowski, P (2018). *A decomposition of the unadjusted gender pay gap using structure of earnings survey data* (Statistical Working Paper EUROSTAT). https://ec.europa.eu/eurostat/documents/3888793/8979317/KS-TC-18-003-EN-N.pdf/3a6c9295-5e66-4b79-b009-ea1604770676

Owen, A. L., & Temesvary, J. (2019). CEO compensation, pay inequality, and the gender diversity of bank board of directors. *Finance Research Letters, 30*, 276–279. https://doi.org/10.1016/j.frl.2018.10.010

PWC. (2019). *Gender pay gap reporting—Spotlight on banking*. https://www.pwc.co.uk/services/human-resource-services/gender-pay/spotlight-on-banking.html

Schneider, M., Iseke, A., & Pull, K. (2021). The gender pay gap in European executive boards: The role of executives' pathway into the board. *The International Journal of Human Resource Management, 32*(14), 2952–2974. https://doi.org/10.1080/09585192.2019.1620307

Stanley, T. D., & Jarrell, S. B. (1998). Gender wage discrimination bias? A meta-regression analysis. *Journal of Human Resources, 33*(4), 947–973. https://doi.org/10.2307/146404

United Nations. (2002). *Gender mainstreaming: An overview*. New York. https://www.un.org/womenwatch/osagi/pdf/e65237.pdf

Usmonova, N. (2020). *Gender pay gap in the banking sector: Has the great recession changed the obvious?* Eastern Michigan University. https://osf.io/preprints/socarxiv/hgzev/download

Vieito, J. P. T. (2012). Gender, top management compensation gap, and company performance: Tournament versus behavioral theory. *Corporate Governance: An International Review, 20*(1), 46–63. https://doi.org/10.1111/j.1467-8683.2011.00878.x

WEF—World Economic Forum. (2021, March). *Global gender gap report*.

Weichselbaumer, D., & Winter-Ebmer, R. (2005). A meta-analysis of the international gender wage gap. *Journal of Economic Surveys, 19*(3), 479–511. https://doi.org/10.1111/j.0950-0804.2005.00256.x

Woodward, A. E. (2001). *Gender mainstreaming in European policy: Innovation or deception?* (WZB Discussion Paper, No. FS I 01-103). Berlin. https://www.econstor.eu/bitstream/10419/44052/1/345123883.pdf

Yanadori, Y., Gould, J. A., & Kulik, C. T. (2018). A fair go? The gender pay gap among corporate executives in Australian firms. *The International Journal of Human Resource Management, 29*(9), 1636–1660. https://doi.org/10.1080/09585192.2016.1255985

Yildirmaz, A., Ryan, C., & Nezaj, J. (2019). *State of the workforce report: Pay, promotions and retention*. The ADP Research Institute. https://www.adpri.org/wp-content/uploads/2020/07/19220244/The-State-of-the-Workforce-Full-Research-Report-2019.pdf

CHAPTER 6

# Gender Diversity in the Insurance Industry: Progress Made and Next Steps

**Abstract** This chapter aims to analyse gender diversity in the insurance sector. It consists of three sections. The first section presents the main evidence from the existing studies and research conducted so far only on insurance companies. The second section reports some data on the current presence of women in the workforce of these financial institutions including managerial and top positions. Finally, the third section highlights the progress that this sector is making towards greater gender equality by presenting three leading insurance companies in the European market (Axa, Zurich Insurance, and Assicurazioni Generali) that are particularly attentive to advancing gender diversity.

## 6.1 Introduction

Addressing gender diversity in the insurance industry is not an easy task. Unlike banks, insurance institutions still seem to receive limited attention from policymakers, practitioners, and academics. Moreover,

---

This chapter is the result of the joint efforts of the two authors. However, Giuliana Birindelli mainly contributed to Sect. 6.3 and Antonia Patrizia Iannuzzi to Sects. 6.1, 6.2, 6.4.



G. Birindelli and A. P. Iannuzzi, *Women in Financial Services*, Palgrave Macmillan Studies in Banking and Financial Institutions, https://doi.org/10.1007/978-3-030-93471-2_6

the insurance regulator (*European Insurance and Occupational Pensions Authority, EIOPA*) appears to have not yet introduced the gender diversity dimension in its recommendations, rules, and standards on corporate governance. To date, the only indication concerning the gender pay gap in pensions (i.e., the difference in retirement income between men and women) was formulated by the Occupational Pensions Stakeholder Group in June 2020 (OPSG, 2020). This is in addition to the diversity of competencies of board members, in terms of knowledge and expertise, provided by the International Association of Insurance Supervisors (IAIS, 2018). There is still much work ahead. In this chapter, we aim to offer an overall picture of women's empowerment and representation in the insurance sector, describing the lights and shadows of this still unexplored topic. To this end, after a brief review of the literature, the chapter presents data on the main roles played by women in the insurance sector and their representation in the corporate governance of a global representative sample of reinsurance and insurance companies (henceforth referred to as re/insurers). Finally, it closes with a discussion on a few interesting and innovative gender diversity initiatives recently put in place by three leading global insurance companies.

## 6.2 Gender Diversity in Insurance Companies: Evidence from the Literature

As shown in Chapter 3, a large body of literature has analysed the effects of board gender diversity (BGD) on bank outcomes in terms of economic-financial performance, risk profile, sustainability results, technical efficiency, and other outcomes. Only a few works so far have investigated these relationships for the insurance industry (Boubakri, 2011). Aside from the information on the size and percentage of outside directors, there is scarce evidence on female representation on the board of insurance firms or women in apical/management positions (Anderloni et al., 2020). Yet, even in the insurance sector, the quality of governance systems, including the efficiency of the board of directors, plays a crucial role in improving economic performance, in attracting more capital and in capturing the institutional investors' interest. For example, the Solvency II Directive (for EU insurance companies) affirms that "*Member States shall require all insurance and reinsurance undertakings to have in place an effective system of governance which provides for sound and prudent management of the business*" (Article 41, Section 2, Chapter IV of the

Directive 2009/138/EC). It is well known that a greater board diversity, inclusive of gender diversity, could improve the efficiency of this body and thus the company's performance (IAIS, 2018).

The few studies conducted so far on the insurance sector reveal the scant presence of female directors and a lack of significant relationships between BGD and corporate performance. These aspects could be interrelated. Given the scarce representativeness of women in management positions, women might not be able to exert a decisive influence on company decisions as stated by Venuti and Alfiero (2016). In their study conducted on 126 European insurance companies from 2009 to 2013, the authors do not find any significant relationship between BGD and the risk-taking attitude of these institutions. It is no coincidence that women directors in the insurance firms analysed are only 23% on average (less than 1 in 4 directors is a woman). Likewise, Fekadu (2015) focusing on 10 Ethiopian insurance companies over the 2007–2014 period, finds that women directors are absent on the board of directors of many companies and represent on average only 13% of the board members in the companies where they are present. Moreover, this author finds that the performance of these insurance companies, measured by return on assets (ROA), is not affected by the board's gender diversity. This again shows that women directors are too few to be able to exercise any influence over corporate outcomes. Different results are found in a more recent study carried out by Pavić Kramarić et al. (2018). These authors, indeed, document that both a greater presence of women directors and a female chair of the supervisory board of the insurance companies significantly and negatively affect the performance of the firms as measured by ROA. This analysis, covering all insurance companies operating in Croatia from 2007 to 2013, does not speak in favour of greater gender diversity in the top positions in the insurance industry. To the best of our knowledge, the only academic study that finds a positive influence of board gender diversity on the performance of insurance companies is the one by Garba and Abubakar (2014). This study, however, suffers from some limitations, namely the sample composition (only 12 listed insurance companies), the country analysed (Nigeria, which is an emerging economy), and the outdated time window (2004–2009).

Yet, when the analysis is extended to larger samples, the effect is confirmed. Research by the Swiss Re Institute, focused on a sample of 170 global insurance, reinsurance, and insurance brokerage companies from 2002 to 2019 and based on Refinitiv ESG data, finds that a higher share of women on company boards and in C-suite positions is associated with a return on equity (ROE) outperformance. In more detail, an insurance company that moves from a low to a high share of women in leadership positions gains 3 to 4 percentage points (ppt) of ROE outperformance compared to the industry average ROE. The benefits are stronger when re/insurers add one or more women to an all-male leadership team. In this case, the increase in ROE is greater than and equal to 3–5 ppt above the industry average (Fan et al., 2021).

Some of the recent evidence speaks in favour of a greater representation of women in the governance of insurance companies. Moreover, numerous positive findings in the banking sector give reason to believe that similar evidence can also be found for insurance companies. We hope that scholars become more involved in this research line in the light of both the growing importance of these institutions in the financial system (especially in the wake of the COVID-19 pandemic) and the increased importance attributed by supervisory authorities to the corporate governance systems of insurance companies.

## 6.3 An Overall Picture of the Gender Diversity in the Insurance Sector

Some research documents that women are significantly underrepresented in board and executive positions in the re/insurance industry. A recent investigation conducted by SpencerStuart (Dubrow et al., 2019) on the top management teams in 29 US insurance companies (16 property and casualty insurers, and 13 life insurers) points out that women make up more than 25% of the executives in only about 10% of companies (3 out of 29, all in life insurance). Additionally, on average, female senior executives represent only 18%. This last position is higher in life insurance companies (20%) than in property and casualty (P&C) companies (16%). Moreover, the figures in Table 6.1 evidence a strong divergence between the roles played by men and women. While men mainly perform "hard tasks" (finance, actuarial, risk, and so on) requiring a technical background, women primarily perform management functions (human resources and general management). This divergence raises a further issue related to gender diversity in the insurance industry, i.e., the lack of specialised technical training among women which may hinder their career paths, and thus the opportunity to reach senior/leadership positions.

**Table 6.1** Functional roles of men and women in the US insurance sector (% values)

| | *Men* | *Women* |
|---|---|---|
| *Human Resources* | 79 | 21 |
| *General Management* | 80 | 20 |
| *Legal* | 90 | 10 |
| *Marketing* | 92 | 8 |
| *Finance* | 93 | 7 |
| *Operations/Technology* | 94 | 6 |
| *Investments* | 94 | 6 |
| *Multiple Functions* | 96 | 4 |
| *Product/Underwriting* | 98 | 2 |
| *Sales/Distribution* | 98 | 2 |
| *Actuarial* | 99 | 1 |
| *Innovation* | 99 | 1 |
| *Risk* | 99 | 1 |
| *Other* | 91 | 9 |

*Source* Dubrow et al. (2019)

Another study by the Swiss Re Institute based on a much larger sample (about 400 insurers and 29 reinsurance companies located in the 12 largest insurance international markets) displays similar findings (Fan et al., 2021). On average, at the end of 2019, women represent only about 23% of C-suite executives, 10% of CEOs, and they chair just 8% of boards of re/insurance companies globally. Except for the share of women as board chairs, women's representation in apical positions is higher in the life insurance segments compared to the non-life ones. The advanced insurance markets show more progress towards board gender diversity compared to emerging insurance markets. Among the advanced markets, France has the highest ratio of women executives (40.6%), whereas New Zealand and Australia have, respectively, the highest ratio of women CEOs (22.7%) and women chairs (23.7%). However, this progress is still far from closing the large gap between women employees and women in top positions. This is a critical issue for the entire financial system—banks included (see Chapter 4). As Table 6.2 shows, most of the insurance markets analysed have a proportion of women employees above 50%, whereas the percentages of women in top positions are on average much lower.

In the last decade, there has been an important advancement. From 2010 to 2019, the percentage of women on the boards and executive committees across 170 global insurance companies increased by 100% and

**Table 6.2** Proportion of women as CEOs, C-suite executives, board chairpersons, and in the workforce of insurance companies (year 2019; % values)

| *Insurance* | *Share of women as CEOs* | | | *Share of women as C-suite executives* | | | *Share of women as board chairpersons* | | | *Women in the workforce* |
|---|---|---|---|---|---|---|---|---|---|---|
| | *Non-life* | *Life* | *Average* | *Non-life* | *Life* | *Average* | *Non-life* | *Life* | *Average* | *Insurance* |
| *France* | 11.8 | 11.8 | 11.8 | 19.4 | 53.6 | 40.6 | 10.0 | 22.2 | 15.8 | 60.8 |
| *New Zealand* | 7.1 | 50.0 | 22.7 | 31.3 | 39.0 | 35.5 | 10.0 | 10.0 | 10.0 | 53.4# |
| *Italy* | 10.0 | 5.6 | 7.9 | 26.0 | 34.6 | 29.3 | 11.1 | 0 | 5.0 | 45.1* |
| *Australia* | 5.6 | 6.3 | 5.9 | 24.6 | 33.3 | 29.0 | 25.0 | 22.3 | 23.7 | 56.5# |
| *US* | 5.0 | 16.7 | 10.5 | 21.1 | 26.9 | 23.8 | 10.0 | 10.1 | 10.1 | 60.1 |
| *UK* | 14.3 | 15.8 | 15.2 | 28.8 | 20.2 | 24.1 | 0 | 0 | 0 | 45.0* |
| *Canada* | 18.8 | 5.3 | 11.4 | 31.2 | 32.4 | 31.7 | 11.8 | 11.1 | 11.4 | 57.7#* |
| *Germany* | 5.0 | 10.0 | 7.5 | 12.6 | 24.2 | 19.3 | 10.0 | 0 | 5.0 | 51.4* |
| *China* | 0 | 22.2 | 10.5 | 14.2 | 19.7 | 16.9 | 0 | 10.1 | 5.1 | 52.0 |
| *Japan* | 5.3 | 0 | 2.6 | 10.6 | 17.7 | 14.5 | 0 | 0 | 0 | 51.3* |
| *India* | 10.0 | 5.0 | 7.5 | 14.5 | 11.2 | 13.0 | 16.7 | 0 | 8.4 | 38.3 |
| *Brazil* | 7.1 | 0 | 3.3 | 11.8 | 5.5 | 10.4 | 0 | 16.7 | 8.4 | 55.6 |
| **Reinsurance** | – | – | 7.4 | – | – | 17.5 | – | – | 3.6 | – |
| ***Overall average*** | **8.0** | **10.6** | **9.6** | **20.2** | **26.3** | **22.7** | **8.7** | **7.8** | **8.0** | – |
| ***Advanced markets*** | **9.7** | **11.0** | **10.4** | **22.9** | **29.9** | **25.6** | **9.7** | **8.1** | **8.3** | – |
| ***Emerging markets*** | **5.9** | **9.3** | **7.2** | **13.5** | **13.2** | **13.8** | **5.9** | **6.8** | **7.1** | – |

*Notes* % values concern a sample of about 400 insurance and 29 reinsurance companies based on information published on the company website and/or in their annual reports. C-suite refers to the executive-level managers within a company, commonly including chief executive officer (CEO), chief financial officer (CFO), chief operating officer (COO), and chief information officer (CIO), as well as other managers included both in the "Management Team" and "Executive Team". #2020 data. *The share of female employment in the insurance and financial sectors combined

*Source* Fan et al. (2021)

70%, respectively (Fan et al., 2021). The "formula" for expanding gender diversity in the insurance industry is no different from that of other financial institutions: adopting gender-related hiring plans, supporting women in their career advancement, expanding flexible working systems, etc. However, even more important is to achieve an optimal synergy between individual company programmes and industry-wide initiatives. Only in this way will women be encouraged to view insurance as a rewarding career choice where they can find the same opportunities for growth that men traditionally enjoy.

## 6.4 Gender Diversity in Some Leading Insurance Companies

In this section, we intend to put forward a brief description of the most important gender diversity initiatives implemented by three of the leading global insurance companies. Reading their documents, we can notice a deep commitment towards the empowerment of women. It should be noted that the following analysis is not to be considered an exhaustive description of all gender diversity strategies and activities implemented by the three insurance companies.

### *6.4.1 AXA*

Among the main insurers that are leaders in promoting gender diversity, one example is the French multinational insurance company AXA. Also offering investment management and other financial services, this leading global insurer boasts remarkable figures: 160,000 employees and 105 million service users in over 54 countries. Corporate documents and the AXA website offer a wealth of interesting information on the gender diversity approach promoted by this company over the last few years. We were readily able to determine the significant progress undertaken by AXA in at least four areas related to gender equality: (a) women's representation on board and in apical positions, (b) the gender pay gap, (c) gender policies and certifications, and (d) other specific women-empowering initiatives. Concerning the first area, AXA has increased its percentage of female representation in senior executive positions by 25% over the past ten years (from 9% in 2009 to 24% in 2016, and 34% in 2020). The ambition is to reach equal representation at the top levels of governance by 2023. To date, female representation in the AXA workplace is considerable, featuring a majority of female employees (54%), a 34% female representation in the Global Leadership Network (the top 250 senior executives working in AXA Group), and a 62.5% representation on the board of directors. In the same vein, to shatter the glass ceiling, AXA has introduced gender equality criteria in its recruitment processes. For example, for each senior position, there must be at least one man and one woman among the shortlisted applicants. Moreover, gender balance is now a goal shared by all CEOs among AXA's entities. Finally, local targets for women's representation at the executive level have also been defined.

Other remarkable advancements include the pay equity between men and women. AXA aims to ensure that every employee is equitably remunerated across the organisation regardless of gender. Many of AXA's entities are progressing towards, or have already reached, pay equity so that the current global potential pay gap is low, at 2%. Here, too, AXA claims to have a very ambitious goal: to remove all unjustified pay gaps with dedicated budgets and to reach full pay equity across all the group entities by 2023 at the latest.

As for gender policies, AXA has not only adopted a specific "Inclusion and Diversity Policy" focused on six areas of priority (gender, LGBT+, disability, origins, multi-generations, and mental health) but in 2017, it also implemented a global parent policy to allow all employees to seek professional and personal balance. Specifically, this policy entitles new parents in all AXA entities worldwide to receive a minimum of 16 weeks and 4 weeks of fully paid maternity and paternity leave, respectively. This is an important tool for increasing the well-being in the workplace and the women's employment rate. This parental policy allows women to avoid leaving their jobs due to their family needs. This has a positive impact also on the gender pay gap (which consequently may tend to lower).

Moreover, in September 2016, AXA launched a specific initiative—"Women in Insurance." This is a full-range approach aimed at increasing the level of women's access to insurance products and services that respond to their needs and expectations. Two years later, in December 2018, it subscribed to the Women's Empowerment Principles (WEPs), which involve seven principles to promote gender equality in the company workforce (see Chapter 2).

Finally, other three important milestones achieved more recently by AXA are: (a) its inclusion for the fourth time in the Bloomberg Gender-Equality Index, (b) its partnership, for the fourth consecutive year, with the "Women's Forum", an international event devoted to ideas and solutions for unleashing women's leadership in the economy and society, and (c) the acquisition (from September 2016) of the Economic Dividends for Gender Equality (EDGE) certification (see Chapter 2), becoming the first French-based global financial services player to be awarded the certification.

### 6.4.2 *Zurich Insurance*

Another European insurance company that is strongly committed to gender diversity is Zurich Insurance Group, a leading multiline insurer headquartered in Zurich (Switzerland) with 55,000 employees in about 215 countries and territories (Zurich Insurance Group, 2020a). Table 6.3 displays female and male representation in the Zurich workplace. Overall, the presence of women in various roles is significant, although it is often lower than that of men. At the end of 2020, women occupied almost 33% of senior management positions, 46% of junior management positions, and 39% of managerial roles. All these percentages are higher than the corresponding values for 2018.

One very interesting and noteworthy initiative is the "Equal Pay for Equivalent Work" (EPEW) policy. It is aimed at ensuring that men and

**Table 6.3** Gender diversity in the workplace at Zurich Insurance Group (data as of 31 December 2018 and 2020; % values)

| | *Men* | *Women* | |
|---|---|---|---|
| | *2020* | *2018* | *2020* |
| Workforce | 49.7 | NA | 50.3 |
| Senior management[a] | 67.4 | 30.7 | 32.6 |
| Junior management | 53.6 | 45.1 | 46.4 |
| Managers | 61.1 | 38.4 | 38.9 |
| Revenue-producing roles[b] | 63.1 | NA | 36.9 |
| STEM workforce[c] | 67.2 | NA | 32.9 |

*Notes* [a]Employees who either report to collaborators of the CEO or directly to the group CEO. [b]Employees working in "Claims", "Underwriting", "Sales and Distribution", or "Life Technical Functions". [c]Employees working in "Risk Engineering", "Engineering and Technology", "Actuarial, Pricing and Analytics", "Application Development", "Platform Management", and "Infrastructure"
*Source* Authors' elaboration on data from Zurich Insurance Group (2020b)

women get equal pay for equivalent work or roles. In detail, this policy has 4 phases:

1. *Commitment*: the application of fair remuneration extended to all resources and processes put in place by Zurich Insurance Group.
2. *Salary Analysis*: all Zurich business units with over 100 employees conduct statistical analyses to measure the impact of gender on the salary disparities and to identify any potential salary differences.
3. *Achievement*: if no pay differences are identified, business units obtain the internal EPEW achievement label.
4. *Monitoring*: when remuneration is not in line with the "equal pay for equivalent work" principle, corrective actions are implemented.

Another interesting initiative implemented in 2012 is the "Women's Innovation Network" (WIN). It is a global employee resource group focused on women and related issues. The WIN's main objective is to meet all female employees and to enable them to share their experiences and needs. By joining such a network, women can benefit from personal and professional support, especially in their career development. Finally, Zurich Insurance Group has also recently introduced a novel parental policy that provides 16 weeks of paid leave for a primary parent and 6 weeks of paid leave for a co-parent. Since 2019, it has also been included in both the "Bloomberg Gender-Equality Index" and the "Forbes list of America's Best Employers for Diversity".

### *6.4.3 Assicurazioni Generali*

Moving to Italy, one leading insurance company on gender diversity issues is Assicurazioni Generali. Established in 1831, this institution currently has more than 72,000 employees and serves 65.9 million service users in about 50 countries worldwide (Assicurazioni Generali, 2021a). First, it features a significant presence of women in its governance bodies. At the end of 2020, the board was made up of 38% women, in addition to 60% women in the risk committee, and 43% in the nomination and remuneration committees. All these committees were chaired by women (Assicurazioni Generali, 2021b). Currently, the level of female representation in managerial positions is 35% (Table 6.4) but the company intends to bring this up to 38% by the end of 2021. To achieve this

**Table 6.4** Gender diversity at Assicurazioni Generali (data as of 31 December of each year; % values)

| *Gender indicator* | *2018* | *2019* | *2020* |
|---|---|---|---|
| Women on the board | 38.4 | 38.4 | 38.4 |
| Women top executives | 11.5 | 16.7 | 16.7 |
| Women managers | 30.0 | 32.4 | 34.8 |
| Women employees | 50.8 | 51.0 | 51.0 |
| Equal pay gap | NA | NA | −2.8 |
| Gender pay gap | NA | NA | −13.9 |
| Accessibility gap to variable remuneration | NA | NA | −5.1 |

*Note* The three indicators for the pay gap (equal pay gap, gender pay gap, and accessibility gap to variable remuneration) refer to about 80% of the total number of employees
*Source* Authors' elaboration on data from Assicurazioni Generali (2019, 2020, 2021a)

goal and to improve the representation of women in leadership positions, Assicurazioni Generali has launched two programmes at the group level, specifically (a) Lioness Acceleration Program, an 18-month journey for female senior managers who are supported through mentoring and coaching and by a panel of international experts on leadership topics, and (b) Elevate, a 12-week programme for female managers including six webinars and two live sessions. The two programmes are complemented by more than 60 actions launched at the local level, such as the Women Mentoring and STEM (Science, Technology, Engineering, and Mathematics) Women Recruitment Programmes.

Concerning the gender pay gap, Assicurazioni Generali has recently adopted an innovative approach. In 2020, it conducted specific assessments to verify the existence of this type of discrimination and establish strategies to eradicate any cases emerging from the analyses. The measures used to assess the pay gap at the group level are: (a) the "equal pay gap", i.e., the pay gap by gender for comparable roles (median base salary of women compared to that of men), (b) the "gender pay gap", i.e., the pay gap by gender across the entire organisation regardless of role (median base salary of women compared to that of men), and (c) the "access to the variable", i.e., the accessibility gap to variable remuneration between women and men, that is, the difference between the rate of access to variable remuneration for women and men. At the end of 2020, in Assicurazioni Generali, the median base salary of women was −2.8% than that of men for comparable roles, while the pay gap calculated regardless of the role was much higher and equal to −13.9%. Additionally, women suffered from discrimination in terms of access to variable payments (Table 6.4).

## References

Anderloni, L., Moro, O., & Tanda, A. (2020). Governance and performance in insurance companies: A bibliometric analysis and a meta-analysis. *International Journal of Economics and Finance, 12*(11), 1–20. https://doi.org/10.5539/ijef.v12n11p1

Assicurazioni Generali. (2019). Annual integrated report and consolidated financial statements 2018, April.

Assicurazioni Generali. (2020). Annual integrated report and consolidated financial statements 2019, April.

Assicurazioni Generali. (2021a). Annual integrated report and consolidated financial statements 2020, April.

Assicurazioni Generali. (2021b). Corporate governance and share ownership report 2020, March.

Boubakri, N. (2011). Corporate governance and issues from the insurance industry. *Journal of Risk and Insurance, 78*(3), 501–518. https://www.jstor.org/stable/23019980

Dubrow, A., Pieroni, B., & Reed, P. (2019). *Increasing gender diversity in insurance leadership. Lessons from women who reached the C-Suite. Spencer Stuart-ACORD.* Retrieved from https://www.acord.org/docs/default-source/research-public/increasing-gender-diversity-in-insurance-leadership.pdf

Fan, I., Krueger, F., Grujovic, A., & Hartmann, J. (2021, February). Gender diversity in the re/insurance industry: For a sustainable future, Swiss Re Institute.

Fekadu, G. W. (2015). Corporate governance on financial performance of insurance industry. *Corporate Ownership & Control, 13*(1–10), 1201–1209. https://doi.org/10.22495/cocv13i1c10p7

Garba, T., & Abubakar, B. A. (2014). Corporate board diversity and financial performance of insurance companies in Nigeria. *Asian Economic and Financial Review, 4*(2), 257–277.

IAIS—International Association of Insurance Supervisors. (2018, November). *Application paper on the composition and the role of the board.* Retrieved from https://www.iaisweb.org/file/77741/application-paper-on-the-composition-and-the-role-of-the-board

OPSG—Occupational Pensions Stakeholder Group. (2020, June 24). *Advice on practices to reduce the gender gap in pension.* Retrieved from https://www.eiopa.europa.eu/sites/default/files/publications/administrative/cvs/opsg/opsg-19-16-gender-gap-paper.pdf

Pavić Kramarić, T., Aleksic, A., & Pejic-Bach, M. (2018). Measuring the impact of board characteristics on the performance of Croatian insurance companies. *International Journal of Engineering Business Management, 10,* 1–13. https://doi.org/10.1177/1847979018765864

Venuti, F., & Alfiero, S. (2016). The impact of corporate governance on risk taking in European insurance industry. *International Scholarly and Scientific Research & Innovation, 10*(1), 188–194.

Zurich Insurance Group. (2020a). Building a better way, Annual report 2020.

Zurich Insurance Group. (2020b). Create a brighter Future together, HR Factbook 2020.

CHAPTER 7

# Women in the Asset Management Sector

**Abstract** This chapter focuses on the role of the asset management (AM) industry in adopting and disseminating gender diversity principles. To this end, the chapter opens with a brief analysis of the rationale behind the importance of gender diversity in the AM industry. Subsequently, it focuses on the significant barriers that women still encounter in this financial sector. The second section analyses the main regulatory initiatives put in place by both European and US regulators to promote gender diversity in the AM sector. The third section deals with the current adoption by US mutual funds of investment strategies focused on the promotion of gender equality. This is followed by an overview of the main "gender diversity funds" that some important asset managers (Nordea, Fidelity, RobecoSAM, UBS Asset Management, and State Street Global Advisors) have chosen to launch recently on the market. Finally, the chapter closes with an in-depth look at the main initiatives adopted by three European AM trade associations (Investment Association, Finance Finland,

This chapter is the result of the joint efforts of the two authors. However, Giuliana Birindelli mainly contributed to Sects. 7.2, 7.4, and Antonia Patrizia Iannuzzi to Sects. 7.1, 7.3.



G. Birindelli and A. P. Iannuzzi, *Women in Financial Services*, Palgrave Macmillan Studies in Banking and Financial Institutions,
https://doi.org/10.1007/978-3-030-93471-2_7

and Assogestioni) aimed at encouraging asset management companies to increase the uptake of gender diversity policies and standards.

## 7.1 Why Does Gender Diversity Matter in the Asset Management Industry?

The asset management (AM) industry mobilises large amounts of capital and can strongly influence the behaviour of companies that are increasingly in need of raising resources in the financial markets, today even more so in the light of the recent crisis caused by the COVID-19 pandemic. Specifically, the AM industry performs three vital functions in the financial market by contributing to the growth of the economy. First, it channels savings towards investment to help finance the economy. Second, it provides the secondary market liquidity and finally, it engages through its asset managers with investee companies to maintain and enhance their long-term value, inclusive of their environmental, social, and governance (ESG) performance (EFAMA, 2020). Accordingly, it is important that the AM industry also increases its involvement in gender diversity actions as it can be a relevant driving force to spread this issue within the financial industry.

In recent years, the AM sector has increased its focus on strategies that broaden gender diversity among the portfolio management teams and the entire industry. However, because there are far fewer women than men entering careers as fund and portfolio managers, this challenge is still open and complex. Despite some evidence of a better performance by asset management teams with greater gender diversity, women-led funds remain a rarity in the investment industry. At present, the AM industry has reached a crossroads. On the one hand, data show the strong barriers women face in entering this financial sector. On the other hand, academic research highlights the harm resulting from the underrepresentation of women, also in the light of the fact that gender diversity in the management of fund portfolios seems to increase investment performance according to recent research findings. It would therefore be suitable for the AM industry to become "pinker" as this would generate more economic value for the players in this financial sector.

### 7.1.1 *The Main Barriers Women Face in the Asset Management Sector*

As widely displayed in other chapters of this book (e.g., Chapter 4), despite some considerable progress, women continue to be the minority across the finance areas, with the gender gap being even wider in the field of investment management (Basilico & Johnsen, 2019). As demonstrated by several studies, women remain significantly underrepresented among mutual fund managers. A 2016 survey by the CFA Institute evidences a male prevalence across the investment management industry worldwide and a female representation below 50% in all the CFA member countries worldwide.[1] The highest percentage of women is reported for Asia and the lowest percentage for Latin America. In the United States, the percentage is slightly above 18%. Moreover, female representation in the global fund industry has remained unchanged over the last twenty years. As shown by a Morningstar analysis using its proprietary databases (including approximately 25,000 fund managers dislocated in 56 countries worldwide), among all fund managers at the end of 2019, only 14% were women—the same percentage as in the year 2000—that is, twenty years ago (Lallos, 2020).

As shown in Table 7.1, reporting the percentage of female fund managers in the international financial markets, the discrepancy among financial centres is impressive. The data evidence the best performance by smaller markets: for example, 23% for Spain and Greece compared to 11 and 13% for the United States and the United Kingdom, respectively.

Overall, it is estimated that just 1.1% of the global wealth of the asset management industry is managed by women. This underrepresentation is likely explained by a combination of structural barriers and implicit biases rather than by a difference in competence and abilities. Several studies suggest that male and female fund managers have similar return, risk, and cost profiles. The only difference appears to be the portfolio turnover, which is lower for female fund managers, a circumstance that

[1] The CFA Institute is a global not-for-profit association with the mission of leading the investment profession. It promotes the highest standards of ethics, education, and professional excellence in the global investment industry through several certifications: the Chartered Financial Analyst (CFA) designation, the Certificate in Investment Performance Measurement (CIPM), the Certificate in ESG Investing, and the Investment Foundations Certificate. To date, the CFA Institute serves more than 186,000 members and 159 member societies around the world. See CFA Institute (2021).

**Table 7.1** Women fund managers in the main financial markets (% values; data as of 31 December 2019)

| *Country* | *% Women* | *Country* | *% Women* |
|---|---|---|---|
| Singapore | 29 | Belgium | 13 |
| Taiwan | 28 | Japan | 13 |
| China | 28 | The United Kingdom | 13 |
| Hong Kong | 28 | Ireland | 12 |
| Greece | 23 | Switzerland | 12 |
| Spain | 23 | Australia | 12 |
| France | 19 | The United States | 11 |
| Italy | 19 | Germany | 10 |
| India | 19 | Norway | 9 |
| Portugal | 18 | The Netherlands | 9 |
| Sweden | 15 | Denmark | 8 |
| Finland | 15 | Poland | 6 |
| **Global mean** | | | **14** |

*Source* www.morningstar.com

favours the funds by avoiding transaction costs detrimental to performance (Basilico & Johnsen, 2019). Moreover, investment performance does not seem to be affected by the gender of fund managers (Babalos et al., 2015; Sargis & Wing, 2018): men and women deliver equally competitive fund performance, as do mixed-gender teams. However, this result is not unanimous. For instance, a recent survey performed by Goldman Sachs on 496 large-cap US equity funds with combined assets of $2.3tn documents that female-managed funds on average delivered returns of −57 basis points (bp) compared with their benchmarks. Conversely, all male-run funds performed worse with average returns of −164 bp. This gap tends to persist even after adjusting for risk[2] (Flood, 2020).

Focusing on the US where the asset management industry is more developed (Epstein, 2019), other criticalities emerge (Fig. 7.1). The first critical issue concerns the gradual decline in the number of women fund managers from 2000 to 2019 within both active and passive open-end mutual funds and exchange-traded funds (ETFs). While women made

[2] Compared to the overall funds analysed by Goldman Sachs, just 14 and 49 were run, respectively, by all women teams and by teams where one-third of the portfolio managers were women. In contrast, 380 of the 496 funds had all-male teams.

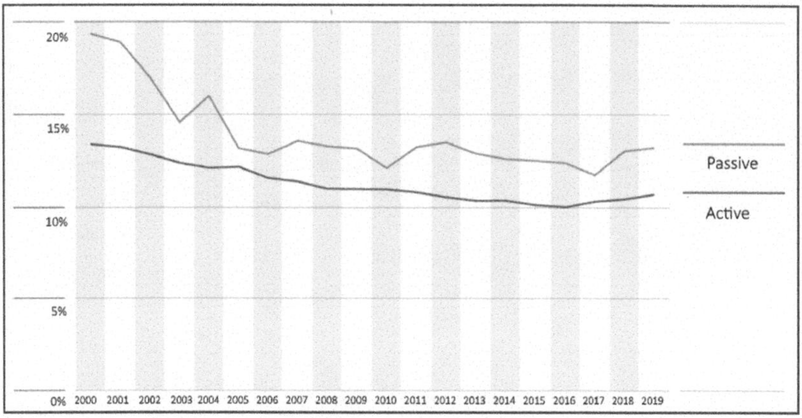


**Fig. 7.1** Women fund managers in active and passive open-end mutual funds (% values; years 2000–2019) (*Note* ETFs are also included. *Source* Lallos [2020])

up 19.4% of US passive fund managers in 2000, they represented only 13.2% in 2019. Likewise, while female representation among active fund managers was 13.4% in 2000, this percentage falls to 10.7% twenty years later (Fig. 7.1).

The second criticality concerns the higher number of women fund managers engaged in passive mutual funds compared to active ones.

As Fig. 7.1 shows, women managers of passive mutual funds have outnumbered those managing active funds in all years from 2000 to 2019. This is despite the massive growth of fund manager jobs that resulted from the broad development of active equity and fixed-income funds over the past 30 years, passed from about 1900 in 1990 to roughly 8500 in 2017. Men have occupied approximately 85–90% of the newly created roles, while women have failed to achieve significant improvements. This circumstance may suggest further discrimination, namely a preconception of a lack of skills among women in active compared to passive fund management, where the fund manager's role is considered much less crucial (Hudson, 2019).

Similar dynamics emerge when analysing funds by asset class. As shown in Fig. 7.2, in the last 20 years, both fixed-income and equity funds experienced a significant reduction in the number of female fund managers. Moreover, while in 2000 the percentage of female fund managers was

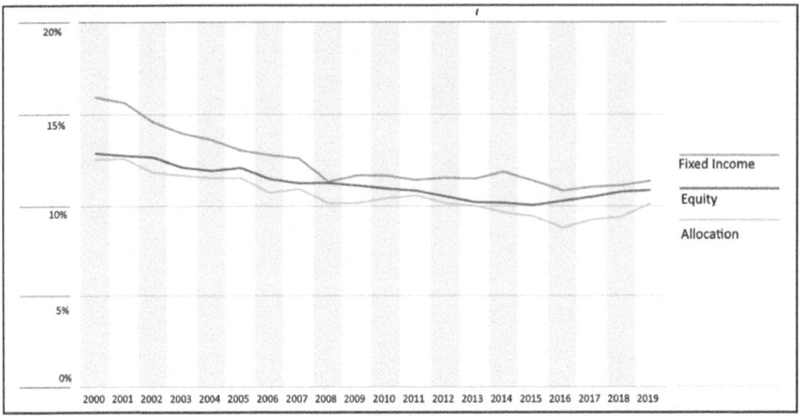


**Fig. 7.2** Women fund managers by asset class (% values; years 2000–2019) (*Note* ETFs are also included. *Source* Lallos [2020])

much higher for the fixed-income universe of funds, this advantage vanishes by 2019, when female representation in both cases (bond and equity funds) is roughly 11% (Fig. 7.2).

Despite these controversial aspects, it is important to highlight the way the asset management industry has been increasingly encouraging companies over the last few years to improve their gender diversity and equal opportunities between women and men. This is evident when analysing the shareholder engagement activities carried out by fund companies, especially the larger ones located in the US. First of all, "*Asset-manager proxy voting support for ESG-related shareholder resolutions has increased considerably over the past five years*" (Cook & Hale, 2020, p. 1). Moreover, the support for resolutions linked to gender diversity issues has significantly expanded. Among these, asset managers have given strong support to the resolutions requesting companies to disclose their gender pay gaps and the steps taken to reduce gender-based pay differences (Cook & Hale, 2020). To this end, Table 7.2 offers an interesting picture of the gender-related resolutions carried out by the largest 10 US fund families between July 2018 and July 2019.

On average, the "gender diversity resolution" is the most supported (59%). This resolution is followed by those for gender pay equity and workplace sexual harassment which have similar values (equal to 21 and

**Table 7.2** Support of the largest US fund families for gender-related resolutions (% values; data refer to July 2018–July 2019)

| | *Gender diversity* | *Gender pay equity* | *Workplace sexual harassment complaints governance* |
|---|---|---|---|
| American Funds | 50 | 3 | 0 |
| BlackRock (incl. iShares) | 9 | 7 | 0 |
| DFA (Dimensional) | 10 | 0 | 0 |
| Fidelity (ex. Geode) | 90 | 35 | 22 |
| Fidelity (Geode) | 91 | 7 | 50 |
| Franklin Templeton | 82 | 13 | 40 |
| PowerShares | 65 | 39 | 12 |
| Pimco | 100 | 98 | 85 |
| State Street (incl. SPDR) | 64 | 25 | 1 |
| T. Rowe Price | 55 | 7 | 10 |
| Vanguard | 36 | 0 | 0 |
| **Mean values** | **59** | **21** | **20** |

*Notes* The percentage values represent the number of gender-related resolutions supported by each fund family compared to the total number of such types of resolutions. Support is calculated as a percentage of all votes cast "for", "against", and "abstain"
*Source* Lallos (2020)

20%, respectively). Among the 10 largest US fund families, the most committed is Pimco, which has supported the highest number of resolutions in all three areas (Diversity, Gender pay equity, and Workplace sexual harassment complaints governance), whereas DFA and Vanguard have failed to support the resolutions for pay equity and sexual harassment. Workplace sexual harassment complaints are becoming an important reputational issue for investors, particularly in technology companies.

## 7.2 Regulatory Initiatives at International and European Level

Another recent Morningstar survey provides interesting insights into the main diversity, equity, and inclusion (DEI) initiatives—inclusive of gender policies—taken by the asset management industry across Europe, Canada, and the US. This survey, conducted in February 2021, covers 11 markets (Canada, Denmark, Finland, France, Germany, Italy, Norway, Spain, Sweden, the US, and the UK) and aims to analyse three main issues, namely (1) the presence, in these markets, of laws/regulations

**Table 7.3** Gender diversity regulations in the AM industry in Europe, Canada, and the US (data as of 26 February 2021)

| *Country* | *Regulation on DEI* | *Regulation on DEI disclosure* | *AM Trade Associations' Guidelines on DEI* |
|---|---|---|---|
| Canada | No | No | No |
| Denmark | No | No | No |
| Finland | Yes | Yes | Yes |
| France | Yes | Yes | No |
| Germany | No | No | No |
| Italy | Yes | No | Yes |
| Norway | Yes | Yes | No |
| Spain | No | No | No |
| Sweden | Yes | Yes | No |
| The US | No | No | No |
| The UK | No | Yes | Yes |
| **Total (%)** | **Yes, 45 No, 55** | **Yes, 45 No, 55** | **Yes, 27 No, 73** |

*Source* Silano (2021)

addressing board diversity, pay equity, and diversity policy that applies specifically to asset management firms,[3] (2) the presence in these markets of laws/regulations regarding the gender diversity disclosure by asset management firms and finally, and (3) the elaboration (or not) of voluntary guidelines on diversity, equity and inclusion by the local AM trade association (Silano, 2021). As we can see from Table 7.3 summarising the main findings of this survey, many markets still do not have diversity and pay gap regulations that apply to asset managers. Only 45% (5 out of 11) of these markets have rules and regulations on gender diversity for these financial intermediaries. Second, in most cases, where there are rules on gender diversity, there are also rules requiring an enhanced disclosure on this issue by the companies. While Canada, Denmark, Germany, Italy, Spain, and the US do not have laws addressing disclosure on diversity policy for asset management firms, the UK has already implemented these disclosure rules but has still to provide specific measures on board diversity. Finally, the AM trade associations setting specific DEI guidelines are still very few (only 3 out of 11, Table 7.3; on this point, see Sect. 7.4).

[3] In this chapter, the terms "asset management firms/companies" and "asset managers" are used interchangeably.

However, this picture is soon to change. The European legislator has published new gender diversity measures for investment firms, namely (a) Regulation (EU) 2019/2033 on the prudential requirements of investment firms, which applies from 26 June 2021 and (b) Directive (EU) 2019/2034 of the European Parliament and of the Council of 27 November 2019 on the prudential supervision of investment firms, which must be transposed at the national level from 26 June 2021. With these acts, the European legislator requires the EU Member States to ensure that investment firms have gender-neutral remuneration policies and that the remuneration committee is established and has a gender-balanced composition.

Differences emerge when looking at individual countries. Although gender diversity is becoming an increasingly important issue in many financial markets, the regulations in place in the asset management industry are still rather heterogeneous across Europe and the US.

The countries with the most advanced positions on this issue are the UK and those in the Scandinavian region. The UK, for example, has 35% women on the boards of asset managers and investment firms belonging to the FTSE 100 and FTSE 250 indexes in December 2020, which is one of the highest percentages of all economic sectors (Hampton-Alexander Review, 2021). In addition, compared to 2019, board gender diversity has increased across most asset management companies. Lower but still significant is the percentage of women in apical and executive positions, at 26%. As for the UK's fund managers, the best in terms of gender diversity performance are: (a) L&G with 36.6% women in middle and senior management positions, 30% women on the board of directors, and an average gender pay gap of 27.6% (although the gender pay gap rises to 45% when it refers to bonus payments alone; data as of December 2020), (b) Insight Investment, with 22 and 17% women, respectively, in middle-top and apical management positions, 18% women on the board[4] and a 26% average gender pay gap (63% for the bonus payments; data as of December 2019), and (c) Standard Life Aberdeen with 37% female executive directors, 45% women on the board, and a 34.5% average gender pay gap (65.9% for the bonus payments; data as of December 2020) (Silano, 2021).

[4] In this chapter, the term "board" refers to the board of directors.

Concerning Finland, asset management and investment companies with at least 30 employees are obliged to set up a gender equality plan that requires, among other things, that the boards of such companies be composed of more than 30% female members. In more detail, the top three best-performing Finnish funds in terms of gender diversity are: (a) Nordea with 40% women in leadership roles, 35% on the board, and 38% as fund managers; (b) Evli with 35% women in leadership roles, 25% on the board, and 50% as portfolio managers; (c) OP with 30% women in leadership roles, 25% on the board, and 25% as managers.

Swedish legislation requires all companies to provide the number of employees by gender. Asset management companies follow these rules as well as general anti-discrimination rules.

The situation in Norway also looks positive. In this country, there are regulations on both diversity policies and disclosure in the asset management industry. The main Norwegian asset management firms more committed to pursuing gender diversity goals are: (a) DNB with 40% women in leadership roles and 50% on the board of directors; (b) Storebrand with 30% women in leadership roles and 40% on the board of directors; (c) KLP with 30% women in leadership roles and 50% on the board of directors. Moreover, these three asset management companies have approved diversity policies. Conversely, in Norway, there are few women among fund managers. According to Morningstar data, Storebrand counts only 9% women fund managers and DNB only 7% of all fund managers. KLP has no female fund managers (Silano, 2021).

In Central Europe, the situation does not appear as rosy. For example, the French AM trade association is working on diversity and inclusion practices but it has not published any clear guidelines to date. Moreover, despite women representing 42% of the overall workforce, they represent only 8% of senior management in the asset management industry where most leadership positions are held by men. Women mainly occupy roles in sales, marketing, and communication but fewer hold front office positions; they are more present in executive committees than on the boards of directors. Overall, the diversity and inclusion objectives in the French asset management and investment sector predominantly concern staff recruitment, coaching, and training.

In the German asset management industry, a KPMG survey conducted in 2017 found that the share of women among total employees was highest in the human resources division (83%), followed by marketing (67%), accounting (56%), and finance (53%). The proportion was lowest in trading (17%), sales (23%), portfolio managers (24%), technology (25%), and digitalization (25%). Looking at the top German asset management companies in terms of gender diversity policies, they are: (a) Union Investment with women representing 16.2% of leadership roles and 22% of portfolio managers; (b) DWS with 13% women in leadership positions and 17% as fund managers; (c) Allianz Global Investors, whose executive committee and portfolio managers count, respectively, 50 and 21% of female members (Silano, 2021).

Moving to the countries of Mediterranean Europe, specifically to Italy, there are contrasting results. As documented by the latest survey conducted by Assogestioni in April 2019 involving 14 of its associated asset managers[5]—that is, 85% of total assets under management (AuM)—at the end of 2017, almost all the asset management companies analysed (13 out of 14) have at least one woman on the board, even though there is only 18% total female representation on corporate bodies.[6] Moreover, only 7% of women hold a top management position, while 30% are in second-level management lines. Finally, Italian asset management companies that have adopted a diversity policy (regarding several diversity aspects: age, gender, experience, and competence) account for 28.6%, while those implementing a gender diversity policy drop to 21.4%. Among the best Italian asset management companies in pursuing gender diversity goals, there are: (a) Eurizon with 28% women in leadership roles, 35% female fund managers, and 20% women directors sitting on the board (this last figure refers to Eurizon Capital SGR); (b) Pramerica with women occupying 23% of leadership roles and representing 25% of fund managers and 11% of board directors; (c) Anima, where women in leadership positions add up to 25% and those involved in fund management to 24%; board gender diversity is equal to 28.57% at Anima SGR and 40% at

[5] These asset managers are Generali Investments Europe SGR, Eurizon Capital SGR, Anima SGR, Pramerica SGR, Fideuram Investimenti SGR, Arca Fondi SGR, Epsilon Associati SGR, Euromobiliare AM SGR, Mediolanum SGR, Amundi SGR, Castello SGR, Pensplan Invest SGR, Hedge Invest SGR, and Etica SGR. See https://www.assogestioni.it/sites/default/files/docs/diversity_04-2019.pdf.

[6] It should be noted that the asset management companies interviewed, being unlisted, were not subject to the obligation introduced by the Golfo-Mosca Law, recently extended by amendments, requiring a minimum representation on the board of directors (and on the board of statutory auditors) of one-third of the underrepresented gender. For more details, see Chapter 10.

Anima Holding. Moreover, these three Italian asset management companies have already adopted gender diversity and inclusion policies (Silano, 2021).

Less information is available on gender diversity within the AM industry in Spain where, according to the latest Morningstar data, the percentage of funds with at least one woman in the management team is 34% (percentage calculated in relation to funds reporting the fund manager's name).

Finally, in the United States, there are no gender diversity laws that apply specifically to asset management companies. These firms are subject to the same rules as all other companies, including (a) the gender pay gap regulation (e.g., Federal Equal Pay Act of 1963 aimed at eliminating pay disparity based on gender; the Civil Rights Act of 1964, which prohibits employers from discriminating based on race, colour, religion, sex, or nationality)[7]; (b) the laws on board gender diversity disclosure (e.g., Nasdaq board diversity rules, updated on 6 August 2021,[8] and the Equal Employment Opportunity Commission-EEOC data collection. This requires companies with more than 100 employees to submit their workforce demographic data, including data by race/ethnicity, sex, and job categories).

## 7.3 The Gender Diversity Funds

In recent years, more and more mutual funds have been planning to embrace the gender diversity lens as an additional screening criterion to select companies in which to invest, deliberately choosing to extend their investment universe to companies with effective diversity and equal opportunity policies. This trend is evident when analysing the "Gender Equality Funds" database realised by "As You Sow", a non-profit foundation chartered in 1992 to promote environmental and corporate social

[7] For some time now, the US has adopted specific pay equity laws aimed at preventing gender and ethnicity from being used as a pay inequality tool. Some of these regulations have recently been updated, such as the California Equal Pay Act, which was amended in 2015 and became effective on 1 January 2016. For more details on the differences between the former and the new version of the Equal Pay Act, see https://www.dir.ca.gov/dlse/california_equal_pay_act.htm.

[8] See https://www.nasdaq.com/press-release/nasdaq-to-advance-diversity-through-new-proposed-listing-requirements-2020-12-01.

responsibility through shareholder advocacy. Since 2015, this organisation has been developing a free online US gender-equality fund screener (www.genderequalityfunds.org) to identify funds that invest in companies with a gender balance among their leadership positions (including the board of directors) and their overall workforce, as well as in companies with sound policies on issues like equal pay. Accordingly, "As You Sow" makes its assessments by combining the data on company gender equality from Equileap[9] with the data on mutual fund holdings from Morningstar. The screening starts with the Equileap company scores which are then cross-referenced with the holdings in each mutual fund. For each holding in a fund's portfolio that is covered by the Equileap Gender Scorecard, the approach adopted by "As You Sow" calculates the average of the company-level scores, weighted by the amount that the fund has invested. In this phase, the market value of the holding is used as a weight.[10] This process leads to an overall gender equality score, which is determined for each fund.[11] Moreover, funds are assigned a grade in letters (A-B-C-D-F) according to the quintile to which their gender score belongs within their assigned group (allocation funds, international equity funds, sector equity funds, or US equity funds). "A grade" funds are in the top 20% of their group, "B grade" funds are in the 60–80 percentile range, "C grade" funds are in the 40–60 percentile range, "D grade" funds are in the 20–40 percentile range, and "F grade" are in the bottom 20% of their

[9] Equileap is an independent specialised data provider that rates over 3500 companies globally based on 19 criteria including gender balance, gender pay gap, paid parental leave, and anti-sexual harassment policies. This assessment is conducted by gathering publicly available information provided by the companies themselves (e.g., annual reports, sustainability reports, and/or websites). Each company is assigned a "gender equality score" between 0 and 100 as result of four sub-scores: (1) gender balance in leadership and workforce (40 possible points), (2) equal compensation and work-life balance (30 possible points), (3) policies promoting gender equality (20 possible points), and finally, (4) commitment, transparency, and accountability (10 possible points). For more details, see the Equileap Gender Equality Global Report and Ranking available at https://equileap.com/equileap-reports/.

[10] This implies that the greater the incidence of a company's assets in the fund's investable universe, the greater the impact of that company's Equileap score on the fund's final gender score.

[11] All funds rated by "As You Sow" and present in its dataset are US-based and are offered as an open-end mutual fund or ETF. At least 40% of total assets of these funds are invested in direct stock holdings, and each fund has at least 33% Equileap coverage. To date, only stock investments are included in the gender score assignment. This means that bond funds and other non-stock-based funds are excluded.

group.[12] To provide an example, we list here the top 10 US mutual funds performers in terms of gender diversity (Table 7.4), along with the cost and financial performance (Table 7.5). As can be seen, there are no cases of negative performance, while the overall cost of these funds is almost always below 1% (Table 7.5).

In Fig. 7.3, we can see the distribution of approximately 8894 US open-end mutual funds and ETFs by their gender equality grade (from A grade to F grade) based on the Equileap gender equality scores of the companies in the portfolio, ranked against peer funds. The data suggest two important considerations. First, the percentage rate of funds with different gender equality grades is quite similar. "A grade" funds represent 20% of the total funds, "B grade" funds represent 19%, "C grade" funds 20%, and finally, "D grade" and "F grade" funds represent, respectively, 18% and 16% of the overall database. This means that the distribution of funds based on their commitment to invest in companies with a better gender diversity performance is quite even. Secondly, very interesting is the percentage rate of "A grade" funds (20%), the highest together with "C grade" funds and only one percentage point higher than "B grade" funds. This shows how the asset management industry is increasing its focus on gender diversity topics. Although these figures relate only to the US funds, given the importance of this market, it can be assumed that this trend will soon affect other geographical areas.

### *7.3.1 An Overview of Some Gender Diversity Funds*

Some asset managers have recently decided to promote mutual funds focused primarily on acquiring securities of leading companies in terms of gender diversity. Accordingly, the high gender diversity performance of firms is no longer one of the fund's investment criteria—as it is for the funds in the previous section—but becomes the main criterion for selecting the target companies by the fund's manager (henceforth these funds will be called "gender diversity funds"). In general, the percentage invested in leading companies in gender diversity practices is very high,

[12] For example, if the fund ranked 926 out of 2371 funds in the US Equity Fund group based on its overall gender score, this means that the percentile ranking of this fund is 61 (i.e., the fund's score is greater than or equal to the score of 61% of funds in this group). Thus, the letter grade of this fund is B as it falls within the group percentile ranking 60–80 band.

**Table 7.4** 10 best-performing US mutual funds in terms of gender diversity

| *Fund name* | *Gender equality grade* | *Gender equality rank, by group* | *Gender equality score* | *Sustainability mandate* | *Net asset $* | *Category* | |
|---|---|---|---|---|---|---|---|
| | | | | | | *Group* | *Category* |
| Pax Ellevate Global Women's Leadership Fund (Instl) | A | 98.2th percentile | 52/100 points | ✓ US-SIF[a] | 821.07 M | International equity fund | World Large-Stock Blend |
| Pax Ellevate Global Women's Leadership Fund (Inv) | A | 98.2th percentile | 52/100 points | ✓ US-SIF[a] | 821.07 M | International equity fund | World Large-Stock Blend |
| Saturna Sustainable Equity Fund | A | 98.8th percentile | 50/100 points | ✓ US-SIF[a] | 22.06 M | International equity fund | World Large-Stock Blend |
| Parnassus Endeavor Fund | A | 98.7th percentile | 49/100 points | ✓ US-SIF[a] | 4.71 M | U.S equity fund | Large Value |
| Parnassus Endeavor Institutional | A | 98.7th percentile | 49/100 points | ✓ US-SIF[a] | 4.71 M | U.S equity fund | Large Value |
| Green Century MSCI International Index Fund (Instl) | A | 86.2th percentile | 48/100 points | ✓ US-SIF[a] | 144.54 M | International equity fund | Foreign Large Value |
| Green Century MSCI International Index Fund (Indvl) | A | 86.2th percentile | 48/100 points | ✓ US-SIF[a] | 144.54 M | International equity fund | Foreign Large Value |

(continued)

**Table 7.4** (continued)

| *Fund name* | *Gender equality grade* | *Gender equality rank, by group* | *Gender equality score* | *Sustainability mandate* | *Net asset $* | *Category* | |
|---|---|---|---|---|---|---|---|
| | | | | | | *Group* | *Category* |
| Calvert International Equity Fund I | A | 84.9th percentile | 48/100 points | ✓ US-SIF[a] | 871.14 M | International equity fund | Foreign Large Growth |
| Calvert International Equity Fund A | A | 84.9th percentile | 48/100 points | ✓ US-SIF[a] | 871.14 M | International equity fund | Foreign Large Growth |
| Calvert International Equity Fund R6 | A | 84.9th percentile | 48/100 points | ✓ US-SIF[a] | 871.14 M | International equity fund | Foreign Large Growth |

*Notes* [a]Member of US-SIF, the Forum for Sustainable and Responsible Investment
*Source* Authors' extrapolation from www.genderequalityfunds.org (last accessed: 31 August 2021)

**Table 7.5** TER and financial performance of the 10 best-performing US mutual funds in terms of gender diversity

| *Fund name* | *TER (Total Expense Ratio)* | *1-year* | *3-year* | *5-year* | *10-year* | *15-year* | *20-year* |
|---|---|---|---|---|---|---|---|
| Pax Ellevate Global Women's Leadership Fund (Instl) | 0.53 | +35.75 | +14.34 | +14.33 | +10.18 | +6.99 | +6.17 |
| Pax Ellevate Global Women's Leadership Fund (Inv) | 0.78 | +35.38 | +14.05 | +14.03 | +9.91 | +6.71 | +5.97 |
| Saturna Sustainable Equity Fund | 0.75 | +28.76 | +16.66 | +15.57 | – | – | – |
| Parnassus Endeavor Fund | 0.94 | +74.28 | +23.22 | +21.48 | +17.53 | +14.78 | – |
| Parnassus Endeavor Institutional | 0.71 | +74.59 | +23.51 | +21.74 | +17.69 | +14.88 | – |
| Green Century MSCI International Index Fund (Instl) | 0.98 | +30.67 | +10.97 | – | – | – | – |
| Green Century MSCI International Index Fund (Indvl) | 1.28 | +30.25 | +10.62 | – | – | – | – |
| Calvert International Equity Fund I | 0.89 | +31.81 | +14.82 | +13.29 | +7.03 | +3.76 | +4.90 |
| Calvert International Equity Fund A | 1.14 | +31.45 | +14.49 | +12.91 | +6.52 | +3.18 | +4.25 |
| Calvert International Equity Fund R6 | 0.85 | +31.86 | +14.77 | +13.07 | +6.60 | +3.23 | +4.28 |

*Source* Authors' extrapolation from www.genderequalityfunds.org (last accessed: 31 August 2021)

between 70 and 80%. This is a very important innovative strategy that will increase the spread of corporate gender diversity policies in line with the most recent data documenting that, within social impact funds, those focusing on gender, diversity, and community development have exhibited a growth of roughly 340% since January 2016 (EFAMA, 2021). Companies that do not comply with these standards risk being excluded from the asset manager's investment choices, therefore, they will try to adapt. At present, the "gender diversity funds" represent a residual category but it is believed that many asset management companies will soon include them in their contractual offering. In the following sub-sections, a brief analysis of some of these funds is carried out with a focus on the

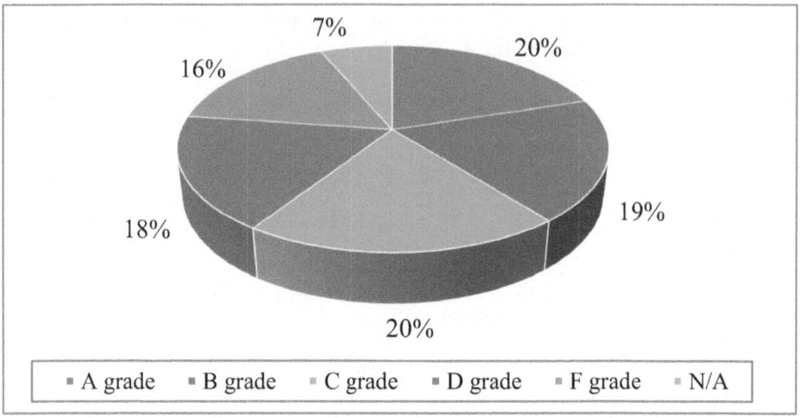


**Fig. 7.3** Distribution of US mutual funds and ETFs by gender equality grade from A to F (data as of 9 August 2021) (*Notes* "A grade" funds are in the top 20% of their group, "B grade" funds are in the 60–80 percentile range, "C grade" funds are in the 40–60 percentile range, "D grade" funds are in the 20–40 percentile range, and "F grade" funds are in the bottom 20% of their group. Percentages are calculated on approximately 8894 US open-end mutual funds and ETFs. *Source* Authors' elaboration on the "Gender Equality Funds" database [www.genderequalityfunds.org])

first gender diversity funds placed on the market, highlighting their main characteristics, including investment strategies and the asset allocation process.

*The Nordea 1-Global Gender Diversity Fund*

The first "gender diversity fund" was promoted by Nordea Asset Management (NAM; €254bn in AuM), which is the asset manager of the Nordea Group, the largest financial services group in Northern Europe.[13] Launched on 21 February 2019 concurrently with International Women's Day, this fund, called "Global Gender Diversity Fund (GGDF)", aims to show that high returns can be achieved by investing in companies with a

[13] The launch of this investment product is in line with another important gender diversity performance achieved by Nordea. This financial group has been part of the Bloomberg Gender-Equality Index since 2019. For more details on this gender diversity index, see Chapter 2.

strong focus on gender balance. As stated by Julie Bech, the co-manager of the fund,[14] "*we privilege companies that include fair gender representation in senior management, executive management and at the board level because we believe that gender diversity drives a company's profitability, thus companies promoting it should be rewarded. While this is a social issue, it is also correlated with business success*" (Nordea 1, 2019, p. 1).

Nordea 1-GGDF is an equity fund. It invests at least 75% of its total assets in equities and equity-related securities of companies worldwide that display a high level of Environmental, Social, and Corporate Governance (ESG) performance and gender diversity, while at the same time appearing to offer high growth prospects. The fund uses NAM's proprietary model to select companies that ensure strong female representation, especially in the upper management team, and actively promote gender diversity at all levels. Potential investments for which insufficient gender diversity data are available are excluded from the fund's investment universe. In addition, the fund applies supplementary negative screening to exclude specific sectors or companies based on ESG criteria and is appropriate for investors with a time horizon of at least 5 years. The base currency is USD (Table 7.6).

Tables 7.7 and 7.8 illustrate the composition of Nordea 1-GGDF's portfolio showing the percentage of securities owned, respectively, by country and top economic sector. Most securities refer to US companies (58.72%) and only a minority percentage refers to European companies (Table 7.7). Moreover, there does not seem to be a prevailing economic sector. The largest weight is in the technology sector (Systems Software, 7.39%). However, this is not much higher than the percentage weight of other economic sectors, such as Pharmaceuticals (Table 7.8).

*The Fidelity Women's Leadership Fund*

If Nordea 1-GGDF is the first European gender diversity fund, the first US gender diversity fund is "Fidelity Women's Leadership Fund" (FWOMX) launched on 1 May 2019 by Fidelity Investment. This is the fourth largest mutual and pension fund company worldwide. The core investment strategy of this "gender diversity fund" is to invest at least 80% of its assets in equity securities of companies that prioritise and promote women's leadership and empowerment. In particular, they are companies

[14] The fund's portfolio managers are both women; their names are Julie Bech and Audhild Asheim Aabø.

**Table 7.6** Nordea 1—Global Gender Diversity Fund: investment strategies and other characteristics

| | |
|---|---|
| Fund inception | 21 February 2019 |
| Benchmark | MSCI ACWI Index (Net Return). For performance comparison only |
| Investment strategy | (a) Preference towards companies that demonstrate a high level of sustainability and gender diversity performance<br>(b) Exclusion of companies active in the production of illegal or nuclear weapons or with exposure to coal mining exceeding a predefined threshold in accordance with NAM's Paris-aligned Fossil Fuel Policy<br>(c) At least 90% of the fund's assets are covered by NAM's ESG scoring framework<br>(d) Suspension of investments in companies involved in violations of, or disputes about, international laws and standards, especially if appropriate shareholder engagement actions fail or are deemed vain |
| Derivatives and techniques | Possible use of derivatives and other hedging techniques to reduce risk, make the portfolio management more efficient and seek investment gains. These investments are not in the scope of the ESG criteria, and they involve costs and superior risks |
| SFDR—Sustainable finance and disclosure regulation | The fund applies baseline ESG safeguards and promotes ESG characteristics according to Article 8 of the SFDR Regulation EU 2019/2088 on "Sustainability-Related Disclosures in the Financial Services Sector" |
| Investor profile | All types of investors who understand the risks of the fund and plan to invest for at least 5 years |
| Shareholder engagement | Engagement of companies in environmental, social, and governance practices is encouraged through a range of activities, including voting, participation in Annual General Meetings, standard-setting, engagement with companies, tabling motions, etc.[a] |
| Base currency | USD |

[a] For a report on the GGDF's engagement activities, see Nordea 1 (2021b). For a detailed description of NAM's engagement process, see NAM (2021)

*Source* Authors' elaboration on information collected from Nordea 1 (2021a)

that, at the time of the initial purchase, (i) include a woman as a member of the senior management team (C-suite), (ii) are administered by a board in which women represent at least one-third of all directors, or (iii) in the adviser's opinion, carry out the best-in-class gender diversity initiatives. These diversity policies include, but are not limited to, those designed to allow parental leave and to monitor the gender pay gap, or those related to the flexible work environment. Securities of both domestic and foreign issuers may be included. At the same time, only target companies with durable earnings growth and income opportunities are included in the

**Table 7.7** Nordea 1-GGDF, breakdown by country (data as of 31 December 2020)

| *Country* | *Weight (%)*[a] | *Country* | *Weight (%)*[a] |
|---|---|---|---|
| The United States | 58.72 | Singapore | 1.36 |
| France | 6.48 | India | 1.29 |
| Sweden | 3.43 | China | 1.10 |
| Canada | 3.42 | The Netherlands | 1.07 |
| Denmark | 2.36 | Israel | 0.95 |
| Taiwan, Province of China | 2.36 | Spain | 0.95 |
| Japan | 2.14 | Norway | 0.90 |
| Cayman Islands | 2.05 | Thailand | 0.74 |
| Switzerland | 1.85 | Philippines | 0.71 |
| The United Kingdom | 1.81 | Germany | 0.67 |
| Australia | 1.80 | Hong Kong | 0.30 |
| Ireland | 1.53 | South Africa | 0.28 |
| **Total** | | | **98.27** |

*Note* [a]in % of net assets
*Source* Authors' elaboration on data collected by Nordea 1 (2020)

**Table 7.8** Nordea 1-GGDF, breakdown by top economic sector (data as of 31 December 2020)

| *Top sectors* | *Weight (%)*[a] |
|---|---|
| Systems Software | 7.39 |
| Pharmaceuticals | 6.57 |
| Diversified Banks | 5.60 |
| Health Care Services | 4.86 |
| Semiconductors | 4.07 |
| Data Processing and Outsourced Services | 3.73 |
| Semiconductor Equipment | 3.58 |
| Personal Products | 3.53 |
| Life and Health Insurance | 3.41 |
| IT Consulting and Other Services | 3.30 |
| Internet and Direct Marketing Retail | 2.79 |
| Integrated Telecommunication Services | 2.77 |
| Movies and Entertainment | 2.58 |
| Electric Utilities | 2.54 |
| Home Improvement Retail | 2.23 |
| Construction and Farm Machinery and Heavy Trucks | 1.98 |

*Note* [a]in % of net assets
*Source* Authors' elaboration on data collected by Nordea 1 (2020)

fund's investment universe. In addition to this main investment strategy, the FWOMX may trade the fund's securities with brokers, dealers, or other counterparts to increase the fund's income. Various techniques, such as buying and selling futures contracts and exchange-traded funds, can be used. These instruments aim to obtain additional returns based on the fund's exposure to changing security prices and other factors that affect security values.

Finally, also ESG criteria are used to construct the best portfolio. Like in Nordea 1-GGDF, the FWOMX's portfolio manager is a woman (Nicole A Connolly, since 1 May 2019). The other characteristics of the fund, including the main investment strategies and risks, are displayed in Table 7.9.

Regarding the portfolio composition, there is a clear prevalence of domestic equities (87%), while the proportion invested in international shares is small (11%) (Fig. 7.4). Most of the latter concern European companies (Table 7.10). No bonds are held by the fund, and only 2% of the fund's assets are held in cash or other net assets (Fig. 7.4).

Finally, the target firms in which FWOMX invests belong principally to the economic sectors of information technology (27.54%), consumer discretionary (15.46%), and health care (14.30%). "Financials" follows with a percentage always above 10% (11.48%, see Table 7.11).

*The RobecoSAM Global Gender Equality Impact Equities*

Another equity gender diversity fund is the "RobecoSAM Global Gender Equality Impact Equities" launched by Robeco Institutional Asset Management on 29 October 2020 to create a positive social impact. This is done by globally investing in leading companies in terms of gender diversity commitment. To select these firms, the fund uses the proprietary "Gender Equality Score" constructed using six gender diversity topics where each is assigned a specific weight. These gender-related items include (1) the adoption of a board gender policy, (2) the percentage of women directors on the board, (3) the percentage of women employees, (4) the gender pay gap and equal remuneration practices, (5) the employee engagement, and (6) the commitment to the well-being of all employees. At the same time, the fund aims to achieve long-term capital growth by trying to overperform the benchmark (MSCI World Index TRN) and currently integrates several ESG criteria in its investment process by excluding companies involved in specific controversial economic sectors (thermal coal, weapons, tobacco, military

**Table 7.9** FWOMX: investment strategies and other characteristics

| | |
|---|---|
| Fund inception | 1 May 2019 |
| Investment strategy | The fund's investment universe includes:<br>(a) Companies with women in key roles in the C-suite<br>(b) Companies with at least 33% women on the board of directors<br>(c) Companies with the best-in-class gender diversity initiatives<br>Moreover, the fund's investment process focuses on companies with strong competitive advantages that can lead to sustained earnings growth, as well as companies that can benefit from growth opportunities |
| Share classes | Multiple classes of shares. All classes of the fund have a common investment objective and investment portfolio |
| Principal investment risks | 1. *Stock Market Volatility*, due to fluctuations in the equity securities value in response to political, market, and economic developments<br>2. *Foreign Exposure*, due to the fluctuations in foreign exchange rates; withholding or other taxes; trading, settlement, custodial, and other operational risks<br>3. *Issuer-Specific Changes*, which can increase the risk of default of an issuer or counterparty, and thus affect the securities' value<br>4. *Management Risk*, which occurs when the adviser's application of the fund's strategy criteria does not achieve the planned outcomes |
| Distribution options | The fund provides the following distribution options:<br>1. *Reinvestment Option*. Both dividends and capital gain distributions can be automatically reinvested in additional shares. This option is automatically assigned when the investor does not indicate any choice<br>2. *Income-Earned Option*. Only capital gain distributions can be automatically reinvested in additional shares. Conversely, dividends can be paid in cash<br>3. *Cash Option*. Both dividends and capital gain distributions can be paid in cash |

*Source* Authors' elaboration on data collected from FWOMX's Factsheet and Prospectus (29 June 2021)

contracting, palm oil, and fossil fuels). Finally, the fund has obtained three sustainable labels and certifications (ISR France, Febelfin, and the European SRI Transparency logo).[15] The current portfolio manager is a man (Michiel Plakman). For more details see Table 7.12.

Similarly to Nordea 1-GGDF and FWOMX, RobecoSAM Global Gender Equality Impact Equities primarily invests in the information technology industry (Software and IT Services) and favours investments in American companies (Table 7.13).

[15] For more information on these labels, see www.lelabelisr.fr/en/, www.towardssustainability.be, and https://www.eurosif.org/transparency-code/, respectively.

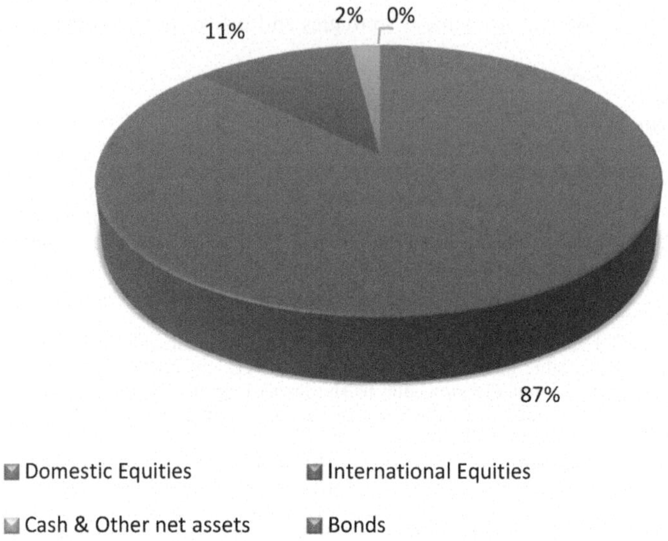


**Fig. 7.4** FWOMX's asset allocation (data as of 30 June 2021) (*Source* FWOMX's Factsheet)

**Table 7.10** Regional diversification of FWOMX (data as of 4 October 2021)

| *Country* | *Weight (%)* |
|---|---|
| The United States | 87.30 |
| Europe | 9.03 |
| Asia-Pacific ex Japan | 0.52 |
| Japan | 0.45 |
| Emerging Markets | 0.37 |
| Other | 2.33 |

*Source* Authors' elaboration on data collected from FWOMX' website (last accessed: 4 October 2021)

*The ETFs on Gender Diversity*

Alongside the active funds above, there also are several passive gender diversity funds. These are the ETFs that seek to provide investment results that, before fees and expenses, match the total return performance of a specific market index (the so-called benchmark). These funds adopt a "replication strategy" as they primarily invest in the securities of the

**Table 7.11** Top economic sectors of FWOMX (data as of 30 June 2021)

| *Top sectors* | *Weight (%)* |
|---|---|
| Information Technology | 27.54 |
| Consumer Discretionary | 15.46 |
| Health Care | 14.30 |
| Financials | 11.48 |
| Industrials | 9.48 |
| Communication Services | 7.93 |
| Consumer Staples | 3.97 |
| Utilities | 2.83 |
| Materials | 2.21 |
| Real Estate | 2.06 |

*Source* Authors' elaboration on data collected from FWOMX's Factsheet

**Table 7.12** RobecoSAM Global Gender Equality Impact Equities: investment strategies and other characteristics

| | |
|---|---|
| Fund inception | 29 October 2020 |
| Benchmark | MSCI World Index TRN |
| Investment strategy | (a) Selection of companies that are leaders in promoting gender equality. These companies must have a high "gender score" based on a proprietary approach covering various criteria such as board diversity, equal remuneration, talent management, and employee well-being<br>(b) Adoption of other ESG criteria to refine the stock selection process<br>(c) An integrated sustainability analysis of financial sectors and target companies is carried out by an in-house Sustainability Investing research team<br>(d) Achievement of a return better than the benchmark |
| SFDR—Sustainable finance and disclosure regulation | This fund features sustainable investment as its objective within the meaning of Article 9 of the Regulation (EU) 2019/2088 of 27 November 2019 on sustainability-related disclosures in the financial sector |
| Investor profile | Informed and/or experienced investors who: (a) wish to attain defined investment objectives, (b) understand the risks of the fund, and (c) plan to invest for at least 5–7 years |
| Shareholder engagement | An active engagement team interacts directly with the management of the holding companies to offer them additional channels for sustainable impact |
| Base currency | EUR |

*Source* Authors' elaboration on data collected from the RobecoSAM Global Gender Equality Impact Equities' Factsheet (August 2021) and Prospectus (June 2021)

**Table 7.13** RobecoSAM Global Gender Equality Impact Equities, breakdown by top economic sector and country (data as of 31 August 2021)

| *Top sectors* | *Weight (%)*[a] | *Country* | *Weight (%)*[a] |
|---|---|---|---|
| Software | 8.3 | America | 68.5 |
| Chemical | 8.0 | Europe | 26.7 |
| IT Services | 7.9 | Asia | 4.8 |
| Machinery | 6.1 | Middle East | 0.0 |
| Capital Markets | 5.2 | | |
| Insurance | 5.1 | | |
| Life Sciences Tools and Services | 4.7 | | |
| Health Care Equipment and Supplies | 3.9 | | |
| Semiconductors and semiconductor equipment | 3.9 | | |
| Health Care Providers and Services | 3.8 | | |
| Commercial Banks | 3.5 | | |
| Personal Products | 3.4 | | |
| Other | 36.2 | | |

*Note* [a]in % of net assets
*Source* Authors' elaboration on data collected by the RobecoSAM Global Gender Equality Impact Equities' Factsheet (31 August 2021)

index with the approximate weightings as in the same index. To date, the best-known ETFs currently focused on gender diversity issues are: (a) the "SPDR SSGA Gender Diversity Index ETF" and (b) the "UBS ETF (IE) Global Gender Equality UCITS ETF".

The first ETF was launched on 7 March 2016 by one of the largest producers of ETFs and indexed investments, namely State Street Global Advisors (SSGA). Its benchmark is the "SSGA Gender Diversity Index" designed to measure the performance of the highest market capitalisation US companies that are leaders on gender diversity issues.[16] Concerning the investment strategies, the "SPDR SSGA Gender Diversity Index ETF" is characterised by having a diversified exposure across economic sectors, although "Information Technology" is preferred (Table 7.15). Finally, the asset allocation does not generally allow for investment in derivatives.

The second ETF on gender diversity issue was promoted by UBS Fund Management (Luxembourg) SA, belonging to UBS SA. It was

[16] For more details on the SSGA Gender Diversity index, see Chapter 2.

launched one year later (19 December 2017). In this case, the benchmark is "Solactive Equileap Global Gender Equality 100 Leaders Net Total Return Index". This includes the 100 leading global companies with a strong track record in gender diversity and sustainability.[17] The "UBS ETF (IE) Global Gender Equality UCITS ETF" invests at least 90% of its total net assets in securities that are constituents of this index to replicate its price and returns. Finally, this ETF also adopts an investment strategy aimed at maximising diversification both geographically and by economic sector. However, in this case, the financial sector is preferred in the asset allocation process (Table 7.15).

Table 7.14 summarises the investment strategies and other features of these two ETFs. Table 7.15 displays the asset diversification by economic sector.

## 7.4 Best Practices and Guidelines to Promote Diversity and Gender Inclusion in the Asset Management Sector: The Case of 3 AM Trade Associations

According to the Morningstar survey (Silano, 2021), to date, only 3 out of 11 AM trade associations (from Canada, Denmark, Finland, France, Germany, Italy, Norway, Spain, Sweden, the UK, and the US) have set up specific guidelines on gender diversity and inclusion addressed to asset management firms. These are Investment Association (IA, in the UK), Finance Finland (FFI, in Finland),[18] and Assogestioni (in Italy).

In detail, in the UK, the Investment Association currently supports diversity and inclusion (D&I) through several internal and external initiatives. The internal gender diversity initiatives concern: (a) the adoption of recruitment policies to attract, retain, and promote talent from a wider pool based on a diverse and inclusive perspective to increase the presence of minority groups and women (who, as outlined in the previous sections, are underrepresented in the AM industry, especially in senior

[17] This index selects companies based on 19 criteria including equal pay, work-life balance, transparency and accountability, gender balance, and sustainability policies. The index includes the 30 highest-rated US stocks but caps individual issuers at 3%.

[18] FFI represents, in addition to fund management companies, Finnish banks, life and non-life insurers, employee pension companies, finance houses, and securities dealers.

**Table 7.14** SPDR SSGA Gender Diversity Index ETF and UBS ETF (IE) Global Gender Equality UCITS ETF: investment strategies and other characteristics

| | *SPDR SSGA Gender Diversity Index ETF* | *UBS ETF (IE) Global Gender Equality UCITS ETF* |
|---|---|---|
| Fund inception | 7 March 2016 | 19 December 2017 |
| Benchmark | The "SSGA Gender Diversity Index", which measures the performance of US large capitalisation companies that are the best performers in terms of "gender diversity", i.e., that exhibit a higher level of female representation in their senior leadership positions | The "Solactive Equileap Global Gender Equality 100 Leaders Net Total Return Index", which includes the top 100 leading global companies with a strong track record in gender diversity and sustainability |
| Investment approach | Achievement of investment results that, before fees and expenses, generally correspond to the total return performance of the benchmark. Specifically:<br>(a) Predominant selection of US companies that demonstrate greater gender diversity within senior leadership positions<br>(b) Adoption of three gender diversity ratios to rank companies in the benchmark within each sector<br>(c) The benchmark seeks to minimise variations in sector weights with respect to the composition of the index's broader investment universe focusing on companies with the highest levels of gender diversity at the leadership level within their sectors | Achievement of investment results that, before fees and expenses, generally correspond to the total return performance of the benchmark. Specifically:<br>(a) Predominant selection of companies worldwide that demonstrate greater gender diversity performance<br>(b) Exclusion of companies involved in weapons, gambling, and tobacco, and those non-compliant with the UN Global Compact and OCSE Guidelines for Multinational Enterprises<br>(c) Exceptional investments in securities that are not yet included but that are expected to be included in the index/benchmark<br>(d) Potential use of derivative instruments to reduce risks or costs, or to generate additional capital or income |

*Source* Authors' elaboration from the SPDR SSGA Gender Diversity Index ETF's Factsheet (30 June 2021) and the UBS ETF (IE) Global Gender Equality UCITS ETF's Factsheet (31 August 2021)

**Table 7.15** Top economic sectors of the SPDR SSGA Gender Diversity Index ETF and the UBS ETF (IE) Global Gender Equality UCITS ETF (data as of 30 June 2021)

| *Top sector* | *SPDR SSGA Gender Diversity Index ETF* <br> *Weight (%)* | *UBS ETF (IE) Global Gender Equality UCITS ETF* <br> *Weight (%)* |
|---|---|---|
| Information Technology | 29.42 | |
| Health Care | 13.35 | 9.79 |
| Consumer Discretionary | 12.91 | 11.06 |
| Financials | 11.22 | 32.24 |
| Industrials | 8.75 | |
| Communication Services | 8.25 | 10.10 |
| Consumer Staples | 5.79 | |
| Real Estate | 3.01 | |
| Materials | 2.65 | |
| Energy | 2.46 | |
| Utilities | 2.21 | |

*Note* We consider only the top 4 sectors for UBS ETF (IE) Global Gender Equality UCITS ETF
*Source* SPDR SSGA Gender Diversity Index ETF' Factsheet (30 June 2021) and Morningstar (https://www.morningstar.co.uk/uk/etf/snapshot/snapshot.aspx?id=0P0001CGXN)

positions), (b) the analysis and understanding of the gender pay gap issue,[19] (c) the definition of a guidance for members to help make the AM industry more inclusive, especially for lesbian, gay, bisexual, and transgender (LGBT) employees, and (d) the growth of the "black voice", emphasising the experience of black people in investment management and providing firms with guidelines for expanding ethnic diversity.[20] Concerning the external initiatives on gender diversity issues promoted by the Investment Association, they aim to encourage investment and

[19] To this end, the Investment Association published two reports: "Closing the Gap" (2019) and "Addressing the Gender Pay Gap" (2020). The first report analyses the factors that may contribute to the gender pay gap and how asset managers can help reduce it. The second report focuses on asset managers' best practices aimed at proactively addressing the gender pay gap issue. These practices range from the development of internal programmes and policies to the support of external initiatives.

[20] To address the underrepresentation of black people in the AM industry, the Investment Association published the report "Black Voices: Building black representation in investment management" (2019) aimed at inducing firms to enhance the ethnic diversity of their workforce by implementing, for example, "ethnicity pay gap reporting".

asset management firms to adopt both the "Women in Finance Charter" (which requires firms to increase female representation in apical positions informing about the progress towards this goal; see Chapter 2) and the "Diversity Project" (designed to achieve equal opportunity and spread a more inclusive culture). Additionally worthy of consideration are: (a) the "Diversity on boards' campaign" arranged by the Investment Association for greater gender diversity on the boards of UK investment and asset management firms, (b) the collaboration with the Hampton-Alexander Review[21] to improve gender balance in FTSE 350 companies, and (c) the establishment of the Institutional Voting Information Service (IVIS), a platform to help shareholders identify companies that are not compliant with the 33% female representation target on boards and in senior leadership teams set by the Hampton-Alexander Review (The Investment Association, 2021). Other important initiatives carried out by the Investment Association consist of the voluntary publication of its gender pay gap and the collection of anonymous data on employees' ethnicity by the annual "Employee Diversity Survey". Finally, in February 2021, the Investment Association announced that it intends to issue warnings to FTSE 350 companies that fail to improve board diversity. An "amber-top" warning will be issued to firms that are non-compliant with the required standards on the disclosure of ethnic and gender diversity of their boards. This is in addition to a "red" warning for firms that exhibit deeper failings in this area (i.e., firms with 30% or fewer female directors).

In Finland, the FFI has developed good operating practices to ensure that all financial market participants work in a transparent, honest, and professional manner according to laws and regulations. The cornerstones of these policies focus on respecting human rights, prohibiting all forms of discrimination, and promoting equal opportunities and diversity in the workplace, including gender diversity. More specifically, the FFI establishes the importance of treating all service users fairly and equally, respecting human rights, not discriminating against anyone (based on gender, nationality, religion, disability, age, sexual orientation, etc.), and promoting equal opportunities and diversity among all staff to increase the level of trust and well-being in the workplace (FFI, 2020).

[21] The origin of the Hampton-Alexander Review lies in the appointment, in February 2016, of Sir Philip Hampton and Dame Helen Alexander to chair an independent review to ensure the promotion of talented women.

Lastly, the strongest actions to promote gender diversity have been taken in Italy by Assogestioni. This AM trade association was the first to approve, in September 2019, specific guidelines on gender and inclusion addressed to asset managers (in Italy, these include SGR, SICAV, and SICAF[22]). The purpose of this guidance is to support Italian asset management companies in defining diversity and inclusion policies and procedures for their corporate boards. Additionally, these standards propose measures and best practices to encourage equal treatment and opportunities between genders within the corporate organisation. These guidelines are structured in three sections. The first section deals with diversity and inclusion policies in corporate bodies, the second section identifies the criteria (age, gender, skills, and experiences) to be used to increase the diversity of corporate bodies, and the third part proposes measures to promote gender diversity among staff members. Among the various recommendations, the one to increase the disclosure of gender diversity policies adopted by the most significant asset managers, or at least by the listed ones, is very relevant. Furthermore, Assogestioni recalls the principle of equal pay with respect to gender (introduced by CRD V, see Chapter 5) and urges asset managers to disclose all measures taken to reduce their gender pay gap. Alongside these standards, to concretely support the promotion of equal treatment and opportunities between genders within the organisation, Assogestioni has also developed several best practices to which all asset managers should conform.[23] Finally, Assogestioni has created a "Diversity & Inclusion Desk" on its institutional website to offer member companies a useful tool to exchange and compare their views on implementing diversity and inclusion guidelines and best practices. The help desk offers the opportunity to create new conversations, respond to open discussions, and share useful documents, with the ultimate aim of promoting the principles of equal treatment and equal opportunities.

[22] In Italian: Società di Gestione del Risparmio (SGR), Società di Investimento a Capitale Variabile (SICAV), Società di Investimento a Capitale Fisso (SICAF).

[23] To consult the standards and best practices on gender diversity elaborated by Assogestioni, see https://www.assogestioni.it/sites/default/files/docs/it-en_linee_guida_politiche_di_diversita_e_inclusione_dei_gestori.pdf.

## References

Babalos, V., Caporale, G. M., & Philippas, N. (2015). Gender, style diversity, and their effect on fund performance. *Research in International Business and Finance, 35*(C), 57–74. https://doi.org/10.1016/j.ribaf.2015.02.020

Basilico, E., & Johnsen, T. (2019). *Smart(er) investing: How academic insights propel the savvy investor*. Palgrave Macmillan.

CFA Institute. (2021). *Annual report 2020.*

Cook, J., & Hale, J. (2020, February 13). *2019 ESG proxy voting trends.* Morningstar Manager Research. https://www.morningstar.com/lp/proxy-voting-esg

EFAMA—European Fund and Asset Management Association. (2020, November). *Asset management in Europe: An overview of the asset management industry.*

EFAMA—European Fund and Asset Management Association. (2021, March). *Market insights: ESG investing in the UCITS market*. https://www.efama.org/sites/default/files/files/Market%20Insights%20Issue4%20ESG%20funds_1.pdf

Epstein, G. (2019). *The asset management industry in the United States.* (Financing for Development Series, No. 271 (LC/TS.2019/81)). Santiago, Economic Commission for Latin America and the Caribbean (ECLAC).

FFI—Finance Finland. (2020, February 13). *Responsible financial sector.* https://www.finanssiala.fi/wp-content/uploads/2020/02/FFI-Responsible-financial-sector-2020.pdf

Flood, C. (2020, September 6). Female-managed US funds outperform all-male rivals. *Financial Times*. https://www.ft.com/content/021a1b60-a5fa-42ad-83b4-482268cac7ac

Hampton-Alexander Review. (2021, February). *Improving gender balance—5-year summary report*. FTSE Women Leaders. https://ftsewomenleaders.com/wp-content/uploads/2021/02/HA-REPORT-2021_FINAL.pdf

Hudson, M. (2019). *Fund managers: The complete guide*. Wiley.

Lallos, L. (2020, February 19). *Women in investing: Morningstar's view.* Morningstar Editorial. https://ioandc.com/wp-content/uploads/2020/03/2-Women_in_Investing_Morningstar.pdf

NAM—Nordea Asset Management. (2021, March). *Responsible investment policy.* https://www.nordea.com/en/doc/namripolicy2021260521.pdf

Nordea 1. (2019, March 7). *On International Women's Day, Nordea asset management announces the launch of global gender diversity strategy*. Press release.

Nordea 1. (2020). *Audited annual report 2020.*

Nordea 1. (2021a, March). *Prospectus and its addendum* (pp. 2–9).

Nordea 1. (2021b). *ESG report, second quarter*. https://www.nordea.co.uk/en/professional/documents/esg---report/ESG-R_GGDF_eng_INT.pdf/

Robeco. (2021, June). *Robeco capital growth funds, prospectus*.

Sargis, M., & Wing, K. (2018, March 8). *Fund managers by gender—Through the performance lens*. Morningstar Research. https://www.morningstar.com/lp/fund-managers-by-gender-performance-lens

Silano, S. (2021, March 10). *Diversity best practices in the asset management industry*. Morningstar website. https://www.morningstar.co.uk/uk/news/210150/diversity-best-practices-in-the-asset-management-industry.aspx

SPDR. (2020, June 30). *Annual report*.

The Investment Association. (2021, February). *The role of investment managers in promoting diversity and inclusion*. https://www.theia.org/sites/default/files/2021-03/The%20role%20of%20asset%20managers%20in%20promoting%20diversity%20and%20inclusion_0.pdf

CHAPTER 8

# How Central Are Women in Central Banks?

**Abstract** The chapter deals with gender issues in Central Banks (CBs). Here, discrimination against women and obstacles to their careers seem even more pronounced than in supervised financial intermediaries. The chapter first discusses the causes of this accentuated difficulty for women and then reviews the scarce literature on the pattern of appointments and promotions of women on CB boards, on the relations between gender and monetary policy decisions, and on the influence exerted by women on the stability of the financial system and the quality of supervision. The focus then shifts to the strengthening of the gender parity policy by the European Central Bank (marked by the setting of targets for the recruitment and promotion of women) and to women governors. In regard to the latter, we attempt to outline a detailed picture of the women who have held such positions in CBs around the world, highlighting both how rare they still are and how patterns change across countries. Finally, the chapter offers a picture of gender policies followed by the EU28 CBs based on

This chapter is the result of the joint efforts of the two authors. However, Giuliana Birindelli mainly contributed to Sects. 8.2, 8.3, 8.4, 8.6 and Antonia Patrizia Iannuzzi to Sects. 8.1, 8.5.



G. Birindelli and A. P. Iannuzzi, *Women in Financial Services*, Palgrave Macmillan Studies in Banking and Financial Institutions, https://doi.org/10.1007/978-3-030-93471-2_8

responses provided by banks to our survey or on information retrieved from the banks' documents, especially their annual reports.

## 8.1 Why Are Women Missing at Central Banks?

Some perhaps remember a famous slip of the tongue by former President Barack Obama addressing the then Vice-Chair of the Federal Reserve, Janet Yellen, as "Mr Yellen" (Perlberg, 2013). The citation is an exemplary representation of the current situation of female presence in Central Banks (CBs), which in many aspects is even more complex and sensitive compared to the issues seen so far for supervised financial intermediaries. Indeed, compared to the latter, CBs present multiple factors that further amplify gender discrimination. In general terms, as we shall see below in some detail, these factors relate to the aspects of experience, relationships, preconceptions, and academic background (Vallet, 2019).

Despite having made some progress in tackling the gender gap, Central Banks still feature predominantly male-dominated career paths. In general, appointment to top positions requires previous experience of serving on collegiate bodies or being an official. Though, given the rare female appointment to these roles, women eventually lack the experience to pass to higher positions. The glass ceiling is further consolidated by the fact that women are less likely than men to build relationships that facilitate their careers.

Another contributing factor is the prejudice against women's approach towards risk and inflation and whether this attitude aligns with the goals pursued by Central Banks. In fact, this aspect has been the object of several works in the literature on women in Central Banks (see next section), analysing the tendency of women to take on a dove-like versus a hawk-like approach against inflation, which relates to a less inflation averse vs more inflation averse approach, respectively.

Finally, another key factor is academic training. Achieving top positions in Central Banks, especially the role of governor, requires a specialisation in economics, especially in macro-economics and finance, also in the form of a Ph.D. The lower number of women pursuing degrees in these fields of education further contributes to the underrepresentation of women (Vallet, 2019). The limited presence of women, in turn, fosters discrimination that hinders their professional development in this field, resulting in their underrepresentation at senior levels.

Remaining in the academic setting, interestingly, several works have evidenced the lower acceptance rates at economic conferences for papers exclusively co-authored by female researchers compared to those exclusively co-authored by male authors. Such outcomes are suggested to be associated with an excessively critical approach of male reviewers towards women authors, especially when they do not belong to a prestigious institution or have no relevant publication record (Hospido & Sanz, 2019). Unfortunately, this low visibility at conferences also affects academic networking and participation as co-author to other possibly relevant research projects, hindering career advancement. Evidence of such bias has been demonstrated by Datta and Vigfusson (2019), who describe co-authorship patterns among economists at the Federal Reserve Board. Given that co-authorship increases scientific productivity and in turn facilitates career advancement, the authors observe a pattern that differs from predictions based on random assignment. Women seem to co-author less in research than men, who co-author more with other people of the same gender. Signs of a critical and patronising attitude towards women are also found by studying the presentation of research by female economists compared to male economists at seminars held at prestigious universities. In particular, although female speakers attract a larger audience, women tend to receive more questions asked by males and more questions classified as hostile (Dupas et al., 2021).

Hence, it is apparent that discriminatory factors and stereotypes still require a lot of action in favour of gender balance, even if current initiatives in Central Banks display encouraging signs, as shown by the findings of the 2021 Official Monetary and Financial Institutions Forum (OMFIF) survey. The study, which covers 50 CBs (including the European Central Bank-ECB) in countries across Africa, Asia Pacific, Europe, Latin America, and North America (OMFIF, 2021), shows an increase in initiatives and a strong focus on this issue. Compared to the 2020 OMFIF survey (OMFIF, 2020), there has been an increase in the number of diversity officers formally assigned to the implementation and monitoring of diversity and inclusion (D&I) practices, in training to support women's career progression (except for mentorship training; the only area to decrease compared to the previous year), in the spread of remote working which has almost doubled since the previous year, and a slight increase in flexibility in working hours especially as a response to the COVID-19 pandemic.

In consideration of the improvements achieved and of those yet to fulfil, efforts now need to be directed towards specific targets. First and foremost, efforts must be focused towards the increase in gender quotas on the board of directors or the monetary policy board (which are present in only 8% of the sample surveyed) or gender quotas when recruiting junior staff (adopted by only 4% of CBs). Other improvements should concern policies ensuring candidates of both genders have equal opportunities for senior management vacancies, adopted by 12% of CBs; measurement of the gender pay gap which occurs in one-third of the respondents, one of which (the Central Bank of Iceland) stands out as the only bank with a pay gap in favour of women; and certification of gender policies by an independent external organisation, currently present in only 27% of the sample.

Focusing briefly on the COVID-19 pandemic, the effects of the current global health crisis are even worse than those caused by the 2017–2018 crisis as unemployment and income loss have affected women more than men. However, the pandemic has triggered changes that in future could alleviate gender inequalities, such as a greater use of remote and flexible working, and a shift in focus to performance rather than time. Nevertheless, such changes need to be carefully managed, since they could have the opposite effect of exacerbating inequality, which, for example, might happen if women worked mainly from home and men mainly in the workplace (OMFIF, 2021, p. 16, interview with Alessandra Perrazzelli, Deputy Governor, Banca d'Italia).

## 8.2 Some Empirical Studies on Women in Central Banks

Despite scant literature on women in Central Banks, we can identify three main strands of research: one addressing the pattern of appointments and promotions of women on Central Bank boards, another addressing the monetary policy approaches, and a third addressing the stability of the financial system and the quality of supervision. Below, we report the main findings from the most representative studies.

As to the research on the pattern of appointments to Central Bank boards, noteworthy is the work by Charléty et al. (2017), which analyses a sample of 26 Organisation for Economic Co-operation and Development (OECD) countries over the period 2003–2015. The findings evidence higher probabilities for appointing women in three settings, namely when

(a) the outgoing member is a woman, (b) a new member is added rather than entered as a replacement of an outgoing member, and (c) female board representation is low. Overall, the research evidences a nomination process that is systematically biased against women. The pattern of appointments to Central Bank boards is also discussed in the work by Bodea (2017) using data from 114 countries spanning from 1998 to 2014. The author analyses different drivers of appointments. In particular, the likelihood of appointing women appears to be higher as the size of boards increases, suggesting that the presence of more "seats" available most likely assigns the seat a lower political value. Moreover, the more women parliamentarians, the more likely women are to be appointed to Central Bank boards, suggesting the role of parliamentarians in supporting the appointment or promotion of the latter. A key role is also played by corruption, being inversely correlated with the presence of women, who are generally excluded from political power and favour distribution networks. Finally, a greater representation of women appears associated (though with low statistical significance) with the independence of the Central Bank. Another study addressing the promotion gap between women and men focuses on the change in gender policy by the ECB (Hospido et al., 2019a). Despite the similar conditions shared by men and women upon entry to the work environment at the ECB, after some years, women experience a wage disparity, as well as a lower probability of promotion. Such disparities, however, appear to have faded following the ECB's measures in 2010 to support gender balance, closing the promotion gap between 2012 and 2017. However, upon closer inspection, the reduction in disparity is due to a match between the lower likelihood of women asking for promotions (the so-called gender promotion gap, Hospido et al., 2019b) and the higher likelihood of women being chosen once they apply for promotions. Another interesting result concerns the underlying motivation for promotion, which appears to be related to the recognition of merit, since promoted women progress more rapidly in terms of wages.

Moving on to the second strand of literature addressing the relationship between gender and monetary policy decisions, the work by Chappell and McGregor (2000) focuses on the voting behaviour of members of the Federal Open Market Committee (FOMC) of the Federal Reserve from 1966 to 1996. During this period, only seven women served on the FOMC, with six ranked among the most dovish members. Women, in essence, generally appear as "doves" (less inflation averse) rather than "hawks" (more inflation-averse). In the same vein, the study by Farvaque et al. (2011) addresses the composition of Monetary Policy Committees (MPCs) in the major OECD countries, divided into inflation targeters and non-targeters, in the years 1999–2008. The aim was to test whether monetary policy decisions are influenced by the composition in terms of demographic characteristics and social attributes. With specific reference to gender, the authors find results opposite to those of Chappell and McGregor (2000): the presence of women in MPCs, especially in targeting countries, is associated with lower levels of inflation and therefore women are more inflation averse than men. According to the authors, the results could be explained "*by the need for women to have higher credentials than their male counterparts in order to be appointed and, once appointed, to mimic the more conservative members to acquire/reinforce reputation and become more influential. As inflation targeting favors a focus on inflation, it may induce this gender effect*" (Farvaque et al., 2011, p. 236). Consistent with this is the finding from the study by Farvaque et al. (2014) which analysed the ability of Monetary Policy Committee members to manage inflation and growth based on nine Central Banks of the world's major economies in the years 1999–2010. In line with the previous finding on women being more inflation averse than their male counterparts (Farvaque et al., 2011), this 2014 study observes that women are less likely to accept a trade-off between inflation and GDP growth volatility. The results of Bennani et al. (2015) are in line with Farvaque et al. (2011, 2014). The research, investigating the gap between the rate preferred by FOMC members and the rate adopted in the meetings that took place between 1994 and 2008 based on the individual characteristics of the members, shows that women are more conservative in their monetary policy preferences and, therefore, shows a high degree of hawkishness. The study by Masciandaro et al. (2015) finds that women have a more hawkish approach, confirming evidence from the more recent literature. Indeed, women seem to express preferences for low inflation rates and limited monetary growth. The study also investigates the institutional drivers relevant to the appointment of women on Central Bank boards, showing, among other things, that Central Bank governance plays a key role: specifically, "*gender representation is more likely to be relevant in countries characterized by better central bank governance (less dovish attitude), i.e. more independent central banks, less involved in banking supervision*" (Masciandaro et al., 2015, p. 19). The findings by Diouf and Pépin (2017), which also address the social (economic and political) conditions underlying the appointments of female chairs in Central Banks, confirm women as hawkish and exhibiting strong conservatism. The authors argue that this attitude can justify the appointment of women as Central Bank chairs as the "*attachment to the ultimate monetary policy goal, reflected by a high degree of conservatism, can be interpreted as a sign of a greater ability to resist political pressures, and hence of independence in the conduct of monetary policy*" (Diouf & Pépin, 2017, p. 206). In some studies (Bordo & Istrefi, 2018), being more inflation averse rather than more focused on output and employment growth does not seem to depend on gender. Policy orientation (hawkish or dovish) seems to depend on other factors, mainly related to the university where one graduated, the economic events in one's life, and the person who appointed the member of the Central Bank. The probability of being a hawk increases in the event a member is born during a period of high inflation, graduates from a university linked to the Chicago School of Economics, and is appointed by a Republican president. A dove, on the other hand, is most likely to be born during a period of high unemployment, graduate from a university with strong Keynesian convictions, and be nominated by a Democratic president.

Concerning the studies on the impact of women on financial system stability and supervisory quality, we shall recall the 2017 International Monetary Fund (IMF) study previously mentioned in Chapter 4, which extends to the regulatory authorities and banking supervision agencies listed by the Bank for International Settlements.[1] The results of the research conducted by the IMF on these organisations, characterised (like the banks) by a low presence of women across 113 countries (higher in many low and middle-income countries), do not show a key role of women; a greater presence of women on the boards of these institutions seems not to impact the quality of supervisory activity. However, controlling for supervisory quality and some bank-level and country-level variables, the study shows a positive relationship between women's share on supervisory boards and banking sector stability (IMF, 2017). In a study conducted the following year, the IMF investigated the role of women sitting on the governing boards of banking supervision agencies in 115 countries. Again, findings confirm a greater representation

[1] The link is the following: https://www.bis.org/regauth.htm.

of women in poorer countries and the evidence found in the previous study. The justification for these empirical results can be found in the fact that the regulatory and supervisory framework is determined by many legal and institutional factors that may be very little affected by the weight of women on supervisory boards (IMF, 2018). Finally, Ozili (2020), focusing on the competencies of Central Bank governors and their relationship with financial stability in 40 countries from 2000 to 2016, evidences a positive association between a male governor's tenure and a more stable financial system, characterised by lower non-performing loans and higher regulatory capital ratios. This result, which is contrary to expectations that women are more risk-averse and conservative than men (see Chapter 3), changes when the author studies the combined effect of gender and cognitive ability/social capital (measured by a variable expressing, respectively, whether the governor had education at an elite university or institution or had a foreign education). The results, in this case, show less financial stability during the tenure of a male governor than a female governor.

In contrast to the considerable amount of literature on women in firms, studies on female representation in Central Banks are limited. Thus, progress in research is expected, though bound to data availability: "*the data available on supervisory boards do not allow us to perform detailed analysis, as was the case for bank boards*" (IMF, 2017, p. 23).

Finally, although not dealing with studies on Central Bank governors, it is worth mentioning an emerging strand of research related to the advantage of women leaders in times of crisis and downturn, in our particular setting in times of COVID-19 (Ryan et al., 2010, 2016). In this vein, a recent research (Sergent & Stajkovic, 2020) assumes that governors influence public health outcomes and examines whether the sex of US governors influences the number of COVID-19 pandemic-related deaths in their states. The results highlight the differences among states, with fewer COVID-19-related deaths in states led by female governors than in states led by male governors. A second important result concerns the impact of early stay-at-home orders; states with female governors who issued an early stay-at-home order had fewer COVID-19-related deaths compared to states with a male governor who issued the same order. To justify these findings, the authors analysed transcripts of government briefings related to COVID-19 that took place between 1 April 2020 and 5 May 2020. Findings evidence that compared to male governors, female governors show more empathy and confidence in their briefings due to a greater understanding of and participation in community sentiments and a greater focus on collective welfare issues, such as employment and financial hardship. On the other hand, gender does not appear to have affected the issuance of stay-at-home orders in that the likelihood of issuance does not change in association with the gender of the governor (Baccini & Brodeur, 2021; Shay, 2020). However, states with a female-headed health agency tend to issue stay-at-home orders earlier than states with a male administrator (Shay, 2020).

## 8.3 European Central Bank Measures to Strengthen Female Representation

Over the last decade, the ECB has taken several steps to address gender equality, starting in 2010 by establishing its diversity strategy. In 2013, it followed up on these intentions by quantifying specific targets for female presence across management positions. At that time, women held 17% of all management positions and 14% of senior positions. Overall, the number of middle and senior management positions held by women should have reached 35% by the end of 2019. A specific target was also set for senior management positions, which was double the percentage at that time (from 14 to 28%). The introduction of gender targets seemed necessary in the light, among other things, of the open letter signed in October 2012 by many distinguished economists denouncing the absence of women on the ECB's Executive Board, pointing out that "*As economists who follow the ECB's work closely, we cannot understand that it will have proven impossible over the last four appointments to find at least one suitable female candidate in the Eurozone. As citizens, we fear that such a situation would be widely and rightly seen as proof of a systemic bias against women when it comes to the highest places in office*".[2]

While the target was reached for senior positions, it was not met for the share of women in all management positions. To further support gender equality, the ECB announced additional measures in May 2020, setting different targets that span until 2026, as outlined in Table 8.1: targets for recruitment and promotion of women expressed as an annual percentage, and targets for the total share of women for the years 2022, 2024, and

[2] See the following link: https://voxeu.org/article/ecb-would-benefit-less-gender-discrimination.

**Table 8.1** New gender targets launched by the ECB

| | *Status quo female (%)* | *Intake targets 2020–2026* | *Targets for the overall share (%)* | | |
|---|---|---|---|---|---|
| *Seniority level (salary bands)* | | | | | |
| Senior management (K-L) | 30.8 | Minimum 50% | 37 | 38 | 40 |
| All management (I-L) | 30.3 | Minimum 50% | 33 | 34 | 36 |
| Principal experts (H) | 33.3 | Minimum 50% | 37 | 40 | 42 |
| Experts (F/G-G) | 41.9 | Minimum 50% | 44 | 45 | 47 |
| Analysts (E/F) | 52.0 | Minimum 50% | 51 | 51 | 51 |
| Period | End 2019 | 2020–2026 | 2022 | 2024 | 2026 |

*Note* Salary bands are classified from the lowest (A) to the highest (L) (see ECB, 2019)
*Source* Targets are drawn from the ECB (2020)

2026. All these targets relate to different seniority levels and different salary bands.

Positive signs of the path followed by the ECB have also come from its advancement in the EDGE (Economic Dividends for Gender Equality) certification process for gender equality in the workplace, passing from the Assess level ("Recognizing commitment"), obtained in February 2019, to the Move level ("Showcasing progress") in February 2021 (on EDGE certification see Chapter 2, Sect. 2.5.2).

Looking at the bodies of the ECB, the gender imbalance is very evident. This is due to, among other things, the low proportion of women graduates in economics, a key source for ECB recruitment (Schnabel, 2020).[3]

Table 8.2 lists the gender composition of the highest decision-making body at the ECB, the Governing Council, including its President, the governors of the National Central Banks—NCBs or also CBs—of the 19 euro area countries, and the six members of the Executive Board.

As can be seen in Table 8.2, while there is a steadily increasing number of members of the Governing Council from 17 in 2003 to 25 in 2020, the number of female representatives remains constantly low, fluctuating from one between 2003 and 2010; to zero between 2011 and 2013;

[3] This is why the ECB launched a scholarship for women in economics in 2019 (see the following link: https://www.ecb.europa.eu/press/pr/date/2019/html/ecb.pr190529_2~cb82990e5d.en.html).

**Table 8.2** ECB: gender of the members of the Governing Council

| | *Number of persons* | | | *% of total* | | |
|---|---|---|---|---|---|---|
| *Year* | *Total* | *Men* | *Women* | *Total* | *Men* | *Women* |
| 2003 | 17 | 16 | 1 | 100 | 94.1 | 5.9 |
| 2004 | 17 | 16 | 1 | 100 | 94.1 | 5.9 |
| 2005 | 17 | 16 | 1 | 100 | 94.1 | 5.9 |
| 2006 | 17 | 16 | 1 | 100 | 94.1 | 5.9 |
| 2007 | 19 | 18 | 1 | 100 | 94.7 | 5.3 |
| 2008 | 21 | 20 | 1 | 100 | 95.2 | 4.8 |
| 2009 | 22 | 21 | 1 | 100 | 95.5 | 4.5 |
| 2010 | 22 | 21 | 1 | 100 | 95.5 | 4.5 |
| 2011 | 23 | 23 | 0 | 100 | 100.0 | 0.0 |
| 2012 | 22 | 22 | 0 | 100 | 100.0 | 0.0 |
| 2013 | 23 | 23 | 0 | 100 | 100.0 | 0.0 |
| 2014 | 24 | 22 | 2 | 100 | 91.7 | 8.3 |
| 2015 | 25 | 23 | 2 | 100 | 92.0 | 8.0 |
| 2016 | 25 | 23 | 2 | 100 | 92.0 | 8.0 |
| 2017 | 25 | 23 | 2 | 100 | 92.0 | 8.0 |
| 2018 | 25 | 23 | 2 | 100 | 92.0 | 8.0 |
| 2019 | 25 | 23 | 2 | 100 | 92.0 | 8.0 |
| 2020 | 25 | 23 | 2 | 100 | 92.0 | 8.0 |

*Source* European Institute for Gender Equality

to two from 2014 onwards. Over the same period, the Presidency was constantly held by males, up until 1 November 2019, when Christine Lagarde replaced the outgoing President, Mario Draghi.

Currently (June 2021) there are two women on the Governing Council: Christine Lagarde, the ECB President, and Isabel Schnabel, member of the ECB's Executive Board since 2020. Both are also members of the Executive Board, which consists of the President, the Vice-President, and four other members—all appointed by the European Council. Finally, the only female representative on the General Council, which comprises the President of the ECB, the Vice-President of the ECB, and the governors of the National Central Banks of the 27 EU Member States, is the President of the ECB.

## 8.4 Female Governors: A Rarity?

To date, information on female representation among governors is extremely hard to come across as there are no official registries or databases collecting such data. This lack of readily accessible sources can be, however, somewhat overcome by extensive research across the web through cross-checking more general information from websites such as the Financial Times with more specific data from websites of individual Central Banks. Although this information can only provide an approximate estimate, we believe that the high number of websites we visited allowed us to sketch a representative picture of the real situation, as can be seen in Table 8.3 which clearly shows a marked gender imbalance: 67 female governors in 51 Central Banks.[4]

Several countries in America have experienced multiple female governors, such as Honduras, Ecuador and, to a lesser extent, Venezuela, and El Salvador. In Europe, only East Germany, Russia, and Belarus have had two women governors (East Germany, according to our data, was the first country to appoint a woman governor). Two female governors have also been appointed in other geographical areas (Israel, Cuba, Malaysia, and Serbia). There are also cases of the same woman appointed twice (this is the case of the São Tomé and Príncipe's Central Bank and the Bank of the Lao PDR-Laos). At present (June 2021), there are 14 women governors in office mainly from smaller countries. They are joined by women who lead three out of twelve US regional Federal Reserve Banks: Loretta J. Mester (Federal Reserve Bank of Cleveland), Esther L. George (Federal Reserve Bank of Kansas City), and Mary C. Daly (Federal Reserve Bank of San Francisco).

Hence, women at top positions in Central Banks are indeed still very few. Although it may be argued that governor appointments depend on decisions made by national governments which leave very little leverage to counter the gender gap, it is also true that the underlying selection processes cannot change until there is a cultural leap to do so. Finally, it is worth remembering that having a limited number of women governors creates a vicious circle to the detriment of women, in the sense that young

[4] We think it is worth stating that the list of governors we have arrived at is in several respects different from the one in Table 1 of the study conducted by Diouf and Pépin (2017), both because the data collection carried out by the authors obviously predates ours and because the sources from which the information was drawn partly differ.

**Table 8.3** Female governors worldwide

| *National Central Bank* | *Female governor* | *Period* |
|---|---|---|
| Central Bank of Cyprus | Chrystalla Georghadji | 2014–2019 |
| Denmark Nationalbank | Bodil Nyboe Andersen | 1995–2005 |
| National Bank of Austria | Maria Schaumayer | 1990–1995 |
| Central Bank of Ireland | Sharon Donnery (acting governor) | June 2019–August 2019 |
| National Bank of East German | Greta Kuckhoff<br>Grete Wittkowski | 1950–1958<br>1967–1974 |
| Central Bank of Finland | Sirkka Hämäläinen | 1992–1998 |
| National Bank of Poland | Hanna Gronkiewicz-Waltz | 1992–2000 |
| National Bank of Ukraine | Valeriia Oleksiivna Hontareva | 2014–2017 |
| Central Bank of the Russian Federation | Tatyana Paramonova<br>Elvira Nabiullina | 1994–1995<br>Since 2013 |
| National Bank of the Republic of Belarus | Tamara Vinnikova<br>Nadezhda Yermakova | 1996–1997<br>2011–2014 |
| Central Bank of the Republic of San Marino | Catia Tomasetti | Since 2018 |
| Central Bank of Aruba | Jeanette R. Semeleer | Since 2008 |
| Cayman Islands Monetary Authority | Patricia Estwick | Since 2021 |
| Central Bank of Curacao and St. Maarten | Leila Matroos | 2017–2019 |
| Central Bank of Nigeria | Sarah Alade (acting governor) | February 2014–June 2014 |
| Central Bank of Madagascar | Vonimanitra Razafimbelo | 2013–2014 |
| Central Bank of Somalia | Yussur A.F. Abrar | September 2013–November 2013 |
| Bank of Botswana | Linah Kelebogile Mohohlo | 1999–2016 |
| São Tomé and Príncipe's Central Bank | Maria do Carmo Trovoada Pires de Carvalho Silveira | 1999–2005<br>2011–2016 |
| Central Bank of Lesotho | Retselisitsoe Matlanyane | Since 2012 |

(continued)

**Table 8.3** (continued)

| *National Central Bank* | *Female governor* | *Period* |
|---|---|---|
| Central Bank of Seychelles | Caroline Abel | Since 2012 |
| South African Reserve Bank | Gill Marcus | 2009–2014 |
| Central Bank of Kenya | Jacinta Wanjala Mwatela (acting governor) | March 2006–March 2007 |
| Central Bank of Argentina | Mercedes Marcó del Pont | 2010–2013 |
| Central Bank of Honduras | Victoria Asfura de Díaz | 1999–2002 |
| | Maria Elena Mondragón | 2002–2006 |
| | Gabriela Núñez | 2006–2007 |
| | Sandra Midence | 2009–2010 |
| | Maria Elena Mondragón | 2010–2014 |
| Central Reserve Bank of El Salvador | Luz María de Portillo | 2002–2009 |
| | Marta Evelyn de Rivera | 2013–2014 |
| Central Bank of Venezuela | Ruth de Krivoy | 1992–1994 |
| | Edmée Betancourt | April 2013–August 2013 |
| Central Bank of Bolivia | Tamara Sánchez Peña | 1985 |
| Central Bank of Belize | A. Joy Grant | Since 2016 |
| Central Bank of Ecuador | Ana Lucía Armijos | 1992–1993 |
| | Jeannette Sanchez | 2012–2013 |
| | Madeleine Abarca | 2016–2017 |
| | Verónica Artola | Since 2017 |
| Banco de Guatemala | María Antonieta Del Cid Navas de Bonilla | 2006–2010 |
| Banco Central del Paraguay | Mónica Pérez | 2005–2007 |
| Bank of Guyana | Dolly Sursattie Singh | 1998–2014 |
| Federal Reserve | Janet Louise Yellen | 2014–2018 |
| Central Bank of The Bahamas | Wendy Craigg | 2005–2015 |
| Central Bank of Cuba | Irma Margarita Martínez Castrillón | 2017–2020 |
| | Marta Sabina Wilson González | Since 2020 |
| Central Bank of Barbados | Marion Vernese Williams | 1999–2009 |
| Maldives Monetary Authority | Azeema Adam | 2014–2017 |
| Bank Negara Malaysia | Zeti Akhtar Aziz | 2000–2016 |
| | Nor Shamsiah Mohd Yunus | Since 2018 |

(continued)

**Table 8.3** (continued)

| *National Central Bank* | *Female governor* | *Period* |
|---|---|---|
| National Bank of the Kyrgyz Republic | Zina Mukaevna Asankojoeva | 2011–2014 |
| Bank of Thailand | Tarisa Watanagase | 2006–2010 |
| Central Bank of Turkmenistan | Shekersoltan Mukhammedova | 2002–2005 |
| State Bank of Vietnam | Nguy˜ên Thị H`ông | Since 2020 |
| State Bank of Pakistan | Shamshad Akhtar | 2006–2009 |
| People's Bank of China | Chen Muhua | 1985–1988 |
| Bank of the Lao PDR (Laos) | Pany Yathotou | 1988–1992<br>1995–1997 |
| Bank of Israel | Karnit Flug | 2013–2018 |
| | Nadine Baudot-Trajtenberg | November 2018–December 2018 |
| Central Bank of Samoa | Maiava Atalina Emma Ainuu-Enari | Since 2011 |
| National Bank of Serbia | Kori Udovički | 2003–2004 |
| | Jorgovanka Tabaković | Since 2012 |
| National Bank of North Macedonia | Anita Angelovska Bezhoska | Since 2018 |
| National Reserve Bank of Tonga | Siosi Cocker Mafi | 2003–2013 |

*Source* Information collected from the *Financial Times*, Wikipedia, and other websites, mainly:
https://www.guide2womenleaders.com/National_Banks.htm
http://www.centralbanknews.info/
https://www.centralbanking.com/
https://www.omfif.org/
https://www.federalreserve.gov/
Last accessed: June 2021

female economists do not have reference points and examples to follow, thus activating a damaging self-feeding mechanism.

Some very interesting indications on how Central Banks around the world are evolving in terms of gender diversity in a broad sense (not only regarding governors) come from the OMFIF reports on the gender balance index. The index is calculated by considering the representation of women at the very top levels (Governors, Deputy Governors, Members of Policy-Setting Committees, and Executive Board Directors) for each CB and by weighing the individual score of each CB by the Gross Domestic Product (GDP) of the corresponding country.

The score is weakly correlated with the size of the economy since the best performers include both small and large countries. Actually,

**Table 8.4** Gender Balance Index score, by region, 2018–2021 (%)

| | *2018* | *2019* | *2020* | *2021* |
|---|---|---|---|---|
| Europe | 34.7 | 38.1 | 37.3 | 42.3 |
| North America | 24.5 | 35.8 | 34.6 | 29.9 |
| Latin America and the Caribbean | 11.3 | 18.8 | 23.1 | 27.9 |
| Africa | 18.9 | 21.0 | 23.3 | 25.2 |
| Asia Pacific | 6.0 | 9.1 | 12.3 | 14.1 |
| Middle East | 11.3 | 10.1 | 7.3 | 5.8 |

*Source* OMFIF (2021)

according to the OMFIF (2021), six out of the 10 top performers are located in countries whose GDP is less than $10bn. This can be explained by the fact that less populated countries have a greater need to draw on their best talents. Also, communist regimes seem to have favoured the presence of female governors (see, e.g., China, Laos, Poland, Kyrgyzstan, Turkmenistan, and Ukraine). Conversely, the weight of religion seems to have yielded a disadvantage for women—with few exceptions represented by countries such as Ecuador, Israel, and Malaysia (Vallet, 2019).

A comparison of GDP-weighted scores by region (Table 8.4) shows an upward trend in 2018–2021 for Latin America and the Caribbean, Africa, and Asia Pacific. On the other hand, the Middle East score continues to fall (the exception to this female sub-representation is Israel). Finally, Europe ranks first on an upward trend, and North America ranks in second place on a downward trend. As we shall see in the following sections, there is considerable divergence among countries in the macro-areas.

## 8.5 Gender Diversity and Central Banks in the EU Member States

In this section, we analyse the evolution of gender composition of Central Bank decision-making bodies from 2003 to 2018. We consider the member countries of the Economic Union, including the aggregate from which the United Kingdom is excluded (therefore, both EU27 and EU28). To count the share of women in the decision-making bodies (listed for each Central Bank in Table 8.5), we consider the total number of members including the Governor.

**Table 8.5** The Central Banks in the EU Member States: the decision-making bodies

| *Country* | *Central Bank* | *Decision-making bodies* |
|---|---|---|
| Belgium | Banque Nationale de Belgique/Nationale Bank van België/Belgische Nationalbank | Board of Directors; Council of Regency |
| Bulgaria | Българска народна банка | Governing Council |
| Czech Republic | Česká národní banka | Bank Board |
| Denmark | Danmarks Nationalbank | Board of Directors; Board of Governors |
| Germany | Deutsche Bundesbank | Executive Board |
| Estonia | Eesti Pank | Supervisory Board; Executive Board |
| Ireland | Central Bank of Ireland | Central Bank Commission |
| Greece | Τράπεζα της Ελλάδος | General Council |
| Spain | Banco de España | Governing Council |
| France | Banque de France | General Council |
| Croatia | Hrvatska Narodna Banka | Council |
| Italy | Banca d'Italia | Directorate; Board of Directors |
| Cyprus | Κεντρική Τράπεζα της Κύπρου | Board of Directors |
| Latvia | Latvijas Banka | Council; Board |
| Lithuania | Lietuvos Bankas | Board |
| Luxembourg | Banque centrale du Luxembourg | Council |
| Hungary | Magyar Nemzeti Bank | Monetary Council |
| Malta | Bank Ċentrali ta' Malta | Board of Directors; Investments Policy Committee |
| The Netherlands | De Nederlandsche Bank | Governing Board |
| Austria | Österreichische Nationalbank | Governing Board |
| Poland | Narodowy Bank Polski | Monetary Policy Council; Management Board |
| Portugal | Banco de Portugal | Board of Directors |
| Romania | Banca Naţională a României | Board of Directors |
| Slovenia | Banka Slovenije | Governing Board |
| Slovakia | Národná Banka Slovenska | Bank Board |
| Finland | Suomen Pankki | Parliamentary Supervisory Council; Board |
| Sweden | Sveriges Riksbank | General Council; Executive Board |

(continued)

**Table 8.5** (continued)

| *Country* | *Central Bank* | *Decision-making bodies* |
|---|---|---|
| The United Kingdom[a] | Bank of England | Court of Directors; Monetary Policy Committee |

[a]As we know, the United Kingdom officially left the European Union on 31 January 2020. The transition period in place ended on 31 December 2020
*Source* European Institute for Gender Equality (2021)

As shown in Table 8.6, there are very diverse situations at a country level. Although female representation is sparse in general, we can observe that some CBs (for instance, in Austria, the Czech Republic, and Slovakia) actually feature a female representation for a few years and then none for the following years, while other CBs (such as in Cyprus, Germany, and Hungary) feature the opposite, with women being represented only after some years into the observation period. The trends across the countries are mostly fluctuating with many showing a strengthening of women representation in more recent years (see Spain, Ireland, and France). In fact, France (like Sweden and the United Kingdom) shows high percentages even in more distant years, which then fall and then rise again. Overall, the EU27 countries show a fluctuating but upward trend over the years; the same consideration applies if we consider the UK and then look at the values referred to the EU28 countries.

The count includes women who assume the role of Governor, namely Chrystalla Georghadji, Governor of the Central Bank of Cyprus from 2014 to 2019; Bodil Nyboe Andersen, Governor of the Denmark Nationalbank from 1995 to 2005; and Sharon Donnery, Governor of the Central Bank of Ireland on an acting basis from June 2019 to August 2019 (see Table 8.3; as noted above, Table 8.6 does not report data for 2019).

**Table 8.6** Female members of all key decision-making bodies (%)

| | *2003* | *2004* | *2005* | *2006* | *2007* | *2008* | *2009* | *2010* | *2011* | *2012* | *2013* | *2014* | *2015* | *2016* | *2017* | *2018* |
|---|---|---|---|---|---|---|---|---|---|---|---|---|---|---|---|---|
| AT | 5.9 | 0 | 5.9 | 5.9 | 12.5 | 0 | 0 | 0 | 0 | 0 | 0 | 0 | 0 | 0 | 0 | 0 |
| BE | 23.5 | 17.6 | 9.1 | 9.1 | 25 | 16.7 | 22.2 | 22.2 | 27.8 | 22.2 | 22.2 | 16.7 | 16.7 | 11.1 | 11.8 | 11.8 |
| BG | 16.7 | 16.7 | 16.7 | 16.7 | 14.3 | 14.3 | 14.3 | 14.3 | 14.3 | 14.3 | 28.6 | 28.6 | 28.6 | 57.1 | 57.1 | 57.1 |
| CY | 0 | 0 | 0 | 0 | 0 | 0 | 0 | 0 | 0 | 0 | 0 | 12.5 | 16.7 | 14.3 | 12.5 | 12.5 |
| CZ | N.A | 16.7 | 16.7 | 16.7 | 0 | 14.3 | 14.3 | 14.3 | 14.3 | 14.3 | 14.3 | 0 | 0 | 0 | 0 | 0 |
| DE | 0 | 0 | N.A | N.A | 0 | 0 | 0 | 0 | 16.7 | 16.7 | 16.7 | 16.7 | 16.7 | 20 | 16.7 | 25 |
| DK | 37.5 | 37.5 | 36 | 32 | 24 | 32.1 | 28.6 | 28.6 | 35.7 | 21.4 | 25 | 28.6 | 35.7 | 28.6 | 28.6 | 28.6 |
| EE | 0 | 12.5 | 12.5 | 12.5 | 12.5 | 8.3 | 16.7 | 18.2 | 18.2 | 18.2 | 18.2 | 18.2 | 18.2 | 18.2 | 18.2 | 18.2 |
| EL | 16.7 | 8.3 | 0 | 0 | 0 | 7.7 | 7.7 | 7.7 | 7.7 | 9.1 | 8.3 | 8.3 | 0 | 0 | 8.3 | 8.3 |
| ES | 0 | 16.7 | 11.1 | 22.2 | 20 | 20 | 20 | 20 | 30 | 22.2 | 20 | 20 | 30 | 30 | 40 | 30 |
| FI | 50 | 50 | 37.5 | 25 | 33.3 | 30.8 | 30.8 | 30.8 | 25 | 41.7 | 41.7 | 25 | 16.7 | 16.7 | 23.1 | 25 |
| FR | 16.7 | 28.6 | 16.7 | 25 | 30 | 33.3 | 30 | 30 | 27.3 | 18.2 | 18.2 | 27.3 | 45.5 | 45.5 | 45.5 | 45.5 |
| HR | N.A | N.A | N.A | N.A | 7.1 | 7.1 | 14.3 | 7.1 | 7.1 | 7.1 | 7.1 | 0 | 0 | 0 | 0 | 0 |
| HU | 0 | 0 | 0 | 0 | 25 | 25 | 33.3 | 28.6 | 28.6 | 28.6 | 22.2 | 11.1 | 11.1 | 11.1 | 11.1 | 11.1 |
| IE | 0 | 9.1 | 9.1 | 9.1 | 7.7 | 7.7 | 15.4 | 15.4 | 10 | 11.1 | 11.1 | 20 | 20 | 30 | 30 | 30 |
| IT | 7.7 | 0 | 0 | 0 | 0 | 0 | 5.6 | 5.6 | 5.6 | 5.6 | 5.9 | 16.7 | 22.2 | 22.2 | 22.2 | 22.2 |
| LT | N.A | 25 | 25 | 25 | 20 | 20 | 20 | 20 | 0 | 0 | 0 | 20 | 20 | 20 | 0 | 0 |
| LU | 12.5 | 12.5 | 12.5 | 12.5 | 11.1 | 11.1 | 0 | 0 | 0 | 0 | 11.1 | 11.1 | 11.1 | 11.1 | 11.1 | 22.2 |
| LV | 28.6 | 28.6 | 28.6 | 28.6 | 25 | 23.1 | 21.4 | 21.4 | 21.4 | 21.4 | 21.4 | 15.4 | 23.1 | 25 | 25 | 22.2 |
| MT | N.A | 25 | 25 | 25 | 20 | 9.1 | 9.1 | 9.1 | 9.1 | 23.1 | 23.1 | 20 | 21.4 | 18.8 | 13.3 | 15.4 |
| NL | 0 | 0 | 11.1 | 11.1 | 20 | 25 | 25 | 25 | 25 | 20 | 20 | 20 | 0 | 0 | 0 | 0 |

(continued)

**Table 8.6** (continued)

| | *2003* | *2004* | *2005* | *2006* | *2007* | *2008* | *2009* | *2010* | *2011* | *2012* | *2013* | *2014* | *2015* | *2016* | *2017* | *2018* |
|---|---|---|---|---|---|---|---|---|---|---|---|---|---|---|---|---|
| PL | N.A | 11.1 | 11.1 | 11.1 | 10 | 11.8 | 5.9 | 23.5 | 23.5 | 23.5 | 25 | 22.2 | 27.8 | 16.7 | 16.7 | 11.8 |
| PT | 0 | 0 | 0 | 0 | 0 | 0 | 16.7 | 16.7 | 16.7 | 0 | 0 | 0 | 0 | 16.7 | 20 | 33.3 |
| RO | 12.5 | 0 | 12.5 | 25 | 22.2 | 22.2 | 22.2 | 11.1 | 11.1 | 11.1 | 11.1 | 11.1 | 11.1 | 11.1 | 11.1 | 11.1 |
| SE | 30 | 30 | 30 | 30 | 45.5 | 41.2 | 41.2 | 35.3 | 23.5 | 29.4 | 29.4 | 29.4 | 29.4 | 29.4 | 35.3 | 35.3 |
| SI | 0 | 0 | 20 | 20 | 0 | 0 | 0 | 20 | 40 | 40 | 40 | 40 | 40 | 40 | 20 | 20 |
| SK | 16.7 | 14.3 | 33.3 | 14.3 | 20 | 20 | 18.2 | 14.3 | 20 | 0 | 0 | 0 | 0 | 0 | 0 | 0 |
| UK | 38.9 | 43.8 | 21.4 | 20 | 16.7 | 12.5 | 11.8 | 11.1 | 5.9 | 5.6 | 5.6 | 0 | 22.2 | 23.5 | 18.8 | 27.8 |
| EU27[a] | 15.4 | 15.1 | 16 | 15.4 | 15.5 | 16.8 | 17.8 | 18 | 18.7 | 17.4 | 18.4 | 18.3 | 20.2 | 19.8 | 20.2 | 20.4 |
| EU28[b] | 17.2 | 17 | 16.3 | 15.6 | 15.6 | 16.5 | 17.5 | 17.6 | 18 | 16.7 | 17.7 | 17.4 | 20.3 | 20 | 20.1 | 20.9 |

*Notes* Here, data for 2019 and 2020 are not reported as they are included in Table 8.7 which summarises actions on gender diversity taken by the Central Banks and related data for that biennium (in Table 8.7, data are disaggregated by each decision-making body, if the CBs have more than one). [a]European Union—27 countries (from 2020) [b]European Union—28 countries (1993–2020) (see EIGE, 2021)

*Source* European Institute for Gender Equality

## 8.6 The Results of a Survey[5]

In April 2021, this research was followed by a questionnaire-based survey involving the EU28 CBs, investigating specific aspects of gender representation within the CBs. The questionnaire was very simple and direct, including a total of 10 questions addressing the representation of women on staff and in the supreme decision-making body/bodies of the bank over the last two years (2019 and 2020), the presence of a formal gender-equality policy document, the measures taken to disseminate a gender-equality culture, to promote the recruitment and career progression of women, to facilitate employees' work-life balance, and to close the gender pay gap. Finally, two questions inquired whether the NCBs had appointed a Diversity and Inclusion manager/body and obtained certification for gender equality (the questionnaire is provided in Box 8.1, at the end of the chapter).

The response rate was 39.29%, with participation from 11 of the total 28 CBs contacted for the survey, namely:

- Oesterreichische Nationalbank (CB of the Republic of Austria)
- Българска народна банка (CB of the Republic of Bulgaria, known as "Bulgarian National Bank")
- Česká národní banka (CB of the Czech Republic, known as "Czech National Bank")
- Banque de France (CB of France)
- Banca d'Italia (CB of Italy)
- Lietuvos Bankas (CB of Lithuania)
- Bank Ċentrali ta' Malta (CB of Malta)
- De Nederlandsche Bank (CB of the Netherlands)
- Banco de Portugal (CB of the Portuguese Republic)
- Hrvatska Narodna Banka (CB of the Republic of Croatia)
- Banka Slovenije (CB of the Republic of Slovenia).

[5] We are very grateful to the Central Banks that took part in the survey and provided us with their valuable feedback. Obviously, any errors in reporting the data and information contained in the questionnaires are our sole responsibility. Likewise, the responsibility for any errors in finding data and information in the documents, some not in English, of the non-responding CBs is ours alone.

Information on the CBs that did not respond to the questionnaires was retrieved both from their 2019 and 2020 annual reports and from a keyword search on their websites and other documents, such as corporate social responsibility reports, gender pay gap reports, and policies on diversity and inclusion. Annual reports were also consulted to integrate information for the responding banks. Data are updated to 30 June 2021.

Table 8.7 summarises the feedback from the survey, while detailed insight is discussed below.

### 8.6.1 *Percentage of Women Working in the CBs*

The first item in the questionnaire concerns the percentage of women employed in the CBs. As shown in Table 8.7, results show a wide percentage range from a minimum of 35% to a maximum of 65% in 2019, with a slightly higher minimum value of 36% in 2020. In seven cases, women represent more than 50% of the workforce almost always in both years. Yet, no clear trends emerge as the percentage of women follows different directions (increasing, decreasing, or remaining stable) in the two years considered. In any case, a trend over two years would not be very meaningful.

### 8.6.2 *Number of Women in the Decision-Making Body*

As to the women sitting on the board of directors, the percentage varies widely across CBs. In particular, the highest percentage is 60% (in both years), reported by the Banco de España (the CB of Spain), which also ranks at the top position in the OMFIF's Gender-Equality Index of the World's Central Banks (OMFIF, 2020)—far ahead of the other European CBs. Another bank has a presence of more than 50% in a single year, while some have no presence at all.

Gender quotas in Central Bank decision-making bodies are rare. One recent case that stands out is that of the National Bank of Belgium (Dutch: Nationale Bank van België, French: Banque nationale de Belgique, German: Belgische Nationalbank), which, since 2020, is subject to a new law aimed at improving the gender balance in the bank's administrative bodies. According to this law, at least one-third of the members of the Council of Regency must be of the opposite sex to that of the other members. In addition, if the Governor is Dutch-speaking, the Regent appointed by the King to chair the Council of Regency must be French-speaking (and vice-versa) and must be of the opposite sex to the Governor (National Bank of Belgium, 2021).

Another distinctive feature of appointments to the decision-making bodies of Central Banks is that this practice cannot be defined as the generalised result of decisions taken in full autonomy. For example, again with reference to the National Bank of Belgium, the 2020 Annual Report states that "*... the Bank is bound by the specific provisions of its Organic Law and its Statutes. It is the King who appoints the Governor. The other members of the Board of Directors are also appointed by the King, upon a proposal from the Council of Regency. The Regents are appointed on the proposal of the Minister of Finance and civil society. In view of the arrangements for appointing the members of its organs, it is therefore not the Bank alone that establishes and implements the diversity policy*" (National Bank of Belgium, 2021, p. 129).

### *8.6.3 Gender-Equality Policy Issued Through a Formal Document*

Based on the responses to the survey and the information drawn from the reports, most CBs state that they have formalised their gender-equality policy or are in the process of doing so. Below we report the details provided in the questionnaires and/or in the banks' documents.

Banque de France's experience dates back to more than 10 years ago. It had signed the Gender Equality Agreement in 2009 (and the updated version in 2014 to be renegotiated in 2021) with focus on the objectives of helping staff to balance work and family life, increasing the share of women in senior positions, supporting women's career progression, and improving the mix of professions.

As to the Central Bank of the Republic of Austria, the Oesterreichische Nationalbank (OeNB) promotes gender equality in the workplace by pursuing an equal opportunities strategy. In particular, the OeNB has adopted its first legally binding action plan for the advancement of women, which defines a set of measures to be implemented between 2016 and 2021. The plan foresees four fields of action, namely: corporate culture and role models, external recruiting, balance of work and family life, and promotion of high-potential employees and career opportunities. The action plan has been regularly monitored and updated as needed (OeNB, 2020b).

In the same vein, the National Bank of Belgium has a gender diversity policy and an action plan aimed at increasing the representation of women among the supervisory staff and management. Moreover, at the end of 2018, it set a 40% quantitative target for female representation among recruits and employees promoted to senior posts (on an annual basis).

Similarly, the Bank of England has a gender-equality policy based on targets for female representation. The targets to be achieved by 31 December 2020 included a 35% proportion of women in senior roles and a 50% target for roles below senior management. The bank shows an upward trend for both representations of women, reaching 32 and 46%, respectively, as shown in its 2020 annual report which covers the period 1 March 2019 to 29 February 2020 (Bank of England, 2020).

The Croatian National Bank (Hrvatska Narodna Banka) has also adopted a formalised policy that ensures the protection and promotion of gender equality, guaranteeing all employees equal opportunities to exercise their employment rights, as well as equal benefits from their achievements. As a result, the bank is obliged to protect employees from discrimination, including discrimination on the basis of gender, in the field of work and working conditions.

Other CBs have adopted policies on diversity and inclusion, which also refer to gender equality. This is the case of the Central Bank of Malta (Bank Ċentrali ta' Malta), which has an Equality, Diversity, and Inclusion Policy in place and is committed to its implementation and maintenance. The policy was approved by the Board of Directors in 2020 and provides guidance to address and successfully manage diversity issues. To this end, the bank is setting up a committee of six employees certified as "diversity officers". The committee will have the task of establishing a strategy for tackling all forms of discrimination and monitoring the actions taken every year.

The CB of the Netherlands, De Nederlandsche Bank (DNB), has several policies in place to promote diversity and has developed a strategy focused on gradually strengthening an inclusive environment. The DNB's diversity policy focuses on three groups of people: (1) those with a non-western cultural background; (2) women in top positions; and (3) people with disabilities. With specific reference to gender equality, the CB strives to achieve a gender balance at all levels of the organisation.

Another example is the Central Bank of Ireland (Banc Ceannais na hÉireann), which in 2018 adopted a Diversity & Inclusion Policy Statement, symbolising its commitment to recognising the value of diversity (including gender diversity) among its staff. The implementation of the D&I Policy Statement, which is reviewed and updated annually, is supported by an action plan (the one currently in force covers the period from 2020 to 2021) and diversity representation goals. The latter tool provides for a balance at all levels of the organisation and a specific goal for the senior leader population (senior leadership teams and heads of division) in that it should be made up of at least 45% of males and females (as of 1 January 2020, this population was composed of a 43% female and a 57% male component).

Also noteworthy is the experience of the Sveriges Riksbank (simply referred to as Riksbank), the Central Bank of Sweden, which has a formalised policy for diversity and equal treatment, the latest version of which was issued in 2020. The policy states that Riksbank's diversity work aims to promote equal rights, possibilities, and obligations for all members of staff. The policy covers many topics, such as working conditions, employee remuneration, recruitment, skills development, employment and parenting, discrimination and harassment, and gender equality. The last topic is the only one for which a numerical target has been set, specifying that the underrepresented sex should account for at least 40% within units and departments (Riksbank, 2020).

Interestingly, the Bulgarian National Bank (Българска народна банка) responded to the questionnaire by stating that according to the Bulgarian Law on Protection against Discrimination, the employer could not establish gender preferences. The bank does not have a gender-equality policy since this policy is regulated at a national level by the Law on Gender Equality. The law does not foresee that the employer must establish a specific institutional policy to ensure the equal treatment of female and male employees. Furthermore, the fundamental principle underlying all HR policies and practices is merit, so professional development and career advancement are based on individual performance and results. Any member of staff or external applicant, regardless of gender, individual characteristics, or facets of diversity, can participate in an open, fair, and transparent competition. As a result, the bank has not implemented any specific gender balance measures, such as those on the promotion of female recruitment and careers.

Equally interesting is the response provided by the Bank of Slovenia (Banka Slovenije). Because it already practices gender equality, as corroborated by its data on female representation, it has not adopted any formal policy. Accordingly, it does not use any means to disseminate a culture on gender equality and to promote female recruitment and careers.

Among the respondents, three Central Banks (Banca d'Italia, Banco de Portugal, and Lietuvos Bankas, respectively, the CBs of Italy, the Portuguese Republic, and Lithuania) have yet to adopt a formalised policy on gender equality but are working to do so. For example, the Banca d'Italia states that despite having a policy for D&I (including gender), it has yet to formalise the policy in a comprehensive document and expects to do so in the coming months.

### 8.6.4 *Culture on Gender Equality*

A separate question in the survey specifically addresses the cultural aspect. Based on the responses to the survey and the information taken from reports, most CBs have activated tools to disseminate a culture of diversity, including gender diversity; among those that still have not done so, one bank currently has a work in progress, while a few others have still not acted in this direction.

One example of a bank already equipped with such tools is the OeNB, which—as previously mentioned—has adopted a plan for female promotion (precisely, the action plan for the advancement of women 2016–2021). In particular, the bank has implemented many measures linked to the field of action 1 ("corporate culture and role models") of this plan. The tools can be listed as follows: opportunities for in-house debate about topics related to diversity management; equality and diversity as an integral part of the seminar programme; regular information in in-house media; use of inclusive language in external corporate communication; and a large-group seminar on diversity management every two years (a group seminar was organised in 2017 and again in 2019, the next is scheduled for 2021) (OeNB, 2020b).

The Banque de France has also aimed to promote a culture on gender equality in several ways. In June 2020, the Banque adopted the charter on Diversity and Inclusion, which details the commitment to reject all forms of discrimination. In particular, through the charter, the Banque undertakes to constantly guard against any discrimination, to guarantee all measures that ensure equal opportunities, to respect differences in the working environment, to raise awareness among staff on the need to combat stereotypes, to inform all staff, service providers, and members of the general public of its commitments, and to encourage them to respect the same principles (Banque de France, 2020b). La Banque also arranged a video entitled "Together we fight against discrimination" (gender, age, disabilities, sexual orientation) and organised training sessions for staff ("Acting on stereotypes and encouraging diversity") and for managers ("Recruiting without discrimination" and "Adopt inclusive management"). Finally, at the end of 2016, it set up a mixed-gender network to acknowledge talent in all its forms. In addition to these tools outlined by the Banque in response to our questionnaire, it is worth mentioning the numerous events, conferences, and meetings organised to provide an opportunity to explore and discuss gender issues, including the economic impact of gender inequality, women in CB governance, gender and financial inclusion, and the impact of digital technology on gender-equality issues (Banque de France, 2020a).

The Banca d'Italia has a D&I strategy whose key elements are the development of an organisational culture on the value of diversity and the building of an inclusive workplace, which therefore imply the promotion of a gender-equality culture. The most used tools are leaflets, seminars, training, and a Management by Objectives (MBO) system that may include objectives based on diversity management. Furthermore, the Banca d'Italia has aimed at spreading the culture externally, such as to supervised banks. First, it invited banks to adopt initiatives aimed at encouraging a greater presence of women in their governing bodies; then after a public consultation, it amended Circular No. 285 of 17 December 2013 (and subsequent updates) concerning the corporate governance of banks and banking groups, introducing, among other things, a 33% minimum gender quota in the management and control bodies of banks (see Chapter 10).

Again, on the topic of D&I, the Diversity & Inclusion Policy Statement of the Central Bank of Ireland specifically states that awareness and understanding of diversity and inclusion are strengthened through learning programmes and communication activities. The statement affirms that an open and inclusive culture is derived from workplace policies, practices, and behaviours. To this end, relevant are events such as panel discussions and information sessions, organised by staff-led networks supported by the bank, including Parents and Carers Network, Rainbow LGBTI+ Network, Women's Network, Cultural Diversity Network, and BankAbility Network (Central Bank of Ireland, 2020b). The CB also plays an important role in overseeing diversity culture outside the bank, particularly in financial firms. Indeed, on the one hand, the bank assessed the approach to diversity and inclusion across a sample of insurance firms in Ireland (Central Bank of Ireland, 2020c), and on the other, it published research on the levels of gender diversity for senior positions in regulated financial services providers.

Also at the DNB, employee networks are focused on cultural diversity (among them, Female Capital aims to empower women). The culture of diversity and inclusion is an integral part of the CB's new multi-year strategy (DNB vision and strategy 2025). The climate of inclusiveness is to be understood in a broad (gender and cultural) sense; in particular, in 2018, the vision on D&I was revisited to include gender balance as a key priority. An important role in the promotion and dissemination of D&I ideas and principles is played by the Diversity Board, which was established at the bank in 2017.

Once again, the promotion of a gender-oriented culture is one of the activities carried out by the governance structure specifically dedicated to diversity and inclusion at the National Bank of Belgium. Internal communication within the bank plays a very important role in this respect, as does the bank's support for and participation in the launch of "Women in Finance Belgium". Joining other financial institutions, the bank is one of the signatories of the Gender Diversity in Finance Charter, which aims to improve gender equality in the financial sector (see Chapter 2). The signing ceremony took place at the bank in June 2019.

The Central Bank of Malta also stands out for promoting an ad hoc culture. The Equality, Diversity, and Inclusion Policy adopted by the CB represents a clear commitment to strengthening an inclusive culture that promotes the diverse backgrounds and experiences of employees while respecting and reinforcing a concept of diversity that is not just gender-based.

Very different feedback was obtained from the Banka Slovenije and the Bulgarian National Bank. The first did not adopt any instruments to disseminate the culture, given that it has already achieved gender equality. The second has not implemented measures to address gender balance in the organisation for the reasons mentioned in the previous point on gender-equality policy (Sect. 8.6.3). In essence, as an employer, it cannot have an institutional policy that ensures that female and male employees are treated on an equal basis and all HR policies are merit-based.

### 8.6.5 Female Recruitment

As for the previous topic, female recruitment among CBs is at different stages, with some CBs having already adopted specific measures, others being in the phase of implementation, and others still not having any initiatives at all.

Among those that have adopted such measures, the Bank of England has a recruitment policy enriched in recent years with gender-equality programmes and arrangements. The bank has implemented the Future Capability programme, which aims to recruit talented young people keen on starting their careers after leaving school helping them develop technical skills useful for working at the bank. In 2018, half of the participants were female. In that same year, the bank also piloted a new name-blind recruitment model, with the belief that assessing candidates without knowing their personal data will help contrast an unconscious bias. This new recruitment model has enabled further progress towards gender equality. One example is the trend of new employees, which shows an increase of women from 40% in 2013 to 45% in 2020 (Bank of England, 2019, 2020).

As to the Central Bank of Sweden, its diversity and equal treatment policy states that recruitment must be based on objective grounds to employ individuals who are deemed to have the right skills. Employment must be granted to the applicant meeting the job qualification requirements with no discrimination. At the same time, an essential principle of recruitment is to achieve a mixed group of people, so in the case of equal competence of job applicants, diversity is a priority. Therefore, no specific measures have been taken in favour of women in recruitment, but the above-mentioned principle safeguards gender equality for women.

The OeNB has implemented the measures related to the field of action 2 ("external recruiting") of its action plan for the advancement of women 2016–2021 (see Sect. 8.6.3). The aim is to recruit qualified female candidates and to attract more job applications from women. As a result, the bank has taken steps in this direction, such as launching a new external recruitment format called "OeNB Insights" addressed to female students of mathematics, informatics, natural sciences, and technology (MINT), which are essential disciplines in the age of digitalisation and, so far, traditionally male-dominated. In addition, at least one woman must be among the potential recruits who are invited for an interview, under the condition that female applicants have the required basic qualifications (OeNB,

2020b). In 2019, the OeNB participated for the first time in Daughters' Day, offering around 40 teenage girls the opportunity to experience a day's work at the bank (OeNB, 2020a). Moreover, it also expanded the range of internships available exclusively for young female students (OeNB, 2021).

In addition to the CBs above, other two CBs have already implemented many recruitment initiatives and are currently working on new measures.

The first is the Banca d'Italia, which promotes female recruitment in several ways by participating in many orientation initiatives (career days and webinars organised by Italian universities), providing information during these events on the recruitment process and career prospects within the bank, and by encouraging the participation of women in public competitions organised by the bank. Interestingly, recruiting commissions are made up of at least one-third female members. In the pre-selection tests featuring several multiple-choice questions, the bank has increased the penalty for answering a question incorrectly (following previous bank's research on the pre-screening phase of the hiring process), based on the assumption that female candidates may be more risk-averse than their male peers. The Banca d'Italia has also activated a dedicated research group to investigate any further reasons for the gender gap in recruitment, with the view of taking further measures if deemed appropriate.

The second bank is the DNB. It encourages managers in charge of hiring to have a diverse (gender) selection committee in the recruitment process and works to make the selection process and interviews more objective and standardised. Moreover, in order to promote equal opportunities and to overcome prejudices, the DNB also puts an effort in adopting inclusive/gender-neutral language in job vacancy posts and trains its Human Resource (HR) personnel, recruiters, and hiring managers to act accordingly.

Other interesting initiatives collected by the survey include the one from the Banque de France, which offers women the opportunity to pursue a high-level scientific training diploma to be a data scientist, an IT architect, an urban planner, or an actuary. Conversely, some CBs claim to have not taken any specific measures towards increasing female recruitment. Among these, the Central Bank of Malta has not implemented any measures because it encourages applications from candidates regardless of their gender, gender identity, ethnicity, sexual orientation, age, religion, disability, or other characteristics. Further, the Equality, Diversity, and Inclusion Policy adopted by the bank qualifies it as an inclusive employer.

Similarly, some CBs (such as the Bulgarian National Bank, the Croatian National Bank, and the Banka Slovenije) have not adopted any specific measures to promote the recruitment of women as these initiatives are considered not necessary since these banks have already reached gender parity in practice and/or they are already prioritising skills and merit, regardless of gender.

### 8.6.6 *Work-Life Balance*

Information collected through the responses provided by CBs and their reports shows a broad consensus among CBs on the provision of actions to facilitate a work-life balance and concerns several measures activated over the years. The banks' documents also refer to the change in working conditions following the coronavirus pandemic, however, we do not consider such changes sufficient to qualify the CBs as active on this front.

For example, the Banca d'Italia lists many measures in terms of flexible working hours and other types of benefits. Regarding the former, the bank has put in place a system for flexible working time since 2014 to meet the personal and professional needs of employees. The system foresees several part-time patterns (horizontal and vertical), remote working, and weekly working hours. In addition, the bank has implemented specific measures to support working parents. For women, the CB foresees a mandatory five-month fully paid maternity leave and an optional six-month additional leave, plus extended remote working during pregnancy. For men, it foresees a 10-day compulsory leave and five days of extraordinary leave for fathers (to be taken immediately after the birth of the child). Since the outbreak of COVID-19, the Banca d'Italia has extended the use of smart working and is working on a new hybrid work model that allows alternating office and remote work to promote a better work-life balance. As to other benefits, it provides nursery and pre-school services to employees. In 2021, it introduced a company-wide flexible benefits plan to allow more flexibility and choice for employees. The programme also provides reimbursement of expenses related to the upbringing of children and to care services for children and elderly family members.

Also, the DNB lists several measures in place: full-time work (i.e., 36 hours per week) 4 days a week; facilitations for parental leave throughout the first eight years after the birth of the child; and the choice to work remotely or from home, part-time, and with flexible hours (e.g., flexible start and end times, compressed hours, annualised hours, staggered hours, and other versions).

Similarly, the Central Bank of Ireland places great emphasis on work-life balance, which is also supported by the initiatives of one of the staff-led networks (the Parents and Carers Network). Work-life balance initiatives have benefited from the progress brought by the recent improvement in flexible working options through the launch of the Home Working Policy in August 2018. Where possible, this policy gives employees greater choice over how and where they work while safeguarding expected productivity and efficiency outcomes. An interesting consequence of flexibility in working (part-time and remote), staff holiday leave, and business trips is the bank's reconsideration of the use of desk estate. Indeed, in assessing the surplus of desks, the CB implemented desk sharing with the ultimate aim of becoming more efficient and effective in the use of its desks and office space (Central Bank of Ireland, 2020a).

The Bank of England has also moved in this direction. It has implemented many work-life balance mechanisms, including flexible working patterns (widely used in senior management positions) and part-time work. Many women use part-time work, with percentages approaching or exceeding 80% of all part-time employees. In addition, the bank has pioneered executive-level job share and has refined technology over time to make remote working (widely used during the COVID-19 crisis) effective. As a result of the many initiatives undertaken, the bank appeared among the top 20 UK companies with the best work-life balance score (Bank of England, 2019) and in 2019 was included in the Working Families annual list of the top family-friendly employers in the UK (Bank of England, 2020).

The Magyar Nemzeti Bank, which is the Central Bank of Hungary, also achieved an important recognition: it was awarded the title of "Family-friendly Workplace" by the Ministry of Human Capacities primarily in virtue of its activation of a child-focused and family-friendly programme, supporting employees with families and children. The bank then obtained the Family-friendly Place Certification in the first round of applications in 2019, achieving the highest certification that could be acquired in that round (Magyar Nemzeti Bank, 2020).

In the same vein, the OeNB has obtained the certification under the "work and family" audit programme, that is, a certification as a family-friendly employer which specifically fulfils the requirements of its action plan for the advancement of women 2016–2021 (OeNB, 2020b) in the field of action 3: "balancing work and family life". Measures include allowing and encouraging fathers of newborns or newly adopted children to take a month's paid leave, the availability of a company kindergarten, guidelines for a return-to-work interview, and flexible working arrangements (such as part-time, teleworking/remote work, and sabbatical).

Also worth mentioning is the experience of the Czech National Bank (Česká národní banka) which reports among its measures a shortened working week and flexible working hours where employees themselves can arrange their shifts around a fixed time between 9 a.m. and 2 p.m., during which all employees have to be available. The bank also offers the opportunity to work from home where possible (some positions, such as cash processing or bank security officers, cannot work from home), and extended holidays beyond the national standard days for the Czech Republic (five weeks instead of four). In addition, the CB provides employees with benefits for payments related to leisure activities, kindergarten or school fees, travel expenses, cultural events, health care, books, and so on, organises cultural and sporting events for employees and their families, and contributes financially to the activities of the employees' sports club.

In addition to the initiatives outlined above, the responses to the questionnaires provide other information on the main measures adopted. The Banco de Portugal indicates flexible working hours and a teleworking policy; the Central Bank of Malta states that the measures include, but are not limited to, parental leave for both genders, additional special leave to care for immediate family members, a system of reduced working hours, social and sports clubs, and the possibility to work remotely. Further, the Lietuvos Bankas states that it has introduced the meeting-free Fridays work format to help employees manage the workweek workload (unfinished tasks and planning of the next week); the Bulgarian National Bank has maternity and paternity leave packages in alignment with legal requirements, flexible working time, part-time work, and teleworking; the Banque de France lists longer periods of maternity and paternity leave than those legally required and facilitates part-time working arrangements; the Croatian National Bank highlights two entitlements of employees including a paid leave of up to seven days per year for personal needs and an additional paid leave for parents; the Banka Slovenije, which was awarded a full Family-Friendly Enterprise certification (Banka Slovenije, 2020) specifies among its other measures additional parental leave for childcare of three days when a child first enters kindergarten and one day when a child first enters primary school; and the Banco de España includes in its Strategic Plan 2024 the objective to achieve greater flexibility in work by implementing more teleworking and streamlining work schedules.

Similarly, many other references to work-life balance measures can be found in the annual reports of some CBs other than those seen so far. The Deutsche Bundesbank, for example, gives an ample description of working from home during the COVID-19 crisis, pointing out how this was facilitated by the fact that many employees already had extensive experience of working remotely through dedicated teleworking arrangements or other means (Deutsche Bundesbank, 2021). In the same way, the Bank of Finland (Suomen Pankki) mentions various flexible working-hour schedules, remote working, and virtual meetings, pointing out that the experience gained by staff before the pandemic from flexible working arrangements and the use of technology for virtual meetings made it easier to adapt to new working practices during the COVID-19 crisis (Bank of Finland, 2021).

### *8.6.7 Women's Career*

Among the 28 CBs, some already have in place programmes to support women's careers, others have begun implementing programmes, and others have yet to put in place initiatives in this direction.

Among the CBs showing the most progress on this front, the OeNB specifically addresses women's careers in its action plan for the advancement of women between 2016 and 2021 (OeNB, 2020b) and has taken measures related to the field of action 4 ("promoting high-potential employees and career opportunities"). In fulfilment of this objective, the bank has put forward many initiatives, among which management shadowing (which involves employees turning into mentees for a brief period during which they get the chance to accompany a manager in charge of a different business area and thus gain insights into various management tasks); special training programmes; raising the share of women in the expert career track via targets (there is a target of 50% for women at all levels); optimising the wording of job advertisements to avoid an unconscious gender bias and to attract more women; diversity on the selection board for positions in the career tracks; systematic criteria to inform decisions by a selection board; transparency by disclosing information on applicants for management positions to the OeNB equalities officers. Indeed, the share of women in the specialist career track has increased between 2017 and 2020 from 33.1 to 35.2%, although it has fluctuated over the years (OeNB, 2021).

On the other hand, the Banca d'Italia has addressed this issue mainly by focusing on female representation and women empowerment training. In particular, it has set a 33% target for women in the director segment to be met by 2023 (currently just over 30%). To date, women account for almost 34% of managerial positions assigned through internal selection procedures, which is an increase of 7 percentage points compared to 2019 (Banca d'Italia, 2021). In addition, in order to promote women's careers, the CB has set up tailored training for the empowerment of women. Training on skills developed in caregiving (including childcare) and their value in the workplace will be delivered in the third quarter of 2021. Finally, the Banca d'Italia has adopted various tools to ensure unbiased evaluation procedures, such as gender balance in the composition of selection panels.

In addition to encouraging internal promotion and developing a pool of female talent from which to draw positions of responsibility, the Banque de France has established an institutional mentoring system: 88 pairs in 2021 with 68% of women. This initiative aims at consolidating the progress that has been made in the share of women in top management positions (from 25 to 27% in just one year between 2018 and 2019).

The DNB also offers mentorship programmes as well as leadership training specifically for female staff to enable women to reach higher positions. The CB has also set a target for women in management positions since 2016 (32% at that time). The current target is to have 37% of women in management positions in 2021; as of 1 January 2021, the share was 35.6%. In any case, the bank's target is effective gender parity (50% women to 50% men), which requires small but steady steps.

The Bank of England has piloted a sponsorship programme to support career progression and strengthen talent. High-potential talent immediately below the level of head of department consists of half women and 16% Black, Asian, and Minority Ethnic (BAME) representation. Those involved in the pilot programme were 84% female and 74% BAME. The feedback has been very positive, and the bank intends to extend the number of people involved in this programme. A good sign of the actions taken to support women's careers is the increase in the number of women promoted compared to overall employees promoted: from 43% in 2013 to 52% in 2019, but with a drop to 48% in 2020.

Finally, the Bank of Finland monitors the career advancement of women. In particular, monitoring is done on the share of management posts of the minority gender within the targets set by the bank on equal career progression and equal skills development. The share of the management staff of the less represented gender is one of the CB's key HR sustainability indicators. It shows an increasing weight of women in recent years: the share has increased from 34% in 2018 to 42% in 2019, and finally to 45% in 2020.

In addition, two CBs have just started to implement measures. One is the Banco de Portugal, which is promoting women's careers through specific courses for women leaders prepared by its training unit. Managerial staff, especially middle management, seem to be unaware of the glass ceiling. As indicated in the annual reports (Banco de Portugal, 2020, 2021), in 2019 and 2020, female representation for middle management was 49.5 and 51.3%, respectively, and 31.7 and 29.5% for senior management. The other bank is the Lietuvos Bankas, which states that, although there are no formal procedures in place, gender balance is taken into account once selecting the candidates for top-level positions.

Finally, no specific measures have been taken by those banks (such as the Banka Slovenije, the Central Bank of Malta, and the Bulgarian National Bank) that, as previously described in relation to recruitment, have already achieved gender equality or already offer equal opportunities to employees regardless of gender and based only on individual performance and achievements.

### *8.6.8 Diversity and/or Inclusion Officer/Team*

Practically one-third of the CBs (9 out of 28) have a D&I officer/body. The organisational configuration varies significantly, either with single or multiple persons in charge, or with more articulated and complex structures, and also in regard to the issues addressed (gender diversity or, in a broader sense, diversity and inclusion).

Concerning gender diversity, the Banque de France has a person designated as a "professional gender equality adviser" and a senior manager who sponsors gender issues.

Similarly, the Bank of England has appointed a gender diversity officer for the bank in compliance with the HM Treasury Women in Finance Charter (see Chapter 2), to which it is a signatory (Carney, 2018).

In addition, some banks have diversity officers or D&I structures of various levels of complexity which usually also deal with gender equality.

This is the case of the OeNB which had to comply with the provisions of the Federal Equal Treatment Act from 1 January 2014, which, inter alia, requires a 50% female quota at all levels of the organisation. To achieve the objectives set out in its action plan for the advancement of women between 2016 and 2021 (OeNB, 2020b), the bank has appointed diversity officers to take effective measures to strengthen gender equality.

It is also the case for the Banca d'Italia, which has a D&I manager who works in the HR function and is assisted by a diversity team.

In the same vein, the Central Bank of Ireland has established the D&I working group. Its tasks include activities related to the action plan (such as monitoring and measuring progress), which supports (as indicated above) the implementation of the CB's Diversity & Inclusion Policy Statement.

In 2019, the National Bank of Belgium set up a governance structure specifically dedicated to diversity and inclusion. The structure is articulated and includes a D&I Council chaired by the Governor, a D&I manager, and finally Diversity ambassadors. Among the tasks assigned, there are the implementation of initiatives to increase female representation at all levels of the organisation and the promotion of a culture open to differences, not only of gender.

Further, the DNB has an articulated structure. Two HR policy advisors work on the CB's D&I policy and activities (for about one-third of their time) as D&I is an integral part of the HR and the organisation-wide strategy. In addition, in 2017, the CB established a Diversity Board including one director, two heads of division, and two heads of department.

The experience of the Lietuvos Bankas is different as it has set up an internal Equal Rights Committee consisting of employees from different units to resolve equal rights issues as they arise.

Finally, Riksbank has no specific person or body responsible for diversity and inclusion issues. However, the HR Unit is responsible for coordinating diversity work at the CB and annually following up the work in cooperation with the trade unions.

The Central Bank of Malta and the Banka Slovenije are working to establish such an appointment. As foreseen by the Equality, Diversity, and Inclusion Policy adopted by the Central Bank of Malta, an Equality, D&I Committee will be established. It will be composed of six diversity officers certified as such by the National Commission for the Promotion of Equality (NCPE is an equality body established in 2004 by Chapter 456 of the Laws of Malta, Equality for Men and Women Act, and with a mandate expanded several times in the fight against discrimination). The bank is currently in the process of forming this Committee. The Banka Slovenije has started to address this issue and is thinking about how to implement changes in this direction.

Finally, among the CBs that have not established or are not in the process of establishing an officer or body, the Banco de Portugal states that it participates, inter alia, in the Commission for Equality in Labour and Employment in Portugal.

### *8.6.9 Gender Equality Certification*

According to the feedback from the survey, CBs are still not familiar with gender equality certification. Only two are involved in the process: the Lietuvos Bankas and the Central Bank of Malta. The latter is in the process of assessing the requirements and inferences for the departments involved within the bank to obtain the Equality Certification, which is not limited to gender but holistically encompasses equality. Similarly, a press release dated 6 January 2021 on the bank's website states that it will be applying to the NCPE for an Equality Mark, a prestigious certification awarded to organisations that make gender equality one of their values.

### *8.6.10 Gender Pay Gap*

The CBs also show a variety of behaviours concerning actions on the gender pay gap. From the information available, two-thirds of the CBs have taken or are taking action on this issue, while one-third have not taken any initiative.

Among the CBs already active on this issue, some of them publish dedicated reports. This is the case of the Bank of England, which publishes a gender (also BAME) pay gap report in its Annual Report, fulfilling its obligation under Schedule 1 (Gender pay gap reporting) of the Equality Act 2010 (Specific Duties and Public Authorities) Regulations 2017. The pay report shows both the mean and the median gender pay gap to support equality through fair pay. Although the gap is still wide (around 20%), both mean and median show a downward trend, most likely due to an increase in the number of women at senior levels and a decrease in the number of women at lower ones. The bank, however, is confident that women and men are paid equally for doing the same work and is pursuing many initiatives on recruitment and career progression that should reduce the pay gap over time.

The Central Bank of Ireland publishes a stand-alone gender pay gap report, which indicates and comments on the results of the analysis based on annualised base pay and on pay grades (attributable to entry-level positions; professional, supervisory, and middle management levels; senior management levels; and other technical salary scales). The pay grades provide the same pay for the same job, regardless of gender. The reports, which have been published since 2018, show that the trend for the gender pay profile is in favour of male employees and is falling, and that the trend for the gender pay gap is consequently narrowing. From 1 January 2018 to 1 January 2021, the former fell from 2.7 to 2.2%, so the gender pay gap narrowed by 0.5% (Central Bank of Ireland, 2021). The gender pay profile is strongly influenced by the timing and impact of employee entry, exit, and promotion activities. The introduction of the above-mentioned gender representation goals for the overall workforce and senior leadership levels supports the bank in monitoring trends and taking any necessary action.

Other CBs have taken measures for employees returning from leave. For example, although the Central Bank of Malta adopts a policy of equal pay based on qualifications, experience, and skills, women on maternity or childcare leave still qualify for their annual performance increases while away from the bank. Thus, when they return, their pay will still be in line with that of their counterparts.

Similarly, the Lietuvos Bankas has taken measures for employees returning from childcare leave, revising their salary to match that of similar employees.

The experience of the Banque de France is also very interesting. The bank calculates a gender equal pay index which was introduced by law in 2018. According to the law, the index should be calculated each year based on five criteria: (1) the pay gap between men and women by age group and equivalent job category; (2) the gap in the increase rate of individual wages between men and women (excluding promotions); (3) the gap in promotions between men and women; (4) the percentage of employees who benefited from a pay increase the year they returned from maternity leave; (5) the number of employees of the underrepresented gender among the top 10 earners. The Banque de France's score for 2020 is 92/100 (the same as that for 2019, and higher than 88/100 for 2018), showing very limited pay gaps. These gaps are mainly attributable to career development, on which the Banque has taken several measures, as seen above.

Other interesting information from the questionnaires and annual reports is as follows: the Croatian National Bank has taken measures to close the gender pay gap following the principle of equal pay regardless of gender, which is incorporated in the internal acts of the CB; the Central Bank of Finland analyses gender pay equality which, as shown in the annual report for 2019 (Bank of Finland, 2020, p. 115), seems to have been achieved ("*The ratio of mean salary for women to mean salary for men of an equivalent skills level was in 2019 an average of 100%*"); finally, salaries at Riksbank are determined in compliance with objective and fair criteria, so the Central Bank carries out annual salary surveys to detect possible inequities.

Currently, two CBs have ongoing initiatives. The Banco de Portugal has been publishing its gender pay gap report since 2019. In the questionnaire, the bank states that it has initiatives in progress to close the pay gap. In this context, the bank carried out a study on the gender pay gap for 2019 and found some interesting results: the study shows "*in general, a gender balance in duties performed, except for management positions. An overall balance is also clear as regards staff members covered by wage increases under the annual performance-related variable pay process*" (Banco de Portugal, 2020, p. 61). Likewise, the Banca d'Italia is moving to take possible measures against the gender pay gap. In particular, the CB is conducting a study on the existence and magnitude of the gender pay gap and possible underlying reasons. The findings of the study, which shall take into account wage dynamics in a sufficiently robust historical depth, will determine the initiatives to be taken to address any gaps that may emerge.

Finally, some CBs claim to have not taken any initiative, yet on closer observation, they have actually implemented some measures. For example, the OeNB replied to the questionnaire stating that it does not take measures to close the gender pay gap. Interestingly, the bank points out that "*due to a rather rigid payment scheme (depending on education and years of experience) the gender pay gap is overall not too large and arises completely out of compositional effects. Hence, measures to promote women in management and expert career tracks serve to close the gender pay gap*". Therefore, although there are no targeted actions on the pay gap, the narrowing of the gap is expected to take place, as in other CBs, through actions focused especially on career progression.

Another case is the DNB. In 2018, the bank performed an analysis to assess whether there were any gender pay gaps among its staff members, finding no significant difference in the payment after adjusting for job scale, age, and years of service. Therefore, it is fair to point out that despite the bank responding in the questionnaire that it had no targeted actions to close the gender pay gap, its study produced more than satisfactory results.

Taken together, the picture that emerges from the answers to the questionnaires and the information obtained from the CBs' documents is heterogeneous. Some CBs are very active and sensitive to gender diversity issues, while others seem to be lagging in adopting measures in favour of women. As expected, we found a greater homogeneity in the promotion of initiatives in favour of a work-life balance.

It must be said though that these findings are inevitably limited by the availability of readily accessible information. While responses to the questionnaires provided direct feedback from 11 of the total CBs contacted, information on the remaining banks was collected from the documents available. Therefore, it is possible that measures are also being taken by other banks for which no information was found.

**Table 8.7** Gender diversity in the EU28 CBs: data, actions taken, and actions in progress

| *National Central Bank* | *Total number of women in the NCB (%)* | *Women in the decision-making body/bodies (%)* | *Formalised gender equality policy adoption* | *Promoting culture on gender equality* | *Support for the recruitment of women* | *Promotion of initiatives to reconcile work and private life* | *Promotion of women's careers* | *Officer/team for diversity and inclusion* | *Certification for gender equality* | *Measures to close the gender pay gap* |
|---|---|---|---|---|---|---|---|---|---|---|
| Oesterreichische Nationalbank* (CB of the Republic of Austria) | 39.3 (2019) 39.6 (2020) | Governing Board: 0 (2019 and 2020) | Yes | Yes | Yes | Yes | Yes | Yes | No | No[a] |
| Nationale Bank van België (Dutch) Banque nationale de Belgique (French) Belgische Nationalbank (German) (CB of Belgium) | 35 (2019) 36 (2020) | Board of Directors: 0 (2019 and 2020) Council of Regency: 7.14 (2019) 38.88 (2020) | Yes | Yes | Yes | Yes | Yes | Yes | N.F | N.F |
| Българска народна банка* (CB of the Republic of Bulgaria) | 65 (2019 and 2020) | Governing Council: 57 (2019) 43 (2020) | No | No | No | Yes | No | No | No | No |

| *National Central Bank* | *Total number of women in the NCB (%)* | *Women in the decision-making body/bodies (%)* | *Formalised gender equality policy adoption* | *Promoting culture on gender equality* | *Support for the recruitment of women* | *Promotion of initiatives to reconcile work and private life* | *Promotion of women's careers* | *Officer/team for diversity and inclusion* | *Certification for gender equality* | *Measures to close the gender pay gap* |
|---|---|---|---|---|---|---|---|---|---|---|
| Κεντρική Τράπεζα της Κύπρου (CB of Cyprus) | N.F | Board of Directors: 12.5 (2019 and 2020) | N.F | N.F | N.F | N.F | N.F | N.F | N.F | N.F |
| Hrvatska Narodna Banka* (CB of the Republic of Croatia) | 64.85 (2019) 64.65 (2020) | Council: 25 (2019) 37.5 (2020) | Yes | Yes | No | Yes | Yes | No | No | Yes |
| Danmarks Nationalbank (CB of Denmark) | 41 (2019 and 2020) | Board of Directors: 28 (2020 and 2021)[b] Board of Governors: 0 (2020) 33 (2021)[b] | N.F | N.F | N.F | N.F | N.F | N.F | N.F | N.F |

(continued)

**Table 8.7** (continued)

| *National Central Bank* | *Total number of women in the NCB (%)* | *Women in the decision-making body/bodies (%)* | *Formalised gender equality policy adoption* | *Promoting culture on gender equality* | *Support for the recruitment of women* | *Promotion of initiatives to reconcile work and private life* | *Promotion of women's careers* | *Officer/team for diversity and inclusion* | *Certification for gender equality* | *Measures to close the gender pay gap* |
|---|---|---|---|---|---|---|---|---|---|---|
| Eesti Pank (CB of Estonia) | 57 (2019) 58 (2020) | Supervisory Board: 25.00 (2019) 10.00 (2020) Executive Board: 33.33 (2019 and 2020) | N.F | N.F | N.F | N.F | N.F | N.F | N.F | N.F |
| Suomen Pankki (CB of Finland) | 46 (2019 and 2020) | Parliamentary Supervisory Council: 22.22 (2020) 20 (2021) Board: 33.33 (2020 and 2021)[c] | N.F | N.F | N.F | Yes | Yes | N.F | N.F | Yes |

| *National Central Bank* | *Total number of women in the NCB (%)* | *Women in the decision-making body/bodies (%)* | *Formalised gender equality policy adoption* | *Promoting culture on gender equality* | *Support for the recruitment of women* | *Promotion of initiatives to reconcile work and private life* | *Promotion of women's careers* | *Officer/team for diversity and inclusion* | *Certification for gender equality* | *Measures to close the gender pay gap* |
|---|---|---|---|---|---|---|---|---|---|---|
| Banque de France* (CB of France) | 46.5 (2019) 46.3 (2020) | General Council: 45.45 (2020 and 2021)[d] | Yes | Yes | Yes | Yes | Yes | Yes | No | Yes |
| Deutsche Bundesbank (CB of the Federal Republic of Germany) | N.F | Executive Board: 33.33 (2019 and 2020) | N.F | N.F | N.F | Yes | N.F | N.F | N.F | N.F |
| Bank of Greece (CB of Greece) | N.F | N.F | N.F | N.F | N.F | N.F | N.F | N.F | N.F | N.F |
| Banc Ceannais na hÉireann (CB of Ireland) | 49 (2019) 48 (2020) | Central Bank Commission: 33.33 (2019) 40 (2020) | Yes | Yes | Yes | Yes | Yes | Yes | N.F | Yes |

(continued)

**Table 8.7** (continued)

| *National Central Bank* | *Total number of women in the NCB (%)* | *Women in the decision-making body/bodies (%)* | *Formalised gender equality policy adoption* | *Promoting culture on gender equality* | *Support for the recruitment of women* | *Promotion of initiatives to reconcile work and private life* | *Promotion of women's careers* | *Officer/team for diversity and inclusion* | *Certification for gender equality* | *Measures to close the gender pay gap* |
|---|---|---|---|---|---|---|---|---|---|---|
| Banca d'Italia* (CB of Italy) | 37.8 (2019 and 2020) | Directorate: 20 (2019 and 2020) Board of Directors: 23 (2019) 31 (2020) | In progress | Yes | In progress | Yes | Yes | Yes | No | In progress |
| Latvijas Banka (CB of Latvia) | 40 (2019) 41 (2020) | Council: 40 (2019) 16.7 (2020) Board: 16.7 (2019) 33.3 (2020) | N.F | N.F | N.F | N.F | N.F | N.F | N.F | N.F |
| Lietuvos Bankas* (CB of Lithuania) | 55.74 (2019) 55.65 (2020) | Board: 25 (2019) 20 (2020) | In progress | In progress | No | Yes | In progress | Yes | In progress | Yes |

| *National Central Bank* | *Total number of women in the NCB (%)* | *Women in the decision-making body/bodies (%)* | *Formalised gender equality policy adoption* | *Promoting culture on gender equality* | *Support for the recruitment of women* | *Promotion of initiatives to reconcile work and private life* | *Promotion of women's careers* | *Officer/team for diversity and inclusion* | *Certification for gender equality* | *Measures to close the gender pay gap* |
|---|---|---|---|---|---|---|---|---|---|---|
| Banque centrale du Luxembourg (CB of Luxembourg) | 37.07 (2019) 36.52 (2020) | Council: 22.22 (2019) N.F (2020) | N.F | N.F | N.F | N.F | N.F | N.F | N.F | N.F |
| Bank Ċentrali ta' Malta* (CB of Malta) | 47.1 (2019) 46.5 (2020) | Board of Directors: 28.6 (2019 and 2020) Investments Policy Committee: 16.7 (2020)[e] 18.2 (2021)[e] | Yes | Yes | No | Yes | No | In progress | In progress | Yes |

(continued)

**Table 8.7** (continued)

| *National Central Bank* | *Total number of women in the NCB (%)* | *Women in the decision-making body/bodies (%)* | *Formalised gender equality policy adoption* | *Promoting culture on gender equality* | *Support for the recruitment of women* | *Promotion of initiatives to reconcile work and private life* | *Promotion of women's careers* | *Officer/team for diversity and inclusion* | *Certification for gender equality* | *Measures to close the gender pay gap* |
|---|---|---|---|---|---|---|---|---|---|---|
| De Nederlandsche Bank* (CB of the Netherlands) | 40.4 (2019) 40.5 (2020) | Governing Board: 40 (2019 and 2020) | Yes | Yes | In progress | Yes | Yes | Yes | No | No[f] |
| Narodowy Bank Polski (CB of Poland) | N.F | Monetary Policy Council: 10 (2019) N.F (2020) Management Board: 25 (2019) N.F (2020) | N.F | N.F | N.F | N.F | N.F | N.F | N.F | N.F |

| *National Central Bank* | *Total number of women in the NCB (%)* | *Women in the decision-making body/bodies (%)* | *Formalised gender equality policy adoption* | *Promoting culture on gender equality* | *Support for the recruitment of women* | *Promotion of initiatives to reconcile work and private life* | *Promotion of women's careers* | *Officer/team for diversity and inclusion* | *Certification for gender equality* | *Measures to close the gender pay gap* |
|---|---|---|---|---|---|---|---|---|---|---|
| Banco de Portugal* (CB of the Portuguese Republic) | 49.8 (2019) 50.4 (2020) | Board of Directors: 20 (2019 and 2020) | In progress | No | No | Yes | In progress | No | No | In progress |
| Bank of England (CB of the UK) | 45 (2019 and 2020) | Court of Directors: 27.27 (2019) 46.15 (2020) Monetary Policy Committee: 11.11 (2019 and 2020) | Yes | Yes | Yes | Yes | Yes | Yes | N.F | Yes |
| Banca Națională a României (CB of Romania) | N.F | Board of Directors: 0 (2019) N.F (2020) | N.F | N.F | N.F | N.F | N.F | N.F | N.F | N.F |

(continued)

**Table 8.7** (continued)

| *National Central Bank* | *Total number of women in the NCB (%)* | *Women in the decision-making body/bodies (%)* | *Formalised gender equality policy adoption* | *Promoting culture on gender equality* | *Support for the recruitment of women* | *Promotion of initiatives to reconcile work and private life* | *Promotion of women's careers* | *Officer/team for diversity and inclusion* | *Certification for gender equality* | *Measures to close the gender pay gap* |
|---|---|---|---|---|---|---|---|---|---|---|
| Česká národní banka* (CB of the Czech Republic) | 48.8 (2019) 48 (2020) | Bank Board and Executive Managers 8.7 (2019) 8.4 (2020)[g] | No | No | No | Yes | No | No | No | No |
| Národná banka Slovenska (CB of the Slovak Republic) | N.F | Bank Board: 0 (2019 and 2020) | N.F | N.F | N.F | N.F | N.F | N.F | N.F | N.F |
| Banka Slovenije* (CB of the Republic of Slovenia) | 53.3 (2019) 53.2 (2020) | Governing Board: 20 (2019) 25 (2020)[h] | No | No | No | Yes | No | In progress | No | No |

| *National Central Bank* | *Total number of women in the NCB (%)* | *Women in the decision-making body/bodies (%)* | *Formalised gender equality policy adoption* | *Promoting culture on gender equality* | *Support for the recruitment of women* | *Promotion of initiatives to reconcile work and private life* | *Promotion of women's careers* | *Officer/team for diversity and inclusion* | *Certification for gender equality* | *Measures to close the gender pay gap* |
|---|---|---|---|---|---|---|---|---|---|---|
| Banco de España (CB of Spain) | 50.23 (2019) 50.70 (2020) | Governing Council (voting members): 60 (2019 and 2020) | N.F | N.F | N.F | Yes | N.F | N.F | N.F | N.F |
| Sveriges Riksbank (CB of Sweden) | N.F (2019) 47 (2020) | General Council: 27.27 (2019) 36.36 (2020) Executive Board: 42.86 (2019) 33.33 (2020) | Yes | Yes | Yes | Yes | N.F | Yes | N.F | Yes |

(continued)

**Table 8.7** (continued)

| *National Central Bank* | *Total number of women in the NCB (%)* | *Women in the decision-making body/bodies (%)* | *Formalised gender equality policy adoption* | *Promoting culture on gender equality* | *Support for the recruitment of women* | *Promotion of initiatives to reconcile work and private life* | *Promotion of women's careers* | *Officer/team for diversity and inclusion* | *Certification for gender equality* | *Measures to close the gender pay gap* |
|---|---|---|---|---|---|---|---|---|---|---|
| Magyar Nemzeti Bank (CB of Hungary) | N.F | Monetary Council: 11.11 (2019 and 2020) | N.F | N.F | N.F | Yes | N.F | N.F | N.F | N.F |

*Notes* N.F means information non found; the National Central Banks that responded to the questionnaire are marked with an asterisk (*)
[a]It is worth noting that, even if the CB states that there are no targeted actions for the gender pay gap, the reduction of the gap appears to take place through actions focused mainly on career progression, as expected for other CBs. Thus, we interpret the answer as "yes". See Sect. 8.6.10
[b]We refer to the composition of the Board of Directors and the Board of Governors shown in Danmarks Nationalbank (2020, 2021): the years are 2020 and 2021, respectively
[c]Values refer to 1 April 2020 and 1 March 2021
[d]Values refer to 1 January 2020 and 1 March 2021
[e]Values refer to 30 March 2020 and 30 March 2021
[f]It is fair to point out that, despite the absence of any targeted action to close the gender pay gap (stated by the bank in the questionnaire) it carried out an ad hoc analysis on the topic which produced more than satisfactory results (see Sect. 8.6.10)
[g]As specified in the questionnaire, the numbers include Bank Board members and Executive Managers (Board-1 level). The breakdown of the numbers is the following: for Bank Board members 0% (31 December 2019 and 31 December 2020); for Executive Directors 12.5% (31 December 2019) and 11.8% (31 December 2020)
[h]As specified in the questionnaire, the figure of 25% as of 31 December 2020 should be interpreted considering that the body was incomplete at that date
*Source* Questionnaires and the CBs documents (such as annual reports, corporate social responsibility reports, and gender pay gap reports)

**Box 8.1: Questionnaire on Gender Diversity**

1. What is the total percentage of women working in the Central Bank (CB) at the end of 2019 and, if available, 2020?

    31 December 2019
    31 December 2020

2. What is the total percentage of women on the Board of Directors at the end of 2019 and 2020?

    31 December 2019
    31 December 2020

3. Has the CB formalised the adoption of any gender equality policies through any official documents?

    Yes
    No
    In progress

Please provide some brief information.

4. Has the CB adopted instruments to disseminate a culture on gender equality?

    Yes
    No
    In progress

Please provide some brief information.

5. Has the CB taken measures to promote female recruitment?

    Yes
    No
    In progress

Please provide some brief information.

6. Has the CB taken measures to promote a balance between work and life?

    Yes
    No
    In progress

Please provide some brief information.

7. Has the CB taken measures to promote women's careers?

Yes
No
In progress

Please provide some brief information.

8. Does the CB have a Diversity and Inclusion officer/dedicated staff?

Yes
No
In progress

Please provide some brief information.

9. Has the CB obtained a certification for gender equality?

Yes
No
In progress

Please provide some brief information.

10. Has the CB taken measures to close the gender pay gap?

Yes
No
In progress

Please provide some brief information.

## References

Baccini, L., & Brodeur, A. (2021). Explaining governors' response to the COVID-19 pandemic in the United States. *American Politics Research*, *49*(2), 215–220. https://doi.org/10.1177/1532673x20973453

Banca d'Italia. (2021). Relazione sulla gestione e sulle attività della Banca d'Italia, anno 2020. Roma, 31 maggio.

Banco de Portugal. (2020). Annual Report. Activities and Financial Statements 2019.

Banco de Portugal. (2021). Annual Report. Activities and Financial Statements 2020.

Bank of England. (2019). Annual Report and Accounts 1 March 2018 to 28 February 2019.

Bank of England. (2020). Annual Report and Accounts 1 March 2019 to 29 February 2020.

Bank of Finland. (2020). Annual Report 2019.

Bank of Finland. (2021). Annual Report 2020.

Banka Slovenije. (2020). Annual Report 2019.

Banque de France. (2020a). Annual Report 2019.

Banque de France. (2020b). Diversity and Inclusion Charter.

Bennani, H., Farvaque, E., & Stanek, P. (2015). *FOMC members' incentives to disagree: Regional motives and background influences* (Narodowy Bank Polski Working Paper No. 221). Economic Institute, Warsaw.

Bodea, C. (2017). *The value of a seat: When are women elevated to central bank boards?* (Working Paper). Michigan State University, V3. May.

Bordo, M. D., & Istrefi, K. (2018). *Perceived FOMC: The making of hawks, doves and swingers* (Working Paper 24650). National Bureau of Economic Research Working Paper Series.

Carney, M. (2018, July 4). Letter to The Rt Hon Nicky Morgan MP, Chair of the Treasury Committee, House of Commons, Committee Office. London.

Central Bank of Ireland. (2020a). Annual Report 2019 and Annual Performance Statement 2019–2020.

Central Bank of Ireland. (2020b). *Corporate social responsibility* (Annual Report).

Central Bank of Ireland. (2020c, July). *Thematic assessment of diversity and inclusion in insurance firms.*

Central Bank of Ireland. (2021). Gender Pay Gap Report.

Chappell, H. W., Jr., & McGregor, R. R. (2000). A long history of FOMC voting behaviour. *Southern Economic Journal, 66*(4), 906–922. https://doi.org/10.2307/1061535

Charléty, P., Romelli, D., & Santacreu-Vasut, E. (2017). Appointments to central bank boards: Does gender matter? *Economics Letters, 155*, 59–61. https://doi.org/10.1016/j.econlet.2017.03.019

Danmarks Nationalbank. (2020). Annual Report 2019.

Danmarks Nationalbank. (2021). Annual Report 2020.

Datta, D. D., & Vigfusson, R. J. (2019, October). *Gender and coauthorship at the Federal Reserve Board.* Federal Reserve Board.

Deutsche Bundesbank. (2021). Annual Report 2020.

Diouf, I., & Pépin, D. (2017). Gender and central banking. *Economic Modelling, 61*, 193–206. https://doi.org/10.1016/j.econmod.2016.12.006

Dupas, P., Modestino, A. S., Niederle, M., & Wolfers, J. (2021). *Gender and the dynamics of economics seminars* (National Bureau of Economic Research, Working Paper 28494).

ECB—European Central Bank. (2019). Conditions of employment for staff of the European Central Bank annex I—Salary structure. Directorate General Human Resources, Last amended 1 January 2019.

ECB—European Central Bank. (2020, May 14). *ECB announces new measures to increase share of female staff members*. Press Release.

EIGE—European Institute for Gender Equality. (2021). *Gender statistics database. Women and men in decision-making*. Methodology. Last updated: 28 January 2021

Farvaque, E., Hammadou, H., & Stanek, P. (2011). Selecting your inflation targeters: Background and performance of monetary policy committee members. *German Economic Review, 12*(2), 223–238. https://doi.org/10.1111/j.1468-0475.2010.00520.x

Farvaque, E., Stanek, P., & Vigeant, S. (2014). On the performance of monetary policy committees. *Kyklos, 67*(2), 177–203. https://doi.org/10.1111/kykl.12049

Hospido, L., Laeven, L., & Lamo, A. (2019a, April). *The gender promotion gap: Evidence from central banking* (European Central Bank Working Paper Series No. 2265).

Hospido, L., Laeven, L., & Lamo, A. (2019b, October 14). *The gender promotion gap: What holds back female economists from making a career in central banking?* (Research Bulletin European Central Bank No. 63).

Hospido, L., & Sanz, C. (2019). *Gender gaps in the evaluation of research: Evidence from submissions to economics conferences*. Documentos de Trabajo, N.° 1918, Banco De España

IMF—International Monetary Fund. (2017). *Banking on women leaders: A case for more?* (Working Paper. WP/17/199). Prepared by Sahay R, Čihák M, N'Diaye P, Barajas A, Kyobe A, Mitra S, Mooi YN, Yousefi SR.

IMF—International Monetary Fund. (2018, September). *Women in finance: A case for closing gaps*. Prepared by Sahay R, Čihák M, and other IMF Staff, SDN/18/05.

Magyar Nemzeti Bank. (2020). Annual Report 2019. Business Report and Financial Statements.

Masciandaro, D., Profeta, P., & Romelli, D. (2015). *Gender and monetary policymaking: Trends and drivers* (Working Paper No. 2015–12). BAFFI CAREFIN Centre Research Paper (Centre for Applied Research on International Markets, Banking, Finance and Regulation).

National Bank of Belgium. (2021). Report 2020. Corporate Report.

OMFIF—Official Monetary and Financial Institutions Forum. (2020). Gender Balance Index.

OMFIF—Official Monetary and Financial Institutions Forum. (2021). Gender Balance Index.

OeNB—Oesterreichische Nationalbank. (2020a). Annual Report 2019 including the Intellectual Capital Report and the Environmental Statement. Sustainability Report 2019.

OeNB—Oesterreichische Nationalbank. (2020b). Equality, diversity and inclusion at the OeNB. Action plan for the advancement of women 2016–2021.

OeNB—Oesterreichische Nationalbank. (2021). Annual Report 2020 including the Intellectual Capital Report and the Environmental Statement. Sustainability Report 2020.

Ozili, P. K. (2020). Does competence of central bank governors influence financial stability? *Future Business Journal, 6*(24), 1–20. https://doi.org/10.1186/s43093-020-00031-y

Perlberg, S. (2013). Obama: Both Yellen and Summers are 'outstanding candidates' for fed chair. *Insider*. https://www.businessinsider.com/obama-speaks-on-yellen-and-summers-2013-8?r=US&IR=T

Riksbank. (2020). Mångfald och likabehandling.

Ryan, M. K., Haslam, S. A., & Kulich, C. (2010). Politics and the glass cliff: Evidence that women are preferentially selected to contest hard-to-win seats. *Psychology of Women Quarterly, 34*(1), 56–64. https://doi.org/10.1111/j.1471-6402.2009.01541.x

Ryan, M. K., Haslam, S. A., Morgenroth, T., Rink, F., Stoker, J., & Peters, K. (2016). Getting on top of the glass cliff: Reviewing a decade of evidence, explanations, and impact. *The Leadership Quarterly, 27*(3), 446–455. https://doi.org/10.1016/j.leaqua.2015.10.008

Schnabel, I. (2020, September 28). Women are central, not just in central banks. Speech by Isabel Schnabel, Member of the Executive Board of the ECB, at the Annual Meeting 2020 of the Verein für Socialpolitik, Frankfurt am Main.

Sergent, K., & Stajkovic, A. D. (2020). Women's leadership is associated with fewer deaths during the COVID-19 crisis: Quantitative and qualitative analyses of United States governors. *Journal of Applied Psychology, 105*(8), 771–783. https://doi.org/10.1037/apl0000577

Shay, L. (2020). Closing time! Examining the impact of gender and executive branch policymakers on the timing of stay-at-home orders. *Politics & Gender, 16*(4), 935–942. https://doi.org/10.1017/s1743923x20000264

Vallet, G. (2019). *Central banks need more women*. inGenere. https://www.ingenere.it/en/articles/central-banks-need-more-women

CHAPTER 9

# Gender Diversity in Banks and Insurance Companies: The State of Art

**Abstract** This chapter is exclusively empirical as it aims to provide an overview of the gender diversity policies adopted by banks and insurance companies worldwide over the last 11 years (2010–2020). This was done by using information collected from the Refinitiv Eikon database. The data considered are (a) the percentage of women employees, (b) the percentage of new women employees, (c) the percentage of women managers, (d) the percentage of female directors on the board, (e) the percentage of female executive members, (f) the gender pay gap, (g) the flexible working hour mechanisms promoting a work-life balance, (h) the board gender diversity policy and, finally, (i) the support for the UN-Sustainable Development Goal (SDG) 5 Gender Equality. The full sample consists of 2064 listed financial intermediaries of which 1427 are banks and 637 are insurance companies (belonging to the following sub-sectors: life & health insurance, multiline insurance & brokers, property & casualty insurance, and reinsurance). Overall, the analysis shows that women are still underrepresented in managerial and especially executive roles in both the banking and insurance sectors. However, it is

This chapter is the result of the joint efforts of the two authors, who contributed equally.



G. Birindelli and A. P. Iannuzzi, *Women in Financial Services*, Palgrave Macmillan Studies in Banking and Financial Institutions, https://doi.org/10.1007/978-3-030-93471-2_9

important to underline that in the last 11 years, there has been a rearrangement of the roles held by women. On the one hand, the number of women employees has decreased. On the other hand, the number of women directors, managers, and executives has increased, although at very different growth rates. In any case, this rebalancing process is still ongoing and will be so for a long time.

## 9.1 Sample and Data

The chapter takes on a purely empirical character in that it presents an analysis using some data on gender diversity in the financial sector from 2010 to 2020. The data, which are first analysed separately for banks and insurance companies and then compared, include: (a) the percentage of female employees, (b) the percentage of new women employees, (c) the percentage of women managers, (d) the percentage of female directors on the board, (e) the percentage of female executive members, (f) the gender pay gap—that is, the percentage of remuneration of women to men for doing the same work, (g) a flexible working hour system promoting a work-life balance, provided by the financial firms, (h) the adoption, by the financial firms, of a policy regarding the gender diversity of the board, and finally, (i) the company's support for the UN-Sustainable Development Goal (SDG) 5 Gender Equality.[1] Data are collected from Refinitiv Eikon. The full sample consists of 2064 listed financial intermediaries of which 1427 are banks and 637 are insurance companies (belonging to the sub-sectors life & health insurance, multiline insurance & brokers, property & casualty insurance, and reinsurance). In essence, all banks and insurance firms surveyed by Refinitiv Eikon are analysed in this chapter. Tables 9.1 and 9.2 display these data for banks and insurance companies, respectively, in particular the average percentage value for each year included in the analysis and the growth (or decrease) rate between 2010 and 2020. Moreover, data are grouped by geographical areas (Africa, the Americas, Asia, and Europe). The following sections deepen the emerging trends and

[1] In the database, these items are called, respectively: (a) Women Employees, (b) New Women Employees, (c) Women Managers, (d) Board Gender Diversity Percent, (e) Executive Members Gender Diversity Percent, (f) Gender Pay Gap Percentage, (g) Flexible Working Hour, (h) Policy Board Diversity, and (i) SDG 5 Gender Equality.

discuss the progress made by banks and insurance companies in adopting gender diversity standards and policies over the last 11 years, as well as the more critical issues and gaps still to be resolved. It should be underlined that the analysis provides a partial picture that should be framed in the light of all the other surveys and studies discussed in the previous chapters (in particular, Chapters 4 and 6). This is because, firstly, the Refinitiv Eikon database focuses only on listed companies (thus, without considering unlisted banks or insurance companies), and secondly, it contains a large number of missing values. Therefore, trends emerging from the indicators considered should be interpreted by taking into account the aforementioned limitations.

## 9.2 Gender Diversity in Banks: International Evidence

Looking at Table 9.1 (Panel A), the first item reported is the percentage of women employees in banks. Regarding this variable, two considerations can be made. Firstly, for all years and geographical areas, the percentage of women employees is almost always above 50%. In addition, 3 out of 4 geographical areas (the Americas, Asia, and Europe) experience a decrease in this value between 2010 and 2020, resulting in an overall 3.15% average decrease in the number of women employed in the banking sector. A similar trend characterises the next item which is the percentage of new women employees (Panel B, Table 9.1). Banks across all geographical areas show a downward trend in the recruitment of new women to the extent that by the end of 2020, on average, this figure is consistently below 50%. On the contrary, women managers seem to have become more representative in banks. This value is the highest in Africa and the Americas where it ranges between 45 and 50%, but the trend is downward in these areas; in the other two geographical areas (Asia and Europe), women managers in the banking industry follow an upward trend, even if the value for 2020 is lower than those calculated for the other two geographical areas (Panel C, Table 9.1). Overall, the growth rate assumed by this variable from 2010 to 2020 is small but positive (+1.5%). The increase of women sitting on the banks' boards is much more marked (Panel D, Table 9.1). Moreover, this growth is recorded across all geographical areas, although it appears to be more pronounced

**Table 9.1** Gender diversity in banks (% values; years 2010–2020; data as of 31 December of each year)

| | *2010* | *2011* | *2012* | *2013* | *2014* | *2015* | *2016* | *2017* | *2018* | *2019* | *2020* | *Δ 2020/2010* |
|---|---|---|---|---|---|---|---|---|---|---|---|---|
| | **Panel A: Women Employees** | | | | | | | | | | | |
| Africa | 54.48 | 61.40 | 57.43 | 55.47 | 55.66 | 56.54 | 55.88 | 56.72 | 52.19 | 51.80 | 58.52 | 7.43 |
| America | 61.07 | 58.60 | 58.25 | 57.63 | 57.62 | 57.75 | 56.79 | 55.38 | 55.67 | 56.60 | 59.83 | −2.02 |
| Asia | 54.99 | 52.54 | 52.83 | 47.05 | 47.88 | 47.40 | 48.45 | 49.59 | 49.45 | 48.74 | 47.67 | −13.31 |
| Europe | 55.72 | 54.41 | 54.19 | 54.69 | 53.76 | 54.61 | 53.84 | 53.92 | 54.34 | 53.85 | 53.10 | −4.70 |
| **Total** | **56.56** | **56.74** | **55.68** | **53.71** | **53.73** | **54.08** | **53.74** | **53.90** | **52.91** | **52.75** | **54.78** | **−3.15** |
| | **Panel B: New Women Employees** | | | | | | | | | | | |
| Africa | NA | NA | NA | 49.60 | 51.00 | NA | 46.68 | 47.95 | 39.79 | 40.03 | 44.70 | −9.88 |
| America | NA | 56.22 | 51.40 | 50.02 | 49.08 | 50.38 | 47.62 | 47.96 | 44.13 | 46.42 | 49.26 | −12.38 |
| Asia | 54.24 | 48.57 | 52.21 | 49.39 | 51.69 | 50.74 | 51.09 | 52.88 | 50.05 | 50.65 | 49.17 | −9.35 |
| Europe | 52.37 | 45.21 | 53.02 | 50.54 | 46.97 | 49.06 | 47.38 | 49.89 | 48.07 | 48.39 | 48.55 | −7.29 |
| **Total** | **53.31** | **50.00** | **52.21** | **49.89** | **49.68** | **50.06** | **48.19** | **49.67** | **45.51** | **46.37** | **47.92** | **−10.10** |
| | **Panel C: Women Managers** | | | | | | | | | | | |
| Africa | 53.60 | 36.25 | 45.46 | 47.91 | 49.07 | 44.83 | 43.17 | 46.46 | 51.16 | 44.51 | 50.43 | −5.91 |
| America | 48.87 | 41.86 | 43.41 | 41.40 | 43.30 | 45.67 | 39.44 | 40.16 | 37.81 | 42.38 | 45.76 | −6.35 |
| Asia | 34.25 | 33.56 | 33.48 | 33.15 | 34.66 | 37.27 | 36.40 | 36.26 | 35.35 | 37.86 | 38.07 | 11.17 |
| Europe | 32.40 | 33.71 | 33.99 | 33.39 | 33.54 | 33.68 | 33.72 | 34.62 | 35.69 | 36.55 | 37.39 | 15.40 |
| **Total** | **42.28** | **36.34** | **39.08** | **38.96** | **40.14** | **40.36** | **38.18** | **39.38** | **40.00** | **40.33** | **42.92** | **1.50** |

| | *2010* | *2011* | *2012* | *2013* | *2014* | *2015* | *2016* | *2017* | *2018* | *2019* | *2020* | *Δ 2020/2010* |
|---|---|---|---|---|---|---|---|---|---|---|---|---|
| | **Panel D: Board Gender Diversity** | | | | | | | | | | | |
| Africa | 11.74 | 11.10 | 13.73 | 14.24 | 14.57 | 14.18 | 15.63 | 16.89 | 20.42 | 18.97 | 22.31 | 90.00 |
| America | 14.98 | 15.82 | 15.66 | 16.34 | 16.52 | 15.31 | 15.54 | 15.56 | 16.76 | 17.61 | 19.05 | 27.16 |
| Asia | 7.19 | 8.27 | 8.42 | 8.40 | 8.48 | 8.80 | 9.10 | 9.76 | 10.90 | 11.07 | 11.44 | 59.17 |
| Europe | 12.98 | 13.06 | 14.89 | 18.47 | 19.75 | 21.66 | 25.31 | 26.27 | 29.00 | 30.34 | 32.05 | 146.96 |
| **Total** | **11.72** | **12.06** | **13.17** | **14.36** | **14.83** | **14.99** | **16.40** | **17.12** | **19.27** | **19.50** | **21.21** | **80.97** |
| | **Panel E: Executive Members Gender Diversity** | | | | | | | | | | | |
| Africa | 17.57 | 18.96 | 18.85 | 18.06 | 19.52 | 21.02 | 21.80 | 23.91 | 24.17 | 24.59 | 24.79 | 41.11 |
| America | 13.94 | 13.60 | 15.03 | 14.41 | 15.08 | 13.94 | 14.43 | 15.19 | 16.08 | 16.94 | 17.22 | 23.54 |
| Asia | 11.72 | 13.47 | 12.89 | 13.41 | 13.09 | 12.83 | 12.48 | 12.34 | 12.41 | 11.17 | 11.62 | −0.88 |
| Europe | 8.85 | 11.66 | 11.86 | 11.93 | 12.59 | 13.58 | 14.55 | 15.32 | 17.00 | 17.38 | 18.60 | 110.18 |
| **Total** | **13.02** | **14.42** | **14.66** | **14.45** | **15.07** | **15.34** | **15.82** | **16.69** | **17.42** | **17.52** | **18.06** | **38.70** |
| | **Panel F: Gender Pay Gap** | | | | | | | | | | | |
| Africa | | | | | | | NA | NA | NA | 100 | 100 | 0 |
| America | | | | | | | NA | 78.50 | 92.33 | 91.50 | 94.18 | 19.97 |
| Asia | | | | | | | NA | 96.30 | 90.20 | 92.74 | 92.85 | −3.58 |
| Europe | | | | | | | 61.4 | 76.38 | 81.17 | 85.30 | 87.52 | 42.55 |
| **Total** | | | | | | | **61.40** | **83.73** | **87.90** | **89.85** | **91.52** | **49.05** |

(continued)

**Table 9.1** (continued)

| | *2010* | *2011* | *2012* | *2013* | *2014* | *2015* | *2016* | *2017* | *2018* | *2019* | *2020* | *Δ 2020/2010* |
|---|---|---|---|---|---|---|---|---|---|---|---|---|
| | **Panel G: Flexible Working Hour** | | | | | | | | | | | |
| Africa (adoption) | 16.67 | 16.67 | 14.29 | 14.29 | 14.29 | 29 | 29 | 29 | 29 | 25 | 25 | 50.00 |
| Africa (non-adoption) | 83.33 | 83.33 | 85.71 | 85.71 | 85.71 | 71 | 71 | 71 | 71 | 75 | 75 | −10.00 |
| America (adoption) | 30.00 | 32.08 | 31.58 | 31.58 | 29.82 | 18.75 | 11.18 | 12.25 | 16.67 | 16.99 | 22.29 | −25.70 |
| America (non-adoption) | 70.00 | 67.92 | 68.42 | 68.42 | 70.18 | 81.25 | 88.82 | 87.75 | 83.33 | 83.01 | 77.71 | 11.01 |
| Asia (adoption) | 8.97 | 11.83 | 10.42 | 11.34 | 10.89 | 15.45 | 20 | 27.78 | 33.08 | 37.93 | 43.51 | 384.79 |
| Asia (non-adoption) | 91.03 | 88.17 | 89.58 | 88.66 | 89.11 | 84.55 | 80 | 72.22 | 66.92 | 62.07 | 56.49 | −37.94 |
| Europe (adoption) | 56.60 | 56.36 | 56.14 | 57.14 | 52.63 | 50.82 | 52 | 53.03 | 51.35 | 58.02 | 64.29 | 13.57 |
| Europe (non-adoption) | 43.40 | 43.64 | 40.35 | 42.86 | 47.37 | 49.18 | 47.54 | 46.97 | 48.65 | 41.98 | 35.71 | −17.70 |
| **Total (adoption)** | **28.06** | **29.23** | **28.11** | **28.59** | **26.91** | **28.40** | **28.05** | **30.41** | **32.42** | **34.49** | **38.77** | **38.17** |
| **Total (non-adoption)** | **71.94** | **70.77** | **71.02** | **71.41** | **73.09** | **71.60** | **71.95** | **69.59** | **67.58** | **65.51** | **61.23** | **−14.89** |

| | 2010 | 2011 | 2012 | 2013 | 2014 | 2015 | 2016 | 2017 | 2018 | 2019 | 2020 | Δ 2020/2010 |
|---|---|---|---|---|---|---|---|---|---|---|---|---|
| **Panel H: Policy Board Diversity** | | | | | | | | | | | | |
| Africa (adoption) | 0 | 0 | 0 | 0 | 0 | 14.29 | 28.57 | 57 | 57 | 75 | 75 | 425.00 |
| Africa (non-adoption) | 100 | 100 | 100 | 100 | 100 | 86 | 71.43 | 42.86 | 42.86 | 25 | 25 | −75.00 |
| America (adoption) | 30 | 35.85 | 38.60 | 6.44 | 40.35 | 62.50 | 73.53 | 78.92 | 83.81 | 83.33 | 85.14 | 183.80 |
| America (non-adoption) | 70 | 64.15 | 61.40 | 59.65 | 59.65 | 37.50 | 26.47 | 21.08 | 16.19 | 16.67 | 14.86 | −78.77 |
| Asia (adoption) | 0 | 0 | 3.13 | 5.15 | 8.91 | 16.36 | 26.67 | 40.48 | 43.85 | 50.34 | 55.84 | 1687.01 |
| Asia (non-adoption) | 100 | 100 | 96.88 | 94.85 | 91.09 | 83.64 | 73.33 | 59.52 | 56.15 | 49.66 | 44.16 | −55.84 |
| Europe (adoption) | 18.87 | 23.64 | 27.27 | 30.36 | 40.35 | 50.82 | 63.93 | 74.24 | 78.38 | 81.48 | 85.71 | 354.29 |
| Europe (non-adoption) | 81.13 | 76 | 72.73 | 69.64 | 59.65 | 49.18 | 36.07 | 25.76 | 21.62 | 18.52 | 14.29 | −82.39 |
| **Total (adoption)** | **12.22** | **14.87** | **17.25** | **10.49** | **22.40** | **35.99** | **48.18** | **62.70** | **65.79** | **72.54** | **75.42** | **517.37** |
| **Total (non-adoption)** | **87.78** | **85.13** | **82.75** | **81.03** | **77.60** | **64.01** | **51.82** | **37.30** | **34.21** | **27.46** | **24.58** | **−72.00** |

(continued)

**Table 9.1** (continued)

| | *2010* | *2011* | *2012* | *2013* | *2014* | *2015* | *2016* | *2017* | *2018* | *2019* | *2020* | *Δ 2020/2010* |
|---|---|---|---|---|---|---|---|---|---|---|---|---|
| | **Panel I: SDG 5 Gender Equality** | | | | | | | | | | | |
| Africa (support) | 0 | 0 | 0 | 0 | 0 | 0 | 0 | 0 | 0 | 33.33 | 37.50 | NA |
| Africa (non-support) | 100 | 100 | 100 | 100 | 100 | 100 | 100 | 100 | 100 | 66.67 | 62.50 | −33.33 |
| America (support) | 0 | 0 | 0 | 0 | 0 | 0 | 0 | 0 | 0 | 2.89 | 8.07 | NA |
| America (non-support) | 100 | 100 | 100 | 100 | 100 | 100 | 100 | 100 | 100 | 97.11 | 91.93 | −2.89 |
| Asia (support) | 0 | 0 | 0 | 0 | 0 | 0 | 0 | 0 | 0 | 12.40 | 46.41 | NA |
| Asia (non-support) | 100 | 100 | 100 | 100 | 100 | 100 | 100 | 100 | 100 | 87.60 | 53.59 | NA |
| Europe (support) | 0 | 0 | 0 | 0 | 0 | 0 | 0 | 0 | 0 | 18.18 | 56.63 | NA |
| Europe (non-support) | 100 | 100 | 100 | 100 | 100 | 100 | 100 | 100 | 100 | 81.82 | 43.37 | −18.18 |
| **Total (support)** | **0** | **0** | **0** | **0** | **0** | **0** | **0** | **0** | **0** | **16.70** | **37.15** | NA |
| **Total (non-support)** | **100** | **100** | **100** | **100** | **100** | **100** | **100** | **100** | **100** | **83.30** | **62.85** | **−16.70** |

*Note* We use the same definitions as in the Refinitiv Eikon database. The term "America" refers to Canada, the United States, and Latin America
*Source* Authors' elaboration on data collected from Refinitiv Eikon

in Europe and Africa. This significant rise in the gender diversity on bank boards (+81% during the last 11 years) is certainly in part due to the several laws on gender quotas that many countries have chosen to issue in recent years (IMF, 2018). However, it may also be ascribed to the greater awareness by banks of the important positive implications of having more women directors, highlighted by many studies (see Chapter 3). Additionally, not only are women more present on the banks' boards—in line with the research by the International Monetary Fund (2017 and 2018) and the European Banking Authority (2016 and 2020) (see Chapter 4)—but they also seem to hold a greater number of executive positions. As shown in Panel E, Table 9.1, the overall average presence of female executives in banks rises from 13.02% in 2010 to 18.06% in 2020 (+38.70%). However, the gap between the total average value of women directors (21.21% at the end of 2020) and the average value of women executives (18.06% at the end of 2020) confirms the prevalence of women in non-executive positions, which is often highlighted in this book.

Another interesting and positive finding concerns the trend of the gender pay gap (GPG) in banks. On the one hand, Panel F in Table 9.1 shows the persistence of this gap in all geographical areas (the values for Africa are not representative given the high number of missing values), on the other hand, its trend reveals the propensity of banks to close this gap[2] (see Chapter 5). The greatest efforts in this direction seem to have been made by European and American banks whose GPG reductions over time appear to be more pronounced (+19.97% in the Americas and + 42.55% in Europe). Regarding the adoption of specific gender policies, the data document a strong increase in both the banks implementing a flexible working hour system aimed at promoting a work-life balance and those adopting a board policy dedicated to increasing the representation of women in this governing body. In more detail, the percentage of banks adopting a flexible working hour system rises by 38% in the last 11 years (Panel G, Table 9.1). The percentage of banks implementing a board gender policy increases by over 500% (Panel H, Table 9.1). Finally, although the percentage of banks supporting the SDG 5 Gender Equality still appears rather low at the end of 2020 (37.15%), it should be noted

[2] These values must be interpreted as follows: the greater the percentage increase in the gender pay gap over a period of time, the more pronounced the process of closing (and thus reducing) said gap. In fact, a gender pay gap equal to 100% means that gender pay discrimination no longer exists.

that the 2019–2020 growth of this percentage is substantial. The banks supporting SDG 5 of the United Nations increase by more than double in 2020 compared to 2019. Specifically, the figure rises from 16.70 to 37.15% (Panel I, Table 9.1).

## 9.3 Gender Diversity in Insurance Companies: Evidence Worldwide

Table 9.2 reports the same variables as Table 9.1, referring to insurance companies. Even in the insurance sector, the proportion of female employees and—especially—that of new female employees decrease over the past 11 years. Additionally, the number of women managers increases, although only by 2% (the growth is even lower in banks). Moreover, as in the case of banks, insurance companies are experiencing a strong growth of the share of women directors and women with executive roles. Upon closer inspection, the growth rate from 2010 to 2020 is 121% in the first case (board gender diversity) and 136% in the second (executive members gender diversity) (Panels D and E, Table 9.2). However, the insurance sector also suffers from a large gap between female employees on the one hand, and female managers and directors on the other. At the end of 2020, on average, female employees make up 53.9%, whereas women managers and directors are equal to 35.99 and 23.22%, respectively. Even lower is the percentage of female executives (14.97%). This means that in the insurance sector, the glass ceiling still seems to be far from being broken.

A stronger growth concerns insurance companies implementing a flexible working hour system and a gender diversity policy regarding the composition of the board of directors. In the latter case, the growth rate over the last 11 years exceeds 1000% (Panel H, Table 9.2). At the end of 2020, only a minority of insurance companies (14.53%) have not yet chosen to adopt a gender diversity policy for their board. The gender pay gap trend is also satisfactory: at a global level, there is a tendency, with varying facets among geographical areas, to narrow this gap (Panel F, Table 9.2). Finally, regarding SDG 5 Gender Equality, the goal has started receiving support from some insurance companies only in 2019—as happened for banks. Most of these financial firms belong to Europe, the first geographical area committed to achieving this important United Nations goal. However, it is worth noting the strong average increase in the number of insurance companies focused on this objective worldwide

**Table 9.2** Gender diversity in insurance companies (% values; years 2010–2020; data as of 31 December of each year)

| | *2010* | *2011* | *2012* | *2013* | *2014* | *2015* | *2016* | *2017* | *2018* | *2019* | *2020* | Δ *2020/2010* |
|---|---|---|---|---|---|---|---|---|---|---|---|---|
| | **Panel A: Women Employees** | | | | | | | | | | | |
| Africa | 56.67 | 57.95 | 58.14 | 58.01 | 58.28 | 59.13 | 58.88 | 58.72 | 59.42 | 59.94 | 59.74 | 5.42 |
| America | 60.42 | 59.44 | 58.52 | 56.77 | 55.11 | 54.77 | 55.99 | 55.69 | 54.71 | 55.53 | 55.26 | −8.55 |
| Asia | 54.48 | 57.49 | 60.29 | 60.66 | 59.99 | 59.85 | 56.84 | 55.68 | 55.74 | 50.78 | 50.23 | −7.79 |
| Europe | 51.60 | 49.91 | 49.93 | 51.52 | 50.68 | 50.68 | 49.99 | 49.74 | 50.11 | 50.21 | 50.36 | −2.39 |
| **Total** | **55.79** | **56.19** | **56.72** | **56.74** | **56.01** | **56.11** | **55.43** | **54.96** | **54.99** | **54.12** | **53.90** | **−3.39** |
| | **Panel B: New Women Employees** | | | | | | | | | | | |
| Africa | NA | NA | 54 | 52 | 86.7 | 55 | 42.83 | 36.67 | 36.81 | 25.78 | 12.72 | −75.54 |
| America | 37.00 | 61.96 | 53.96 | 60.43 | 66.73 | 67.90 | 46.32 | 54.56 | 50.55 | 51.71 | 52.12 | −15.88 |
| Asia | 94.85 | 94.92 | 95.17 | 75.06 | 75.32 | 72.62 | 65.87 | 62.82 | 62.24 | 63.15 | 62.08 | −34.55 |
| Europe | 48.87 | 52.09 | 49.80 | 50.78 | 54.19 | 50.56 | 49.10 | 49.03 | 49.65 | 46.42 | 46.19 | −5.48 |
| **Total** | **71.86** | **69.66** | **66.31** | **59.57** | **70.73** | **61.52** | **51.03** | **50.77** | **49.81** | **46.76** | **43.28** | **−39.77** |
| | **Panel C: Women Managers** | | | | | | | | | | | |
| Africa | 55.56 | 51.92 | 40.19 | 39.80 | 44.26 | 46.10 | 41.01 | 41.74 | 37.03 | 34.90 | 36.33 | −34.61 |
| America | 49.30 | 56.07 | 52.92 | 45.03 | 42.82 | 42.61 | 42.83 | 39.47 | 41.75 | 43.19 | 41.88 | −15.04 |
| Asia | 5.78 | 6.47 | 14.89 | 21.15 | 20.77 | 31.09 | 28.99 | 29.61 | 28.12 | 31.32 | 30.81 | 433.43 |
| Europe | 30.52 | 31.78 | 34.22 | 33.15 | 31.48 | 31.76 | 30.81 | 31.21 | 33.15 | 33.24 | 34.93 | 14.44 |
| **Total** | **35.29** | **36.56** | **35.56** | **34.78** | **34.83** | **37.89** | **35.91** | **35.51** | **35.01** | **35.66** | **35.99** | **1.98** |

(continued)

**Table 9.2** (continued)

| | *2010* | *2011* | *2012* | *2013* | *2014* | *2015* | *2016* | *2017* | *2018* | *2019* | *2020* | Δ *2020/2010* |
|---|---|---|---|---|---|---|---|---|---|---|---|---|
| | **Panel D: Board Gender Diversity** | | | | | | | | | | | |
| Africa | 8.89 | 14.67 | 16.17 | 15.70 | 16.48 | 15.67 | 17.19 | 17.86 | 23.17 | 25.57 | 24.11 | 171.26 |
| America | 14.13 | 13.54 | 13.87 | 14.50 | 15.80 | 16.92 | 16.14 | 17.64 | 19.04 | 20.38 | 21.60 | 52.91 |
| Asia | 2.29 | 4.05 | 3.76 | 3.35 | 3.58 | 4.87 | 5.45 | 7.67 | 7.91 | 9.01 | 12.83 | 459.77 |
| Europe | 16.69 | 16.92 | 19.00 | 23.11 | 27.24 | 29.65 | 30.56 | 30.54 | 31.80 | 33.43 | 34.32 | 105.60 |
| **Total** | **10.50** | **12.30** | **13.20** | **14.17** | **15.77** | **16.78** | **17.33** | **18.43** | **20.48** | **22.09** | **23.22** | **121.09** |
| | **Panel E: Executive Members Gender Diversity** | | | | | | | | | | | |
| Africa | 1.45 | 13.37 | 12.10 | 12.97 | 13.56 | 13.57 | 16.58 | 19.16 | 18.89 | 15.77 | 14.84 | 924.08 |
| America | 11.53 | 11.84 | 11.97 | 11.91 | 11.55 | 11.38 | 13.38 | 14.73 | 15.11 | 15.71 | 16.24 | 40.81 |
| Asia | 4.17 | 6.73 | 6.69 | 8.31 | 9.32 | 9.70 | 8.77 | 8.75 | 8.95 | 8.79 | 10.22 | 145.08 |
| Europe | 8.21 | 9.27 | 9.23 | 9.19 | 10.07 | 10.47 | 13.01 | 13.59 | 13.78 | 15.52 | 18.59 | 126.42 |
| **Total** | **6.34** | **10.30** | **10.00** | **10.60** | **11.13** | **11.28** | **12.93** | **14.06** | **14.18** | **13.95** | **14.97** | **136.14** |
| | **Panel F: Gender Pay Gap** | | | | | | | | | | | |
| Africa | | | | | | | NA | NA | NA | NA | NA | |
| America | | | | | | | NA | 106.50 | 84.53 | 89.82 | 91.05 | −14.50 |
| Asia | | | | | | | NA | NA | 100 | 100 | 95 | 5.26 |
| Europe | | | | | | | 80.00 | 79.28 | 77.75 | 78.10 | 80.14 | 0.18 |
| **Total** | | | | | | | **80.00** | **92.89** | **87.43** | **89.31** | **88.73** | **10.92** |

| | *2010* | *2011* | *2012* | *2013* | *2014* | *2015* | *2016* | *2017* | *2018* | *2019* | *2020* | Δ *2020/2010* |
|---|---|---|---|---|---|---|---|---|---|---|---|---|
| | **Panel G: Flexible Working Hours** | | | | | | | | | | | |
| Africa (adoption) | 0 | 0 | 0 | 14.29 | 14.29 | 14 | 14 | 43 | 43 | 43 | 42.85 | 200.00 |
| Africa (non-adoption) | 100 | 100 | 100 | 85.71 | 85.71 | 86 | 86 | 57 | 57 | 57 | 57.14 | −42.86 |
| America (adoption) | 36.00 | 36.54 | 40.38 | 40.38 | 40.38 | 36.21 | 29.63 | 30.68 | 36.56 | 37.37 | 42.34 | 17.62 |
| America (non-adoption) | 64.00 | 63.46 | 59.62 | 59.62 | 59.62 | 63.79 | 70.37 | 69.32 | 63.44 | 62.63 | 57.66 | −9.91 |
| Asia (adoption) | 44.44 | 29.41 | 41.18 | 38.89 | 36.84 | 33.33 | 36 | 45.45 | 60.87 | 54.84 | 58.82 | 32.35 |
| Asia (non-adoption) | 55.56 | 70.59 | 58.82 | 61.11 | 63.16 | 66.67 | 64 | 54.55 | 39.13 | 45.16 | 41.18 | −25.88 |
| Europe (adoption) | 66.67 | 63.64 | 60.61 | 64.71 | 58.33 | 62.16 | 59 | 60 | 69.77 | 68.75 | 75.51 | 13.27 |
| Europe (non-adoption) | 33.33 | 36.36 | 39.39 | 35.29 | 41.67 | 37.84 | 40.54 | 40 | 30.23 | 31.25 | 24.49 | −26.53 |
| **Total (adoption)** | **36.78** | **32.40** | **35.54** | **39.57** | **37.46** | **36.50** | **34.93** | **44.75** | **52.51** | **50.95** | **54.88** | **49.23** |
| **Total (non-adoption)** | **63.22** | **67.60** | **64.46** | **60.43** | **62.54** | **63.50** | **65.07** | **55.25** | **47.49** | **49.05** | **45.12** | **−28.64** |

(continued)

**Table 9.2** (continued)

| | *2010* | *2011* | *2012* | *2013* | *2014* | *2015* | *2016* | *2017* | *2018* | *2019* | *2020* | Δ *2020/2010* |
|---|---|---|---|---|---|---|---|---|---|---|---|---|
| | **Panel H: Policy Board Diversity** | | | | | | | | | | | |
| Africa (adoption) | 0 | 17 | 29 | 43 | 43 | 42.86 | 57.14 | 100 | 100 | 100 | 100 | 133.33 |
| Africa (non-adoption) | 100 | 83 | 71 | 57 | 57 | 57 | 42.86 | 0 | 0 | 0 | 0 | −100.00 |
| America (adoption) | 8 | 11.54 | 17.31 | 23.08 | 25.00 | 46.55 | 65.43 | 76.14 | 81.72 | 81.82 | 85.59 | 969.82 |
| America (non-adoption) | 92 | 88.46 | 82.69 | 76.92 | 75.00 | 53.45 | 34.57 | 23.86 | 18.28 | 18.18 | 14.41 | −84.33 |
| Asia (adoption) | 0 | 0 | 0 | 5.56 | 10.53 | 19.05 | 36.36 | 50 | 60.87 | 64.52 | 70.59 | 1170.59 |
| Asia (non-adoption) | 100 | 100 | 100 | 94.44 | 89.47 | 80.95 | 63.64 | 50 | 39.13 | 35.48 | 29.41 | −70.59 |
| Europe (adoption) | 15.15 | 42.42 | 48.48 | 50.00 | 55.56 | 64.86 | 72.97 | 80 | 83.72 | 85.42 | 85.71 | 465.71 |
| Europe (non-adoption) | 84.85 | 58 | 51.52 | 50.00 | 44.44 | 35.14 | 27.03 | 20 | 16.28 | 14.58 | 14.29 | −83.16 |
| **Total (adoption)** | **5.79** | **17.66** | **23.59** | **30.37** | **33.48** | **43.33** | **57.98** | **76.53** | **81.58** | **82.94** | **85.47** | **1376.74** |
| **Total (non-adoption)** | **94.21** | **82.34** | **76.41** | **69.63** | **66.52** | **56.67** | **42.02** | **23.47** | **18.42** | **17.06** | **14.53** | **−84.58** |

| | *2010* | *2011* | *2012* | *2013* | *2014* | *2015* | *2016* | *2017* | *2018* | *2019* | *2020* | Δ *2020/2010* |
|---|---|---|---|---|---|---|---|---|---|---|---|---|
| | **Panel I: SDG 5 Gender Equality** | | | | | | | | | | | |
| Africa (support) | 0 | NA | NA | 0 | NA | 0 | 0 | 0 | 0 | 0 | 14.29 | NA |
| Africa (non-support) | 100 | NA | NA | 100 | NA | 100 | 100 | 100 | 100 | 100 | 85.71 | −14.29 |
| America (support) | 0 | 0 | 0 | 0 | 0 | 0 | 0 | 0 | 0 | 2 | 10.81 | NA |
| America (non-support) | 100 | 100 | 100 | 100 | 100 | 100 | 100 | 100 | 100 | 98 | 89.19 | −10.81 |
| Asia (support) | 0 | 0 | NA | 0 | 0 | 0 | 0 | 0 | 0 | 10 | 35.29 | NA |
| Asia (non-support) | 100 | 100 | NA | 100 | 100 | 100 | 100 | 100 | 100 | 90 | 64.71 | −35.29 |
| Europe (support) | 0 | 0 | 0 | 0 | NA | 0 | 0 | 0 | 0 | 26 | 48.98 | NA |
| Europe (non-support) | 100 | 100 | 100 | 100 | NA | 100 | 100 | 100 | 100 | 74 | 51.02 | −48.98 |
| **Total (support)** | **0** | **0** | **0** | **0** | **0** | **0** | **0** | **0** | **0** | **9** | **27.34** | NA |
| **Total (non-support)** | **100** | **100** | **100** | **100** | **100** | **100** | **100** | **100** | **100** | **91** | **73.66** | **−27.34** |

*Note* We use the same definitions as in the Refinitiv Eikon database. The term "America" refers to Canada, the United States, and Latin America
*Source* Authors' elaboration on data collected from Refinitiv Eikon

over the last two years. From 9% at the end of 2019, they have risen to 27.3% in one year (Panel I, Table 9.2).

## 9.4 Banks Versus Insurance Companies: A Few Considerations

By comparing data on female representation in banks and insurance companies, we can evidence that they share similar trends. First, as shown in Table 9.3, the broadest women professional categories in both these financial intermediaries at the end of 2020 are—as expected—women employees, followed by women managers, and women sitting on the board of directors. At the bottom position, there are women executives. In any case, while at the end of 2020 there is a greater presence of women managers in banks compared to insurance companies, the opposite is true for women directors, who are more numerous in insurance companies.

**Table 9.3** Gender diversity in banks and insurance companies: a comparison (% values; years 2010, 2015, and 2020; data as of 31 December of each year)

| | *Banks* | | | *Insurance companies* | | |
|---|---|---|---|---|---|---|
| | *2010* | *2015 (2016 for GPG)* | *2020* | *2010* | *2015 (2016 for GPG)* | *2020* |
| Women Employees | 56.56 | 54.08 | 54.78 | 55.79 | 56.11 | 53.90 |
| New Women Employees | 53.31 | 50.06 | 47.92 | 71.86 | 61.52 | 43.28 |
| Women Managers | 42.28 | 40.36 | 42.92 | 35.29 | 37.89 | 35.99 |
| Board Gender Diversity | 11.72 | 14.99 | 21.21 | 10.50 | 16.78 | 23.22 |
| Executive Members Gender Diversity | 13.02 | 15.34 | 18.06 | 6.34 | 11.28 | 14.97 |
| Gender Pay Gap | NA | 61.40 | 91.52 | NA | 80.00 | 88.73 |
| Flexible Working Hours | 28.06 | 28.40 | 38.77 | 36.78 | 36.50 | 54.88 |
| Policy Board Diversity | 12.22 | 35.99 | 75.42 | 5.79 | 43.33 | 85.47 |
| SDG 5 Gender Equality | 0 | 0 | 37.15 | 0 | 0 | 27.34 |

*Note* We use the same definitions as in the Refinitiv Eikon database
*Source* Authors' elaboration on data collected from Refinitiv Eikon

However, the percentage differences are not high, especially for female directors, and they may suffer from a high number of missing values for both categories of financial firms.

Concerning the adoption of a flexible working hour system and a policy on board gender diversity, insurance companies seem to be more advanced. In both 2015 and 2020, the percentage values of these firms are much higher than the respective values referred to banks. Conversely, for the gender pay gap, banks perform better in 2020. Indeed, the last available figure shows that there is a smaller gender pay gap in banks (91.52%) than in insurance companies (88.73%). Similarly, SDG 5 Gender Equality seems to be supported more by banks than by insurance firms. In 2020, the percentages are 37.15 and 27.34%, respectively (Table 9.3).

## References

EBA—European Banking Authority. (2016). Report on the Benchmarking of diversity practices at the European Union level. EBA-Op-2016-10, July.

EBA—European Banking Authority. (2020). Report on the Benchmarking of diversity practices at European Union level, under Article 91(11) of Directive 2013/36/EU (2018 Data). EBA/REP/2020/05.

IMF—International Monetary Fund. (2017). Banking on women leaders: A case for more? Prepared by Sahay R, Čihák M, N'Diaye P, Barajas A, Kyobe A, Mitra S, Mooi YN, Yousefi SR (Working paper. WP/17/199).

IMF—International Monetary Fund. (2018). Women in Finance: A Case for Closing Gaps, Prepared by Sahay R, Čihák M, and other IMF Staff. September, SDN/18/05.

CHAPTER 10

# A Case of Temporary (Extended) "Hard Quotas": Gender Diversity in Italian Banks

**Abstract** The chapter analyses gender diversity in Italian banks starting from the regulatory framework, first by looking at the Golfo-Mosca Law, which was reiterated with amendments by the 2020 Budget Law. Alongside these regulations, the chapter illustrates numerous additional initiatives, such as the establishment of an Observatory that studies and promotes gender equality by the Bank of Italy, together with the Department for Equal Opportunities of the Italian Presidency of the Council of Ministers and the Italian Companies and Exchange Commission (Commissione nazionale per le società e la Borsa, CONSOB). Another initiative is the charter by the Italian Banking Association inviting signatories to strengthen their governance following the principles of inclusiveness and equal opportunities. Not least, the proposal by the Bank of Italy, following its 2015 diversity benchmark, of introducing a gender quota in the administrative and control bodies of banks. The chapter ends with an analysis and commentary on the female presence and the gender

This chapter is the result of the joint efforts of the two authors. However, Giuliana Birindelli mainly contributed to Sects. 10.1, 10.2, 10.3 and Antonia Patrizia Iannuzzi to Sect. 10.4.



G. Birindelli and A. P. Iannuzzi, *Women in Financial Services*, Palgrave Macmillan Studies in Banking and Financial Institutions,
https://doi.org/10.1007/978-3-030-93471-2_10

pay gap in Italian banks (with a focus on listed banks) based on data extrapolated from corporate governance and remuneration policy reports.

## 10.1 Regulatory Excursus: Where Is Italy Heading?

In Chapter 2, we reviewed the process that led the European legislator to strengthen governance rules by aiming at a policy promoting diversity, a concept which, we shall recall, is not limited to the principle of gender equality alone, but extends to heterogeneity in terms of cultural origin, education, experience, and cultural growth, and to actions that foster the exchange of views and debate, make control action more effective, and improve quality of decisions.

In Italy, the implementation of diversity in banks has been prompted by the transposition of Directive 2013/36/EU (known as CRD IV, see Chapter 2) at the Italian level, which entailed significant changes to the supervisory rules for banks (Bank of Italy, Circular No. 285 of 17 December 2013 and subsequent updates) in the Title dedicated to "Corporate governance, internal controls, risk management" (Title IV, Part one: Transposition of CRD IV in Italy). In particular, this title's section on "Composition and appointment of corporate bodies" states that the bodies with strategic supervisory and management functions must include persons who will fulfil an adequate degree of diversification (in terms of gender, age, and geographical origin) and favour multiple viewpoints and diversified analytical perspectives in the bank's decision-making process. Concurrently, the appointments committee must establish a target share of the least represented gender and meanwhile prepare an action plan to bring that share to target. This is required without prejudice to the alignment with the obligations under the rules for listed banks.

In the case of listed banks, the provisions of the Consolidated Law on Finance (in Italian, "Testo Unico della Finanza" or, by using the acronym, TUF) apply. In particular, the provision contained in Article 147-ter, subsection 1-ter of the TUF states that the bylaws foresee the directors on the boards be elected in line with the principle that ensures a balance between genders. In the version prior to the entry into force of the Italian 2020 Budget Law (Law No. 160 of 27 December 2019), the TUF had established that the least represented gender had to make up at least one-third (33%) of the directors elected. This criterion of distribution between the two genders was applied for three consecutive terms of office. This provision was also extended to the management board under the reference in Article 147-quater, sub-section 1-bis: "*If the Management Board consists of at least three members, it shall be subject to the provisions of Article 147-ter, sub-section 1-ter*" (our translation from Italian). Similarly, TUF Article 148, sub-section 1-bis (prior to the 2020 Budget Law) extended the 33% gender allocation also to the effective members of the board of statutory auditors. The amendments to the TUF on equal access to the boards of directors and auditors of companies listed on regulated markets had been established by the Golfo-Mosca Law (Law No. 120 of 12 July 2011) regarding gender balance in the bodies of listed companies, foreseeing a minimum 20% female presence quota for the first renewal, and a minimum 30% presence in the second and third renewals. Although we will not focus on this point, it should be noted that Article 3 of Law No. 120/2011 provided for the application of the same provisions also to companies established in Italy, controlled by public administrations and not listed on regulated markets, postponing the related implementation of rules to the issuing of a specific regulation, adopted by Presidential Decree No. 251 of 30 November 2012.

Interestingly, despite its temporary nature, the Golfo-Mosca Law has generated long-lasting effects, which go beyond the period of its validity, encouraging further initiatives over time (Profeta et al., 2014). The reach of the law has also been recognised in an article published in 2017 (D'Ascenzo, 2017), citing the law as one of the best practices at a European level alongside initiatives from Finland, France, and Sweden. In particular, the article states that the objective of the Italian law had been substantially achieved and would be further consolidated in the upcoming three-year renewal period (on the effects of gender quotas introduced in Italy, see also Paoloni et al., 2019; Pastore & Tommaso, 2016). As portrayed by the article, the number of women sitting on company boards has increased in absolute terms, even if the effect on top management appears far less significant since the percentage of female CEOs in companies, including financial and non-financial ones, has actually decreased. Moreover, women are on average younger than men (50.9 years old compared to 58.9 years) and have fewer ties to the majority shareholder family (13.1% compared to 16.9% referred to men). They are also most often university-educated (88.5% vs. 84.5%) and have undertaken postgraduate education (29.7% vs. 16.7%). They are less often managers (54.1% vs. 76.5%) as there are few women among the executives of the companies they are directors of, while they are more often professionals (33.2% vs. 16.6%) and academics (12.2% vs. 6.4%). In essence, women appear to be younger, more educated, and mostly come from an external work environment.

In 2019, the Golfo-Mosca Law was extended with some amendments by Law No. 160 of 27 December 2019 (aka the "2020 Budget Law") to newly address gender balance in the bodies of listed companies, modifying the provisions of TUF Articles 147-ter and 148 on gender balance in the bodies of listed companies. The new provisions, effective from 1 January 2020, stipulate that for reaching the gender balance, the least represented gender must obtain at least two-fifths (40%) of both the elected directors and effective members on the board of statutory auditors. The provisions also extend the time frame for the applicability of the balance criterion, from three to six consecutive terms. On the other hand, they maintain the gradualness for the newly listed companies, providing for a minimum one-fifth (20%) threshold allocation criterion upon the first renewal following the start date of trading.

These extensions, which were introduced with amendments, were intended to allow women who were gaining relevant experience in the governance of listed companies (thus banks as well) to consolidate their skills and refine them towards a future entry into top positions. As commented by Genovese, the extension also seemed proportionate "*because it is 'time-limited', as is appropriate for regulatory measures that steer market development towards objectives that, due to a number of obstacles, including cultural ones, companies do not yet seem able to achieve spontaneously. The 'time-based' approach, in practice, obliges Parliament, as the new deadline approaches, to reconsider the measure*" (our translation from Italian, Genovese, 2019).

In a press release dated 30 January 2020, the public authority responsible for regulating the Italian financial markets—the Italian Companies and Exchange Commission (Commissione nazionale per le società e la Borsa—CONSOB)—provided an interpretative clarification on how to apply the new provisions in the scenario of three-member corporate bodies. In such cases, firms should apply the rule of rounding down rather than rounding up, in agreement with provisions of the Regulation on stock market issuers (adopted by Resolution No. 11971 of 14 May 1999 and subsequent amendments). Article 144-undecies.1, sub-section 3, of the Regulation on stock market issuers states that "*If the application of the gender distribution criterion does not result in a whole number of members of the administrative or control bodies belonging to the least represented gender, this number shall be rounded up to the nearest whole number, except for corporate bodies consisting of three members for which the rounding down shall be to the nearest whole number*" (our translation from Italian). For corporate bodies consisting of more than three members, rounding up to the higher unit shall remain valid.

Alongside these hard quotas established ex lege in consideration of what was happening in other countries (Norway was the first in Europe in 2003), we then have what are known as soft quotas, deriving from self-regulation. Indeed, the previous version of the self-regulatory code (Comitato per la Corporate Governance, 2018) invited issuers to adopt gender diversity criteria for the composition of both the board of directors and the board of statutory auditors from the beginning of the first term of office of such bodies following the termination of the effects of Law 120/2011 (i.e., after three consecutive terms). Further, comments in the code called for the principles of gender equality to be applied within the overall company organisation. In the current version of the Corporate Governance Code (Comitato per la Corporate Governance, 2020), Recommendation No. 8 states that at least one-third (33%) of the board of directors and the board of statutory auditors should be made up of members of the least represented gender. This recommendation is applied from the first renewal after the termination of the effects of legal provisions imposing a quota equal to or higher than that recommended by the Code. The reason for such a postponement was the adoption of the Corporate Governance Code before the latest amendments to the Consolidated Law on Finance concerning gender quotas in corporate bodies, which increased the quotas reserved for the less represented gender from one-third to two-fifths.

Also worth mentioning is the Bank of Italy's initiative of July 2015 (Banca d'Italia, 2015). In the application of CRD IV, the Bank of Italy carried out a monitoring activity on the degree of diversity (understood in a broad sense) of the boards of directors, supervisory boards, and management boards of Italian banks. In terms of gender diversity, this control activity revealed a gradually decreasing female presence as the size (measured by total assets) of banking intermediaries decreases. However, as for the top positions (chair of the board of directors, chief executive officer, and general manager), women were absent in the largest banks while they were present (in low percentages) in the other size classes. Given this situation, the Bank of Italy invited banks to adopt initiatives aimed at encouraging a greater presence of women in their governing bodies, especially in executive and top positions. The minimum value of the female presence indicated was 20% and, for the largest banks (with assets over €10 billion), 33% as a consolidated market practice partly resulting from the application of the "pink" quota for listed companies provided for by the Golfo-Mosca Law in force at that time.

More recently, in December 2020, the Bank of Italy put out for public consultation (ended on 22 February 2021) some amendments to the Circular No. 285 of 17 December 2013 and subsequent updates concerning the corporate governance of banks and banking groups with the intention of better linking the current provisions with the evolution of the national and European regulatory frameworks (Banca d'Italia, 2020b). Among other innovations, the introduction of a gender quota in the administrative and control bodies of banks should be considered as a proposal in continuity with the supervisory expectations expressed in 2015. According to the quota, 33% of the members must belong to the least represented gender. In the impact analysis carried out by the Bank of Italy (Banca d'Italia, 2020a), this percentage was found to be optimal: a lower percentage would have not favoured a beneficial internal dialectic and, therefore, would have not effectively influenced the decision-making processes; a higher percentage would have entailed an excessively onerous adjustment compared to the initial situation. The option that was chosen implies the replacement of 551 men by women on the boards of directors in 305 banks (for details see Banca d'Italia, 2020a, Table 5.1), and the replacement of one man by one woman on the boards of statutory auditors in 206 banks. Also, in the attempt to further foster gender diversity, the Consultation Document contains other recommendations, considering "good practices" that banks can follow evaluating the most appropriate configurations with flexibility. One concerns the presence of at least one member of the least represented gender in the internal board committees; the other concerns the opportunity for the chair of the board with strategic supervision function/management function, the chair of the control body, the CEO, and the general manager to be of different genders. Additionally, the non-delegable tasks assigned to the board with strategic supervision function include the approval of the policy for the promotion of diversity and inclusiveness (the so-called diversity policy). These proposals, which have become an integral part of Circular No. 285/2013 through update no. 35 of 30 June 2021, indicate the strong attention to gender diversity profile shown on several occasions by the

Bank of Italy. The Central Bank has chosen an application regime that will allow banks time to adapt to the new provisions. Specifically, it requires reaching the gender quota on the occasion of the first full renewal of the body and, in any case, by 30 June 2024; if the full renewal should occur in 2021, banks can wait until 2024.

The Bank of Italy, together with the Department for Equal Opportunities of the Italian Presidency of the Council of Ministers and CONSOB, launched another important initiative. We refer to the signing of a Protocol of Understanding on 22 November 2018 establishing the "Inter-institutional Observatory on women's participation in the management and control bodies of Italian companies", with effect from 1 January 2019 and a 5-year renewable term. The Protocol specifies the functions of the Observatory: to jointly promote initiatives aimed at concretely achieving the objective of female participation on boards, verifying the progressive trend of gender equality over time, and carrying out analyses that allow the identification of potential critical and attention profiles. The first report drawn up by the Observatory is dated 8 March 2021 (Osservatorio interistituzionale sulla partecipazione femminile negli organi di amministrazione e controllo delle società italiane, 2021).

Finally, as anticipated in Chapter 2, the Italian Banking Association (Associazione Bancaria Italiana—ABI) approved the Charter "Women in Banks: enhancing gender diversity" in June 2019, which aims to enhance gender equality in the banking sector on the assumption that this principle is a key resource for development, sustainable growth, and value creation in firms. Since the percentage of women decreases with increasing levels of qualification, prestige, and salary, the charter issued by the ABI commits signatories to strengthen their corporate policies according to the following five equal opportunity principles (which form an integral part of the ABI Code of Ethics, by resolution of its Executive Committee of 12 July 2019): (a) constantly promoting an inclusive work environment open to the values of diversity, including gender diversity; (b) strengthening selection and development methods suitable for promoting equal gender opportunities throughout the organisation, also to encourage qualified female candidatures where they are lacking; (c) spreading full and effective female participation, with particular reference to the highest positions, in an organisational framework oriented at all levels towards equal role opportunities and equal treatment; (d) committing to promoting gender equality also outside the ABI and for the benefit of the relevant communities; and (e) carrying out under the responsibility of high-level figures appropriate initiatives to address and enhance organisational policies on gender equality—involving testimonials and awareness-raising activities on the motivations and expected benefits.

As of 9 March 2021, there were 37 signatories of the charter (with more than 10 being a listed parent company of a banking group and slightly fewer unlisted parent companies) representing 90% of the banking system in terms of total assets and 88% in terms of employees (ABI, 2021). Here we report the updated list indicating the listed parent companies by specifying "listed" in brackets: Associazione Bancaria Italiana, Banca Agricola Popolare di Ragusa (parent company of a banking group), Banca Consulia, Banca del Piemonte, Banca di Cividale, Banca di Credito Popolare (parent company of a banking group), Banca di Piacenza, Banca Macerata, Banca Mediolanum (listed), Banca Monte dei Paschi di Siena (listed), Banca Nazionale del Lavoro (parent company of a banking group), Banca Popolare Etica (parent company of a banking group), Banca Progetto, Banca Sella Holding S.P.A. (parent company of a banking group), BPER Banca (listed), Banco BPM (listed), Banco Desio (listed), Cassa di Risparmio di Bolzano (parent company of a banking group), Cassa di Risparmio di Cento (parent company of a banking group), Cassa di Risparmio di Fossano, CBI, Credem (listed), Crédit Agricole Italia (parent company of a banking group), Creval S.P.A. (listed), Findomestic (parent company of a banking group), FinecoBank (listed), Gruppo Bancario Cooperativo Iccrea (banking group), illimity Bank S.P.A. (listed), Ing Bank N.V., Intesa Sanpaolo (listed), La Cassa di Ravenna (parent company of a banking group), Mediobanca (listed), Mediocredito Centrale - Invitalia, Société Générale Securities Services, State Street Bank International Gmbh - Succursale Italia, Banca UBI (listed), UniCredit (listed).

Taken together, all the initiatives above represent great achievements, especially if they are considered in their political, social, and cultural context, still affected by stereotypes and prejudices about women and by a backward gender culture. Not surprisingly, a report focusing on financial firms in Italy (Oliver Wyman, 2016a) poses a provocative question: "*Will it be necessary to wait another 15 years to achieve an effective balance in top management*?". If the financial industry really wants to attract the best talent regardless of gender and encourage balanced and productive work environments, radical discontinuity solutions are needed. In particular, the report (Oliver Wyman, 2016a) highlights five priorities for action aimed at facilitating a full awareness of the phenomenon: (1) "Believing with all your heart", driving change from the top down; (2) "Flexibility as an asset", that is, putting corporate flexibility initiatives into practice; (3) "From personnel management to talent management", that is, professionalising and making performance appraisal processes more objective; (4) "Don't leave us alone", that is, establishing coaching and mentoring relationships between top management and the best female talents; and (5) "Seeing change", that is, measuring the results of gender initiatives and making them transparent within the company.

In this regard, it is important to recall Italy's position as reported by the Global Gender Gap Index, drawn up by the World Economic Forum around the four dimensions of Economic Participation and Opportunity, Political Empowerment, Health and Survival, and Educational Attainment. Italy often occupies a place in the middle of all the countries ranked (Table 10.1) and is experiencing a process of gradual, albeit fluctuating, advancement in its position compared to other countries, accompanied by a slight upward trend in its overall score.

**Table 10.1** Global gender gap index: Italy's ranking

| *Year* | *Rank (compared to the total number of countries)* | *Overall Score*[a] |
|---|---|---|
| 2021 | 63 out of 156 | 0.721 |
| 2020 | 76 out of 153 | 0.707 |
| 2018 | 70 out of 149 | 0.706 |
| 2017 | 82 out of 144 | 0.69 |
| 2016 | 50 out of 144 | 0.719 |
| 2015 | 41 out of 145 | 0.726 |
| 2014 | 69 out of 142 | 0.6973 |
| 2013 | 71 out of 136 | 0.6885 |
| 2012 | 80 out of 135 | 0.6729 |
| 2011 | 74 out of 135 | 0.6796 |
| 2010 | 74 out of 134 | 0.6765 |
| 2009 | 72 out of 134 | 0.6798 |
| 2008 | 67 out of 130 | 0.6788 |
| 2007 | 84 out of 128 | 0.6498 |
| 2006 | 77 out of 115 | 0.6456 |

*Note* [a]It varies between 0 (total absence of parity) and 1 (gender parity)
*Source* World Economic Forum, The Global Gender Gap Report, various years (the value for 2019 is missing)

Also, significant progress has been made for a few indicators of Goal 5 "Achieve gender equality and empower all women and girls", one of the 17 Sustainable Development Goals (SDGs) in the 2030 Agenda for Sustainable Development, adopted in September 2015. In particular, as reported by Istat (2019), there has been an increase in the proportion of seats held by women in the Senate of the Republic and the Chamber of Deputies (35.4 in 2018), by women on the boards of companies listed in the stock exchange (36.0 in 2018) and, to a lesser extent, by women on Regional Councils (21.2 in 2019), and by women in decision-making bodies: Privacy Authority, Autorità per le Garanzie nelle Comunicazioni, Antitrust Authority, Constitutional Court, Superior Council of the Magistracy, Ambassadors, and CONSOB (15.8 in 2019). In comparison with other EU countries, Italy ranks first in terms of change in the rate of the presence of women on the boards of the largest listed companies (+31.9% in the period October 2010–October 2018), most likely in response to the entry into force of the law on gender quotas (Law no. 120 of 12 July 2011): in fact, the countries that have recorded the highest increases are those that have moved towards binding, rather than non-mandatory, quotas (Italy, France, Belgium, and Germany; see European Commission, 2019; European Parliament, 2015). However, this effect on board composition has not been paralleled by an impact on board positions, and disparity in professional development persists, as can be seen by the slight increase in female representation in top management roles, not least by the sparse number of women sitting as board chairs or CEOs (European Commission, 2019). In essence, there are more women but few in top positions (see Chapter 4).

## 10.2 Insight into the Italian Scenario: How Is Female Representation Evolving?

The large body of research and reports discussed so far (particularly in Chapter 4) represent a valuable source for extracting data on gender diversity in Italian financial institutions. Here those studies will be integrated by further works to provide as detailed a picture as possible on the evolution of female representation in these firms.

Country-specific data from the 2017 International Monetary Fund study (IMF, 2017 and excel file in supplementary material) show a 16.5% average female presence on Italian bank boards for 2013 (Chapter 4, Table 4.1) in agreement with the 16.54% European average in the IMF survey (Table 4.1 in Chapter 4 reports the European and non-European countries together with the associated average share). It is worth noting that despite only 13 Italian banks participating in the 2017 IMF survey, these are the largest and most important institutions in the country.

In the 2016 EBA report, the number of Italian credit institutions and investment firms rise to 67. Of these, 16.42% have a gender diversity policy, which is below the European average of 24.54% (the countries considered in the report belong to the European Union and European Economic Area).

As documented in the report, the percentage of female participation as executive and non-executive directors in the management body in Italy is below the total sample average, with 7.35% versus 13.63% and 15.98% versus 18.90%, respectively (EBA, 2016, Fig. 12). Therefore, the largest negative gap is for female executive directors (see Table 10.2). However, the comparison between Italian female directors recruited from 2010 to 2013 and those recruited in 2014 shows a very small increase in female

**Table 10.2** EBA reports: Italian data

| *Items* | *Average value for Italy (%)* | *Gap with the average of all countries considered by the EBA (%)* |
|---|---|---|
| EBA (2016) | | |
| Italian institutions with a gender diversity policy | 16.42 | −8.12 |
| Female executive directors in the management body | 7.35 | −6.28 |
| Female non-executive directors in the management body | 15.98 | −2.92 |
| EBA (2020) | | |
| Italian institutions with a gender diversity policy | 28.57 | −12.08 |
| Italian significant institutions with a gender diversity policy | 73.33 | +1.96 |
| Female executive directors in the management body | 10 | −5.11 |
| Female non-executive directors in the management body | 22.11 | −0.23 |

*Source* EBA (2016) and EBA (2020)

executives (0.15%) and a decrease in female non-executives (−3.89%). Hence, despite "pink" quotas being in force since 2011 for listed companies, both financial and non-financial, the push for a rearrangement of bodies in favour of women still seems weak for companies excluded from the application of the Golfo-Mosca Law. As for the moral suasion rules, these cannot be discussed as they were dictated by the Bank of Italy in 2015 (see Sect. 10.1).

A second EBA study published in 2020 (EBA, 2020) features 70 Italian institutions. Of these, 28.57% have a gender diversity policy, indicating an expansion of this practice compared to the previous report. Yet, when comparing the average for Italy to the European average (40.65%), we can observe a 12% difference, signalling a greater distance from other EU countries (Table 10.2). Conversely, the trend is very different for the significant institutions (15 out of 70), among which 73.33% adopted such a policy, showing greater attention to gender issues. This figure for Italy is slightly higher than the EU value (71.37%, EBA, 2020, Fig. 4). However, the absence of this information in the previous EBA report prevents us from making any comparisons on these percentages.

Both executive and non-executive female directors increase over time: the former from 7.35 to 10%, the latter from 15.98 to 22.11% (for the most recent data see EBA, 2020, Fig. 17). Although also the figures in the second report are lower than the EU averages (15.11 and 22.34%, respectively), the gaps between the Italian data and the EU averages are narrower, especially regarding female non-executive directors (see Table 10.2). The averages calculated for the governance system (1-tier system and 2-tier system) of credit institutions and investment firms indicate a greater alignment with EU averages for the latter than for the former (EBA, 2020, Figs. 8 and 9).

Table 10.2 shows the main Italian data included in the two EBA reports discussed above.

A comparison between women in executive committee positions in Italy and other European and non-European countries can be found in Oliver Wyman's reports, the main findings of which are outlined in Chapter 4. For 2013, Italy features one of the lowest percentages (below 10%) for these positions, similarly to other EU countries such as Germany and Spain (Oliver Wyman, 2014, Exhibit 2). In 2016, the percentage increases to 16%, reaching the global average (Oliver Wyman, 2016b, Exhibit 2). Finally, in the last report, the figure falls to 13%, well below the global average (20%, Oliver Wyman, 2020, Exhibit 3). It should be noted that the trend must be interpreted with due caution, as the sample of companies under observation changes across the three reports: as specified in Chapter 4, the sample of companies consists of more than 150 companies in the 2014 report, 381 in the 2016 report, and 468 in the last report. An important observation concerns the placement of Italy among the countries called in these reports "hitting a ceiling", "beyond the ceiling", "stuck in the mud", and "getting there" (see the definitions in Sub-section 4.3.1, Chapter 4) based on two variables: the number of women on executive committees in 2013 (and 2016) and the growth rate between 2013 and 2016 (and 2016–2019). In the 2016 report, considering the number of women on executive committees in 2013 and the growth rate between 2013 and 2016, Italy is among the "getting there" countries—that is, countries with a low percentage of women in 2013 but high growth rates (Oliver Wyman, 2016b, Exhibit 5). Looking at the 2016–2019 growth rate and the number of women in 2016, the worsening of Italy's position featuring few women on the executive committees and a negative 2016–2019 growth rate results in the country's fall to the "stuck in the mud" position (Chapter 4, Fig. 4.1). Thus, the evolution is still marked by great difficulties in promoting female talent to positions of responsibility.

In order to understand the effectiveness of measures to support the presence of women, very relevant is the study by Capone (2020) which analyses the board composition of all 426 Italian banks (23 listed) operating as of 30 June 2018. The study allows us to obtain indications on the impact of the diversity benchmark moral suasion indicated by the Bank of Italy for unlisted banks on the one hand, and of the minimum quota established by law for listed banks on the other. While the overall presence of women on the boards of listed and unlisted banks increased over the period considered in the research (2014–2018), the weight of women on the boards of listed and unlisted banks has followed different patterns, increasing on average from 10% in 2014 to just over 14% in 2018 in unlisted banks, and from 25% in 2014 to over 33% in 2018 in listed banks (Capone, 2020). Going into more detail, in 2018, about 25% of the boards of unlisted banks do not have women, evidencing the limited effectiveness of the measure adopted by the Bank of Italy: about 29% of banks exceed the 20% threshold of female presence on boards, showing only a 10% increase compared to 2014—before the publication of the benchmark; among the largest banks, for which the Bank of Italy had indicated a minimum 33% share of women, only 14% reach this result (they were 6% in 2014). In contrast, the threshold set by law was much more effective: not surprisingly, the minimum threshold is met by all listed banks and exceeded in 25% of cases.

The analysis of all Italian banks confirms the clear prevalence of women among non-executive directors rather than among executive directors: in 2018, women in the unlisted banks account for 16% of all non-executive directors, compared to 11% of all executive directors, whereas the percentages of women among non-executive directors in the listed banks rise to 43% and to 18% among executive directors. In addition to the strong growth of female non-executive directors in the listed banks (up from 27 to 43% between 2014 and 2018), these banks also show a strong growth of female board chairs (from 0 to 16% from 2014 to 2018), while they have no female CEOs. This last information contrasts with what has been found for the unlisted banks where female CEOs in 2014 and 2018 were 5 and 7%, respectively (Capone, 2020, Fig. 3).

The significantly greater weight of women on the boards of larger banks (including listed banks to which gender balance rules apply) is confirmed by the data for 2019. Interestingly, the age of the majority of women in these roles ranges from 41 to 60 years. The almost total absence of women over the age of 60 likely reflects the different career paths taken in the past. Lastly, the data on the type of positions held by women also show that, in 2019, the most important positions (chief executive officer and board chair) are very rarely held by women (Osservatorio interistituzionale sulla partecipazione femminile negli organi di amministrazione e controllo delle società italiane, 2021).

Basically, the results found in Capone's study highlight a clear dichotomy between unlisted and listed banks: in the former, the underrepresentation of women in corporate bodies persists and, therefore, the glass ceiling and tokenism phenomena against women continue; in the latter, on the other hand, the presence of women is not a symbolic gesture but is substantial, since reaching a critical mass of women can have the power to influence male members. This dichotomy is the result of the different degree of effectiveness of two dissimilar measures: on the one hand, a 20% reference target dictated by the supervisory authority (namely the Bank of Italy), on the other, a quota that is compulsory by law and matched by a system of sanctions against non-compliant companies (Capone, 2020). The research also reveals the absence or scarce presence of women in key decision-making roles, such as CEO and general manager, as well as the substantial prevalence of non-executive positions on boards of directors meaning women are not involved in the operational management of the bank. Yet, women are better educated and younger than men (D'Ascenzo, 2017; De Vita & Magliocco, 2018), so there would certainly be a pool of female talent to draw from for leadership roles. In addition to the disadvantages above, women also have a shorter seniority of office compared to men: elaborations by the Bank of Italy (Banca d'Italia, 2020a) show that the length of time women serve on boards of directors is about half in both listed and unlisted banks (3.2 years for women versus 6.1 for men, and 5 years for women versus 9.4 for men, respectively). Similarly, with regard to the board of statutory auditors, the average tenure of men is 9.2 years in unlisted banks compared to 5.8 for women; in listed banks, the gap narrows, but remains strong (5.2 vs. 3.2).

The financial crisis that originated in 2008 did not, therefore, lead to the "feminisation of management", nor to the disappearance of vertical discrimination (the so-called glass ceiling), nor to the horizontal segmentation, as inferred from the complete lack of female CEOs in listed banks (De Vita & Magliocco, 2018). Ultimately, it does not seem to have led to any important signs of cultural change or manifestations of the "glass cliff"—a term used to indicate another tough battle that women are called to face when assuming leadership positions in poorly performing firms, where the possibility of failure is higher (Ryan & Haslam, 2005, 2007).

In the next section, we shall continue to illustrate data on gender representation, in particular data extracted from documents of Italian listed banks. In this regard, Legislative Decree No. 254/2016—implementing Directive 2014/95/EU on non-financial information—amended art. 123-*bis* of the Consolidated Law on Finance by introducing the obligation to include diversity-related policies applied to the composition of corporate bodies, objectives, implementation methods, and results in the "Report on Corporate Governance and Ownership Structures", published by listed companies on an annual basis (see Article 123-*bis*, paragraph 2, letter d-*bis* of the Consolidated Law on Finance). These disclosure requirements are governed by the "comply or explain" principle: a company that does not adopt any diversity policy must adequately justify the reasons for such choice. Finally, it is useful to recall that Legislative Decree No. 254/2016 provides that public interest entities (listed companies, banks, insurance companies, and reinsurance companies) that comply with certain size requirements publish each year the Non-financial Statement, which must include a description of the social aspects and those pertaining to personnel management, including the actions put in place to ensure gender equality, the measures aimed at implementing the conventions of international and supranational organisations on the matter, and the way the dialogue with the social partners is carried out. Also in this case, the "comply or explain" criterion is followed. For the sake of completeness, with regard to size requirements, these must be public interest entities that have had, on average, more than 500 employees during the financial year and, at the balance sheet date, have exceeded at least one of the two following size limits: (a) balance sheet total: €20,000,000; and (b) total net revenues from sales and services: €40,000,000. Regarding the expected development of this type of disclosure, we refer to Chapter 2, Section 2.4.

## 10.3 Focus on Female Presence in Italian Listed Banks

We now turn to the presence of women in the corporate bodies of Italian listed banks. As is well known, listed banks are banking intermediaries subject to the hard quotas in force in Italy, i.e., first to the quotas provided for by the Golfo-Mosca Law and then to those in force with its extension, which took place, with amendments, with the enactment of Law No. 160 of 27 December 2019. In particular, here we will consider 22 banks that are parent companies of banking groups. Following the same order in which they appear in Table 10.3, these are: Banca Generali, Banca Ifis, Banca Intermobiliare di Investimenti e Gestioni (BIM), Banca Mediolanum, Banca Monte dei Paschi di Siena (MPS), Banca Popolare di Sondrio, Banco BPM, Banco Desio, BPER Banca, Banca Carige, Credito Emiliano (Credem), Credito Valtellinese (Creval), FinecoBank, Intesa Sanpaolo, Mediobanca, UniCredit, UBI Banca, Banca Finnat, Banca Sistema, Banca Farmafactoring (BFF), illimity Bank, and doBank. The timeframe considered spans from 31 December 2017 to 31 December 2019 (with the exceptions indicated in the notes to Table 10.3), therefore we assume that all banks were already compliant with the Golfo-Mosca Law.

Our evaluation is based on information collected from the Corporate Governance and Ownership Structures yearly reports prepared by the parent companies of each banking group. In detail, we consider the following 14 items:

**Table 10.3** Female representation in the bodies of Italian listed banks (parent companies of banking groups)

| *Italian listed banks* | *Female CEO (not = 0, yes = 1)* | *Female chair (not = 0, yes = 1)* | *Women on the board of directors (%)* | *Executive women (%)* | *Non-executive women (%)* | *Women in the risk committee (%)* | *Female president of the risk committee (not = 0, yes = 1)* | *Women in the appointments committee (%)* | *Female president of the appointments committee (not = 0, yes = 1)* | *Women in the remuneration committee (%)* | *Female president of the remuneration committee (not = 0, yes = 1)* | *Women on the board of statutory auditors (%)* | *Women on the board of statutory auditors (including alternate auditors) (%)* | *Female president of the board of statutory auditors (not = 0, yes = 1)* |
|---|---|---|---|---|---|---|---|---|---|---|---|---|---|---|
| **Banca Generali** | | | | | | | | | | | | | | |
| *2017*[1] | 0 | 0 | 44.44 | 0 | 100 | 50 | 1 | 0 | 0 | 66.66 | 0 | 33.33 | 40 | 0 |
| *2018*[2] | 0 | 0 | 44.44 | 0 | 100 | 50 | 1 | 33.33 | 0 | 33.33 | 0 | 33.33 | 40 | 0 |
| *2019*[3] | 0 | 0 | 44.44 | 0 | 100 | 50 | 1 | 33.33 | 0 | 33.33 | 0 | 33.33 | 40 | 0 |
| **Banca Ifis** | | | | | | | | | | | | | | |
| *2017* | 0 | 0 | 33.33 | 0 | 100 | 50 | 0 | 0 | 0 | 33.33 | 1 | 33.33 | 40 | 0 |
| *2018* | 0 | 0 | 33.33 | 0 | 100 | 50 | 0 | 0 | 0 | 33.33 | 1 | 33.33 | 40 | 0 |
| *2019* | 0 | 0 | 33.33 | 0 | 100 | 60 | 0 | 33.33 | 0 | 66.66 | 1 | 33.33 | 40 | 0 |
| **BIM** | | | | | | | | | | | | | | |
| *2017* | 0 | 0 | 37.50 | 0 | 100 | 66.66 | 0 | 33.33 | 0 | 66.66 | 1 | 33.33 | 40 | 0 |
| *2018* | 0 | 0 | 33.33 | 0 | 100 | 75 | 1 | 25 | 1 | 60 | 1 | 33.33 | 40 | 0 |
| *2019* | 0 | 0 | 33.33 | 0 | 100 | 100 | 1 | 33.33 | 1 | 66.66 | 1 | 33.33 | 40 | 1 |
| **Mediolanum** | | | | | | | | | | | | | | |
| *2017* | 0 | 0 | 9.09[4] | 0 | 100 | 0 | 0 | 33.33 | 0 | 0 | 0 | 33.33 | 20 | 1 |
| *2018* | 0 | 0 | 30.76 | 0 | 100 | 33.33 | 0 | 50 | 0 | 33.33 | 0 | 33.33 | 50 | 0 |
| *2019* | 0 | 0 | 30.76 | 0 | 100 | 33.33 | 0 | 66.66 | 0 | 33.33 | 0 | 33.33 | 50 | 0 |
| **MPS** | | | | | | | | | | | | | | |
| *2017* | 0 | 1 | 35.71 | 0 | 100 | 40 | 1 | 40 | 1 | 20 | 0 | 66.66 | 60 | 1 |
| *2018* | 0 | 1 | 35.71 | 0 | 100 | 20 | 0 | 40 | 1 | 40 | 1 | 66.66 | 50 | 1 |
| *2019* | 0 | 1 | 35.71 | 0 | 100 | 20 | 0 | 40 | 1 | 40 | 1 | 66.66 | 60 | 1 |

(continued)

Table 10.3 (continued)

| *Italian listed banks* | *Female CEO (not = 0, yes = 1)* | *Female chair (not = 0, yes = 1)* | *Women on the board of directors (%)* | *Executive women (%)* | *Non-executive women (%)* | *Women in the risk committee (%)* | *Female president of the risk committee (not = 0, yes = 1)* | *Women in the appointments committee (%)* | *Female president of the appointments committee (not = 0, yes = 1)* | *Women in the remuneration committee (%)* | *Female president of the remuneration committee (not = 0, yes = 1)* | *Women on the board of statutory auditors (%)* | *Women on the board of statutory auditors (including alternate auditors) (%)* | *Female president of the board of statutory auditors (not = 0, yes = 1)* |
|---|---|---|---|---|---|---|---|---|---|---|---|---|---|---|
| **Pop. Sondrio** | | | | | | | | | | | | | | |
| *2017* | 0 | 0 | 33.33 | 40 | 60 | 25 | NA | 66.66 | NA | 66.66 | NA | 33.33 | 20 | 0 |
| *2018* | 0 | 0 | 40 | 50 | 50 | 25 | NA | 100 | NA | 66.66 | NA | 33.33 | 20 | 0 |
| *2019* | 0 | 0 | 40 | 50 | 50 | 25 | NA | 100 | NA | 66.66 | NA | 33.33 | 20 | 0 |
| **Banco BPM** | | | | | | | | | | | | | | |
| *2017* | 0 | 0 | 36.84 | 0 | 100 | 50 | 0 | 25 | 0 | 75 | 0 | 40 | 50 | 0 |
| *2018* | 0 | 0 | 36.84 | 0 | 100 | 50 | 0 | 25 | 0 | 75 | 0 | 40 | 50 | 0 |
| *2019* | 0 | 0 | 35.29 | 0 | 100 | 50 | 0 | 25 | 0 | 75 | 0 | 40 | 50 | 0 |
| **Desio** | | | | | | | | | | | | | | |
| *2017* | NN[5] | 0 | 33.33 | 25 | 75 | 33.33 | 0 | 100 | 1 | 0 | 0 | 33.33 | 33.33 | 1 |
| *2018* | NN[5] | 0 | 33.33 | 25 | 75 | 33.33 | 0 | 100 | 1 | 0 | 0 | 33.33 | 33.33 | 1 |
| *2019* | 0 | 0 | 33.33 | 25 | 75 | 33.33 | 0 | 66.66 | 1 | 33.33 | 0 | 33.33 | 33.33 | 1 |
| **BPER** | | | | | | | | | | | | | | |
| *2017* | 0 | 0 | 33.33 | 0 | 100 | 100 | 1 | 66.66 | 1 | 66.66 | 1 | 40 | 42.85 | 0 |
| *2018* | 0 | 0 | 46.66 | 14.28 | 85.72 | 75 | 1 | 66.66 | 0 | 100 | 1 | 60 | 57.14 | 0 |
| *2019* | 0 | 0 | 46.66 | 14.28 | 85.72 | 75 | 1 | 66.66 | 0 | 100 | 1 | 60 | 71.42 | 0 |
| **Carige** | | | | | | | | | | | | | | |
| *2017* | 0 | 0 | 33.33 | 20 | 80 | 33.33 | 0 | 0 | 0 | 66.66 | 0 | 33.33 | 40 | 0 |
| *2018* | 0 | 0 | 33.33 | 0 | 100 | 33.33 | 0 | 75 | NA | 33.33 | 0 | 33.33 | 50 | 0 |
| *2019*[6] | 0 | 0 | 40 | 0 | 100 | 25 | 0 | 66.66 | 1 | 33.33 | 0 | 33.33 | 40 | 0 |
| **Credem** | | | | | | | | | | | | | | |
| *2017* | NN[5] | 0 | 33.33 | 0 | 100 | 33.33 | 1 | 33.33 | 0 | 66.66 | 1 | 66.66 | 60 | 1 |
| *2018* | NN[5] | 0 | 33.33 | 25 | 75 | 20 | 1 | 33.33 | 1 | 66.66 | 1 | 66.66 | 60 | 1 |
| *2019* | NN[5] | 0 | 33.33 | 25 | 75 | 20 | 1 | 33.33 | 1 | 66.66 | 1 | 66.66 | 40 | 1 |

| Italian listed banks | Female CEO (not = 0, yes = 1) | Female chair (not = 0, yes = 1) | Women on the board of directors (%) | Executive women (%) | Non-executive women (%) | Women in the risk committee (%) | Female president of the risk committee (not = 0, yes = 1) | Women in the appointments committee (%) | Female president of the appointments committee (not = 0, yes = 1) | Women in the remuneration committee (%) | Female president of the remuneration committee (not = 0, yes = 1) | Women on the board of statutory auditors (%) | Women on the board of statutory auditors (including alternate auditors) (%) | Female president of the board of statutory auditors (not = 0, yes = 1) |
|---|---|---|---|---|---|---|---|---|---|---|---|---|---|---|
| **Creval** | | | | | | | | | | | | | | |
| *2017* | NN[5] | 0 | 40 | 16.7 | 83.3 | 33.33 | 1 | 100 | 1 | 66.66 | 1 | 33.33 | 20 | 0 |
| *2018* | 0 | 0 | 40 | 0 | 100 | 33.33 | 1 | 100 | 1 | 66.66 | 1 | 33.33 | 20 | 0 |
| *2019* | 0 | 0 | 46.66 | 0 | 100 | 60 | 0 | 100 | 1 | 66.66 | 1 | 33.33 | 40 | 1 |
| **FinecoBank[7]** | | | | | | | | | | | | | | |
| *2017* | – | – | – | – | – | – | – | – | – | – | – | – | – | – |
| *2018* | – | – | – | – | – | – | – | – | – | – | – | – | – | – |
| *2019* | 0 | 0 | 33.33 | 0 | 100 | 0 | 0 | 66.66 | 1 | 33.33 | 0 | 66.66 | 60 | 1 |
| **Intesa[8]** | | | | | | | | | | | | | | |
| *2017* | 0 | 0 | 36.84 | 0 | 100 | 40 | 1 | 20 | 0 | 20 | 0 | 40 | 40 | 0 |
| *2018* | 0 | 0 | 36.84 | 0 | 100 | 40 | 1 | 20 | 0 | 20 | 0 | 40 | 40 | 0 |
| *2019* | 0 | 0 | 36.84 | 0 | 100 | 20 | 1 | 40 | 1 | 20 | 0 | 40 | 40 | 0 |
| **Mediobanca[9]** | | | | | | | | | | | | | | |
| *2017* | 0 | 0 | 35.71 | 20 | 80 | 60 | 1 | 40 | 0 | 25 | 0 | 33.33 | 33.33 | 0 |
| *2018* | 0 | 0 | 33.33 | 20 | 80 | 60 | 1 | 40 | 0 | 25 | 0 | 33.33 | 33.33 | 0 |
| *2019* | 0 | 0 | 33.33 | 20 | 80 | 60 | 1 | 40 | 0 | 25 | 0 | 33.33 | 33.33 | 0 |
| **UniCredit[10]** | | | | | | | | | | | | | | |
| *2017* | 0 | 0 | 35.29 | 0 | 100 | 33.33 | 0 | 28.57 | 0 | 20 | 0 | 40 | 55.56 | 0 |
| *2018* | 0 | 0 | 40 | 0 | 100 | 57.14 | 0 | 33.33 | 0 | 50 | 0 | 40 | 55.56 | 0 |
| *2019* | 0 | 0 | 35.71 | 0 | 100 | 75 | 0 | 40 | 0 | 66.66 | 0 | 40 | 55.56 | 0 |
| **UBI[11]** | | | | | | | | | | | | | | |
| *2017* | 0 | 1 | 42.86 | 66.66 | 33.33 | 60 | 1 | 20 | 0 | 50 | 1 | 33.33 | 33.33 | 0 |
| *2018* | 0 | 1 | 42.86 | 66.66 | 33.33 | 60 | 1 | 20 | 0 | 66.66 | 1 | 33.33 | 33.33 | 0 |
| *2019* | 0 | 1 | 40 | 0 | 100 | 33.33 | 0 | 20 | 1 | 33.33 | 0 | 60 | 60 | 0 |

(continued)

**Table 10.3** (continued)

| *Italian listed banks* | *Female CEO (not = 0, yes = 1)* | *Female chair (not = 0, yes = 1)* | *Women on the board of directors (%)* | *Executive women (%)* | *Non-executive women (%)* | *Women in the risk committee (%)* | *Female president of the risk committee (not = 0, yes = 1)* | *Women in the appoint-ments committee (%)* | *Female president of the appoint-ments committee (not = 0, yes = 1)* | *Women in the remuner-ation committee (%)* | *Female president of the remuner-ation committee (not = 0, yes = 1)* | *Women on the board of statutory auditors (%)* | *Women on the board of statutory auditors (including alternate auditors) (%)* | *Female president of the board of statutory auditors (not = 0, yes = 1)* |
|---|---|---|---|---|---|---|---|---|---|---|---|---|---|---|
| **Finnat** | | | | | | | | | | | | | | |
| *2017* | 0 | 1 | 36.36 | 0 | 100 | 0 | 0 | 33.33 | 1 | 33.33 | 0 | 33.33 | 40 | 0 |
| *2018* | 0 | 1 | 36.36 | 0 | 100 | 0 | 0 | 33.33 | 1 | 33.33 | 0 | 33.33 | 40 | 0 |
| *2019* | 0 | 1 | 36.36 | 0 | 100 | 0 | 0 | 33.33 | 1 | 33.33 | 0 | 33.33 | 40 | 0 |
| **Banca Sistema** | | | | | | | | | | | | | | |
| *2017* | 0 | 1 | 25[12] | 50 | 50 | 50 | 0 | 50 | 0 | 0 | 0 | 33.33 | 40 | 0 |
| *2018* | 0 | 1 | 33.33 | 0 | 100 | 50 | 1 | 33.33 | 0 | 0 | 0 | 33.33 | 40 | 0 |
| *2019* | 0 | 1 | 33.33 | 0 | 100 | 50 | 1 | 33.33 | 0 | 0 | 0 | 33.33 | 40 | 0 |
| **BFF** | | | | | | | | | | | | | | |
| *2017* | 0 | 0 | 20[13] | 0 | 100 | 25 | 1 | 33.33 | 0 | 33.33 | 1 | 66.66 | 40 | 0 |
| *2018* | 0 | 0 | 33.33 | 0 | 100 | 33.33 | 1 | 50 | 0 | 66.66 | 1 | 66.66 | 40 | 1 |
| *2019* | 0 | 0 | 44.44 | 0 | 100 | 66.66 | 1 | 33.33 | 0 | 100 | 1 | 66.66 | 40 | 1 |
| **illimity**[14] | | | | | | | | | | | | | | |
| *2017* | – | – | – | – | – | – | – | – | – | – | – | – | – | – |
| *2018* | – | – | – | – | – | – | – | – | – | – | – | – | – | – |
| *2019* | 0 | 1 | 33.33 | 0 | 100 | 75 | 1 | 33.33 | 0 | 33.33 | 0 | 33.33 | 40 | 0 |
| **doBank**[15] | | | | | | | | | | | | | | |
| *2017* | – | – | – | – | – | – | – | – | – | – | – | – | – | – |
| *2018* | 0 | 0 | 22.22 | 0 | 100 | 0 | 0 | 0 | 0 | 0 | 0 | 33.33 | 60 | 1 |
| *2019* | – | – | – | – | – | – | – | – | – | – | – | – | – | – |
| **Average values** | | | | | | | | | | | | | | |
| *2017* | 0 | 0.21 | 28.33 | 9.12 | 90.88 | 42.31 | 0.50 | 35.91 | 0.28 | 23.33 | 0.39 | 40.00 | 39.29 | 0.21 |
| *2018* | 0 | 0.20 | 40.00 | 6.67 | 93.33 | 41.07 | 0.53 | 46.07 | 0.33 | 37.00 | 0.42 | 45.00 | 42.67 | 0.25 |
| *2019* | 0 | 0.24 | 40.00 | 6.00 | 94.00 | 45.00 | 0.45 | 50.63 | 0.50 | 51.43 | 0.35 | 48.00 | 43.53 | 0.33 |

**Table 10.3** (continued)

*Notes* [1]Data refer to 1 March 2018, except for the board of statutory auditors, whose data refer to 10 March 2017; [2]Data refer to 8 March 2019; [3]Data refer to 1 April 2020; [4]Banca Mediolanum SpA, as a listed company, was created on 30 December 2015 from the merger by incorporation with the former parent company Mediolanum SpA. Previously, the bank was only a subsidiary, not listed on the stock exchange. In 2017, therefore, the board of the unlisted company appointed for the three years 2015–2017 (appointed in April 2015) remained in office, naturally with the approval of CONSOB; [5]Not nominated; [6]Data for the year 2019 refer to the date on which the extraordinary administration of the bank ends (31 January 2020); [7]FinecoBank became a parent company in 2019. Data for the year 2019 actually refer to 12 March 2020; [8]Intesa Sanpaolo adopts the "one-tier" management and control model, whereby the administration and control duties are performed, respectively, by the board of directors and the management control committee set up within it; [9]The data for the years 2017–2019 refer to 30 June 2018, 30 June 2019, and 30 June 2020, respectively; [10]The data for the years 2017–2019 refer to the date of approval of the Report on Corporate Governance and Ownership Structures (5 March 2018, 5 March 2019, 5 March 2020); [11]The UBI Group had a "two-tier" governance system, where the policy, strategic supervision, and control functions were assigned to the supervisory board, and the corporate management functions were assigned to the management board, but in 2019, the group moved to a "one-tier" management and control model; [12]The composition of the board does not comply with gender quota regulations following the resignation of a female director, as explained in the Report on Corporate Governance and Ownership Structures for 2017; [13]The Report on Corporate Governance and Ownership Structures for 2017 states that, with regard to diversity policies, in 2017, the bank did not adopt any formalised ad hoc policies on the diversity of corporate bodies, considering them to be included, inter alia, in the statute, the regulations of the board of directors, and the regulations of the board of statutory auditors. As for the board of directors, the report outlined that it should be noted that the outcomes of these policies were reflected inter alia in the guidelines for shareholders published on the website in the section "Investor Relations/Shareholders' Meeting Documentation". For this reason, the percentage is lower than the minimum value required by Italian law; [14]The bank listed during 2019; [15]doBank applied for listing in June 2017. It should be noted that one female director resigned in 2018, as stated in the Report on Corporate Governance and Ownership Structures for that year

*Source* Authors' elaboration on data collected from the reports on corporate governance and ownership structures of banks

1. The gender of the CEO, represented as a dummy variable that takes the value 0 or 1 depending on whether the CEO is, respectively, male or female.
2. The gender of the chair of the body that carries out administration duties, usually represented by the board of directors: also, in this case we have a dummy variable that takes the value 0 if the chair is male, or 1 otherwise.
3. The percentage of women on the board of directors (or other similar body) over the total number of directors.
4. The representation of women in executive roles, expressed as a percentage of the number of executive women on the board.
5. The presence of non-executive women, expressed as a percentage of the number of non-executive women on the board so that the sum of executive and non-executive women is 100%.
6. The presence of women in the risk committee (or similarly named), expressed as a percentage of the total number of committee members.
7. The gender of the risk committee chair: the dummy is 0 if the chair is a man, otherwise 1.
8. The percentage of women on the appointments committee (or similarly named), expressed as a percentage of the total number of committee members.
9. The gender of the appointments committee chair, represented as a dummy variable taking the value of 0 or 1 depending on whether the chair is male or female, respectively.
10. The percentage of women on the remuneration committee (or similar name) over the total committee members.
11. The gender of the remuneration committee chair, represented as a dummy variable taking the value of 0 or 1 depending on whether the chair is male or female, respectively.
12. The percentage of women in the control body (in most cases represented by the board of statutory auditors) compared to the total number of effective auditors.
13. The percentage of women in the control body over the total number of auditors, both effective and alternate.
14. The gender of the control body chair, represented as a dummy variable taking the value of 0 or 1 depending on whether the chair is male or female, respectively.

The above-mentioned board committees were chosen as they are expressly recommended by the Corporate Governance Committee (Comitato per la Corporate Governance, 2018, 2020). The data are shown in Table 10.3. Further details are provided in the notes to the table.

Upon examining Table 10.3, we can see that the data confirm much of the evidence highlighted so far: first and foremost, the absence of female CEOs, contrasted by a discrete presence of female chairs on the board (in four banks from 2017 to 2019 and in one bank—illimity Bank—in the only year of observation). Specifically, executive women are completely absent over the entire observation period in 13 of the 22 banks considered (59.09% of the total banks); additionally, female executive directors are absent for one/two years from a number of other banks (BPER in 2017, Carige in 2018 and 2019, Credem in 2017, Creval in 2018 and 2019, UBI in 2019, and Banca Sistema in 2018 and 2019). In force of the "pink" quotas for listed companies, all banks reach or exceed the 33.33% quota on the board of directors, with the exceptions explained in the notes under Table 10.3. Few banks are already compliant with the new percentage envisaged in the 2020 Budget Law (40%), with only three banks reaching or exceeding this percentage in 2017, and some other institutions reaching or exceeding it in one or both the following years (in 2018 and/or 2019). The maximum percentage of female presence on the board of directors is close to 50%, precisely 46.66%, in BPER (in 2018 and 2019) and Creval (in 2019).

The same considerations made about the board of directors also apply to the control body, which is subject to gender quotas: banks are compliant if they reach or exceed the 33% quota. In detail, thirteen banks (59.09%) feature a 33.33% presence of women in the control body for all three years considered, while other banks feature percentages higher than those reported for the board of directors, with the maximum share being 66.66%. When comparing the data for the two bodies (board of directors and board of statutory auditors), we notice that most banks exceed 33.33% for the first body, whereas they often remain stationary at 33.33% for the second body. However, in the cases where the quota is exceeded, the percentages are lower for the administrative body than for the control body. Then, taking into account alternate auditors, we can see that a few banks feature female quotas falling below the minimum. Yet, given the seniority of the effective auditors, we expect quotas have been met at subsequent boards. Women chairs of the control body are few, as is the case for the administrative body, being present for all years only in five banks, and present in one or two years in four other banks.

It is interesting to assess whether the data collected on the risk committee, appointments committee, and remuneration committee reflect the recent recommendation of the Bank of Italy on the presence of at least one member of the less represented gender on the committees within the board, which was put out for public consultation and has become an integral part of Circular No. 285/2013.

Almost all risk committees have at least one woman: the only banks to have no female representation in the years considered are FinecoBank, Finnat, and doBank; Mediolanum has no women in 2017, whereas more than half of the risk committees (twelve banks) have a female chair at least for some period over the three years considered. A similar situation is found for the appointments committee: despite the strong dissimilarity among banks across all committees, only four banks do not have women (Banca Generali in 2017, Banca Ifis in 2017 and 2018, Carige in 2017, and doBank in 2018). Similarly, female chairs are present in eleven banks. Regarding the last committee, there are no women on the remuneration committee of four banks: Mediolanum in 2017, Desio in 2017 and 2018, Banca Sistema in 2017–2019, and doBank in 2018. The number of women chairs fall for this committee, being present in less than half of the sample (eight banks).

It is important to underline both the strong dissimilarity among banks and the absence of a clear trend in the female presence in the various bodies and committees considered: in a few cases, the trend is upward, in others downward.

Finally, the data collected allow us to evaluate whether the increase in women on the board of directors corresponds to an increase in women on the board committees and the board of statutory auditors. In other words, we can check whether the banks that are most inclined to appoint women to the board of directors show this greater propensity also for appointments in other bodies. In this regard, we can calculate the correlation index, which is an index measuring the association between two variables; more specifically, it measures the degree to which two variables "move together". As we know, a positive correlation means that if the values in one matrix increase, so do the values in the other matrix; the opposite is true if the correlation is negative. A correlation coefficient close to 0 indicates a weak value or no correlation at all. Our data display that there is a positive correlation with respect to women on the board of directors in all cases, but the values diverge significantly showing a strong correlation in the case of the remuneration committee (+0.77), a medium correlation in the case of the risk committee (+0.47), a weak correlation in the case of the appointments committee (+0.23), and an even weaker correlation in the case of the board of statutory auditors (+0.21). Therefore, there are no clear indications as to the behaviour of the banks in the various processes of appointment of the members of the corporate bodies.

Leaving aside the peculiarities of individual banks and focusing on the average values of the sample, split by year, we can outline the growth/decrease trends for all banks (see average values in Table 10.3). The lack of women CEOs is accompanied by both a weak increase in the number of chairwomen on boards—close to 25% in 2019—and a sustained growth—up to 40% overall—in the number of women directors especially in non-executive roles (94% in 2019). The trend in control bodies is even more in favour of women: the percentage of women rises to 48% in 2019, and that of chairwomen to 33% in the same year. The trend in internal board committees is also positive: the proportion of women increases, in some cases significantly, to 45–50%. This positive sign is contrasted by the downward trend of female chairs on two committees.

## 10.4 The Gender Pay Gap in Italian Listed Banks

Table 10.4 discloses the average remuneration paid to male and female members of the management and control bodies of all Italian listed banking groups between the years 2017 and 2019. To make a fair comparison between men and women, remuneration has been broken down according to the role held. Specifically, the following positions have been identified: chief executive officer, general manager, chairperson of the board of directors (or the management board in the "two-tier" governance system), members of the board of directors or the management board, chairperson of the board of statutory auditors (or the management control committee or the supervisory board in the "one-tier" and "two-tier" governance system, respectively), and statutory auditors/members of the management control committee or the supervisory board. For each of these roles, Table 10.4 also displays the share attributable to participation in board committees.

**Table 10.4** Remuneration paid to male and female members of governance bodies in the Italian listed banks (parent companies of banking groups) (mean values; thousands of euros)

| | *2017* | | | *2018* | | | *2019* | | |
|---|---|---|---|---|---|---|---|---|---|
| | *Male* | *Female* | *difference male–female* | *Male* | *Female* | *difference male–female* | *Male* | *Female* | *difference male–female* |
| ***CEO and GM*** | 899,956 | 457,014 | +442,942 | 963,080 | 529,698 | +433,382 | 1,208,194 | 529,698 | +678,496 |
| *for participation in committees* | *31,100* | *0* | *+31,100* | *20,320* | *0* | *+20,320* | *12,467* | *0* | *+12,467* |
| ***Chair of the management body*** | 404,602 | 266,338 | +138,264 | 429,228 | 228,179 | +201,049 | 411,454 | 169,087 | +242,368 |
| *for participation in committees* | *27,977* | *4658* | *+23,319* | *61,813* | *20,000* | *+41,813* | *26,287* | *26,338* | *−50* |
| ***Member of the management body*** | 149,751 | 104,589 | +45,163 | 141,492 | 96,348 | +45,144 | 120,630 | 103,396 | +17,233 |
| *for participation in committees* | *26,374* | *27,264* | *−890* | *23,804* | *23,971* | *−166* | *28,070* | *26,869* | *+1201* |
| ***Chair of the control body*** | 168,385 | 114,818 | +53,567 | 172,259 | 85,613 | +86,646 | 169,662 | 106,360 | +63,303 |
| *for participation in committees* | *23,675* | *10,000* | *+13,675* | *23,744* | *0* | *+23,744* | *20,438* | *23,650* | *−3213* |
| ***Member of the control body*** | 102,164 | 97,881 | +4283 | 74,244 | 67,342 | +6902 | 84,788 | 91,158 | −6370 |
| *for participation in committees* | *43,635* | *41,044* | *+2591* | *9183* | *7825* | *+1358* | *36,627* | *41,390* | *−4763* |

*Notes* CEO: chief executive officer; GM: general manager (including deputies). The sample of banks in this table is the same as in Table 10.3

*Source* Authors' elaboration on data collected from the remuneration reports of banks according to Table 1 of the Regulation on stock market issuers, CONSOB, annex 3

Looking at Table 10.4, at least three main considerations can be made. Firstly, the data confirm that there is a clear pay gap between men and women running the same function. Indeed, in general, men tend to earn more than women except for a few cases related to participation in board committees, which, as mentioned, increased significantly for women, and—as we shall see—a case related to the control body. Moreover, this gap increases in the years 2017–2019 for senior/apical roles (CEOs and GMs, and chairs). In particular, the male–female difference in CEO and GM remuneration (in thousands of euros) was +€ 442,942 in 2017, and the corresponding value became +€ 678,496 in 2019. The second consideration arises from a comparison of the gender pay gap between the above top positions and the members of the management and control bodies. The male–female pay gap increases for CEOs and GMs, and chairs over time, while it gradually narrows for the members of the management and control bodies. Finally, another feature concerns the comparison between remuneration paid to the members of the management body and that paid to the members of the control body. The data in Table 10.4 highlight that the pay gap between men and women is greater for the members of the management body than the members of the control body. Actually, it should be noted that in 2019, women with control functions earned more than men with the same function.

The differences, almost always in favour of men, can be due to various reasons. Among the hypotheses that can be advanced, the higher remuneration of men for the two positions of CEO and GM might be explained by the fact that the first position (CEO) has never been held by women in the period considered (see previous section). Another explanation could be that men hold their positions in the largest banks in our sample, which most likely pay a higher remuneration for the same functions performed. Finally, it is likely that the gap may also be caused by a lower rate of participation of women in meetings. This last motivation raises the frequently mentioned difficulty of reconciling private life and work, which is a central issue for the mitigation of the gender gap, including the pay gap.

In any case, the correct estimation of the gender pay gap is very complex in the banking sector, as a director can take on several roles and functions. In this respect, the EBA states that further investigation and more granular data collection are needed to identify the exact consistency of the gender pay gap in the banking sector, stripped of any possible conditioning linked to the type and size of the bank, and the role held (EBA, 2020).

It is likely (and desirable) that the pay gap will narrow over time, also to avoid reputational penalties due to misalignment with a principle of equality that is much more strongly felt than in the past and is at the centre of socio-political debate and media attention (see, e.g., the policy statements of Mario Draghi, Prime Minister of Italy, and former President of the European Central Bank; Draghi, 2021).

## References

ABI—Associazione Bancaria Italiana. (2021). Carta "Donne in banca: valorizzare la diversità di genere". Elenco degli aderenti in ordine alfabetico. Aggiornamento al 9 marzo.

Banca d'Italia. (2015). Benchmark di diversity per il sistema bancario italiano. Luglio.

Banca d'Italia. (2020a). Analisi di Impatto della Regolamentazione. L'introduzione delle Quote di Genere nelle Disposizioni sul Governo Societario delle Banche e dei Gruppi Bancari. 24 dicembre.

Banca d'Italia. (2020b). Documento di consultazione sulle disposizioni della Banca d'Italia in materia di "Governo societario delle banche e dei gruppi bancari". 24 dicembre.

Capone, D. (2020). Diversità e inclusione nelle banche italiane: un'analisi empirica delle misure a sostegno della presenza femminile nei board. Questioni di Economia e Finanza (Occasional Papers), Banca d'Italia, Numero 552 – Marzo.

Comitato per la Corporate Governance. (2018). Codice di autodisciplina. Luglio.

Comitato per la Corporate Governance. (2020). Codice di corporate governance. Gennaio.

D'Ascenzo, M. (2017). Italia ai vertici europei per donne nei cda. Ma cosa accadrà allo scadere della legge sulle quote? Il Sole 24 Ore, 30 Gennaio.

De Vita, L., & Magliocco, A. (2018). Effects of gender quotas in Italy: A first impact assessment in the Italian banking sector. *International Journal of Sociology and Social Policy, 38*(7–8), 673–694. https://doi.org/10.1108/IJSSP-11-2017-0150

Draghi, M. (2021). Le dichiarazioni programmatiche del Presidente Draghi. Mercoledì, 17 Febbraio.

EBA—European Banking Authority. (2016). Report on the Benchmarking of diversity practices at the European Union level. EBA-Op-2016-10 | 08 July 2016.

EBA—European Banking Authority. (2020). Report on the Benchmarking of diversity practices at European Union level, under Article 91(11) of Directive 2013/36/EU (2018 Data). EBA/REP/2020/05.

European Commission. (2019). Report on equality between women and men in the EU.

European Parliament. (2015). Report on the EU Strategy for equality between women and men post 2015. (2014/2152[INI]) Committee on Women's Rights and Gender Equality, 13.5.2015.

Genovese, A. (2019). Audizione della CONSOB, SENATO DELLA REPUBBLICA Commissione 6ª (Finanze e tesoro). Roma, 7 maggio.

IMF—International Monetary Fund. (2017). Banking on Women Leaders: A case for more? Prepared by Sahay R, Čihák M, N'Diaye P, Barajas A, Kyobe A, Mitra S, Mooi YN, Yousefi SR. Working paper. WP/17/199.

ISTAT—Istituto Nazionale di Statistica. (2019). Italian data for UN-SDGs Sustainable Development Goals of the 2030 Agenda. Goal 5.

Oliver Wyman. (2014). Women in Financial Services.

Oliver Wyman. (2016a). Women in Financial Services in Italia. Come accelerare il percorso verso una leadership più al femminile.

Oliver Wyman. (2016b). Women in Financial Services.

Oliver Wyman. (2020). Women in Financial Services. A Panoramic Approach.

Osservatorio interistituzionale sulla partecipazione femminile negli organi di amministrazione e controllo delle società italiane. (2021). La partecipazione femminile negli organi di amministrazione e controllo delle società italiane. 8 marzo.

Paoloni, M., Paoloni, P., & Lombardi, R. (2019). The impact on the governance of the gender quotas legislation: The Italian case. *Measuring Business Excellence, 23*(3), 317–334. https://doi.org/10.1108/MBE-02-2019-0019

Pastore, P., & Tommaso, S. (2016). Women on corporate boards: The case of 'gender quotas' in Italy. *Corporate Ownership and Control, 13*(4), 132–155. https://doi.org/10.22495/cocv13i4p13

Profeta, P., Amidani Aliberti, L., Casarico, A., D'Amico, M., & Puccio, A. (2014). *Women directors: The Italian way and beyond*. Palgrave Macmillan.

Ryan, M. K., & Haslam, A. S. (2005). The glass cliff: Evidence that women are over- represented in precarious leadership positions. *British Journal of Management, 16*(2), 81–90. https://doi.org/10.1111/j.1467-8551.2005.00433.x

Ryan, M. K., & Haslam, A. S. (2007). The glass cliff: Exploring the dynamics surrounding the appointment of women to precarious leadership positions. *Academy of Management Review, 32*(2), 549–572. https://doi.org/10.2307/20159315

CHAPTER 11

# Proposing a Framework for Calculating an Index on Gender Equality in Financial Firms

**Abstract** This chapter opens by underlining the importance of a model that allows the assessment of the gender diversity of financial firms under several analysis profiles widely discussed in the previous chapters. We propose a model of analysis that is suitable for the construction of an index of gender diversity based on a set of items predetermined according to standards, legal acts, and best practices relevant to the topic. More in detail, the framework consists of 24 items that can be divided into four categories: (1) gender balance in governance bodies and employees; (2) policies promoting gender equality; (3) transparency of the company's actions towards the community; and (4) equal compensation. In the case of comparison among intermediaries of the same country, the proposed framework can be integrated by taking into account further elements peculiar to each country. It is a first attempt to fill a gap in the gender diversity literature, where—to the best of our knowledge—there is no framework to calculate a gender equality index that goes beyond the composition of governance bodies and the gender of the board chair and/or CEO.

This chapter is the result of the joint efforts of the two authors, who contributed equally.



G. Birindelli and A. P. Iannuzzi, *Women in Financial Services*, Palgrave Macmillan Studies in Banking and Financial Institutions, https://doi.org/10.1007/978-3-030-93471-2_11

## 11.1 Is There Truly the Need for a Gender Equality Framework?

To date, a number of studies in literature have addressed the relationship between female representation on the boards of financial institutions, especially banks, and financial, social, and environmental performance (see Chapter 3). Other studies have analysed financial products and services addressing Sustainable Development Goals (SDGs) (among others, Weber, 2018) or bank endorsements of the SDGs in accordance with Global Reporting Initiative (GRI) performance indicators (Avrampou et al., 2019). However, to the best of our knowledge, so far there are no studies on the construction of a gender diversity index for financial institutions and their positioning with regard to this index.

In the previous chapters, we described gender diversity in multiple dimensions of analysis; here, we will now seek to fill the literature gap by developing a multi-perspective assessment model on gender equality. The framework we propose is not limited to the GRI Standards, which we have illustrated in discussing the disclosure of non-financial information (Chapter 2, Sect. 2.4). The framework, as we will see in the next section, considers many other elements of assessment. In particular, it will be interesting to see the behaviour of financial institutions in response to the establishment of hard quotas and see whether they have acted to conform with minimum requirements or whether they have gone beyond, moving along a path to enhance and develop the professional role of women. Our framework tries to meet this purpose—though in no case does the proposal claim to be exhaustive. Rather, it is a first attempt to develop a framework to measure a gender equality index that goes beyond the composition of governance bodies or the gender of the board chair or the CEO, and to fill a gap in the gender diversity literature.

## 11.2 The Analysis Framework

Measurement of a company's orientation towards gender equality is generally based on the gender composition of management and control bodies, and the gender of the board chair and of the CEO.

Here, we propose an analysis model that constructs a gender diversity index based on a broader set of predetermined items in accordance with relevant standards, legal acts, and best practices on the topic (Coy & Dixon, 2004; Jain et al., 2015). These sources of information integrate commonly used items with multiple perspectives to achieve a unified view of the company's orientation. In particular, the framework consists of 24 items, which are grouped into four categories (see Table 11.1).

1. Gender balance in governance bodies and employees (nine items);
2. Policies promoting gender equality (three items);
3. Transparency of the company's actions towards the community (eight items);
4. Equal compensation (four items).

The first category includes nine items (1a–1i) related to the proportion of women in the governance bodies, i.e., on the board of directors (item 1a) and in the control body (item 1d), which—as is well-acknowledged—may take different names; board committees (such as the risk committee, the appointments committee, and the remuneration committee) may be added, especially in countries where these committees are subject to specific rules and/or recommendations, such as Italy (see Chapter 10); the gender of the chairpersons of the administrative and control bodies (1b and 1e) and, where applicable, of the above-mentioned committees; the CEO's gender (1c); the proportion of female staff, also specified for each employee category (1f and 1h) as required by the GRI Standard on Disclosure 405-1 (diversity of governance bodies and employees); the number of female recruits (1g); and the number of career advancements by gender (1i). This last item was added in consideration of the commitments specified in various charters (such as the HM Treasury Women in Finance Charter launched by the UK government, the Italian Charter "Women in Banks: enhancing gender diversity", and the Belgian "Gender Diversity in Finance" Charter, illustrated in Chapter 2, Sect. 2.3).

The second category (items 2a to 2c) concerns the policies and initiatives undertaken to ensure gender equality (Directive 2014/95/EU, recital 7, in reference to the disclosure of non-financial and diversity information). In particular, the items address the presence of any policies adopted by the financial institution setting out principles to ensure equal opportunities for all employees, regardless of gender (item 2a), of a D&I manager or team (as specifically recommended by the UK and Belgian charters mentioned above) (2b), of any work-life balance tools

**Table 11.1** Gender diversity framework

| *Item* | *Description* | *Score* |
|---|---|---|
| **1. Gender balance in governance bodies and employees** | | |
| 1a) Female directors | Total number of women on the board of directors (or other denomination of the body that supervises management) divided by the total number of board members | Score 0: percentage of women on the board below or equal to the hard/soft quota (alternatively, below or equal to the average value by country or geographical area)<br>Score 1: percentage of women on the board above the hard/soft quota (alternatively, above the average value by country or geographical area) |
| 1b) Gender of chair of the board of directors (or other denomination) | Presence of a chairman or chairwoman | Score 0: chairman<br>Score 1: chairwoman |
| 1c) CEO's gender | Presence of a female or male CEO | Score 0: male CEO<br>Score 1: female CEO |
| 1d) Female members on the control body | Total number of women on the control body divided by the total number of body members | Score 0: percentage of women in the body below or equal to the hard/soft quota (alternatively, below or equal to the average value by country or geographical area)<br>Score 1: percentage of women in the body above the hard/soft quota (alternatively, above the average value by country or geographical area) |
| 1e) Gender of the control body's chair | Presence of a chairman or chairwoman | Score 0: chairman<br>Score 1: chairwoman |
| 1f) Female employees | Women employed divided by the total employees | Score 0: more men than women<br>Score 1: more women than men |
| 1g) Number of recruits by gender | Women recruited divided by the total recruits | Score 0: more men than women<br>Score 1: more women than men |

(continued)

**Table 11.1** (continued)

| *Item* | *Description* | *Score* |
|---|---|---|
| 1h) Distribution of employees by category and gender | Female executives and female middle managers divided by the total female employees | Score 0: ratio below or equal to the average value by country or geographical area<br>Score 1: ratio above the average value by country or geographical area |
| 1i) Number of career advancements by gender | Women having a promotion divided by the total career advancements | Score 0: more men than women<br>Score 1: more women than men |
| **2. Policies promoting gender equality** | | |
| 2a) Policy on gender equality | The institution has a policy that sets out principles and guidelines to ensure equal opportunity for all employees, regardless of gender | Score 0: No<br>Score 1: Yes |
| 2b) Diversity and inclusion manager | The institution has a manager/committee that monitors initiatives on gender equality and the progression of the diversity targets set by the institution | Score 0: No<br>Score 1: Yes |
| 2c) Work-life balance | The institution adopts tools for a better work-life balance (e.g., smart working and flexible working hours) | Score 0: No<br>Score 1: Yes |
| **3. Transparency of the company's actions towards the community** | | |
| 3a) Report on gender diversity (e.g., gender pay gap report) | The institution systematically publishes details on issues concerning women in the workforce and the progress in achieving internal targets | Score 0: No<br>Score 1: Yes |
| 3b) Sponsoring award | The institution sponsors awards in support of gender equality and the development of the role of women in the business world | Score 0: No<br>Score 1: Yes |
| 3c) Prize | The institution was awarded a prize in support of gender equality and the development of the role of women in the business world | Score 0: No<br>Score 1: Yes |

(continued)

**Table 11.1** (continued)

| *Item* | *Description* | *Score* |
|---|---|---|
| 3d) Gender diversity index | The institution is included in an index that tracks the performance of the companies most committed to advancing women through gender diversity | Score 0: No<br>Score 1: Yes |
| 3e) Commitment to women's empowerment by signing ad hoc principles | The institution is a signatory of the Women's Empowerment Principles or other sets of principles aiming to protect women from discrimination, marginalisation, and exclusion | Score 0: No<br>Score 1: Yes |
| 3f) Gender equality certification | The institution has obtained a gender equality certification | Score 0: No<br>Score 1: Yes |
| 3g) Female entrepreneurship | The institution adopts development-oriented policies that support female entrepreneurship | Score 0: No<br>Score 1: Yes |
| 3h) Investment fund | The institution has launched a fund that invests in companies that actively seek to improve the gender balance and support women | Score 0: No<br>Score 1: Yes |
| **4. Equal compensation** | | |
| 4a) Pay of the senior executive team | The institution ensures that the remuneration of the senior executive team is linked to the achievement of internal gender diversity targets | Score 0: No<br>Score 1: Yes |
| 4b) Actions for closing the gender pay gap | The institution adopts measures to fill the pay gap between men and women | Score 0: No<br>Score 1: Yes |
| 4c) Gender pay gap (1) | Ratio of basic salary of women to men | Score 0: the ratio recorded by the intermediary indicates a higher gender pay gap than the official figure used in the analysis<br>Score 1: the ratio recorded by the intermediary indicates a lower gender pay gap than the official figure used in the analysis |

(continued)

**Table 11.1** (continued)

| *Item* | *Description* | *Score* |
|---|---|---|
| 4d) Gender pay gap (2) | Ratio of remuneration of women to men | Score 0: the ratio recorded by the intermediary indicates a higher gender pay gap than the official figure used in the analysis<br>Score 1: the ratio recorded by the intermediary indicates a lower gender pay gap than the official figure used in the analysis |
| **Index (sum of scores)** | | **Value of the index** |

*Source*: Authors' elaboration

(2c) (as indicated in Chapter 2, Sect. 2.2, a directive was recently issued on this topic, namely Directive (EU) 2019/1158 on work-life balance for parents and carers).

The third category includes eight items (3a–3h) concerning the transparency of the company's actions towards the community. Some of these items come from legal acts and recommendations, others from best practices in the financial sector. Among the items: the publication of the gender diversity report in compliance with the social dialogue recalled by Directive 2014/95/EU (item 3a); the adoption of credit policies that support female entrepreneurship, in line with Goal 8 of the SDGs (3g); the sponsorship of awards addressed to companies that excel in the support of gender equality (3b) (for instance, the award established by Intesa Sanpaolo—a leading banking group in Italy—together with the Marisa Bellisario Foundation[1]); being awarded for the commitment to developing the role of women in business (3c) (e.g., IMB Bank has been recently nominated by the Workplace Gender Equality Agency as an Employer of Choice for Gender Equality[2]); being included in gender equality indexes (3d) (such as the Bloomberg Gender-Equality

[1] See the following link: https://www.intesasanpaolo.com/it/business/landing/premio-fondazione-marisa-bellisario.html.

[2] https://www.imb.com.au/news-imb-bank-celebrates-international-womens-day-announcing-prestigious-workplace-gender-equality-citation.html.

Index and the European Women on Boards Gender Diversity Index, see Chapter 2, Sect. 2.5.1); adhering to gender equality principles, including the Women's Empowerment Principles (3e) (Chapter 2, Sect. 2.5.3); obtaining a gender equality certification (3f) (such as the Economic Dividends for Gender Equality certification and the Winning Women Institute certification, see Chapter 2, Sect. 2.5.2); and the launch of funds that invest in companies that are leaders in promoting gender equality (3h) (Chapter 7).

The last category includes four items on equal pay for women and men. Following the GRI Standard on Disclosure 405-2, the items are the ratios of the basic salary and remuneration of women to men for each employee category (4c and 4d). Here, we have added the potential measures taken for hindering the disparity in pay (4b) and an item recommended by the UK Women in Finance Charter on whether the remuneration of the senior executive team is linked to the achievement of goals on gender diversity (4a).[3]

The valuation of the items is based on the assumption that the higher the index value resulting from the sum of the values assigned to each item, the higher the gender parity. The score/index is based on a binary scale assigning the value 1 when an item is present, and 0 otherwise (e.g., the value is 1 if the firm obtained a certification or adopted a gender equality policy; otherwise its value is 0). Dummy variables are also used for the gender of the chair of the governance bodies and of the CEO (0 in the presence of a man, 1 otherwise), for the number of female employees, for the recruitment by gender, and for career advancement by gender (0 if men outnumber women, 1 otherwise).

For other items, for which quantification is more complex, we provide a set of solutions specific for the setting of financial firms. In our view, the number of employees by category and gender can take into account average values at a country/geographic level or values calculated for representative samples of financial firms performing the same activity as the firms under analysis (available, as we know, mainly in research carried out by regulatory authorities). As for the items related to the number of women in the bodies, the value 1 could be used when women exceed the hard or soft quota (if present in the country) and 0 otherwise; if absent, again average values could be used here, too. Finally, the gender pay gap

[3] This item, which in itself is not directly related to the issue of equal compensation, is a tool to provide incentives to close the various forms of gender gaps.

could take a value linked to the gender pay gap calculated by the Eurostat for financial and insurance activities, or by regulatory authorities such as the European Banking Authority (Chapter 5): thus, the score would be 0 if the pay gap shown by the financial intermediary is even more unfavourable to women, 1 otherwise.

Furthermore, the framework can be supplemented with additional items when needed, such as in the case of comparisons among intermediaries from the same country. In this case, the proposed framework can be integrated with other country-specific elements, such as provisions on board committees and/or their chairs.

The framework proposed is described in detail in Table 11.1.

## References

Avrampou, A., Skouloudis, A., Iliopoulos, G., & Khan, N. (2019). Advancing the sustainable development goals: Evidence from leading European banks. *Sustainable Development, 27*(4), 743–757. https://doi.org/10.1002/sd.1938

Coy, D., & Dixon, K. (2004). The public accountability index: Crafting a parametric disclosure index for annual reports. *The British Accounting Review, 36*(1), 79–106. https://doi.org/10.1016/j.bar.2003.10.003

Jain, A., Keneley, M., & Thomson, D. (2015). Voluntary CSR disclosure works! Evidence from Asia-Pacific banks. *Social Responsibility Journal, 11*(1), 2–18. https://doi.org/10.1108/SRJ-10-2012-0136

Weber, O. (2018, November). *The financial sector and the SDGs: Interconnections and future directions* (Centre for International Governance Innovation Papers No. 201).

# Index





G. Birindelli and A. P. Iannuzzi, *Women in Financial Services*, Palgrave Macmillan Studies in Banking and Financial Institutions, https://doi.org/10.1007/978-3-030-93471-2

The manufacturer's authorised representative in the EU is Springer
Nature Customer Service Centre GmbH, Europaplatz 3, 69115 Heidelberg,
Germany. If you have any concerns regarding our products, please
contact ProductSafety@springernature.com

Printed and bound by CPI Group (UK) Ltd, Croydon, CR0 4YY
30/09/2026
02225661-0011